Current Research
in Natural Language
Generation

Cognitive Science Series

Collections

1 Reasoning and Discourse Processes   *T. Myers, K. Brown and B. McGonigle (eds), 1986*
2. New Directions in Semantics   *E. Le Pore (ed.), 1987*
3. Language Perception and Production: Relationships between listening, speaking, reading and writing   *A. Allport, D. G. MacKay, W. Prinz and E. Scheerer (eds), 1987*
4. Current Research in Natural Language Generation   *R. Dale, C. Mellish and M. Zock (eds), 1990*

Monographs

Agreement and Anaphora   *P. Bosch, 1983*
Temporal Representation and Inference   *B. Richards, I. Bethke, J. van der Does and J. Oberlander, 1989*

Current Research in Natural Language Generation

Edited by

Robert Dale

Human Communications Research Centre,
University of Edinburgh, Edinburgh, UK

Chris Mellish

Department of Artificial Intelligence,
University of Edinburgh, Edinburgh, UK

Michael Zock

LIMSI-CNRS, Paris, France

ACADEMIC PRESS
Harcourt Brace Jovanovich, Publishers
London   San Diego   New York   Boston
Sydney   Tokyo   Toronto

ACADEMIC PRESS LIMITED
24–28 Oval Road,
LONDON NW1 7DX

U.S. Edition Published by
ACADEMIC PRESS INC.
San Diego, CA 92101-4311

British Library Cataloguing in Publication Data is available

ISBN 0-12-200735-2

Printed in Great Britain by
St Edmundsbury Press Limited, Bury St Edmunds, Suffolk

List of Contributors

Eduard H. Hovy, Information Sciences Institute of the University of Southern California, 4676 Admiralty Way, Marina del Rey, CA 90292-6695, USA
Email: hovy@isi.edu

Donia R. Scott, Philips Research Laboratories, Cross Oak Lane, Redhill, Surrey RH1 5HA, UK
Email: scott@prl.philips.co.uk

Clarisse Sieckenius de Souza, Departamento de Informática, PUC/RJ, Rua Marquês de São Vicente 225, 22453 Rio de Janeiro, RJ, Brazil
Email: usercsds@lncc.bitnet

Alison Cawsey, Department of Artificial Intelligence, University of Edinburgh, 80 South Bridge, Edinburgh EH1 IHN, Scotland
Email: ajc@aipna.ed.ac.uk

Kathleen McKeown, Michael Elhadad, Yumiko Fukumoto, Jong Lim, Christine Lombardi, Jacques Robin and **Frank Smadja**, Department of Computer Science, 450 Computer Science Building, Columbia University, New York, NY 10027, USA
Email: kathy@beach.cs.columbia.edu

Gertjan van Noord, OTS RUU, Trans 10 Utrecht, The Netherlands
Email: vannoord@hutruu59.bitnet

Koenraad J. M. J. De Smedt, Nijmegen Institute for Cognition research and Information technology (NICI), University of Nijmegen, Postbus 9104, NL-6500 HE Nijmegen, The Netherlands
E-mail: desmedt@hnykun53.bitnet

Helmut Horacek, Universität Bielefeld, Fakultät für Linguistik und Literaturwissenschaft, Postfach 8640, D-4800 Bielefeld 1, West Germany

Robert Dale, Human Communication Research Centre, University of Edinburgh, Edinburgh EH8 9LW, Scotland
Email: R.Dale@ed.ac.uk

Ehud Reiter, Aiken Computation Laboratory, Harvard University, Cambridge, MA 02138, USA; currently at Department of Artificial Intelligence, University of Edinburgh, 80 South Bridge, Edinburgh EH1 IHN, Scotland
Email: E.Reiter@ed.ac.uk

Hiroaki Kitano, Center for Machine Translation, Carnegie Mellon University, Pittsburgh, PA 15213, USA
Email: Hiroaki.Kitano@a.nl.cs.cmu.edu

George Houghton, MRC Applied Psychology Unit, 15 Chaucer Road, Cambridge CB2 2EF, UK
Email: george@uk.ac.cam.mrc-apu

Contents

6 An Overview of Head-driven Bottom-up Generation 141
Gertjan van Noord

7 IPF: An Incremental Parallel Formulator 167
Koenraad J. M. J. De Smedt

8 The Architecture of a Generation Component in a Complete Natural Language Dialogue System 193
Helmut Horacek

9 Generating Recipes: An Overview of Epicure 229
Robert Dale

1 Introduction

Robert Dale, Chris Mellish, and Michael Zock

1.1 Background

Natural language generation is the computer production of natural language utterances—anything from a single sentence to an entire discourse—on the basis of a given input. Although there are some systems which produce synthesised speech, the output is usually in the form of printed text; the input tends to vary from one system to another, although there is an increasing consensus that the input to a complete language generation system (rather than a system which deals specifically with the construction of a surface linguistic form on the basis of some fully specified semantic content) should be of the form of a **communicative intention**, i.e., some goal that the speaker program is to attain by means of a communicative act.

Approached in this way, the process of language generation becomes a process of choice at many levels. A fully specified model of the generation process has to consider at least the following decisions:

- what the content of an utterance or set of utterances should be;
- how to organise that content in a coherent discourse;
- what tone or degree of formality should be adopted in the language used;
- how the material should be broken down into sentences and clauses;
- what syntactic constructions should be used;
- how entities should be described; and
- what words should be used.

No single generation system confronts all of these problems, but each has been addressed at one time or another in existing systems. In order to cut down the size of the task, many researchers adopt a distinction (first put forward by Thompson [1977]) between two stages of the language production process: deciding 'what to say' (the **strategic** level) and deciding 'how to say it' (the **tactical** level). Although there is some controversy as to the validity of such a distinction (see, for example, [Appelt 1985; Danlos 1987]), it has proved useful in making the generation task more manageable. Researchers can then focus their attention on strategic issues such as the organisation of discourse, or on

tactical issues such as word choice. The papers in the present volume address
issues on both sides of this distinction.

Looking at the field of natural language processing as a whole, it is still the
case that more work is being done in natural language *understanding* (NLU)
than in natural language *generation* (NLG). It is not entirely clear why this
imbalance should exist; but, for whatever reason, it would be fair to say that
work in natural language generation got off to a slow start. One possible
reason for the imbalance is that there are few applications which are rich
enough in terms of what they want to express to justify the construction of a
facility which makes sophisticated use of natural language. This situation is
changing; in particular, the increasing sophistication of intelligent knowledge
based systems requires just such facilities.

Although there was some important work done in the 1970s (in particular, see [Goldman 1974] and [Davey 1978]), the seminal PhD theses which
did so much to shape the direction of research in natural language generation
appeared at the beginning of the 1980s (see, in particular, [McDonald 1980;
McKeown 1982; Appelt 1982]). The 1980s have seen a tremendous surge in
interest in natural language generation. It would be a little premature to say
that the field has *matured*, but it should be noted that the increase in interest
has not just manifested itself as an increase in the number of papers appearing
at conferences and in journals; there have also been significant shifts in the
foci of interest pursued by researchers. Thus, whereas much of the research
pursued in the 1970s involved relatively simple approaches to isolated sentence
generation (based, for example, on augmented transition networks: see [Sim-
mons and Slocum 1972] and [Shapiro 1975, 1979]), work in the 1980s has seen
a move towards (on the one hand) an increased interest in the construction of
texts larger than a sentence, and (on the other hand) a stream of research that
focuses on the problems of using particular linguistic formalisms in generation.
In both these areas, the kinds of questions asked by generation researchers are
also beginning to influence the work of those involved in natural language
understanding.

As evidence of this increase in interest over the last decade, witness the
appearance of gatherings whose single focus is research in natural language
generation: in particular, 1990 sees the fifth biennial International Natural
Language Generation Workshop, and 1991 will see the third biennial European Natural Language Generation Workshop. It is in this second series of
workshops that the present volume has its origins.

The first European Natural Language Generation Workshop was held at
the Abbaye de Royaumont, near Paris, in 1987; the work reported there is
published in [Zock and Sabah 1988]. The present volume derives from the
Second European NLG Workshop, held in Edinburgh in April 1989. Not all
the papers presented at that workshop appear in this volume, and not all the

papers in this volume were presented at the workshop: instead, we invited those who participated in the workshop to provide revised papers for peer review, the result of which is the present book. The papers collected together here were selected not only for their quality but also for their contribution to a coherent picture of the field. The book is, therefore, more than a conference proceedings: it is a snapshot of the state-of-the-art in a number of important research themes in NLG.

We have deliberately structured the book to follow through four particular themes. We begin with a number of papers [Hovy, Scott and Souza, Cawsey] that focus on the topic of **text planning**: the strategic level as we distinguished it above. These are followed by a paper by McKeown *et al.*, which discusses both work on the strategic level and work on the tactical level, and thus leads to our second theme: **linguistic realisation**. We include two papers which focus specifically on tactical level issues [van Noord, De Smedt].

The remainder of the book contains papers on two particular themes which are currently the focus of a considerable amount of attention: the process of **building descriptions** [Horacek, Dale, Reiter] and **connectionist approaches** to language generation [Houghton, Kitano]. The remainder of this introduction describes each of these sections in turn.

1.2   Text Planning

As we noted above, one of the more obvious shifts over the last decade has been the gradual evolution of the goals of the NLG community from the generation of isolated sentences to the production of coherent and purposeful texts. Various approaches have been taken in order to achieve this goal. Some researchers [Meehan 1975, 1976; Appelt 1982, 1985] have attempted to view the generation process as a kind of planning in the AI sense, driven by the communicative goals of the speaker. Achieving textual coherence seems, however, to involve satisfying stylistic and aesthetic goals, which are at a rather different level and are difficult to describe precisely.

Over the last ten years, two principal contenders for the structuring of text above the level of the sentence have arisen: the use of **text schemas** (see, in particular, [McKeown 1985]) which describe conventional textual structures in terms of patterns which specify the overall structure of a text, and the use of **rhetorical relations** to state the relationships that may hold between individual elements of a text. The latter approach is most well known in the form of Rhetorical Structure Theory (RST) [Mann and Thompson 1987]. Whereas schemas capture domain-dependent patterns of discourse well, the aim of RST is to explain the structure of all coherent discourses using the same set of primitive relations. Although this is a significant distinction, in practice much current research on the generalisation of schemas and the encoding of RST relations as planning operators reveals that there are close connections between the two approaches.

RST in its pure form is intended to be purely descriptive; however, Hovy's paper shows how to operationalise RST relationships in order to allow the organisation of the material to be conveyed, in agreement with a set of discourse goals, into a coherent whole. In his system, the text structure planner (a limited top-down hierarchical expansion planning system) takes as input one or more discourse goals along with a set of (unordered) clauses, and organises these data into a tree structure. More precisely, given a goal, the system looks for an RST relation that ensures the achievement of this goal. The structure planner then searches the base of information to be conveyed for material that matches the requirements imposed by this discourse plan.

Since different RST relations can be used to achieve different goals, it is straightforward to think of RST relations not only as text organising devices but also as plans for achieving particular goals. Thus, RST combines intentionality with coherence: this method ensures that the texts built are both well-formed (coherent) and to the point (goal sensitive).

Hovy also compares the two principal approaches to text structuring distinguished above (i.e., the use of schemas *vs* planning using rhetorical relations), and analyses some of the theoretical and computational problems that have to be solved in order to enable a planner to build texts which are well organised, of good style and to the point.

Scott and Souza also rely on RST as a basis for the generation of texts. However, their method focuses on psycholinguistic and computational constraints. Their goal is to produce texts which are easy to read, to remember and to understand; their contribution lies in their attempt to operationalise 'style'. Scott and Souza suggest that the notion of style (in the sense of clarity and readability) is better understood in terms of cognition (i.e., ease of processing a text) than in terms of taste (i.e., aesthetic well-formedness).

In order to ensure the production of texts that can easily be processed, Scott and Souza propose a set of heuristics, of which the following are some examples: make rhetorical structure relationships explicit; avoid the destruction of textual units by embedding one rhetorical relation inside another; and express each rhetorical relation in one sentence. These rules are extremely useful in controlling embedding (i.e., deciding when to use a relative clause), avoiding dangling modifiers, and in generally improving the clarity of texts.

Cawsey's concern is not so much the generation of coherent, natural sounding texts, as the problem of tailoring the text to the user in a truly interactive setting. The constraints of interactive operation have forced her to generalise a schema-based approach using a discourse planner.

EDGE (Explanatory Discourse Generator) provides interactive explanations of the behavior of electrical components. Two features are particularly interesting:

1. The system is capable of adapting its behavior to the user's needs. As it receives feedback, the explanations given are geared to the level of the user's needs: what does she know? What does she need or want to know?

2. The output consists of both textual and graphical elements.

These two features—interactivity and multi-modal output—allow the system to determine dynamically what is relevant at any given moment (i.e., what should be said), and how a given message should be conveyed (i.e., the level of detail, the order of information, and the use of graphical output). These characteristics are important prerequisites for the use of such a system in real life.

The paper by McKeown *et al.* also presents a system which provides explanations in a multi-modal way. However, the choice of the output mode here (textual *vs* graphical) is additionally grounded on psychological evidence. COMET (CoOrdinated Multimedia Explanation Testbed) produces explanations for equipment maintenance and repair. For example, if the user suspects that a piece of equipment has suffered a loss of memory, the system describes the procedure for troubleshooting loss of memory on request.

In order to produce well formed text, the system uses text schemas. A well known problem with this approach is that schemas are generally domain specific; thus, every time the domain or discourse purpose is changed, new schemas have to be identified. In order to minimise this need McKeown *et al.* have generalised a schema across domains: the common features are encoded in generic schemas at various levels of abstraction. The result of this generalisation process is a hierarchical schema library useful in a wider range of domains.

1.3   Linguistic Realisation

Once the desired content of a discourse has been planned, it is necessary to consider how this might be realised in a natural language. The tactical component of a natural language generation system must have knowledge of the resources of the target natural language, that is, a **grammar** of that language, and a **lexicon** relating elements in the application domain to those resources. Devising grammars or grammar formalisms that support natural language generation and natural language analysis (parsing) equally well (so-called **bidirectional** grammars) is an active research aim, one which van Noord's paper contributes to directly. Nevertheless, in practice natural language generation researchers have often used different grammatical formalisms from those researchers working on natural language analysis. Especially popular in this respect have been **functional** frameworks, for instance Functional Systemic Grammar [Halliday 1985], which emphasise the set of independent choices that a language generator has to make and the syntactic and semantic functions of the parts of an utterance in the whole. Since a generation system has the aim of *using* language for a specific purpose (and choosing a good way of doing this from the set of alternatives available), it is not surprising that such an approach has had its attractions.

Many modern grammatical formalisms have adopted a framework where linguistic categories are complex descriptions consisting of attributes and values, whose information can be combined by an operation of **unification**. Such unification grammar formalisms (for a good introduction, see [Shieber 1986]) include McKeown *et al.*'s FUF formalism (which is close to Kay's Functional Unification Grammar [Kay 1984]), the logic-based formalism of van Noord (which is close to Pereira and Warren's Definite Clause Grammars [Pereira and Warren 1980]) and the Segment Grammar of De Smedt (which is derived from earlier work of Kempen [1987]), all of which are described here. The fact that unification is commutative and associative means that the information computed about a phrase (for instance, as a result of taking into account successive aspects of its semantic structure) does not depend on the order in which that information arrives. This makes unification grammars attractive computationally: order independence means a flexibility of operation and leads to a system that satisfies some of the prerequisites of bidirectionality. Kay's Functional Unification Grammar (FUG) [Kay 1984] combines a functional grammar approach with a unification formalism.

It is valuable to consider the abstract problem of linguistic realisation in a unification framework in order to see how the work of McKeown *et al.*, van Noord and De Smedt are related. Linguistic realisation starts off with some semantic information about an utterance (perhaps a complete logical form), and the aim is to extend this partial description to be one which also specifies a complete phrase structure and sequence of words that is acceptable to the grammar. This is done by comparing the description with the set of options defined in the grammar. At an abstract level, the grammar can be seen as an infinite expression built using the binary operators $\vee$, $\wedge$ and : [Kasper and Rounds 1986]. $\wedge$ indicates that both subexpressions must apply and $\vee$ indicates that at least one must apply. The : symbol is used to specify that the value of an attribute (whose name is written before it) must satisfy some condition (which is written after it). So, for instance, the simple phrase structure grammar:

$$s \rightarrow np, vp$$
$$np \rightarrow \text{``john''}$$

$$vp \ \rightarrow \ v, \, s$$
$$vp \ \rightarrow \ v$$
$$v \ \rightarrow \ \text{``}saw\text{''}$$

could be written as the following expression Γ:

$(cat : s \, \wedge \, d_1 : cat : np \, \wedge \, d_2 : cat : vp \, \wedge \, d_1 : \Gamma \, \wedge \, d_2 : \Gamma) \vee$
$(cat : np \, \wedge \, d_1 : john) \vee$
$(cat : vp \, \wedge \, d_1 : cat : v \, \wedge \, d_2 : cat : s \, \wedge \, d_1 : \Gamma \, \wedge \, d_2 : \Gamma) \vee$
$(cat : vp \, \wedge \, d_1 : cat : v \, \wedge \, d_1 : \Gamma) \vee$
$(cat : v \, \wedge \, d_1 : saw)$

where each Γ is a copy of the whole expression. In this example, a description of a phrase can just have the attributes *cat* (syntactic category), d_1 (first subphrase) and d_2 (second subphrase). For generation, of course, we are interested in grammars that specify values for semantic, as well as syntactic, attributes. This example also does not show how a unification grammar can specify sharing between attribute values.

Given such a grammar and a description of a phrase that specifies (only) the value of semantic attributes, extending the description could then involve something like the partly defined algorithm shown in Figure 1.1. The algorithm maintains an 'agenda' of pairs $< D, G >$, where D is some part of the description to be extended and G is a 'subexpression' of the grammar. The agenda starts off containing a single pair consisting of the whole description and the whole grammar. If the agenda can be successfully emptied, then the extended description that arises is a possible way of realising the desired semantics.

In the work of McKeown and her colleagues, a similar algorithm is performed by 'unification'[1] of the initial description with the grammar. Their FUF grammars have constructs corresponding to our three operators; for instance, the ALT structure corresponds to the $\vee$ above. It is interesting to note how similar in spirit their transitivity system (a subpart of the grammar) is to work done in the Systemic Grammar tradition. It is also interesting that they have applied the same unification algorithm to other parts of the generation process, for instance lexical choice. Thus FUF unification seems to give access to a more generally useful 'programming language' (rather similar in spirit to Prolog).

Van Noord's paper deals with linguistic realisation within a more conventional phrase-structure grammar framework, in spirit quite similar to the example above, except that his categories are complex feature bundles. He

---

[1]This is a slightly non-standard use of the term 'unification' because of the range of constructions it handles, though this is the standard usage within FUG.

Top-Down Generation:
Do the following until the agenda is empty:

1. Remove a pair $< D, G >$ from the agenda.

2. (a) If G is $G_1 \vee G_2$,
   Add either $< D, G_1 >$ or $< D, G_2 >$ to the agenda

   (b) If G is $G_1 \wedge G_2$,
   Add both $< D, G_1 >$ and $< D, G_2 >$ to the agenda

   (c) If G is $F : G_1$,
   Extend D to have attribute F, with value D_1
   (fail if D is already defined as something else)
   Add $< D_1, G_1 >$ to the agenda

   (d) If G is an atom,
   Extend D to be this atom
   (fail if D is already defined as something else)

Figure 1.1: An algorithm for top-down generation

shows that in this setting top-down generation algorithms can get into infinite loops similar to the kinds of loops one encounters in Prolog. Whereas in McKeown *et al.*'s system the order in which pairs are retrieved from the notional 'agenda' is built into the unification algorithm, van Noord considers general principles for ordering the realisation subtasks. A key feature of the approach is a strong bottom-up flavour in addition to some remaining element of top-down guidance.

Since the order of a sequence of unifications does not affect the result, an interesting option is to do some of them in parallel, and this idea is followed up interestingly by De Smedt in pursuit of a model of human sentence generation. Indeed, De Smedt's tactical component is conceived as operating in parallel with a content planning component that can provide conceptual input in any order (in contrast to both McKeown and van Noord, whose strategic and tactical components are temporally distinct). It thus shares common features with Kitano's parallel translation system.

1.4 Building Descriptions

Natural language generation systems have to find ways of describing the things they are talking about. The problem of building descriptions or constructing referring expressions[2] has long been a theme of interest in natural language generation, with some of the more well known work being that of Davey [1978] and Appelt [1985].

Solutions to this general problem are constrained by a number of principles, which we might call principles of **sensitivity, efficiency** and **adequacy**. These are very like Gricean conversational maxims [Grice 1975]. The **principle of sensitivity** requires that a speaker should always be *sensitive* to her hearers: in constructing a description, the speaker must pay heed to what the hearer can be presumed to know. The **principle of adequacy** requires that a description should identify the intended referent unambiguously, and provide sufficient information to serve the purpose of the reference or description. The adequacy of an act of reference or description is dependent upon its purpose: an expression which is sufficient to permit the hearer to construct or retrieve a mental entity corresponding to the intended referent may not be adequate for actually locating the referent in the real world. The **principle of efficiency** requires that the expression used must not contain more information than is necessary for the task at hand: as such, it pulls in the opposite direction from the principle of adequacy. This is not just a question of the speaker saving her breath; saying more than is necessary is likely to mislead the hearer into thinking that something else is encoded in the message.

In many generation systems, these problems are sidestepped by using a carefully handcrafted mapping from conceptual objects to lexical items or phrases so that there is only ever one way of describing each entity or relation. In more sophisticated systems, this restriction is unacceptable. The papers in this section each address the problems that arise when richer underlying knowledge structures are used.

Although Horacek presents an architecture for a system covering the generation process as a whole, his main emphasis is on those components which are responsible for building descriptions. As the generator is part of a complete natural language dialogue system, the other components of the system have considerable influence on this process. The consequence is one of the central themes of this paper: an explicit distinction between cognitive and lexical representational levels, where the former is more appropriate for representing and reasoning about real-world matters. A potential problem here is the possibility that the information content associated with the meanings of lexical

---

[2]We take the view here that, from the point of view of generation, a referring expression is just a description constructed for the specific purpose of identifying a referent.

items and grammatical functions may not be provide an even coverage of the
information maintained in the cognitive representational level; in view of this,
Horacek's objective is to provide mechanisms that permit a mapping between
the two levels. Horacek defines the transition between these levels explicitly in
a compositional fashion, permitting both ontological and structural differences
between the representational levels. The particular contributions of the paper
lie in

- the use of **terminological transformations** to mediate choices between alternative expressions of facts on the cognitive level, these being
  carried out on the basis of the user's knowledge; and

- the realisation of the content of a message specification on the cognitive
  level by lexical means (the verbalisation procedure), which is based on
  the user's knowledge as well as on (general) stylistic preferences.

Dale also describes a complete generation system, EPICURE. In this system,
which uses a simple top-down plan expansion algorithm in order to determine
which propositions have to be conveyed to the user, the primary focus is the
construction of subsequent referring expressions (definite noun phrases, pronouns and *one*-anaphoric expressions) in a domain where the entities to be
referred to are constantly undergoing change. This requires, on the one hand,
the use of a representational language which makes it easy to model changes
of state, while at the same time being sensitive to the kinds of distinctions
required from a linguistic point of view. The model Dale develops makes
use of three distinct levels of representation: the representation of the underlying knowledge base entities themselves, a level of **recoverable semantic
structure** which represents the semantic content to be communicated to the
hearer, and a more linguistically oriented abstract syntactic structure. The
resulting mechanism, like Horacek's, relies on processes that map from one
level of representation to another. The central contributions of Dale's work
here are:

- a language which permits the representation of non-singular entities (i.e.,
  masses and sets) as easily as it does individual entities; and

- an explicit mechanism for the construction of a referring expression,
  based on a notion of **discriminatory power**, that is consistent with
  the principles of efficiency and adequacy defined above,

The result is a mechanism that can generate a wide range of referring expressions.

Whereas Horacek and Dale both describe complete generation systems that
embody mechanisms for constructing descriptions as subtasks, Reiter focuses
directly on the content determination component of a generation system. His

main concern is to avoid unintended conversational implicatures when informing the hearer that an object has certain attributes, or that it belongs to
certain classes. For example, suppose I want to warn someone that swimming
in a particular area is not a good idea because of the presence of sharks: if I
say *There is a shark in the water*, a hearer who knows about sharks will infer,
amongst other things, that there is a dangerous fish in the water, and that
swimming is probably not a sensible thing to do. If the hearer does not know
about sharks, then *There is a dangerous fish in the water* might be a more
appropriate utterance. However, if I use this second utterance when speaking to someone who knows about sharks, she might take this to mean that,
whatever it is that is in the water, it isn't a shark; for it it were a shark, then
surely I would have used that term. Reiter develops an approach that takes
considerations of this kind on board. His system, FN, is intended to adhere
to three constraints: the descriptions it builds should be truthful (**accurate**),
should trigger the desired inferences in the hearer (be **valid**), and should not
lead the hearer to draw incorrect conversational implicatures (be **free of false
implicatures**). These notions themselves are not, of course, particularly new;
however, Reiter's work is original in providing a formal treatment of this kind
for use in a generation system. He specifies his algorithm in considerable
detail, and provides some formal complexity results.

1.5 Connectionist Approaches

The final two papers in the book explore aspects of a relatively new direction
in natural language generation research: the use of approaches that are based
on connectionism.

Houghton starts from the observation that while current work done on text
generation in the framework of AI has allowed the achievement of impressive
results, 'little of it sheds much, if any, light on the fundamental psychological, or neurophysiological, mechanisms which underlie the human capacity
to produce sequentially structured behavior such as language.' For example,
practically none of this work has very much to say about speech errors, the
tip of the tongue phenomenon, etc. (a notable exception being the work done
on incremental sentence production: see [Kempen and Hoenkamp 1987; De
Smedt 1990]).

In order to gain some insights into these fundamental problems, Houghton
suggests working within the connectionist paradigm, rather than the symbolic
processing paradigm. However, there have been problems with the representation of sequencing in previous connectionist models, and sequencing of output
is obviously vital for any model of language generation.

Houghton's paper deals with the learning and recall of phonemic sequences, i.e. monosyllabic English words. His model respects the following constraints:

1. Words are not stored literally, but are recreated on-line as dynamic activity patterns.

2. There is no position-specific coding of elements.

3. Upcoming phonemes in a word should be pre-activated, i.e., active before being produced (anticipation).

An important element in Houghton's model is the notion of **competitive queuing**. This idea is based on the intuition that serial order can be effected by the activation of a node (representing, for example, a word) whose elements (in our case phonemes) will start to compete. The order of arrival—i.e., the order in which each component (phoneme) will surface—depends on their respective level of activation.

The learning process takes place in two steps: exposure and practice. The first stage of learning involves associating the phonemes comprising each word to be learned with a particular node pair in the network. During the practice phase the network is instructed to produce a given word by activating the appropriate node. Since learning within the connectionist paradigm consists in computing incremental weight changes, the practice phase consists in adjusting the weights until the words to be learned are adequately reproduced.

It should be noted that the performance of Houghton's system with respect to speech errors is in line with psycholinguistic evidence; hence, it deserves further study in order to determine the extent to which it can be applied to other tasks in generation.

Kitano's work also falls within the framework of connectionism. However, unlike Houghton, Kitano's work is focused at a much higher level, namely the simulation of a simultaneous interpreter. The ultimate goal of this work is to produce simultaneous speech-to-speech translation between English and Japanese in real time. Unlike traditional work on automatic translation, Kitano's system allows for concurrent parsing and generation: parsing and generation are carried out in parallel, so that a part of the utterance being translated can be generated while parsing the remainder of the utterance is still in progress.

Kitano's approach makes sense both for practical and psychological reasons. On the practical side, if translation could only be begun once the input message had been completed, there would be undesirable delays for both the speaker and the hearer. However, incremental translation is justified not only because of the need to minimise the delay between the utterance of the source text and its translation, but also because of cognitive constraints [Zock 1988]. If translation can start only once all of the content of the source utterance is known, one would be confronted with severe memory problems; and people, unlike computers, can hold only limited amounts of information in short-term memory.

In Kitano's system, both parsing and generation are carried out by using a parallel marker-passing scheme and a connectionist network. The memory network incorporates knowledge at all levels, from morphophonetics to the plan hierarchies of each participant in the dialogue. Each node in the network represents either a concept, a sequence of concepts, a plan, or a sequence of plans. The system can perform certain inferences about the information contained in the network: it can make predictions about which nodes (events) are likely to be activated next (i.e., what could be said next), speculate how this piece of information could be verbalised (i.e., the creation of lexical and phrasal hypotheses), and so on. When a concept is recognised by the parser, hypotheses for its translation will be activated.

Other features of Kitano's system are the following:

- The time at which translation can commence is parameterisable. Since commencing translation too early may yield poor stylistic results, Kitano's system can be tuned so that translation is delayed until a whole clause is parsed.

- The translations produced by the system are supported by the transcripts from real simultaneous interpetation sessions.

- The system uses opportunistic planning techniques in order to avoid syntactic dead ends.

Currently Kitano is trying to improve the efficiency of the system by investigating methods (a) to solve the conflicts that may arise from the different knowledge sources, and (b) to prevent over-generation, i.e., the production of sentences that are well-formed but which in reality never occur, as they are not produced by a native speaker.

1.6 Conclusions

In this introduction, we have attempted to lay out some of the research themes addressed by the papers in this collection. The links between the papers are rich, and what we have sketched is only one of many possible ways of organising them. Well-defined specialist concerns in NLG are certainly beginning to emerge, and this is an important step in its evolution as a discipline. A number of areas are, however, still insufficiently well understood for a definitive map to be drawn. For instance, the problem of building descriptions seems to interact in a complex way with both text planning and linguistic realisation. Moreover, the impact of connectionist work remains to be taken into account, as it might cause us to redraw some of the traditional boundaries in new ways. These are some of the issues that face NLG researchers as we enter the 1990s.

References

Appelt, D E [1982] Planning Natural-Language Utterances to Satisfy Multiple Goals. Technical Note No. 259, SRI International, Menlo Park, Ca., March, 1982.

Appelt, D E [1985] *Planning English Sentences.* Cambridge: Cambridge University Press.

Danlos, L [1987] *The Linguistic Basis of Text Generation.* Cambridge: Cambridge University Press.

Davey, A [1978] *Discourse Production.* Edinburgh: Edinburgh University Press.

De Smedt, K [1990] Incremental sentence generation: a computer model of grammatical encoding. PhD Thesis, NICI TR No. 90–01, Nijmegen Institute of Cognition Research and Information Technology, 1990.

Goldman, N M [1974] Computer Generation of Natural Language from a Deep Conceptual Base. PhD Thesis, Stanford AI Laboratory Memo AIM–247, Stanford University.

Grice, H P [1975] Logic and conversation. In P Cole and J L Morgan (eds.) *Syntax and Semantics,* Volume 3: *Speech Acts,* pp41–58. New York: Academic Press.

Halliday, M A K [1985] *An Introduction to Functional Grammar.* London: Edward Arnold.

Kasper, R T and Rounds, W C [1986] A logical semantics for feature structures. In *Proceedings of the 24th Annual Meeting of the Association for Computational Linguistics,* Columbia University, New York, 10–13 June 1986, pp257–266.

Kay, M [1984] Functional Unification Grammar: a formalism for machine translation. In *Proceedings of the 10th International Conference on Computational Linguistics and the 22nd Annual Meeting of the Association for Computational Linguistics,* Stanford University, Stanford, Ca., 2–6 July 1984, pp75–78.

Kempen, G [1987] A framework for incremental syntactic tree formation. In *Proceedings of the Tenth International Joint Conference on Artificial Intelligence,* Milan, Italy, 23–28 August 1987, pp655–660.

Kempen, G and Hoenkamp, E [1987] An incremental procedural grammar for sentence formulation. *Cognitive Science,* **11**, 201–258.

Mann, W and Thompson, S [1987] Rhetorical Structure Theory: A theory of text organisation. In L Polanyi (ed.) *The Structure of Discourse.* Norwood, NJ: Ablex.

McDonald, D D [1980] Natural Language Generation as a Process of Decision-Making under Constraints. PhD Thesis, Department of Computer Science and Electrical Engineering, MIT.

McKeown, K R [1982] Generating Natural Language Text in Response to Questions about Database Structure. PhD Thesis, Department of Computer and Information Science, University of Pennsylvania.

McKeown, K R [1985] *Text Generation: Using Discourse Strategies and Focus Constraints to Generate Natural Language Text.* Cambridge: Cambridge University Press.

Meehan, J [1975] Using planning structures to generate stories. *American Journal of Computational Linguistics*, Microfiche **33**.

Meehan, J [1976] TALE-SPIN: an interactive program that writes stories. Research Report No. 74, Department of Computer Science, Yale University, 1976.

Pereira, F C N and Warren, D H D [1980] Definite Clause Grammars for language analysis—a survey of the formalism and a comparison with Augmented Transition Grammars. *Artificial Intelligence*, **13**, 231–278.

Shapiro, S C [1975] Generation as parsing from a network into a linear string. *American Journal of Computational Linguistics*, Microfiche **35**.

Shapiro, S C [1979] Generalized augmented transition network grammars for generation from semantic networks. In *Proceedings of the 17th Annual Meeting of the Association for Computational Linguistics*, University of California at San Diego, La Jolla, Ca., 11–12 August, 1979, pp25–29.

Shieber, S M [1986] *An Introduction to Unification-based Approaches to Grammar.* Chicago, Illinois: The University of Chicago Press.

Simmons, R F and Slocum, J [1972] Generating English discourse from semantic networks. *Communications of the ACM*, **15**, 891–905.

Thompson, H [1977] Strategy and tactics in language production. In W A Beach, S E Fox, S Philosoph (eds.) *Papers from the Thirteenth Regional Meeting of the Chicago Linguistics Society*, Chicago, 14–16 April, 1977.

Zock, M and Sabah, G (eds.) [1988] *Advances in Natural Language Generation.* London: Francis Pinter.

Zock, M [1988] Natural languages are flexible tools; that's what makes them hard to explain, to learn and to use. In M Zock and G Sabah (eds.) *Advances in Natural Language Generation*, Volume 1, pp181–196. London: Francis Pinter.

2 Unresolved Issues in Paragraph Planning

Eduard H. Hovy

Abstract

What is involved in the planning of multi-sentence paragraphs of text? Until a few years ago, the only way we could control the production of coherent multi-sentence paragraphs by computer was by instantiating a schema and linking the schema traverser to a single-sentence generator. Recently, various attempts have been made to develop a new, more flexible, method of planning paragraphs by dynamically assembling and manipulating the basic building elements of coherent paragraphs. All these attempts employ a construct one can call the paragraph structure tree. A number of issues pertaining to the nature and construction of the tree remain unresolved. This chapter first briefly describes the paragraph structure planning method developed at ISI and then, using this method as an example, attempts to draw together the major problems currently confronting the dynamic paragraph construction paradigm and, in some cases, to outline possible forms of solutions.

2.1 Introduction

2.1.1 The basic questions

There is more to building coherent paragraphs than the mere generation of single sentences. When one studies the building of coherent multi-sentence paragraphs, two principal questions arise:

1. What is it that makes multi-sentence text coherent?

2. What algorithm is most suited to construct such text?

In order to produce a clear definition of coherence, one requires an understanding of the interrelationships between the parts of a paragraph. With respect to the algorithm, one would like a method that is computationally well-founded and that handles paragraph-size issues without becoming overly cumbersome or slow.

Research on the automatic production of multi-sentence paragraphs has had a history somewhat similar to that of the generation of single sentences. One of the earliest techniques for producing single sentences relied on templates, in which slots of a predefined template were filled in with appropriate

17

values (lexical items or other templates, filled recursively). Though useful in certain domains, the template technique is limited in flexibility and extensibility because it cannot support the dynamic construction of new types of sentences from the basic elements. Thus, during the last decade, generators have moved away from templates, to the point where the most powerful systems today deal with large numbers of very detailed grammatical features which together specify a sentence.

One of the first systems to produce paragraphs of text used so-called schemas which mandated the content and order of the clauses in paragraphs (see McKeown [1985]). A schema is a fixed representation of a stereotypical discourse strategy that people employ in communication; each schema produces a different type of paragraph. Though early schemas afforded some variation, and later methods were developed to provide additional types of variation [Paris 1987], these structures do not contain the information required for dynamic reassembly of the basic parts into new types of paragraphs.

In order to address this shortcoming, two responses are possible: either generalise schemas and build a hierarchy of increasingly general schema types which can be filled in recursively, or identify the basic building elements from which coherent paragraphs (and thus also schemas) are composed and develop a method of assembling them dynamically into paragraphs on demand. Both approaches have advantages and disadvantages. The former approach is currently being investigated by McKeown [this volume]; the latter by a number of researchers, including the work in this chapter, as well as Cawsey [this volume] and Scott and Souza [this volume]. This chapter briefly describes one of the first attempts at paragraph construction using the dynamic assembly paradigm, and then discusses, with reference to similar work by various people, a number of open questions that remain to be addressed before this method and these ideas can crystallise into a theory.

2.1.2   Some previous work

The question 'what makes text coherent?' has a long history, going back at least to Aristotle [1954]. A number of researchers have recognised that in coherent text successive pieces of text are related in particular ways. Hobbs [1978, 1979, 1982] produced a set of relations organised into four categories, which he postulated as the four types of phenomena that occur during communication. Both Grimes [1975] and Shepherd [1926] categorised typical intersentential relations. The structure of coherent dialogue has been the focus of much study; see for example Reichman [1978], Polanyi [1988], Grosz [1977], and Grosz and Sidner [1986], who outline a theory of how interlocutors' changing intentions and focus of attention give shape to coherent discourse. Extending to longer texts, Van Dijk [1972] discusses large-scale text organisation and defines the notion of macro-structures; and Rumelhart [1975] develops the idea of story grammars. None of this work, however, has led to extensive automatic production of multi-sentence text.

The earliest computational approaches to multi-sentence text production relied on the underlying semantic organisation of the material to enforce coherence; a good example is provided in Meehan [1976]. However, it has become clear that coherence is a function of communicative intent, meaning that the same material can be organised differently to achieve different communicative effects, and that no single 'correct' underlying semantic organisation exists. One of the first attempts to isolate the problem and provide a thoroughly described and computationally sound approach to producing coherent paragraphs was that of McKeown [1985]. She defined four schemas that represent the structure of stereotypical paragraphs for describing objects. Coherence was enforced by the correct nesting and filling of the schemas.

In an effort to identify the basic building elements of coherent text, Mann and Thompson [1986, 1988] conducted a wide-ranging study of hundreds of texts of different types and genres. They proposed that a set of approximately 25 relations suffice to represent the relations that hold within the texts that normally occur in English. Their theory, called Rhetorical Structure Theory (RST), holds that the relations are used recursively, relating ever smaller blocks of adjacent text, down to the single clause level; it assumes that a paragraph is only coherent if all its parts can eventually be made to fit under one overarching relation. Thus each coherent paragraph can be described by a tree structure that captures the rhetorical dependencies between adjacent clauses and blocks of clauses. Most relations have a characteristic cue word or phrase which informs the hearer or reader how to relate the adjacent parts; for example SEQUENCE is signalled by *then* or *next* and PURPOSE by *in order to*. The RST relations include most of Hobbs's, Shepherd's, and Grimes's relations and support McKeown's schemas.

In recent years, a number of computationally oriented research projects have addressed problems that involve generating coherent multi-sentence paragraphs. Almost all of these use a tree of some kind to represent the structure of the paragraph. In some cases, a predefined tree is tailored to the current communicative requirements, such as in the work of Carcagno and Iordanskaja [1989], who generate paragraphs describing the utilisation of a computer. The paragraph is built up by pruning out unfilled options from a fixed structure that contains a space for everything the system could communicate. Maybury [1989] describes the use of interclausal relations within an explanation schema to produce coherent explanations. Jullien and Marty [1989] use a tree to represent the structures of dialogues with possible interruptions and deviations. In other cases, the tree arises as the result of some other processing and doubles as a paragraph structure, as in Dale [this volume], who generates text from a recipe (the cooking plan is represented as a tree). A similar approach, in which the tree is a house-building plan, is taken in Mellish [1988]. Zuckerman and Pearl [1986] use the proof of a mathematics solution as a text tree structure, and Weiner [1980] the hierarchical structure of a tax form. In other cases, the tree is built up dynamically as the result of text planning or other processing. Rankin [1989] describes the use of RST in producing a critique of an expert system user's text for solving a problem. Cawsey [this volume], concerned with the effects of hearer knowledge and resultant interactions in explanatory dialogue, also uses a tree structure to represent the dialogue as it progresses. Moore and Swartout [1988, 1989], Moore and Paris [1989], and Paris [1988] built a text planner using RST and other relations and plans to construct short explanatory dialogues for an expert system. Scott and Souza [this volume] provide rules governing the expression of clauses related by RST relations for maximal clarity, and Souza *et al.* [1989] describe enhancements to RST relations required to produce high-quality Portuguese and English paragraphs. Simonin [1988] describes a bottom-up method for collecting, ordering, and interrelating material before generating it, in which the ordering and interrelation produce a paragraph tree.

Based on such experience, it seems fairly likely that all approaches to the problem of dynamically constructing coherent texts will use a tree to capture the dependencies among and order of the clauses. Depending on the specific tasks they address, the systems above all encountered the same types of problems, which therefore seem likely to be endemic to this paradigm. This chapter attempts to draw together the major problems currently confronting the dynamic paragraph construction paradigm and, in some cases, to outline possible forms of solutions.

2.2 Planning Paragraphs with RST Operators

2.2.1 The method

The planning of multi-sentence paragraphs by computer requires both a sound theory of text organisation and an algorithm that can make efficient use of it. In recent years, an investigation into the planning and generation of multi-sentential paragraphs has been carried out at ISI. Since Rhetorical Structure Theory was developed at ISI, much of this work uses plans which are operationalisations of some RST relations. A text structure planner, a limited top-down hierarchical expansion planning system patterned on NOAH [Sacerdoti 1977], was built to plan coherent paragraphs which achieve communicative goals of affecting the hearer's knowledge in some way. The structure planner operates after some application program (such as an expert system) and before the sentence generator PENMAN [Penman 1989; Mann and Matthiessen 1983].

From the application system, the planner accepts one or more communicative goals along with a set of clause-sized input entities that represent the material to be generated. It assembles the input entities into a tree that embodies the paragraph structure, in which nonterminals are RST relations and terminal nodes contain the input material. It then traverses the tree, submitting the input entities to PENMAN. A short review of the planning process occupies the rest of this section; it is described in much more detail in Hovy [1988a, 1988b].

The plans used are formulations of RST relations. Each relation/plan has two primary parts, a **nucleus** and a **satellite,** and recursively relates some unit(s) of the input, or another relation (cast as nucleus), to other unit(s) of the input or another relation (cast as satellite). (A simple relation/plan, SEQUENCE, is shown in Figure 2.1). In order to admit only properly formed relations, nuclei and satellites contain requirements that must be matched by characteristics of the input. In addition, nuclei and satellites contain **growth points**: collections of goals that suggest the inclusion of additional input material in the places where they frequently occur in typical paragraphs (such as found, for example, in an experiment carried out by Conklin and McDonald [1982]).

On finding (an) RST relation/plan(s) whose effects include achieving (one of) the system's communicative goal(s), the structure planner searches for input entities that match the requirements holding for its nucleus and satellite. If fulfilled, the planner then considers the growth points of the relation/plan. It tries to achieve each newly activated growth point goal by again searching for appropriate relation/plans and matching their nucleus and satellite requirements to the input, recursively, adding successfully instantiated relations to the paragraph tree structure. The planning process bottoms out when either all of the input entities have been incorporated into the tree, or no extant goals can be satisfied by the remaining input entities. The tree is then traversed in a depth-first left-to-right manner, adding the relations' characteristic cue words or phrases to the appropriate input entities and transmitting them to PENMAN to be generated as English clauses. This process is described in detail in Hovy [1988b].

2.2.2   Experiences with the structure planner

The paragraph structure planner has been applied to three domains: two expert systems (one application described in Hovy [1988a]) and a database information display system (Arens *et al.* [1988]). We take here an example from the latter, the Integrated Interfaces program, a multi-modal system that uses maps, tables, and paragraphs of text to answer users' requests for the display of information from a database of naval information about ships. In the example, the Integrated Interface display planner furnishes the RST text

```
Name: SEQUENCE

Results:
  ((BMB SPEAKER HEARER (SEQUENCE-OF ?PART ?NEXT)))

Nucleus requirements/subgoals:
  ((BMB SPEAKER HEARER (TOPIC ?PART)))

Satellite requirements/subgoals:
  ((BMB SPEAKER HEARER (TOPIC ?NEXT)))

Nucleus+Satellite requirements/subgoals:
  ((NEXT-ACTION ?PART ?NEXT))

Nucleus growth points:
  ((BMB SPEAKER HEARER (CIRCUMSTANCE-OF ?PART ?CIR))
   (BMB SPEAKER HEARER (ATTRIBUTE-OF ?PART ?VAL))
   (BMB SPEAKER HEARER (PURPOSE-OF ?PART ?PURP)))

Satellite growth points:
  ((BMB SPEAKER HEARER (ATTRIBUTE-OF ?NEXT ?VAL))
   (BMB SPEAKER HEARER (DETAILS-OF ?NEXT ?DETS))
   (BMB SPEAKER HEARER (SEQUENCE-OF ?NEXT ?FOLL)))

Order: (NUCLEUS SATELLITE)
Relation-phrases: ("" "then" "next")
Activation-question:
  "Could ~A be presented as start-point, mid-point, or end-point
  of some succession of items along some dimension? -- that is,
  should the hearer know that ~A is part of a sequence?"
```

This plan guarantees (the Results field) that both speaker and hearer will mutually believe that the relationship sequence-of holds between two input entities (i.e., that one entity follows another in temporal, ordinal, or spatial sequence). One input entity is bound to the variable ?PART in the Nucleus requirements field and the other to the variable ?NEXT in the Satellite requirements field; no other semantic requirements hold on the input entities individually. However, to ensure that that ?PART does in fact precede ?NEXT, the Nucleus+Satellite requirements specify that they be semantically related by the sequential link NEXT-ACTION (a relation from the Navy domain). Additional material related to the nucleus is suggested in the Nucleus growth points field, calling for circumstantials (time, location, etc.), attributes (size, colour, etc.) and purpose. The typical order of expression in the text is nucleus first and then satellite, using either no cue word, *then*, or *next*.

Figure 2.1: The RST relation/plan SEQUENCE

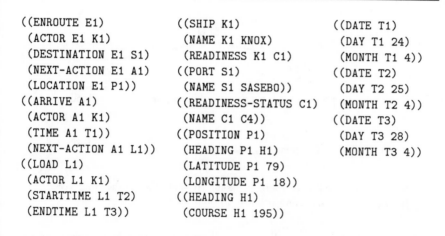

```
((ENROUTE E1)              ((SHIP K1)                ((DATE T1)
 (ACTOR E1 K1)              (NAME K1 KNOX)            (DAY T1 24)
 (DESTINATION E1 S1)        (READINESS K1 C1)         (MONTH T1 4))
 (NEXT-ACTION E1 A1)       ((PORT S1)                ((DATE T2)
 (LOCATION E1 P1))          (NAME S1 SASEBO))         (DAY T2 25)
((ARRIVE A1)              ((READINESS-STATUS C1)      (MONTH T2 4))
 (ACTOR A1 K1)             (NAME C1 C4))             ((DATE T3)
 (TIME A1 T1))            ((POSITION P1)              (DAY T3 28)
 (NEXT-ACTION A1 L1))      (HEADING P1 H1)            (MONTH T3 4))
((LOAD L1)                 (LATITUDE P1 79)
 (ACTOR L1 K1)             (LONGITUDE P1 18))
 (STARTTIME L1 T2)        ((HEADING H1)
 (ENDTIME L1 T3))          (COURSE H1 195))
```

Figure 2.2: Example Navy domain input

structure planner with a set of six related entities, along with the following goal to describe a sequence of events (starting with the first event, and including as much of the given information as possible):

(1) (BMB SPEAKER HEARER (SEQUENCE-OF E1 ?NEXT))

which can be paraphrased as: achieve the state in which both the speaker and the hearer mutually believe that input entity E1 is followed by some other input entity. The notation is explained in Section 2.3.1.

After rewriting the input into a standard form (called here input entities, and shown in Figure 2.2), the structurer proceeds to plan a paragraph, producing the resulting tree shown diagrammatically in Figure 2.3. It then traverses the tree and supplies the input entities at the leaves to PENMAN to be generated as sentences, one by one. This example will be used throughout the chapter for exposition.

In developing this method, we have discovered that RST relation/plans are an ideal tool for planning paragraphs, for the following reasons:

- RST relation/plans support reasoning about the communicative goals of speaker and hearer in a very natural way, since their contents can be formulated in terms of the intentions and beliefs of the speaker and hearer. This formulation recognises explicitly the goal-directed nature of communication, and the way part-to-part relations in the text are used to carry out those intentions.

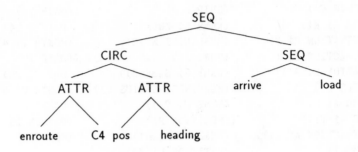

Knox, which is c4, is en route to Sasebo. It is at 79N 18E heading ssw.
It will arrive on 4/24, and will load for four days.

Figure 2.3: A Navy example paragraph structure tree and corresponding
text

Left branches of the tree are nuclei and right branches are satellites. C4 is an
operational readiness status.

- Planning with RST relation/plans affords more flexibility than with schemas, because individual relation/plans typically mandate less of the
  paragraph than schemas do. However, we have found that it is possible to formulate and treat RST relation/plans as schemas when necessary (this issue is discussed in Section 2.3.4). This is desirable because
  schemas are easy to define and use; in many situations they are more
  convenient than relation/plans.

- This method of planning paragraphs builds a tree structure that represents the internal organisation and rhetorical dependencies between
  clauses in the text. The paragraph structure tree makes possible some
  powerful reasoning about the text. First, it contains the derivation of
  each part of the paragraph, enabling one to reason about the part each
  clause plays with respect to the whole, and thus to identify and repair
  mistakes. Second, by inspecting the internal balance and bushiness of the
  tree, one can regroup its parts to achieve a different balance, add additional material into sparse parts, or elide material in bushy parts. Third,
  one can examine the tree to trace the development of the theme, which
  helps decide questions of reference such as pronominalisation. Though
  we have not yet pursued any of these avenues of research, we believe

them to be rich with possibility.

2.3 Seven Unsolved Problems

The use of a tree to represent the paragraph structure enables various new possibilities. However, its content and construction pose a set of hitherto unaddressed questions. The rest of this chapter describes seven currently open problems, where each section lists a number of particular questions that should be addressed. Though the problems are presented using RST as the example, they seem endemic to the dynamic paragraph planning paradigm and will have to be faced by all particular implementations in this paradigm. The problems, which can be organised into two groups, are:

- Theory and representation of coherence relations:

    1. A formalism for relation/plans
    2. The content of relation/plans
    3. The ontology of relations
    4. Relation/plans and schemas

- Algorithm:

    1. Controlling tree growth with focus
    2. Additional function: collecting material
    3. Additional function: organising sentence content

Each section following is dedicated to one problem area, and each contains a number of open questions. For concreteness, the questions are usually posed in terms of RST and the RST structure planner, though their general form will be apparent.

2.3.1 A formalism for relation/plans

As used to plan paragraphs, RST is a goal-based theory: its descriptions are organised around the intentions of the speaker and the rhetorical relations that can be used to achieve those intentions. The effect field of each relation/plan contains a description of the intended effect of the relation, which must be interpreted as the inferences that the speaker is licensed to make about the hearer's knowledge after the successful generation of the relation in the text. Thus the goals of the planner are identified with the effects on the hearer's knowledge state. Employing RST relations as plans was the central insight which made possible this style of text planning with RST.

In order to ensure that each relation links appropriate material, each relation/plan's nucleus, satellite, and joint nucleus and satellite requirements fields prescribe the features required of material to be used in the nucleus or satellite positions in the text. How should these features be represented? Obviously, the requirements must relate to semantic properties of the material as well as to the hearer's knowledge and beliefs. Also, these requirements must be expressible in the particular ontology used by the application to represent the domain.

A suitable notation for reasoning about hearer's beliefs and speaker's intent in various ontologies is the set of modal operators used in the formal theory of rational interaction being developed by, among others, Cohen, Levesque, and Perrault. The operators are:

(2)   a   (BEL x p)
            p follows from x's beliefs

       b   (BMB x y p)
            p follows from x's beliefs about what x and y mutually believe

       c   (GOAL x p)
            p follows from x's goals

       d   (AFTER a p)
            p is true in all courses of events after action a

as well as the logical operators AND and OR.

It is no accident that these terms are well suited for paragraph planning. Cohen and Levesque have been trying to derive speech acts from the basic modal operators following a theorem-oriented research paradigm, and in their derivations they construct intermediate proofs or lemmas that resemble RST relation/plans. For example, Cohen and Levesque [1985] present a proof (later retracted) that the indirect speech act of requesting can be derived from the above basic modal operators. In doing so, they define **summaries** as, essentially, speech act operators with activating conditions (**gates**) and **effects**. These summaries are useful intermediate steps in the production of large-scale effects such as speech acts. The summaries closely resemble, in structure, the RST relation/plans, with gates corresponding to satellite and nucleus constraints and effects to intended effects. This obvious correspondence suggests the possibility of using rhetorical operators such as RST relations as 'lemmas' in formal 'proofs' or derivations of the meanings of paragraphs. (Though Cohen and Levesque have subsequently retracted the conclusions of their 1985 paper, and hold instead that one requires also a notion of commitment when performing such derivations, the utility of the notation remains unaffected for informative statements such as those on which we performed the text structuring experiments.)

An implicit INFORM speech act is present at each leaf of the paragraph structure tree. To this, QUESTION, ORDER, REQUEST, and other speech acts can be added. How to incorporate them within the functionality of RST, as it is currently stated, is an open problem.

Though at present the RST structure planner does not perform sophisticated reasoning about the speaker's and hearer's beliefs, the speech act notation was chosen for its eventual utility in that regard. Its potential, and the experience of planning out coherent paragraphs, give rise to the following questions:

- Are the following two basic requirements sufficient for a notation in which to represent the contents of relation/plans: the ability to support reasoning about the hearer's and the speaker's beliefs and knowledge, and to represent the semantics of the application domain?

- Will RST relation/plans prove to be useful as intermediate steps in deriving various speech acts?

- Can the relation/plans fruitfully be used in constructing coherent interactive dialogues? The possibility of something resembling RST relation/plans being put to such use was raised in 1986 by Grosz and Sidner [1986], and is evident in the work of Moore and Swartout [1989] (and see Section 2.3.6), Cawsey [this volume], and Jullien and Marty [1989].

2.3.2   The content of relation/plans

Questions arise also in the operationalisation of RST relations, where one has to formulate 'semantic' descriptions for such complicated notions as, for example, SEQUENCE, PURPOSE, and SOLUTIONHOOD. To the extent that one's relations are to be used in a computational system which has a representation for such notions, this task is simple; for example, the essential term in the nucleus and satellite requirements in Figure 2.1 is the term

(3)   (NEXT-ACTION ?PART ?NEXT)

since NEXT-ACTION is the way the Navy domain represents temporal sequence. However, in general, formulating a characterisation of an RST relation sufficiently abstract to have some semblance to its original intent, while remaining concrete enough to hint at a viable implementation, is not an easy task. Consider the relation SOLUTIONHOOD, which can be defined as in Figure 2.4.

Roughly, the nucleus requirements specify some state ?STATE-A which is good (or which the speaker has the goal to bring about) and which is achieved by some action ?ACT-A. The satellite requirements specify some other state ?STATE-B which is bad and which is somehow the inverse of ?STATE-A (for

```
Nucleus requirements/subgoals
   ((STATE ?STATE-A)
    (OR (BMB SPEAKER HEARER (OPINION SPEAKER ?STATE-A GOOD))
        (AND (BMB SPEAKER HEARER (HAVE-GOAL SPEAKER ?GOAL-A))
             (BMB SPEAKER HEARER (DESIRE ?GOAL-A ?STATE-A))
             (GOAL ?GOAL-A)))
    (ACTION ?ACT-A)
    (BMB SPEAKER HEARER (RESULT ?ACT-A ?STATE-A)))
Satellite requirements/subgoals
   ((STATE ?STATE-B)
    (BMB SPEAKER HEARER (OPINION SPEAKER ?STATE-B BAD)))
Nucleus+Satellite requirements/subgoals
   ((INVERSE-STATES ?STATE-A ?STATE-B))
```

Figure 2.4: A tentative definition for the RST relation/plan SOLUTIONHOOD

example, the state of a car being filled with gasoline being desirable compared to the state of the car being empty). This last requirement, namely

(4) (INVERSE-STATES ?STATE-A ?STATE-B)

is pure wishful shorthand (in the 'wishful mnemonics' spirit of McDermott [1981]) for some formulation of the opposition of the two states, a matter not at all clear (in the example, capturing somehow the fact that both states pertain to the same car and that, except for the gasoline and some related details such as time of consideration, all other details remain unaffected). For such very difficult representational issues no adequate representation terminology has been found thus far.

The relation/plan builder should be aware of the fact that a definition may be adequate for the task at hand but still fall a long way short of being general, or even of applying in the next domain. On the other hand, one should guard against formulating such general definitions that they do not seem to apply to the specific relations desired for a particular domain. Hence the questions:

- How can one develop adequate definitions for RST relation/plans, some of which express very complex notions such as solutionhood, purpose, and concession?

- How can one ensure that the definitions are general enough to relate easily to the ontologies of arbitrarily different domains while not being so general as to lose their uniqueness and utility?

A further issue pertains to the nature of the content of the nucleus and satellite fields. As illustrated in Figure 2.1, most terms in the requirements fields relate to the semantics of the domain, since they have to differentiate usable input entities from unusable ones; while in the growth point fields, most terms relate to other RST relation/plans, since they control coherent growth. Thus, in traditional planning jargon, nucleus and satellite requirements are treated as preconditions while growth point goals are plan steps (and, parenthetically, the 'side-effect' of generating text from the nucleus and satellite fillers corresponds to the actual actions!). This is not the only possible treatment, however. There is no reason why nucleus and satellite requirements must always be satisfied directly, in the manner of preconditions; it is quite reasonable to allow the planner to plan to bring about the satisfaction of unsatisfied requirements by the inclusion of further material, in exactly the way it includes material as suggested by growth point goals. In this case, questions arise about the freedom a planner should have in violating (or simply not fully satisfying) its requirements, and about the planning of repair moves. The optimal treatment of requirements and growth points is not yet clear; in the current implementation, semantically oriented requirements and rhetorically oriented requirements are separated into the two different fields as a useful notational simplification. Some open questions are:

- Under which conditions can growth be spawned by unsatisfied nucleus and satellite requirements? How should the planning then be controlled? What does this imply for coherence?

Yet another issue pertains to the intentionality expressed in relation/plans. Moore and Swartout [1989] and Moore and Paris [1989] claim that using RST-based relation/plans to govern whole paragraphs constitutes a conflation of the intentional and rhetorical function of text planning for communication. This claim poses an interesting question about the intentionality expressed by RST relation/plans. Does the plan labeled PERSUADE, containing a step labeled EVIDENCE (from Paris [1988]), have intentional overtones which an RST relation/plan such as SEQUENCE, with essential requirement NEXT-ACTION, completely lacks? That is to say, when the planner operates under the goal to persuade, does it exhibit more intentional behaviour than when it operates under the goal to express sequentiality? Certainly, as Moore and Paris point out, the goal to persuade can be achieved by various rhetorical means—even, under the right circumstances, by expressing a sequence of events. But the nature of intentionality remains intuitive and unclear. Perhaps texts are planned using plans with an intentional nature, which then find their coherent interclausal realisation by means of rhetorical relation/plans. An analogy to the distinction between high-level programming languages and assembly language may be apt: there is a similar intuitive difference between the construct DO-WHILE,

on the one hand, and the instructions SUBTRACT, BRANCH-IF-ZERO, JUMP (all
three of which are necessarily contained in a DO loop), on the other. The results reported by Jullien and Marty [1989], whose plans (used in a plan revision
system performing dialogue) are of two kinds, overall strategies and particular
primitive actions, tend to support this view. The pertinent questions are:

- Can one differentiate the rhetorical from the intentional effects of rela-
  tion/plans? Does it matter?

- What is the intentional force of RST relation/plans? How can plans with
  some intentionality be assembled out of plans without any?

- What other operators in addition to the RST relation/plans are required
  to perform text planning in various domains? How will they be tax-
  onomised?

2.3.3   The ontology of relations

The third problem area pertains to the specific set of relation/plans used.
As postulated in RST (in, say, Mann and Thompson [1988]), about 25 relations suffice to explain coherence in English. Practical text structure planning
experience accumulated so far indicates that some reorganisation of the RST relations is necessary. Depending on the application domain's needs, certain relations seem naturally to subdivide into sets of similar relations (such as ELAB-
ORATION, which gives rise to ELABORATION-PART/WHOLE, ELABORATION-
ABSTRACT/INSTANCE, ELABORATION-ATTRIBUTE, etc.), and other relations
seem indistinguishable due to our current inability to represent notions such as
intention adequately (such as NON-VOLITIONAL-RESULT, VOLITIONAL-RESULT,
and PURPOSE). Fortunately, not all application domains require all relations
to be equally finely distinguished: some may require more detailed representations of causality, others may concentrate on object descriptions or historical
narrations. In order to accommodate various domain needs, the solution seems
to be to structure relations into a hierarchical taxonomy of progressively finer
detail.

   Furthermore, as is described in Section 2.3.6, evidence is mounting that
the relations provided by RST are not sufficient for all types of text structure
planning, and that for certain kinds of explanation and argumentation, additional plans such as PERSUADE and MOTIVATE are required: see Paris [1988],
Moore and Swartout [1988], and Sections 2.3.6 and 2.3.2; Maybury [1989]
uses the plans EXPLAIN, SUPPORT, RECOMMEND, IDENTIFY-PROBLEM; Cawsey
[this volume] uses terms such as TEACH-HOW-IT-WORKS and TEACH-WHAT-IT-
DOES. Assuming that the RST relation/plans constitute the most basic interclausal relations, this work seems to suggest the existence of a level of more expressive, perhaps more intentional, plans, which usually control slightly larger

spans of text.

Continuing along the scale of text size, one may then surmise the existence of a taxonomy of even more expansive plan/schemas to govern the planning of such stereotypical multi-paragraph texts as reports, letters, etc. The text planner would have access to all these schema/plan/relations and be able to expand them in terms of each other in order to produce appropriate texts. While the development of these ideas is future work, the idea can be summarised by the taxonomy in Figure 2.5. The basic question is simply:

- What relations/plans/schemas are necessary to support the dynamic planning of coherent multi-sentence and multi-paragraph texts in English? What layers of complexity do they form?

2.3.4 Relation/plans and schemas

As was implied in the previous section, a close relationship exists between relation/plans and schemas. This is fortunate, because both the structure planning and the schema instantiation paradigms have distinct advantages and disadvantages. Schemas have the great advantage of being simple to understand and easy to use computationally. However, they do not support the adaptive requirements of interactive systems that can be called upon dynamically to elaborate or replan any particular piece of a paragraph at any time, because they do not contain the motivations under which each clause (or group of clauses) appears in the paragraph. In contrast, a paragraph tree does provide this information, but at a cost—paragraph tree assembly can be considerably more difficult than schema instantiation. Clearly, a melding of the two techniques is desirable.

In 1987, an argument was made in Mann [1987] that schemas are nothing else than stereotypically appearing collections of RST relations, or conversely, that RST relations are simply the elemental building blocks of schemas. This characterisation was carried further by Hovy [1988b], who addressed the computational aspects of schemas and relation/plans. Hovy showed that a melding can be achieved by exercising appropriate control over optional additional material—the material, in the current RST structure planner implementation, whose order and inclusion is captured in the growth point goals.

This works as follows. As shown, treating growth point goals as *suggestions* to include additional material, rather than as *injunctions* to do so, makes the difference between a relation/plan that acts like a very flexible minimum-sized relation and one that acts like a schema. In this treatment, some growth point goals can be made required and others optional. Relation/plans can thus simultaneously incorporate both fixed structural options that are not justified by reasoning (i.e., act as schemas), as well as relational patterns that

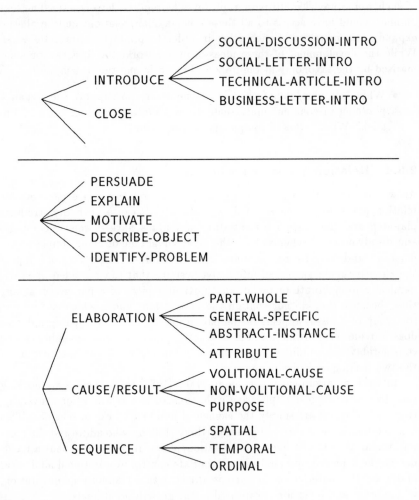

Figure 2.5: A layered taxonomy of schema/plan/relations

are developed dynamically (i.e., support opportunistic planning). This hybrid approach is eminently adapted to such texts as letters in which some parts (the salutation and first paragraph) are relatively structured, while other parts (the body) are relatively free. The ease of such hybridisation is very encouraging, because it makes available for paragraph structuring applications that are otherwise difficult or impossible to handle. That is to say, relation/plans are useful primarily when a large amount of flexibility is desired over a relatively small number (in the order of 10 to 30) of clause-sized units of information to be conveyed. However, in large collections of information, a less flexible method with more structure is required, if planning time is to be kept manageable— and this is exactly the strength of schemas.

When treating growth point goals merely as suggestions for additional paragraph growth, two problems are immediately introduced:

- Which growth point goals should be considered?

- In what order should new growths be added to the tree?

Some criteria for determining inclusion and ordering of growth point goals are given in Hovy [1988b]. They depend on (the planner's attitude toward) the hearer's knowledge and opinions, external constraints on the length and complexity of the text, the desired textual balance of the paragraph, and the method of introduction and development of the material (that is, thematisation or focus). Other than the issue of focus (see Section 2.3.5), none of these criteria has been addressed yet by a computational system (to the author's knowledge). Thus the following open questions remain:

- In converting from a schema-like structure to a relation/plan, how should the optional growth point material be handled? What decision criteria can be brought to bear? When should a relation be used as a schema and when not?

2.3.5 Controlling tree growth with focus

The remaining four problem areas pertain to the procedural and functional aspects of paragraph planning.

To produce the paragraph in Figure 2.3, the structurer relied on a very important assumption: relation/plans' growth points were treated as injunctions, making the relation/plans essentially mini-schemas. But, as discussed in Section 2.3.4, the order and inclusion of growth point goals can be made optional, which of course enables the structurer to build many more paragraph trees from the same input material. This introduces a problem: allowing free ordering of growth point fillers gives rise to some paragraphs that do not seem

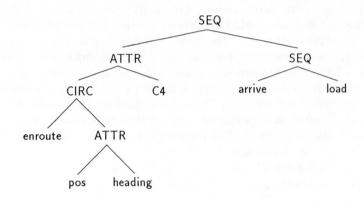

Knox is en route to Sasebo. It is at 79N 18E heading SSW. It is C4. It
will arrive on 4/24, and will load for four days.

Figure 2.6: Another version of the Navy text, treating growth points in free
order

coherent. For example, structure planning with the same six Navy input elements used before produces (among others) the tree shown in Figure 2.6.
The fact is that RST relation/plans alone, under free growth point ordering,
simply do not provide enough information to produce coherent paragraphs in
all cases.

On reflection, this is not surprising, since coherence is a not unitary phenomenon, capturable simply in a single knowledge structure. Coherence results
from the confluence of a number of considerations.

One such consideration, as illustrated in McKeown [1985], is focus (i.e.,
method of development of the theme). In order to take focus into account, we
are collaborating with McCoy from the University of Delaware, who is developing a theory of **Focus Trees** (a technique of managing perspective shifts;
see McCoy and Cheng [1988], McCoy [1985]). We are investigating merging
RST structure planning with the constraints imposed by Focus Tree building
rules (this work is reported in Hovy and McCoy [1989]). Under this joint
regime, the RST planner constructs the paragraph structure tree and a Focus
Tree in tandem. During the expansion of a node in the RST tree, the structurer applies all the growth point goals active at that point and collects the
resulting candidate relations and their associated clause-sized input entities.

Each candidate growth entity is then checked against the currently allowed focus shifts in the Focus Tree, and invalid candidates are simply removed from consideration. One of three possibilities ensues:

1. Only one candidate remains. In this case, growth proceeds straightforwardly with this candidate.

2. More than one candidate remains. In this case all candidates are coherent based on rhetorical structure and focus but additional measures, still to be developed, must be employed to select the best of these. (As an interim practical solution, the growth points in the RST relation/plan can be ordered by typical occurrence, and the tree can be grown in this default order.)

3. No candidates remain. In this case, depending on the overall stylistic goals of the system, two options ensue:

    (a) Tree growth is simply stopped at this point.
    (b) Tree growth is continued at this point, in the default order as above, but the text is linguistically marked to indicate a focus shift.

This approach is promising: unacceptable trees are not built, or, in some cases, are made accessible by a reordering of their parts. That is to say, when an RST tree is unacceptable to the Focus Tree criterion in its initial form, but can be made acceptable by reordering its parts (which may involve generating appropriate linguistic focus words in the text). The paragraph structure tree in Figure 2.6 is such a case; under the additional control of the Focus Tree, the C4 clause is required to precede the **enroute** clause in the text. The RST planner handles this requirement by inverting the ATTRIBUTIVE relation nucleus and satellite in the RST tree, giving a linguistically marked text by focusing on the readiness status. The resulting tree, with accompanying text, is shown in Figure 2.7.

Since this is work newly begun, a number of questions remain unaddressed:

- In the example shown, focusing is not a goal-directed process but derives passively, as it were, from the Focus Tree. The treatment of focus as a passive restraint rather than an active protagonist makes it easy to incorporate with planning motivated by RST, but is it an adequate model of thematisation?

- How do other theories of thematisation (such as Daneš [1974], Fries [1981], Halliday [1967, 1970], Thompson [1985]) relate to Focus Trees? How can they be integrated with this method of paragraph structure planning?

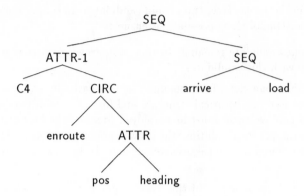

With readiness C4, Knox is en route to Sasebo. It is at 79N 18E heading SSW. It will arrive on 4/24 and will load for four days.

Figure 2.7: Joint RST and focus generated Navy text

- In what ways can the signalling of focus (such as inverted order of sentence constituents and realisation as independent and dependent clauses) be made responsive to RST relation/plans?

2.3.6 Collecting material

As initially conceived, the RST structurer builds coherent paragraphs from input provided by some source. But very early on, Moore, Paris, and Swartout from ISI (see Moore and Swartout [1988, 1989], Paris [1988], Moore and Paris [1988]) recognised that the same planning method could be used simultaneously to *collect* the material to be generated from a suitably structured collection of information (in their case, from the knowledge underlying an expert system; though databases do just as well). In fact, Paris makes the claim that the task of choosing what is to be said cannot be separated from the task of organising it into a coherent whole; each task influences the other. This is true in many cases, especially for tasks such as explaining an expert system's reasoning interactively to a user. Here the explanation constructor should perform the paragraph planning in parallel with its determination of what to include, because the communicative nature of the explanation task places strong constraints on the material to be said. In other cases, however, it is more convenient to separate the application system and the structure planner, usually when the application task is more remote from language than explanation generation. In our experiment with the Integrated Interfaces Navy project (and, initially, our joint work with Moore and Paris, before they built their own text planner), the application program determines what is to be generated, and the text structure planner organises it into a coherent body of text. A similar task division is described in Maybury [1989] and in Carcagno and Iordanskaja [1989].

Following their avenue of investigation, Moore and Paris have produced very interesting results (this brief summary does not do justice to the work they have done). They have investigated using the text plan in dialogue to answer vaguely articulated follow-up questions, and have tried to associate attentional information (in the sense of Grosz and Sidner [1986]) in with the text plan. They have also developed a set of approximately 50 text plans that serve to select, from the traces produced by their expert systems, just that material that is pertinent to the current communicative goals. These plans are used in addition to those provided by RST; as described in Section 2.3.4, their plans seem to have a more intentional flavour.

In summary, then, some questions to be addressed are:

- How can text relation/plans be formulated so as to control the search through the knowledge base for appropriate material? Though Moore and Paris have made a beginning, much more work remains to be done before adequately expressive plan languages and formalisms have been developed.

- What is the proper relationship between host system and text planner? Which system decides what is to be said? Under which conditions?

- How can RST relation/plans and plans such as developed by Moore and Paris be used together?

2.3.7   Organising sentence content

Even after taking into account the constraints imposed by focus, the paragraph structure tree does not contain all the information required for the successful realisation of text. For example, the first ATTRIBUTIVE relation in Figure 2.3 has the following realisational alternatives:

(5)   a   Knox, which is C4, is en route.

     b   Knox is en route and it is C4.

     c   Knox is en route. It is C4.

and the final SEQUENCE has at least the following:

(6)   a   It will arrive on 4/24 and will load for 4 days.

      b   It will arrive on 4/24. It will load for 4 days.

In addressing this question, a number of issues must be taken into account. Focus (the amount of attention accorded to material) can help determine dependent or independent clauses, as can the complexity of the remainder of the paragraph tree, the desired overall style of the text—a general preference for short or long sentences, for example, and the rhythm of sentences (long alternating with short, as suggested in numerous books on good style, such as Shepherd [1926]). The issues can be summarised by the following questions:

- When should the parts of a relation be realised as a single sentence, and when as separate sentences?

- If the parts are realised in a single sentence, when should the two clauses by related hypotactically (i.e., one as a dependent clause) and when paratactically (i.e., as two independent clauses linked by a conjunction)?

The problem of delimiting and organising sentence content has a counterpart within the noun phrase. Three issues are particularly relevant.

The first issue relates to pronominalisation. Though it is a common belief that pronominalisation is a linear phenomenon (that is, that it depends only on the previous occurrence of some entity in the text), studies suggest that pronominalisation is sensitive to rhetorical groupings, since it seems to respect boundaries between relatively major blocks of text but not minor ones (see, for example, Björklund and Virtanen [1989]). The availability of the paragraph's rhetorical structure as an RST tree, in which rhetorical groupings manifest themselves as subtrees, enables the development of more sophisticated pronominalisation strategies. Exactly which group boundaries permit pronominalisation, however, remains an open question.

One promising approach to handling pronominalisation is to use Discourse Representation Structures (DRSs) from the Discourse Representation Theory (DRT) of Kamp [1981] in RST paragraph trees. A preliminary description of such use of DRSs is reported in Hovy [1989]. Relevant information about each entity mentioned in a clause can be captured in a DRS in the normal way, and the structure can then be propagated upward in the RST tree during tree traversal (just before sentence generation), from nucleus to relation to satellite, where it determines pronominalisation in the satellite clause and merges with relevant information from the satellite. Further propagation proceeds recursively.

The second issue arises in cases where material in a dependent clause can be realised instead within the noun phrase proper (as an adjective, say). Again from Figure 2.3, *Knox, which is C4,* ... could have been realised as *the C4 Knox* ...; in Figure 2.7, we deemed the clause-sized *Being C4, Knox* ... (which was realised by default) unacceptable, preferring the realisation *With readiness C4, Knox* ... Determining the optimal syntactic class of material that can be realised in various ways might depend, among other things, on the balance of the paragraph structure tree, on focus, and on the stylistically desired density of information in the noun phrase. This question has been addressed by Scott and Souza [this volume], who provide a grammar for controlling the realisation of RST relations into high-quality English at places where multiple realisations are possible.

The third issue, aggregation, appears frequently, and is a direct result of the fact that disparate pieces of information can often be grouped when they have pertinent features in common. In the example domain, the Integrated Interface display manager deals with one ship at a time, since this is how ship information is organised in the database. This organisation imposes a serious limitation on the quality of the text produced, as illustrated by PENMAN:

(7) Fanning is en route in order to rendezvous with Task Group 70.1, arriving on 4/27, to perform operations until 4/30.
Passumpsic is en route in order to rendezvous with Task Group 70.1, arriving on 4/24, to perform operations until 4/31.
Whipple is en route in order to rendezvous with Task Group 70.1, arriving on 4/27, to perform operations until 4/30.

In order to improve the text, the following simple rule was applied to alter the grouping of the input entities:

If input elements A and B contain the same action, the same ending date or time, and the same location, and they contain different actors, then merge element B with element A.

The result, also generated by PENMAN, is better:

(8) Fanning, Passumpsic, and Whipple are en route in order to rendezvous with Task Group 70.1, arriving 4/27. Fanning and Whipple will perform operations until 4/30. Passumpsic will perform operations until 4/31.

Though this grouping rule is obviously very specific, it is easily generalised and appears useful in many and varied applications. Similar grouping tasks to improve texts are described in the text structuring work of Dale [this volume] and of Cargano and Iordanskaja [1989].

Grouping rules of this type can clearly be applied either before or after the paragraph structure has been planned out. The major difference lies in the amount of work to be done in the two cases. If aggregation is performed before structure planning, the aggregator has to inspect every pair of input

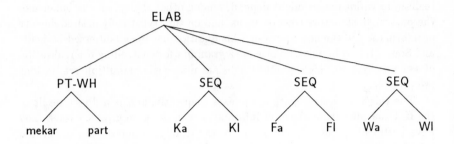

Figure 2.8: A tree configuration for which aggregation is possible

elements for each aggregation rule it has, an order n^2 operations per rule for n elements. If aggregation is performed after structuring, the aggregator need only inspect the pairs of elements within each leaf of the paragraph structure tree, since the overall structure has been determined. Typically, by the nature of RST text structuring, this number is in the order of to two or three elements.

Another type of aggregation involves RST relations directly. Before aggregation, PENMAN generated the following example (MEKAR-87 is a naval exercise):

(9) MEKAR-87 takes place in the South China Sea from 10/20 until 11/13. Knox, Fanning, and Whipple are participating. Knox arrives on 10/20. It leaves on 10/31. Fanning arrives on 10/20. It leaves on 11/13. Whipple arrives on 10/29. It leaves on 11/13.

The paragraph structure, involving three parallel ELABORATION relations, is shown in Figure 2.8.

In order to improve this text, we applied a second aggregation rule, namely,

> If two instances of the same RST relation emanate from a single nucleus, then merge the two instances into one relation, and append their satellites.

to the above tree, followed by the application of the first rule, which resulted in:

(10) MEKAR-87 takes place in the South China Sea from 10/20 until 11/13. Knox, Fanning, and Whipple are participating. Knox and Fanning arrive on 10/20. Whipple arrives on 10/29. Knox leaves on 10/31. Fanning and Whipple leave on 11/13.

Of course, the problem of aggregation is not limited to instances such as these; as discussed in Van Dijk and Kintsch [1983] and in Hovy [1987], aggregation rules can also be based upon concept subsumption (as when *he sold his house and threw away his books* becomes *he got rid of his goods*) or on world knowledge (as in *Joe hit Mike. Mike hit Joe back. Joe kicked Mike* ... becomes *Mike and Joe fought*). But structural aggregation, with the types of benefits shown here, can only be performed using a paragraph structure tree with appropriate rules.

To conclude this section, some questions:

- How does pronominalisation relate to the paragraph structure tree? Do specific RST relations for pronoun boundaries, or are large enough leaps in the tree enough?

- If DRSs are incorporated into an RST tree, do they provide acceptable pronominalisation? What are the rules for DRS propagation in the tree?

- When should material in a noun phrase be realised as dependent clauses, and when as other constituents, for example as adjectives? Do RST relations play a role in the decision?

- What general rules of aggregation exist? How can the internal structure—symmetry, bushiness, etc.—of the paragraph structure tree be used to guide the application of such rules?

2.4 Conclusion

Though the seven unresolved problem areas outlined here have always been latent in text generation, they have been brought to the forefront by the development of the dynamic paragraph planning paradigm, exemplified in this chapter by the RST structure planner and relation/plans. The number of recent papers identifying and addressing these issues testify to their topicality.

The availability of the paragraph structure tree as a central construct with which to work makes the task of addressing these questions and evaluating the answers much easier than it was a decade ago, when it was often difficult even to formulate the problems. Though we have but taken the first step toward the eventual ability to plan coherent paragraphs dynamically, the issues we have encountered, summarised by the questions listed in this chapter, will require our attention for a considerable time. Answers to these questions will enable the flexible planning and generation of coherent, high-quality paragraphs, and greatly facilitate the next step: multi-page multi-paragraph texts.

Acknowledgements

This work was supported in part by the Advanced Research Projects Agency monitored by the Office of Naval Research under contract N00014-82-K-0149, and by the Rome Air Development Center under RADC contract FQ7619-89-03326-0001.

References

Arens, Y, Miller, L, Shapiro, S C and Sondheimer, N K [1988] Automatic construction of user-interface displays. In *Proceedings of the 7th National Conference on Artificial Intelligence*, St Paul, Minnesota, 1988, pp808–813. Also available as USC/Information Sciences Institute Research Report RR-88-218.

Aristotle [1954] The Rhetoric. In W R Roberts (trans) *The Rhetoric and the Poetics of Aristotle*. New York: Random House.

Björklund, M and Virtanen, T [1989] Variation in narrative structure: A simple text *vs* an innovative work of art. Presented at the *16th International Systemics Congress*, Helsinki, June 1989.

Carcagno, D and Iordanskaja, L [1989] Content determination and text structuring in Gossip. In *Extended Abstracts of the Second European Natural Language Generation Workshop*, University of Edinburgh, 6–8 April, 1989, pp15–22.

Cawsey, A [1990] Generating explanatory discourse. This volume.

Cohen, P R and Levesque, H [1985] Speech acts and rationality. In *Proceedings of the 23rd Annual Meeting of the Association for Computational Linguistics*, University of Chicago, Chicago, Illinois, 8–12 July, 1985, pp49–59.

Conklin, E J and McDonald, D D [1982] Salience: the key to the selection problem in natural language generation. In *Proceedings of the 20th Annual Meeting of the Association for Computational Linguistics*, University of Toronto, Toronto, Ontario, Canada, June, 1982, pp129–135.

Dale, R [1990] Generating recipes: An overview of Epicure. This volume.

Daneš, F [1974] Functional sentence perspective and the organization of the text. Pages 106–128 in F Daneš (ed) *Papers on Functional Sentence Perspective*. The Hague: Mouton.

Fries, P H [1981] On the status of theme in English: Arguments from discourse. *Forum Linguisticum*, 6, 1–38.

Grimes, J E [1975] *The Thread of Discourse*. The Hague: Mouton.

Grosz, B J [1977] The representation and use of focus in a system for understanding dialog. Technical Note No. 151, SRI International, Menlo Park, Ca.

Grosz, B J and Sidner, C L [1986] Attention, intentions, and the structure of discourse. *Computational Linguistics*, 12, 175–204.

Halliday, M A K [1967] Language structure and language function. *Journal of Linguistics*, **3**, 177–274.

Halliday, M A K [1970] *An Introduction to Functional Grammar*. Baltimore, Md.: Edward Arnold Press.

Hobbs, J R [1978] Why Is Discourse Coherent? Technical Note No. 176, SRI International, Menlo Park, Ca., November, 1978.

Hobbs, J R [1979] Coherence and coreference. *Cognitive Science*, **3**, 67–90.

Hobbs, J R [1982] Coherence in discourse. In W G Lehnert, and M H Ringle (eds) *Strategies for Natural Language Processing*, pp223–243. Hillsdale, NJ: Lawrence Erlbaum Associates.

Hovy, E H [1987] Interpretation in generation. In *Proceedings of the 6th National Conference on Artificial Intelligence*, August 1987, pp545–549. Also available as USC/Information Sciences Institute Research Report RS-88-186.

Hovy, E H [1988] Planning coherent multisentential text. In *Proceedings of the 26th Annual Meeting of the Association for Computational Linguistics*, State University of New York at Buffalo, Buffalo, NY, 7–10 June 1988, pp163–169.

Hovy, E H [1988] Approaches to the planning of coherent text. Presented at the *4th International Workshop on Text Generation*, Los Angeles, 1988. Also in C L Paris, W R Swartout, and W C Mann (eds), *Natural Language in Artificial Intelligence and Computational Linguistics*, to appear.

Hovy, E H and McCoy, K F [1989] Focusing your RST: A step toward generating coherent multisentential text. In *Proceedings of the 11th Cognitive Science Conference*, Ann Arbor, August 1989, pp667–674. Also available as USC/Information Sciences Institute Research Report RS-89-246.

Hovy, E H [1989] Notes on dialogue management and text planning in the LILOG project. Unpublished working document, Projekt LILOG, Institut für Wissensbasierte Systeme, IBM Deutschland, Stuttgart, May 1989.

Julien, C and Marty, J-C [1989] Plan revision in person-machine dialogue. In *Proceedings of the 4th Conference of the European Chapter of the Association for Computational Linguistics*, University of Manchester Institute of Science and Technology, Manchester, UK, 10–12 April 1989, pp153–160.

Kamp, H [1981] A theory of truth and semantic representation. In J A G Groenendijk, T M V Janssen, and M B J Stokhof (eds) *Formal Methods in the Study of Language*, Volume 136, pp277–322. Amsterdam: Mathematical Centre Tracts.

Mann, W C [1987] Text Generation: The Problem of Text Structure. Technical Report No. RS-87-181, USC/Information Sciences Institute, Marina Del Rey, Ca., March, 1987.

Mann, W C and Matthiessen, C M I M [1983] Nigel: A systemic grammar for text generation. Technical Report No. RR-83-105, USC/Information Sciences Institute, Marina Del Rey, Ca.

Mann, W C and Thompson, S [1986] Rhetorical Structure Theory: Description and Construction of Text. RS-86-174, USC/Information Sciences Institute, Marina Del Rey, Ca., October, 1986.

Mann, W C and Thompson, S A [1988] Rhetorical structure theory: Toward a functional theory of text organization. *Text*, **8**, 243–281. Also available as USC/Information Sciences Institute Research Report RR-87-190.

Maybury, M T [1989] Enhancing explanation coherence with rhetorical strategies. In *Proceedings of the 4th Conference of the European Chapter of the Association for Computational Linguistics*, University of Manchester Institute of Science and Technology, Manchester, UK, 10–12 April 1989, pp168–173.

McCoy, K F [1985] Correcting object-related misconceptions. PhD Thesis, Department of Computer and Information Science, University of Pennsylvania.

McCoy, K F and Cheng, J [1988] Focus of attention: Constraining what can be said next. Presented at the *4th International Workshop on Text Generation*, Los Angeles, 1988. Also in C L Paris, W R Swartout, and W C Mann (eds), *Natural Language in Artificial Intelligence and Computational Linguistics*, to appear.

McDermott, D [1981] Artificial Intelligence meets Natural Stupidity. In J Haugeland (ed), *Mind Design*, pp143–160. Bradford Books: Montgomery, Vermont.

McKeown, K R [1985] *Text Generation: Using Discourse Strategies and Focus Constraints to Generate Natural Language Text*. Cambridge: Cambridge University Press.

McKeown, K R, Elhadad, M, Fukumoto, Y, Lim, J, Lombardi, C, Robin, J, and Smadja, F [1990] Natural language generation in COMET. This volume.

Meehan, J [1976] The Metanovel: Writing Stories by Computer. PhD Thesis, Yale University.

Mellish, C [1988] Natural language generation from plans. Chapter 7 in M Zock and G Sabah (eds) *Advances in Natural Language Generation*, Volume 1, pp131–145. London: Pinter Publishers Ltd.

Moore, J D and Paris, C L [1988] Constructing coherent text using rhetorical relations. In *Proceedings of the 10th Cognitive Science Conference*, Montreal, June 1988, pp199–204.

Moore, J D and Paris, C L [1989] Planning text for advisory dialogues. In *Proceedings of the 27th Annual Meeting of the Association for Computational Linguistics*, Vancouver, Canada, June 1989, pp203–211.

Moore, J D and Swartout, W R [1988] Dialogue-based explanation. Presented at the *4th International Workshop on Text Generation*, Los Angeles, 1988. Also in C L Paris, W R Swartout, and W C Mann (eds), *Natural Language in Artificial Intelligence and Computational Linguistics*, to appear.

Moore, J D and Swartout, W R [1989] A reactive approach to explanation. In *Proceedings of the Eleventh International Joint Conference on Artificial Intelligence*, Detroit, August 1989, 1504–1510.

Paris, C L [1987] The use of explicit user models in text generation: Tailoring to a user's level of expertise. PhD Thesis, Department of Computer Science, Columbia University.

Paris, C L [1988] Generation and explanation: Building an explanation facility for the Explainable Expert Systems framework. Presented at the *4th International Workshop on Text Generation*, Los Angeles, 1988. Also in C L Paris, W R

Swartout, and W C Mann (eds), *Natural Language in Artificial Intelligence and Computational Linguistics*, to appear.

Penman [1989] The Penman Documentation. Unpublished documentation for the Penman language generation system, USC/Information Sciences Institute.

Polanyi, L [1988] A formal model of the structure of discourse. *Journal of Pragmatics*, **12**, 601–638.

Rankin, I [1989] The Deep Generation of Text in Expert Critiquing Systems. Licentiate thesis, University of Linköping, Sweden.

Reichman, R [1978] Conversational coherency. *Cognitive Science*, **2**, 283–327.

Rumelhart, D [1975] Notes on a schema for stories. In D G Bobrow and A M Collins (eds) *Representation and Understanding: Studies in Cognitive Science*, pp 75–93. London: Academic Press.

Sacerdoti, E D [1977] *A Structure for Plans and Behavior*. New York: North Holland.

Shepherd, H R [1926] *The Fine Art of Writing*. New York: The Macmillan Co.

Scott, D and Souza, C S [1990] Getting the message across in RST-based text generation. This volume.

Simonin, N [1988] An approach for creating structured text. In M Zock and G Sabah (eds) *Advances in Natural Language Generation*, Volume 1, pp146–160. London: Francis Pinter.

Souza, C S, Scott, D R and Nunes, M G V [1989] Enhancing text quality in a question-answering system. Unpublished manuscript, Pontificia Universidade Católica de Rio de Janeiro.

Thompson, S. A. [1985] Grammar and written discourse: initial vs final purpose clauses in English. *Text*, **5**, 55–84.

Van Dijk, T A [1972] *Some Aspects of Text Grammars*. The Hague: Mouton.

Van Dijk, T A and Kintsch, W [1983] *Strategies of Discourse Comprehension*. New York: Academic Press.

Weiner, J L [1980] BLAH: A system which explains its reasoning. *Artificial Intelligence*, **15**, 19–48.

Zukerman, I and Pearl, J [1986] Comprehension-driven generation of meta-technical utterances in Math tutoring. In *Proceedings of the 5th Annual Meeting of the American Association for Artificial Intelligence*, Philadelphia, Pa., August 1986, pp606–611.

3 Getting the Message Across in RST-based Text Generation

Donia R. Scott and Clarisse Sieckenius de Souza

Abstract

This chapter examines the problem of generating texts that achieve their communicative goals in an effective way. We discuss an approach to producing effective text that is geared towards ensuring that the rhetorical aspects of a message are not only preserved but enhanced in the text. This approach is strongly influenced by research in psycholinguistics and the psychology of memory, and is based on a view of stylistics as a matter having rather more to do with cognition than aesthetics.

3.1 Introduction

Text generation can be characterised as a process of transforming a message into a text. This process is successful if, and only if, the reader of the text is able to derive its intended message. The ultimate criterion of what it means for a text to be good is thus a cognitive rather than a strictly linguistic one: the easier it is for the reader to decode the intended message from the text, the better the text will be. Given this, it is therefore important to be able to specify just what are the characteristics of a text whose message is easily retrievable. Grice [1975] addresses this issue in his Manner maxim:

> Be perspicuous: avoid obscurity of expression, avoid ambiguity, be brief and be orderly.

Clearly, if it is our aim to generate text that conforms to this directive then it is crucial for us to be able to determine just what are the defining features of the characteristics that Grice so strongly recommends. When, for example, is a text brief and when is it not? Unfortunately, Grice provides us with no more than a quick glimpse of what these directives amount to in practice. Neither do other potential sources of information provide us with much more to go on; essays and textbooks on good writing tell us what we should and should not do, but give us next to no indication about how we could or should go about doing it. For example, Mark Twain, in his critical essay on the art of good writing (*Fenimore Cooper's Literary Offences*), simply tells us that the writer must:

- say what he is proposing to say, not merely come near to it;
- use the right word, not its second cousin;
- employ a simple and straightforward style;
- not omit necessary details;
- avoid slovenliness of form;
- eschew surplusage; and
- use good grammar.

Similarly, Strunk and White [1979], in what is perhaps the most popular book of the genre of writing textbooks, define conciseness in the following terms:

> A sentence should contain no unnecessary words, a paragraph no unnecessary sentences, for the same reason that a drawing should have no unnecessary lines and a machine no unnecessary parts. This requires not that the writer make all his sentences short, or that he avoid all detail and treat his subjects only in outline, but that every word tell.

In the absence of clearer guidelines, we are thus left with the task of specifying these directives by hypothesising their meaning, implementing our hypotheses in working systems, and judging the validity of the hypotheses by their effect on the goodness of the resulting text. Given the cognitive nature of our stated criterion for good text, it makes obvious sense to look to cognitive models of reading to provide the foundation for our hypotheses. That is, our hypotheses should be based on psycholinguistic models of language comprehension. In the work presented here, we discuss some of the hypotheses we have developed in this way for planning the generation of good text. The hypotheses we discuss are based on a general model of text understanding suggested by Clark and Clark [1977]. They are aimed at achieving clarity and conciseness in the textual expression of the message at the rhetorical level.

In our approach, the message of a text is comprised of a set of propositions which form the leaves of a hierarchical rhetorical structure that expresses the writer's intentions behind the inclusion of each proposition. If the message is coherent, then each of its constituent propositions contributes to the overall intention—that is, to the writer's communicative goal. We have chosen to represent messages within the framework of Rhetorical Structure Theory (RST) [Mann and Thompson 1985, 1987a, 1987b]. RST provides a number of extremely useful features for text generation, many of which are discussed at length in Hovy [this volume]. Most important among them for the present discussion is that RST can be used to represent both the message and the text plan and that it provides a means for capturing the notions of relevance and coherence within the representation of messages. The advantage of these is that, taken together, they provide the basis for maintaining the control that is required during the generation process to ensure that the necessary mappings from message to discourse and syntax are meaning-preserving. Like many other text planning systems (e.g. McKeown [1985]; Paris [1987]; Hovy [1988a], [1988b]) the basic elements of our messages are verb-based, clause-sized propositions, each of which can be expressed as a single sentence.[1]

Our particular concern here is that of ensuring that the texts we generate convey the rhetorical structure of the message in an effective manner.[2] This means that our texts must conform to the following three basic requirements. First, they must be sensitive to the communicative context in which they are set, i.e., one where the writer is an artificial interlocutor, with few resources for predicting or judging the impact of the text on the reader. Second, the chosen expression of the message must be a valid and unambiguous textual rendition of its rhetorical structure (i.e. the rhetorical structure of the message must be derivable from the text). Third, the chosen expression must be the most easily processable member of the set of all valid and unambiguous expressions of the message.

3.2 Making the Text Sensitive to the Communicative Setting

Clearly an important factor in effective writing is the tailoring of the expression of the message to suit one's intended audience. The need to provide tailored communication is now well recognised among designers of cooperative human-computer interfaces, and there are a growing number of dialogue systems which attempt to provide just this sort of interaction by incorporating a model of the user (see Kobsa and Wahlster [1989] for a detailed discussion of these systems). Although user models provide a useful basis for tailoring a system's contribution to a dialogue, they cannot be expected to be reliable representations of the user. Since artificial interlocutors clearly have fewer possibilities to make reliable assessments of their audience's ability to 'get the message' than do their human equivalents, their expressions of the message often need to be more explicit than would be ideal. This is particularly the case with respect to the rhetorical aspects of messages, whose understanding generally relies heavily on common-sense knowledge. Also of relevance is the

---

[1]It is worth noting that this also accords with the prevailing view in psycholinguistics. See Clark and Clark [1977] and van Dijk [1977] for a discussion of this, and Johnson Laird [1983] and Garnham [1985] for an alternative view.

[2]Meteer [1988a, 1988b, 1989] presents a rather different approach for planning text that is clear and concise at the propositional level.

fact that although most user models attempt to represent the overlap between the system's knowledge base the user's beliefs, few attempt to represent the user's beliefs about the relationship between the facts in the knowledge base.

It follows from the above that since the present generation of computer systems cannot reliably determine whether their users will be able to correctly infer the rhetorical structure of a message from its constituent facts, they should therefore make this structure explicit to the user. Our first hypothesis is thus:

> Hypothesis: Readers are unlikely to retrieve the rhetorical structure of a message unless it is stated explicitly.

To account for this factor, one of our heuristics for guiding generation is therefore:

> Heuristic 1: Always generate accurate and unambiguous textual markers of the rhetorical relations that hold between the propositions of the message.

Our examination of two unrelated languages, British English and Brazilian Portuguese (see Souza, Scott and Nunes [1989]), shows that at least in these languages all rhetorical relations of the set proposed by Mann and Thompson [1987b] can be marked textually. These rhetorical markers may be lexical, phrasal or purely syntactic, and their roles in the language are strictly pragmatic. For example, the ANTITHESIS relation can be signalled in a number of ways: *rather than, instead of, however,* and *yet.* Similarly, the EVIDENCE relation can be signalled by *since, because,* and *therefore,* RESTATEMENT by *in other words* and PURPOSE by *in order to.* Some relations, in particular ELABORATION, can only marked by syntax.

A requirement of text generators, then, is that they include information about the appropriate textual markers of each rhetorical relation.

3.3 Generating Valid and Unambiguous Textual Markers of Rhetorical Relations

In order to ensure that only valid and unambiguous markers are generated, it is important for the generator to know not only what the markers of each relation are, but also how they can be used in the target language. It must know, for example, that as a marker of EVIDENCE, *since* can only be attached to the satellite of the relation, and can only be used intrasententially, but with any ordering of the satellite and nucleus, whereas *therefore* can only be attached to the nucleus, can be used intersententially and can only be used with the satellite presented before the nucleus. This type of information permits the

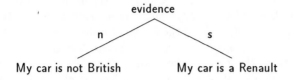

Figure 3.1: An instance of the EVIDENCE relation

generation of a message, such as that shown in Figure 3.1, as sentences (1)–(3), all of which are valid expressions of the message and therefore ones from which the message is retrievable. It also prevents the generation of sentences such as (4)–(8), none of which are valid expressions of the message and some of which (sentences (6)–(8)) are valid expressions of some other message and therefore likely to 'give the wrong message'.

(1) Since my car is a Renault, it's not British.

(2) My car is not British since it's a Renault.

(3) My car is a Renault, therefore it's not British.

(4) *Therefore my car is not British, it's a Renault.

(5) *My car is not British. Since it's a Renault.

(6) *My car is not British, although it's a Renault.

(7) *Since my car is not British, it's a Renault.

(8) *My car is not British, therefore it's a Renault.

In addition to the above constraints on the use of rhetorical markers, there are also situations where strong constraints are placed on the tense that can be used to express elements of a relation in conjunction with particular markers. For example, in Brazilian Portuguese, the satellite of a CONCESSION relation marked by *embora* can only be expressed in the subjunctive.

Avoiding the generation of ambiguous markers can often prove difficult, since there are a number of markers that apply to more than one relation.

When this happens, however, it is generally the case that the set of applicable relations form a superclass. One such superclass involves the above-mentioned markers of EVIDENCE, which also happen to be markers of what Mann and Thompson [1987a] call the **cause cluster**: the VOLITIONAL CAUSE, VOLITIONAL RESULT, NON-VOLITIONAL CAUSE, NON-VOLITIONAL RESULT and PURPOSE relations. That the marker *because* (i.e., *be* + *cause*) should validly apply to them all is hardly surprising, since they are all organised around the concept of causation. Although not considered to be part of the cause cluster, it can be argued that EVIDENCE properly belongs to it, since it too involves the notion of causation. Given all this, the applicability of *because* to all of six rhetorical relations does not prove problematic, since it narrows down the choice of applicable relations to a well-defined set whose differences are not so great as to lead the reader off-track.

There are other markers, however, which are so ambiguous as to be almost meaningless; *and* is a case in point. *And* can be used to link the elements of most, if not all, rhetorical relations. It is a strong marker of only a few of these relations (to be discussed below) and an extremely weak marker of the rest, where it tends to mark not a rhetorical relation between the elements that it is linking, but merely the fact that they are part of the same piece of discourse [Gleitman 1965; Lakoff 1971]. Its weak use is rather more prevalent in speech than in text, and this may well be related to the fact that the transient and immediate nature of speech, as compared to text, means that it is rather more difficult to undo errors of omission without disrupting the comprehension of the message. But the real point to be made here is that rhetorical markers are better thought of as strong clues to the presence of a specific relation than as proof of its presence, and that although some degree of ambiguity will have to be tolerated, ambiguities that arise from the generation of a very weak marker that also happens to be a stronger marker of another rhetorical relation should not count among them. There are good reasons why this should be the case. Firstly, there is a wealth of psycholinguistic evidence from studies performed in the 1970s which suggest that ambiguities can produce quite severe disruptions to the comprehension process (e.g. [Lackner and Garrett 1972; Foss and Jenkins 1973]). Secondly, there is also strong evidence to suggest that rhetorical markers have such a powerful influence on language comprehension that people will try to make sense of what they read purely on the basis of the marker, even when what they are reading makes no sense at all [Fillenbaum 1971, 1974a, 1974b].

Having established the means by which we can provide the reader with strong clues to the identity of rhetorical relations, we are well on our way to being able to generate texts whose message is *retrievable*. But it must be remembered that we are aiming for more than this—for texts whose message is *easily* retrievable. So, the obvious question here is: given the range of possibilities for signalling a rhetorical relation, what is the most effective way to do so? Clearly, the answer to this will be related to the psychology of language comprehension.

The task of comprehending a text involves transforming a linear string (the text) into its underlying, hierarchical structure (the message). This holds for texts (and messages) of all levels of complexity—from those consisting of a single clause (one proposition, no rhetorical relations) to those of paragraph or even book length (many propositions, any number of rhetorical relations). Psycholinguistic studies suggest that readers interpret text by reconstructing its propositions and using them to continually build onto a hierarchical representation of propositions.[3] The ease with which this construction process occurs is heavily dependent on the effect it has on the consumption of working memory resources.

Working memory is the mental work space we use during comprehension [Newell and Simon 1972]. During reading, it is where we reconstruct the message in order to interpret its meaning. Comprehension proceeds by processing the basic constituents of the message and then using them to build coherent units with previously-processed constituents that are being stored in working memory. Once a coherent unit is formed, it is added to the main structure (the interpreted message so far) in episodic memory. There is known to be a rather direct relationship between the processing and storage resources of working memory: the more storage that is required at any particular moment, the fewer the resources available for processing the incoming data [Baddely 1986; Daneman and Carpenter 1980]. Because of this trade-off, the human comprehension process is organised so as to minimise the number of partial products that need to be held in working memory. This means that the more structured the input is, the easier it will be for the reader to derive its underlying message. Syntax plays a major role in helping structure the incoming information so that it can be retained in working memory until the parts needed to complete it have been processed. Textual features such as long distance dependencies, digressions, or constituents that involve a lot of processing, will place heavy demands on working memory and thus slow down the comprehension process. Similarly, undoing previously built structures will be costly. Related to this is the suggestion that readers typically purge working memory, retaining only the gist of what was stored, at sentence boundaries [Jarvella 1970, 1971]. This view of language comprehension presents at least two immediate tips for us. The first is:

> Hypothesis: The greater the amount of intervening text between the propositions of a relation, the more difficult it will be to reconstruct its message.

---

[3] See Clark and Clark [1977] for a review of the literature on this topic.

which leads us to include the heuristic:

> Heuristic 2: Keep the propositions of a rhetorical relation together
> in the text.

Failure to keep the propositions of a rhetorical relation together in the text will result in the introduction of long-distance dependencies. As mentioned above, long-distance dependencies hinder comprehension. One reason for this is that the closer the propositions of a relation are in the text, the less time they will need to be stored in working memory before their rhetorical link can be recovered. Another reason is that there is a natural tendency for readers to attach each new constituent to the one that came immediately before it [Kimball 1973]. This explains why the ordering of unlinked sentences in a text has such a strong effect on its overall interpretation. For example, by producing Hovy's example message about the ship Knox (Hovy, this volume, Figure 2.3) as:

(9) Knox is heading SSW. It is of readiness C4. It is at 79N 18E. It
     will arrive on 4/24. It will load for 4 days. It is en route to Sasebo.

instead of the suggested

(10) Knox is en route to Sasebo. It is of readiness C4. It is at 79N 18E.
      It is heading SSW. It will arrive on 4/24. It will load for 4 days.

we end up conveying the wrong message, since the text incorrectly implies that the place where Knox is intended to arrive on 4/24 for 4 days loading is not Sasebo, but some place on Knox's route between 79N 18E and Sasebo.

The second tip we get from the cognitive model is:

> Hypothesis: Rhetorical relations that are expressed within a single
> sentence are more easily understood than those expressed in more
> than one sentence.

This hypothesis is suggested by the finding that readers tend to purge working memory at or soon after the end of a sentence. If this is the case, then it makes obvious sense to include the heuristic:

> Heuristic 3: Make a single sentence out of every rhetorical relation.

The question of how to distribute the propositions of a message as sentences in the text is one which Hovy [this volume] poses as one of the unresolved issues in paragraph planning. It has a major bearing on the style of the final text, especially in approaches (such as ours, and those mentioned above) where the input units to the generator are clause-sized propositions. In such cases, the text can, in principle, contain any number of sentences: from one to as many as there are propositions.

The above heuristic addresses this issue rather directly. It proposes that parts of a rhetorical relation should not be realised as individual sentences; neither should they be combined as sentences with parts of other rhetorical relations. Rather, they should all together form a sentence.

Application of this heuristic will increase the efficacy of the generated text in the following ways. First, the text will be more concise, since it will contain fewer sentences. Second, its message will be clearer since (a) there will be more opportunities for generating the textual markers of its rhetorical relations (most rhetorical markers can only be used intrasententially) and (b) sentence scoping will be guaranteed not to distort the hierarchical structure of the message since sentence boundaries will be conterminous with boundaries of rhetorical relations. Finally, the text will be easier to understand since the presentation of rhetorical units as sentence units will require less storage and processing in working memory, thus making its underlying rhetorical structure easier to rebuild.

In summary, this heuristic not only provides an effective approach to the problem of determining sentence scope, but it also provides one that is theoretically motivated. Decisions about where to place sentence boundaries are not based on *ad hoc* aesthetic criteria to do with how good the text will look, but rather on criteria which ensure that sentence allocations enhance rather than disturb the accessibility of the message, and on psycholinguistic factors that are known to facilitate the processing of a piece of text. This is not to say, however, that the issue of sentence scoping is now resolved. Although we have a fairly clear idea of what sort of text we should not generate in this respect, we have little idea of what we should generate. In particular, two outstanding problems remain: that of when to stop adding propositions to sentences, and that of how best to combine our clause-sized propositions to form complex sentences.

The first problem arises from the fact that the rhetorical relations of a message may be complex structures comprised of a number of other relations. It goes without saying that a coherent text can only be produced from a coherent message, which, in terms of RST, is a message that is spanned by a single rhetorical relation. Given Heuristic 3, this means that any message could, in principle, be packed in its entirety into a single sentence. Such complete freedom would be undesirable, since there is clearly a point where a sentence becomes 'too long'. Although as writers we seem to be able to recognise, and thus avoid producing, overly lengthy sentences, it is difficult to specify what the criterion of 'too long' actually is. Again, it is easier to say what it is not. It is clearly not the number of words *per se*. For example, (11a) below is more acceptable than (11b), even though it has more than double the number of words.

(11)   a   Mary's son Lawrence, the difficult one that everyone always said would come to a bad end, was fatally attacked by piranhas in the Pantanal last month, despite having been warned repeatedly by the local fishermen that it was dangerous to swim in the Cuiaba river.

   b   Lawrence, who married the very elegant young Austrian woman who used to run a boarding school for the illegitimate children of aspiring back-benchers, is a solicitor.

Neither does it seem to have much to do with number of rhetorical relations or number of propositions *per se*, since (11a) also has more of both of these than (11b). Rather, the answer seems to lie in some complex combination of factors which include number of words, number of relations, number of propositions, and syntax; factors such as the 'balance' of the text also seem to play a role. Just what the magic algorithm is, is unclear to us, and we do not know of any empirical studies on this topic.[4]

The second problem arises from the fact that there is more than one way to make a complex sentence from a set of clauses: through embedding, paratactic coordination or hypotactic coordination. Not surprisingly, there is a strong correlation between the syntactic specification of a complex sentence and its perceived rhetorical structure. This means that certain types of complex sentences are likely to be better expressions of a given rhetorical relation than others, and that the wrong choice of sentence type may lead to the wrong interpretation of the underlying rhetorical relations. So in addition to knowing *when* we must combine propositions to form complex sentences, we also need to know *how* we should combine them.

The remainder of this chapter presents an approach to the problem of producing only the most appropriate choice of complex sentence for a given rhetorical configuration. In what follows, we will be discussing only two of the three types of clause combining: embedding and paratactic coordination. Our approach to the generation of hypotactically coordinated sentences is discussed in greater detail in Scott [in preparation].

3.3.1   Embedding

Although embedding is considered by some linguists[5] to be a separate activity from clause combining, we do not adhere to that distinction here, on the purely practical grounds that our propositions are always clausal units.

---

[4]There are, however, a number of studies which examine the individual effect of some of these factors.

[5]See Matthiessen and Thompson [1987] for a discussion of this.

Following from Heuristic 3, that only valid and unambiguous markers should be generated, our investigations have led us to apply the following heuristic for embedding:

> Heuristic 4: Embedding can only be applied to the ELABORATION relation.

We restrict embedding to the ELABORATION relation since this relation appears to us to be the only one of the set of existing relations for which it is appropriate. It is also significant that embedding provides the only valid means by which the propositions of an ELABORATION relation can be combined to form a complex sentence. It is also the only available textual marker of ELABORATION.[6]

Embedding provides an extremely reliable syntactic cue to the semantic subordination of the embedded material to that of its matrix. It marks the embedded material as being less relevant to the message. The implication of this for RST is clear:

> Heuristic 5: When embedding, the nucleus of the relation must form the matrix of the sentence, and the satellite the embedded clause.

This heuristic guarantees that embedding preserves the hierarchical relationship of the propositions to which it is applied. So, for example, an ELABORATION relation with (12) as nucleus and (13) as satellite could result in (14) or (15) but not (16) or (17).

(12) The substance is fatal.

(13) The substance is illegal.

(14) The illegal substance is fatal.

(15) The substance, which is illegal, is fatal.

(16) The fatal substance is illegal.

(17) The substance, which is fatal, is illegal.

If, on the other hand, (13) were the nucleus and (12) the satellite, then (16) or (17) could be produced, but never (14) or (15).

In cases where the nucleus of the ELABORATION relation is complex, then there may be more than one candidate matrix proposition. Some direction for choosing among them is therefore required. This is provided by:

---

[6]That is, with the possible exception of phrases like *by the way* or *to be specific*. These, however, are more likely to be repair markers, for introducing information that has been erroneously left out, than rhetorical ones.

Heuristic 6: When embedding, the matrix proposition must be the earliest occurring candidate in the immediate nucleus of the to-be-embedded proposition.

This means that given the RST structures in Figure 3.2 with both (a) and (b) as candidate matrix clauses for (c), the chosen proposition will be (a) in structures (i)–(iv) and (b) in all others.

The impact of this heuristic on the prevention of stylistic blunders is considerable. For example, suppose the following instantiations were made to the elements in Figure 3.2:

(18)   a   My car is French
       b   My car is a Renault
       c   My car is new
       R1 EVIDENCE
       R2 ELABORATION

Then Heuristic 6 would ensure that only sentences like (19) and (20) could result from embedding, and never ones like (21) or (22):

(19)   Since my new car is a Renault, it's French.

(20)   My new car is French, since it's a Renault.

(21)   Since my car is a Renault, it, which is new, is French.

(22)   My car is French since it, which is new, is a Renault.

Not only does the complexity of the nucleus provide opportunities for producing stylistic blunders when embedding, but so too does the complexity of the satellite. This occurs when embedding has the side effect of destroying the integrity of another relation. An example of this arises in cases where the embedded proposition is an element of a LIST relation and the result of embedding it is a LIST containing only one element. Heuristic 7 acts to prevent such an occurrence.

Heuristic 7: Propositions of a LIST relation should not be embedded if doing so would make the number of remaining propositions in the relation equal to 1.

This heuristic not only preserves the integrity of the message (since the LIST relation requires more than one proposition), but it prevents the production of dangling sentences.

Dangling sentences occur when information that is only weakly relevant to the message is produced as a separate sentence. This is always the case

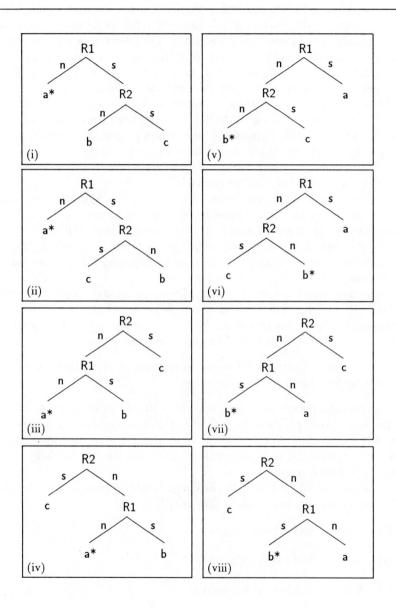

Figure 3.2: Structures involving embedding

when satellites of an ELABORATION relation are not subject to embedding. ELABORATION is the weakest of all rhetorical relations in that its semantic role is simply one of providing 'more detail'. The information contained in its satellite is thus only weakly relevant to the message. Since embedding is the only textual marker of ELABORATION, the only alternative to not applying it is to generate the satellite as a separate, and thus dangling, sentence.

Dangling sentences can have a severely disruptive effect on the comprehensibility of a text. They give the impression of having been included as an afterthought, or of introducing a new topic which is then abruptly abandoned. Integrating the content of such sentences with the preceding text is made difficult by the fact that their content is made more perceptually prominent in the text than it actually is in the message.

Stylistic blunders can also arise from the choice of syntactic realisation for the embedded satellite. Embedded clauses can be realised as nominals, adjectivals or adverbials. Although the choice between these realisation classes will be determined by strictly semantic aspects of the propositions, there is still a choice to be made regarding the most appropriate syntactic form within the chosen class.

Adjectivals can be expressed as an adjective, a relative clause or a prepositional phrase, adverbials as an adverb or prepositional phrase, and nominals as a noun or an appositive phrase. Within each class, some expressions will lead to better text than others. This can be expressed as:

> Heuristic 8: Syntactically simple expressions of embedding are to
> be preferred over more complex ones.

We use the notion of syntactic complexity here for want of a better term to refer to the move from lexicalised to phrasal and clausal modifiers. This heuristic biases the generation process towards expressing the embedded clause as an adjective or adverb. The impact of this heuristic on the resulting text can be seen in the following examples.

When embedding (24) in (23), preference would be given to a rendition as (25) over the equally grammatical (26) or (27):

(23)   A man bought the picture.

(24)   The man had blond hair.

(25)   A blond man bought the picture.

(26)   A man with blond hair bought the picture.

(27)   A man who had blond hair bought the picture.

Similarly, preference would be given to the production of (28) over (29):

(28)   Paula danced with Peter willingly.

(29)   Paula danced with Peter with willingness.

Heuristic 8 enhances the readability of the resulting text in two important
ways. Firstly, it reduces the possibility of generating ambiguities, since relative
clauses can be restrictive or non-restrictive, and prepositional phrases can be
adjectival or adverbial. Secondly, it necessarily makes the text more concise,
since lexicalised modifiers involve fewer words than phrasal or clausal ones:
(25) is clearly more concise than (26) and (27), and (28) is more concise than
(29).

   It should be noted, however, that there are exceptional cases where the
application of Heuristic 8 may lead to stylistic blunders. Notable among them
are those resulting from the generation of low-frequency adjectives or adverbs
over their more commonplace, wordy equivalents: for example, *rancourously*
instead of *with rancour*.

   There are strong similarities between our use of Heuristic 8 and Meteer's
[1988a, 1988b, 1989] treatment of the expression of verbal predicates in SPOKES-
MAN, which has the effect of preferring simple verbs over their corresponding
complex ones or verb phrases (e.g. *decided* over *made a decision*, or *fed* over
gave food to).

   Our final heuristic for embedding controls the types of multiple embeddings
that are allowed.

> Heuristic 9: Self-embedding is only allowed in cases where the
> proposition that is the deeper of the two embeddings is expressed
> as an adjective or adverb.

This heuristic ensures that self-embeddings do not lead to comprehension difficulties. So, for example, it allows sentences like (30) to be generated, but
not ones like (31) with the same number of self-embeddings.

(30)   The dog [that likes the [black] cat] is sad.

(31)   *The dog [that likes the cat [that disappeared]] is sad.

Even more important, it guarantees that double centre embedded sentences
are never generated. Double centre embedded sentences (e.g. *The dog that
the cat that the rat saw chased died*) are definitely to be avoided since they
are notoriously difficult to process [Miller and Isard 1963, 1964; Schlesinger
1968; Freedle and Craun 1970; Carpenter and Just 1989], and are known to

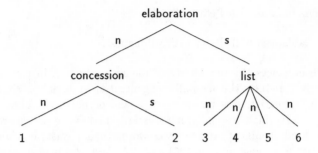

[1] George received a letter from Peter.

[2] George had told Peter never to contact him.

[3] George and Peter are brothers.

[4] George and Peter are estranged.

[5] The letter was long.

[6] George is my friend.

Figure 3.3: A message to which the embedding heuristics can be applied

slow down the comprehension process by as much as 58% [Larkin and Burns 1977].

The global impact of the heuristics controlling embedding can be demonstrated by their effect on the process of transforming the message shown in Figure 3.3. Taken together, their application would result in embedding that provides for the possibility of generating:

(32)   My friend George received a long letter from his estranged brother Peter, even though he had told Peter never to contact him.

which is a stylistically good rendition of the message. The heuristics prevent the generation of alternative, equally grammatical but less easily understood renditions such as (33)–(37):

(33)   *My friend George received a long letter from his estranged brother Peter, who he had told never to contact him.

(34)   *George, who received a long letter from his estranged brother Peter even though he had told Peter never to contact him, is my friend.

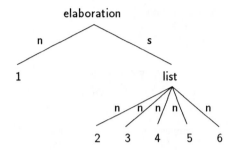

Figure 3.4: The message conveyed by example (33)

(35) *My friend George received a long letter from his brother Peter, even though he had told Peter, from whom he is estranged, never to contact him.

(36) My friend George received a letter from his estranged brother, Peter even though he had told Peter never to contact him. The letter was long.

(37) My friend George received a letter from Peter, who is his brother and from whom he is estranged, even though he had told Peter never to contact him.

In (33), the embedding of proposition [2] in proposition [1] results in the loss of the CONCESSION relation to which they belong. As a result, the text does not convey the message shown in Figure 3.3. Rather, it conveys the message shown in Figure 3.4. The possibility of generating this text from the given message is prevented by Heuristic 4.

Again, the text in (34) does not convey the message in Figure 3.3. By having [6] as the main clause, the text expresses instead the message in Figure 3.5. Such a possibility is prevented by Heuristic 5.

Although the message in Figure 3.3 is, in fact, derivable from the text in (35), the stylistic blunder that is created by the embedding of [4] in [2] instead of [1] makes message retrieval rather more difficult than it need be. The possibility of producing this stylistic blunder is prevented by Heuristic 6.

Like (35), (36) is a valid expression of the desired message. However, extracting this message is made difficult by the presentation of [5] as a separate, dangling sentence. This is prevented by Heuristic 7.

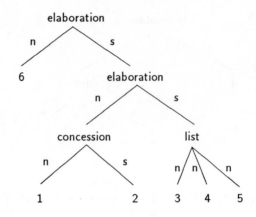

Figure 3.5: The message conveyed by example (34)

Sentence (37) is another valid expression of the desired message but one that is made unnecessarily difficult to process. This difficulty is caused by presenting [3] and [4] as relative clauses instead of adjectives. The production of this type of stylistic blunder is prevented by Heuristic 8.

The possibility of providing an example message to demonstrate all 6 embedding heuristics has only been prevented by our lack of imagination in constructing examples.

3.4 Paratactic Coordination

Paratactic constructions are complex sentences involving the *coordinate* conjoining of one or more sentential units linked by a coordinating conjunction (*and, or, but*).[7] The use of the coordinate conjunctions as rhetorical markers is not, however, restricted to paratactic conjunctions. They are also often used as weak rhetorical markers in hypotactic constructions, as can be seen in (38)–(40), where the (a) versions involve a coordinate conjunction and the (b) versions a subordinate one.

---

[7]Our use of the term **parataxis** is thus wider than that of Quirk *et al.* [1985].

(38) a The printer is broken and the chapter is due tomorrow.

    b The printer is broken and I haven't been able to print out the chapter.

(39) a The laser printer is broken but the line printer is working.

    b The laser printer appears to be broken but it does work.

(40) a Turn off the printer or unplug it at the wall.

    b Turn off the printer or it will overheat.

This overuse of coordinating conjunctions means that it is not always easy, or even possible, to identify the rhetorical relationship that they are intended to be signalling. For example, our understanding of the (b) versions above is heavily reliant on extralinguistic information; it is only our knowledge of the possible consequences of a broken printer that allows us to recognise the subordinate role of the second part of (38b) to the first, and thus to recover the underlying NON-VOLITIONAL RESULT relation. Similarly, it is only our knowledge of the possible consequences of not turning off an electrical appliance in certain circumstances that allows us to recover the underlying OTHERWISE relation in (40b).

Given our generation goal to convey the rhetorical role of all propositions of a message, and the previously discussed constraints imposed by the communicative setting in which generation is performed, it is therefore important for us to ensure that the syntactic operation of paratactic coordination is only ever used in genuine cases of the conjoining of rhetorically coordinate propositions. By being precise in our usage, we increase the chances of the reader recovering the intended rhetorical relation between the coordinated propositions. Our first heuristic for paratactic coordination identifies the criterion for determining which rhetorical relations it can be applied to:

> Heuristic 10: Paratactic Coordination can only be applied to multi-nuclear relations.

Mann and his colleagues identify three multi-nuclear relations: SEQUENCE, CONTRAST and LIST [Mann and Thompson 1987b; Matthiessen and Thompson 1987]. We have added a fourth, ALTERNATIVE, to this set. ALTERNATIVE is one of the two relations that Grimes [1975] considers to be 'purely paratactic'. It is closely related to Mann and Thompson's OTHERWISE relation, the crucial difference being that it does not involve a dependency relationship between its elements. This difference is shown in (40) above, where (40a) involves the ALTERNATIVE relation and (40b) OTHERWISE.

Heuristic 10 ensures the unambiguous mapping between propositions that are coordinate at the rhetorical level, and coordinate structures at the syntactic

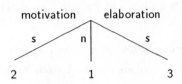

[1] John wants to be a diplomat.

[2] John likes travelling.

[3] John will take the Foreign Office exams tomorrow.

Figure 3.6: A message to which Heuristic 10 can be applied

level. It guarantees the possibility of producing all the (a) versions of (38)–(40) but none of the (b) versions as expressions of the same message, even though they are grammatical and semantically non-anomalous.

By restricting paratactic coordination to information units that are not only coordinate but nuclear, this heuristic also prevents the undesirable coordination of some multi-satellite structures. Consider, for example, the message in Figure 3.6.

Although propositions [2] and [3] are coordinate with respect to [1]), the fact that they belong to different rhetorical relations makes them unsuitable candidates for joint membership of the multi-nuclear LIST relation. Heuristic 10 thus prevents them from being generated as a paratactically coordinated complex sentence like (41) or (42).

(41)   *John wants to be a diplomat because *he likes travelling and will take the Foreign Service exams next week.*

(42)   *John wants to be a diplomat so *he will take the Foreign Service exams next week and he likes travelling.*

If, however, [3] were replaced in the message by *John likes going to diplomatic parties*, also in a MOTIVATION relation with [1], then (43), which is clearly appropriate, could be generated.

(43)   John wants to be a diplomat because *he likes travelling and going to diplomatic parties.*

Having determined which rhetorical links can be expressed through paratactic coordination, we now need to stipulate which members of the set of coordinating conjunctions can be applied to which rhetorical relations.

> Heuristic 11: The paratactic marker *and* must only be applied to SEQUENCE and LIST, *but* to CONTRAST, and *or* to ALTERNATIVE.

This heuristic guarantees that the paratactic coordination of propositions does not result in the generation of invalid or rhetorically ambiguous text. For example, it will ensure that only the unstarred sentences could be generated as expressions of the following:

SEQUENCE:

(44) Put the loose tea in the teapot and pour in the boiling water.

(45) *Put the loose tea in the teapot but pour in the boiling water.

(46) *Put the loose tea in the teapot or pour in the boiling water.

LIST:

(47) John likes apples and bananas.

(48) *John likes apples but bananas.

(49) *John likes apples or bananas.

CONTRAST:

(50) The meal looked good but tasted like poached cardboard.

(51) *The meal looked good and tasted like poached cardboard.

(52) *The meal looked good or tasted like poached cardboard.

ALTERNATIVE:

(53) John wants to go to Sussex or Essex.

(54) *John wants to go to Sussex and Essex.

(55) *John wants to go to Sussex but Essex.

Clearly, (45) and (46) are not synonymous with (44). Neither are (48) and (49) with (47), (51) and (52) with (50), or (54) and (55) with (53).

A characteristic feature of multi-nuclear rhetorical relations is that the order of appearance of their elements in the text tends not to affect the message. The only exception to this is SEQUENCE, which involves the notion of temporal priority.[8] Heuristic 12 allows for a different ordering of the propositions of multi-nuclear relations in the text than in the message in situations where this is appropriate.

> Heuristic 12: Propositions of all relations except SEQUENCE can be reordered during paratactic coordination.

This heuristic provides the flexibility for generating (56), (57) and (58) as synonyms of (47), (50) and (52) respectively, and prevents the generation of (59) as a synonym of (44).

(56)   John likes bananas and apples.

(57)   The meal tasted like poached cardboard but looked good.

(58)   John wants to go to Essex or Sussex.

(59)   *Pour the boiling water in the teapot and put in the loose tea.

This flexibility is often useful, especially in cases where the order of presentation of the propositions affects the thematic flow of the text. For example, (38a) would be more appropriate than its alternative (60) if the preceding sentence were (61), and *vice versa* if the preceding sentence were (62).

(60)   The chapter is due tomorrow and the printer is broken.

(61)   The printer always fails when I most need it.

(62)   I doubt that I'll be able to finish this chapter on time.

It should be noted, however, that there are cases where the linguistic realisation of the individual propositions will rule out certain otherwise permissible orderings. For example, the alternative ordering of propositions [2] and [3] in (43), which would lead to:

(63)   *John wants to be a diplomat because *he likes going to diplomatic parties and travelling.*

---

[8]See Lakoff [1971] and Schmerling [1975] for a more detailed discussion of this.

would clearly not be desirable. Situations like these do not become apparent until quite late in the generation process and thus cannot be taken into account when the message itself is being planned. It is therefore important to have the flexibility for reordering that is provided by Heuristic 12.

It is also important that this flexibility should *not* be extended to the SEQUENCE relation, since the resulting text would violate Grice's directive that the text be 'orderly', and lead to an erroneous interpretation of the message (see also Schmerling [1975]). Reorderings of the propositions of SEQUENCE must be marked by hypotactic coordination.

It follows from Heuristic 12 that the number of orderings of the relevant propositions that are possible during the construction of paratactically coordinated complex sentences is the factorial of the number of propositions of the relation. As we have just seen, some of these will lead to better text than others. This is especially true in cases where there are a fair number of propositions to be considered, and thus often more than one sentence to be formed. In such situations there will be a need to bias the generation process towards the production of the best combination of coordinated propositions. Heuristic 13 provides one way of doing this.

> Heuristic 13: The greater the number of shared elements between propositions, the more desirable it is to coordinate them.

This heuristic biases paratactic coordination towards complex sentences which, to use Lakoff's [1971] terms, share a common topic. By promoting the generation of paratactically coordinated complex sentences with similar propositions, this heuristic has a direct bearing on the conciseness of the resulting text, since it encourages coordinations which provide the greatest opportunities for ellipsis.

A broad view of the operation of the heuristics for paratactic coordination can be seen with reference to the message shown in Figure 3.7. Taken together, the above heuristics will provide the possibility for expressing this message as (64).

(64)   In order to change the oil in the tank, one must drain the tank and sump of oil, replace the oil filter, and refill the tank with oil.

The possibility of applying coordination to propositions [1] and [2], thereby generating something like (65) is prevented by Heuristic 10.

(65)   *Change and drain the oil in the tank ...

Heuristic 11 blocks the possibility of generating an incorrect paratactic marker, thereby conveying the wrong message, as in (66):

(66)   *... drain the tank or sump ...

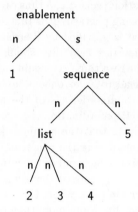

[1] Change the oil in the tank.

[2] Drain the oil in the tank.

[3] Replace the oil filter.

[4] Drain the oil in the sump.

[5] Refill the oil in the tank.

Figure 3.7: A message to which the heuristics for paratactic coordination can be applied

---

Changing the order of the elements of the SEQUENCE relation in the text would result in something like (67). Although clearly grammatical, (67) would be undesirable since, like (66), it conveys the wrong message. This is prevented by Heuristic 12.

(67)   *... refill and drain the oil in the tank ...

Finally, by biasing the generation process towards the paratactic coordination of propositions [2] and [4], Heuristic 13 prevents the production of the stylistic blunder that would occur if [3] were chosen over [2], thereby giving (68):

(68)   *... drain the oil from the tank and replace the oil filter, drain the oil from the sump ...

3.5 Summary

There is little need to argue for the importance of stylistic factors in the readability of a text. Until now, the problem has always been that of determining just how we should go about giving our texts good style. One approach to this problem is to allow the process of text production to be guided by what is known about the way in which readers understand texts. We have shown here that this approach is effective, at least with regard to the rhetorical aspects of text generation. It allows us to maximise the possibility that the message will be retrieved from the text by ensuring that the rhetorical structure of the message is enhanced by the choice of discourse structure for the text, which is in turn reflected in the choice of syntactic structures. An added advantage of this approach is that it provides us with a sound theoretical basis for dealing with some aspects of the issue of sentence content and organisation (see Hovy [this volume]).

Acknowledgements

We are extremely grateful to Graça Volpe Nunes, Patrizia Tabossi and Richard Cole for their helpful discussion of many of the ideas discussed in this chapter.

References

Baddely, A D [1986] *Working Memory*. Oxford: Oxford University Press.

Carpenter, P A and Just, M A [1989] The role of working memory in language comprehension. In D Klahr and K Kotovsky (eds) *Complex Information Processing*, pp31–68. Hillsdale, NJ: Lawrence Erlbaum Associates.

Clark, H H and Clark, E V [1977] *Psychology and Language*. New York: Harcourt Brace Jovanovich.

Daneman, M and Carpenter, P A [1980] Individual differences in working memory and reading. *Journal of Verbal Learning and Verbal Behaviour*, 19, 450–466.

Fillenbaum, S [1971] On coping with ordered and unordered conjunctive sentences. *Journal of Experimental Psychology*, 87, 93–98.

Fillenbaum, S [1974a] Pragmatic normalization: Further results for some conjunctive and disjunctive sentences. *Journal of Experimental Psychology*, 102, 574–578.

Fillenbaum, S [1974b] Or: Some uses. *Journal of Experimental Psychology*, 103, 913–921.

Foss, D J and Jenkins, C M [1973] Some effects of context on the comprehension of ambiguous sentences. *Journal of Verbal Learning and Verbal Behaviour*, 12, 577–589.

Freedle, R O and Craun, M [1970] Observations with self-embedded sentences using written aids. *Perception and Psychophysics*, 7, 247–249.

Garnham, A [1985] *Psycholinguistics: central topics.* London: Methuen.

Gleitman, L R [1965] Coordinating conjunctions in English. *Language*, **41**, 260–293.

Grice, H P [1975] Logic and conversation. In P Cole and J L Morgan (eds) *Syntax and Semantics*, Volume 3: *Speech Acts*, pp41–58. New York: Academic Press.

Grimes, J E [1975] *The Thread of Discourse.* The Hague: Mouton.

Hovy, E H [1988] Planning coherent multisentential text. In *Proceedings of the 26th Annual Meeting of the Association for Computational Linguistics*, State University of New York at Buffalo, Buffalo, NY, 7–10 June 1988, pp163–169.

Hovy, E H [1988] Approaches to the planning of coherent text. Presented at the *4th International Workshop on Text Generation*, Los Angeles, 1988. Also in C L Paris, W R Swartout, and W C Mann (eds), *Natural Language in Artificial Intelligence and Computational Linguistics*, to appear.

Hovy, E H [1990] Unresolved Issues in Paragraph Planning. This volume.

Jarvella, R J [1970] Effects of syntax on running memory span for connected discourse. *Psychonomic Science*, **19**, 235–236.

Jarvella, R J [1971] Syntactic processing and connected speech. *Journal of Verbal Learning and Verbal Behavior*, **10**, 409–416.

Johnson-Laird, P N [1983] *Mental Models.* Cambridge: Cambridge University Press.

Kimball, J P [1973] Seven principles of surface structure parsing in natural language. *Cognition*, **2**, 15–47.

Kobsa, A and Wahlster, W (eds) [1989] *User Models in Dialog Systems.* Berlin: Springer-Verlag.

Lackner, J R and Garrett, M F [1972] Resolving ambiguity: Effects of biasing context in the unattended ear. *Cognition*, **1**, 359–372.

Lakoff, R [1971] If's, And's, and But's about conjunction. In C J Fillmore and D T Langendoen (eds.), *Studies in Linguistic Semantics*, pp114–149. New York: Holt, Rinehart and Winston.

Larkin, W and Burns, D [1977] Sentence comprehension and memory for embedded structure. *Memory and Cognition*, **5**, 17–22.

Mann, W and Thompson, S A [1985] Assertions from discourse structure. *Proceedings of the Eleventh Annual Meeting of the Berkeley Linguistics Society*, Berkeley, California, 16–18 February 1985.

Mann, W C and Thompson, S A [1987a] Rhetorical Structure Theory: A Framework for the Analysis of Texts. USC/Information Sciences Institute Research Report RS-87-185.

Mann, W and Thompson, S [1987b] Rhetorical Structure Theory: A theory of text organisation. In L Polanyi (ed.) *The Structure of Discourse.* Norwood, NJ: Ablex.

Matthiessen, C M I M and Thompson, S A [1987] The structure of discourse and 'subordination'. In J Halman and S A Thompson (eds), *Clause Combining in Discourse and 'Subordination'.* Amsterdam: John Benjamins Publishing Company.

McKeown, K R [1985] *Text Generation.* Cambridge: Cambridge University Press.

Meteer, M W [1988a] Defining a vocabulary for text planning. *Proceedings of the AAAI-88 Workshop on Text Planning and Generation*, St. Paul, Minnesota, 25 August 1988.

Meteer, M W [1988b] The implication of revisions for natural language generation. *Proceedings of the Fourth International Workshop on Natural Language Generation*, Catalina Island, California, 17–21 July 1988.

Meteer, M W [1989] The SPOKESMAN Natural Language Generation System. Bolt, Beranek and Newman Technical Report No. 7090.

Miller, G A and Isard, S D [1963] Some perceptual consequences of linguistic rules. *Journal of Verbal Learning and Verbal Behavior*, **2**, 217–228.

Miller, G A and Isard, S D [1964] Free recall of self-embedded English sentences, *Information and Control*, **7**, 292–303.

Newell, A and Simon, H A [1972] *Human Problem Solving*. Englewood Cliffs, NJ: Prentice-Hall.

Paris, C L [1987] The Use of Explicit User Models in Text Generation: Tailoring to a User's Level of Expertise. PhD Thesis, Department of Computer Science, Columbia University.

Quirk, R, Greenbaum, S, Leech, G, and Svartvik, J [1985] *A Comprehensive Grammar of the English Language*. London: Longman.

Schlesinger, I M [1968] *Sentence Structure and the Reading Process*. The Hague: Mouton.

Schmerling, S F [1975] Asymmetric conjunction and rules of conversation. In P Cole and J L Morgan (eds) *Syntax and Semantics*, Volume 3: *Speech Acts*, pp211–231. New York: Academic Press.

Scott, D R [In preparation] A cognitive approach to the generation of hypotaxis.

Souza, C S, Scott, D R and Nunes, M G V [1989] Enhancing text quality in a question-answering system. In J Siekmann (ed) *Lecture Notes in Artificial Intelligence*. Berlin: Springer-Verlag.

Strunk, W and White, E B [1979] *The Elements of Style*, 3rd Edition. New York: The Macmillan Co.

van Dijk, T A [1977] *Text and Context*. London: Longman.

4   Generating Explanatory Discourse

Alison Cawsey

Abstract

This chapter examines the problem of generating text and discourse to achieve communicative objectives. This involves much more than generating coherent, natural sounding textual descriptions. It requires considering the knowledge and interests of the particular audience, and how information may be presented in such a way that it may be understood by them.

One important criterion for effective (human-computer) communication is to allow an active dialogue with the user, allowing follow-up questions, interruptions and checks on understanding. Yet current work on generating multi-sentence text has largely ignored the potential of computers to generate textual descriptions which are interactive, this work being based more on the analysis of written rather than verbal communication. The model developed in this chapter is based on studies of verbal, interactive explanations of the behaviour of physical systems. It integrates theories of text structure, dialogue structure and user modelling. The system is fully implemented, allowing graphical/textual explanations to be generated which take into account the likely prior knowledge of the user while allowing interactions with the user as the explanation progresses.

4.1   Introduction

The main criterion for generating effective text is that the text should achieve the communicative objectives of the speaker or writer. This involves satisfying a number of subsidiary criteria, such as that it should be coherent, understandable by the particular hearer and contribute to the hearer's goals. If there is a possibility of interaction, then the generation of text should furthermore take into account the discourse context, and use the interactive situation to monitor the hearer's understanding and acceptance of the text.

Recent work on text generation has shown how coherent, multi-sentence text may be generated [McKeown 1985] and how it can take into account the prior knowledge of the hearer [Paris 1988]. Rhetorical Structure Theory suggests how the structure and coherence of the text may be linked to the goals of the speaker [Mann and Thompson 1987] and this has led to a number of

plan-based approaches to text generation [Hovy 1988; Moore and Paris 1989].
Yet none of these systems make explicit all of the constraints on generating
communicative multi-sentence text, and only Moore and Paris consider the
interactive nature of human-computer interaction.

The remainder of this chapter will examine some of the criteria for generating communicative discourse, and show how more flexible text planners can be
developed by making these criteria explicit, rather than implicit, in compiled
schemas which satisfy the criteria in constrained situations. This flexibility is
especially important for interactive discourse, where the discourse situation is
continually changing.

The EDGE[1] discourse planner will be presented, which emphasises how
text may be generated which is interactive and which depends on the hearer's
knowledge. This model started with an analysis of human verbal explanations
in a limited domain. However, the stereotypic sequences of text (and interaction) types observed could be explained by more general constraints such as
precondition relations between concepts and **coherence** relations between
discourse segments. By beginning to make these relations explicit, the system is better able to adapt to the (changing) knowledge of the user, and to
unpredicted situations.

However, before discussing this particular model, the general criteria for
generating effective communicative discourse will be discussed.

4.2   Criteria for Communicative Discourse

The following criteria are adapted from de Beaugrande and Dressler's [1981]
principles for communicative text, extended to consider features of human-
computer interaction. The description of each criterion will be followed by a
discussion about how far existing systems explicitly satisfy it.

4.2.1   Cohesion: surface level ties

The first criterion discussed by Beaugrande and Dressler is cohesion. Unless
appropriate surface level ties are made between textual elements, then not only
will the text be unnatural and inefficient, but incorrect discourse structures
(and intentions) may be inferred. The most important cohesive tie is perhaps
the use of pronominalisation. Grosz and Sidner show how pronoun use may be
linked to an underlying discourse model [Grosz and Sidner 1985] and a version
of this model has been used as the basis for some generation systems (e.g.,
[Dale, this volume]).

---

[1]EDGE stands for Explanatory Discourse GEnerator.

4.2.2   Coherence: semantic relations between utterances

The next criterion for communicative text is that it should be coherent. There should be inferrable links between the ideas and objects in the text. Several systems (such as [McKeown 1985]) have used the notion of local focus to aid in the generation of coherent text: there should be links between the objects in focus in successive sentences, or in successive discourse segments. This idea has been extended by McCoy and Cheng [1988], who discuss the use of **Focus Trees** in generation. However, as well as relations between objects in focus, there are also a restricted set of relations that can apply between the ideas in successive discourse segments [Mann and Thompson 1987]. For example, successive segments may be used to 'compare and contrast' or to describe a cause and resultant effect. Both focus and such **rhetorical relations** may influence the order of textual elements, and a combination of the two have recently been used by Hovy and McCoy [1989].[2]

4.2.3   Intentionality: the speaker's goal

If a text is to succeed in its objective then the intention of the speaker must normally be inferrable from the text. For example, the indirect speech act *The door's open* will only succeed if the hearer recognises the speaker's intention to get her to shut the door. Multi-sentence text must be organised in such a way that these intentions can be recognised. One way to achieve the appropriate organisation is to plan text starting from some overall goal (or goals), and to explicitly represent the resultant intentional structure. This has many advantages over schema-based approaches, as it is possible to reason about the goals resulting in the text when dealing with follow-up questions and interruptions, and to insert appropriate markers to make the segmentation of the text clearer.

Rhetorical Structure Theory attempts to combine its account of textual coherence with a description of the goals which the different relations may be used to achieve, and this has resulted in planners which use these relations to both select and order information given an underlying goal (e.g., [Moore and Paris 1989; Moore 1989b]). Moore shows how this representation allows follow-up questions to be dealt with take into account the previous planned utterance.

---

[2]Note that some of these relations have been discussed in terms of cohesive TIES between utterances [Halliday and Hasan 1976]. However, in this chapter we will use the term **cohesion** for the surface level ties observable in the text, and **coherence** for the existence of underlying semantic relations as they influence the selection and ordering of utterances.

4.2.4   Acceptability: the hearer's goal

No-one is going to read a text which does not address her own goals (even if
these goals are somewhat indirect, such as to please the speaker). Generating
communicative text should therefore consider the overall goals of the hearer.
For example, someone interested in mending her car might want a different
explanation of how an engine works from someone interested in running it
efficiently, passing a test, or impressing the speaker! Ideally, therefore, there
should be some attempt to infer the goals which motivate questions, and to
use these in tailoring the explanation. McKeown *et al.* [1985; McKeown 1988]
have shown how simple expert system explanations can be influenced by the
hearer's assumed (and inferred) goal.

4.2.5   Informativity: the hearer's knowledge

Text content should obviously depend on the hearer's prior knowledge. If the
hearer is told too much that she already knows, then the text will be boring,
while if complex ideas are referenced which are unfamiliar to the hearer, then
it will not be understood.   Several early text generation systems used the
heuristic of not telling users facts that they should know already (e.g., [Mann
and Moore 1981; Weiner 1980]). However, this oversimplifies the problem.
For example, in a causal explanation another heuristic is to use only known
concepts in an explanation [Wallis and Shortliffe 1984]. Furthermore, neither
heuristic considers the extra anchoring or prerequisite information which is
needed when conveying complex information if it is to be understood [Draper
1987].   Work on curriculum design in Intelligent Tutoring Systems provides
ideas about how information can be selected and ordered so that it may be
understood [Peachey and McCalla 1986; Murray 1989].

4.2.6   Situationality: the discourse context

Text generation should also take into account other aspects of the discourse
context, such as the type of discourse (e.g., tutorial or advice) and more directly, what is going on at that moment, and what has been said so far. Hovy
[1985] shows how the 'conversational setting' can influence text generation,
while Moore [1989b] uses the context (or **co-text**) defined by the plan of
the past explanation to influence responses to follow-up questions. Both of
these—the immediate and more general discourse context—are important in
generating appropriate text. The immediate discourse context may be used
to infer knowledge about the user which may in turn be used to generate
informative and acceptable text.

4.2.7   Intertextuality: text types

The term **intertextuality** refers to how texts provide the context for other texts. Interpreting or generating text must take into account this context. Some types of text may refer directly to other texts (e.g., reviews), but normally the influence is more subtle. One way texts establish the context for other texts is by the development of certain text types: standardised conventions for text structure applying in particular situations (e.g., formal letters or scientific papers). While these conventions may have been originally influenced by the criteria above, it may not be efficient or even possible to generate appropriate texts without considering such specialised forms. However, as mentioned before, applying stereotypic sequences indiscriminately will result in inflexible generation which is hard to adapt to the changing situation.

There has been much analysis of text types within psycholinguistics, such as the extensive discussion about story grammars (e.g. [Rumelhart 1975; Black and Wilensky 1979]). A distinction should be made between domain dependent orderings (content schemas) and conventions for structuring texts of different types (text grammars) [Kieras 1985].

4.2.8   Interactivity

The above criteria (adapted from de Beaugrande and Dressler [1981]) apply to written text. However, human-computer interaction is as much like verbal interaction as it is like written interaction.[3] Therefore, a further criterion for communicative text generation is that it should be **interactive**, allowing interruptions, follow-up questions and checks on understanding. There is much evidence that human verbal explanations involve negotiation and checking moves [Pollack *et al.* 1982; Ringle and Bruce 1981] and that human-computer interaction could be improved by considering these issues. Moore [1989b] begins to approach the problem by allowing follow-up questions after explanations. However, there are many more types of interaction which should be considered. Allowing a range of interactions within an explanation both provides for more robust communication and allows a model of the user's goals and knowledge to be built up, improving later generation. Such 'execution monitoring' has been discussed by Moore, but not yet incorporated in her system.

---

[3]Of course, keyboard interaction is really unlike both written and spoken interaction. The details of how we structure interactive discourse will inevitably depend on the particular mode and style of interaction, but the basic principle of *interactivity* will still apply.

4.2.9   Graphical actions in discourse planning

The final criterion for generating communicative discourse is that it should
be possible (where appropriate) to integrate textual and graphical actions.
Many types of explanations can be improved by reference to a diagram, and
in human-computer interaction it is possible to coordinate pointing and other
graphical actions with the associated proposition in the text (e.g., [Neal *et
al.* 1988; Reithinger 1987]). Several attempts at generating qualitative causal
descriptions of device behaviour have combined text and graphics [Forbus and
Stevens 1981; Falkenheimer and Forbus 1988].

4.2.10   Conclusion: satisfying multiple criteria

This section has reviewed a number of criteria for generating communicative
discourse, discussing work that has been done in each area. Some of the approaches mentioned satisfy several criteria; for example, Rhetorical Structure
Theory (RST) combines intentionality with coherence, while Paris [1988] combines text types with informativity. Many approaches (including RST) implicitly satisfy criteria by using standard orderings of textual elements abstracted
from an analysis of a particular text type.

Flexible text generation involves making more of these criteria or constraints explicit. For example, ordering of information in the text depends
on coherence, informativity and standard text types. A text planner should
use these constraints to generate appropriate text. Selection of information
depends further on acceptability and the speaker's goal. The planner should
be able to use all these principles to influence the selection of what to say, so
that this may depend on several aspects of the discourse situation.

Hovy and McCoy's recent work [Hovy and McCoy 1989] illustrates one
example of default orderings being replaced by more flexible rules. Here, focus
rules are used as an additional constraint on ordering in an under-constrained
RST-based generation system (see also [Hovy, this volume]). Making such
ordering constraints explicit gives increased flexibility, especially where the
focus may change unpredictably, as in a dialogue.

The model discussed in the next section emphasises how informative, graph-
ical/textual interactive explanations may be generated given a high-level goal
of what to explain. By making prerequisite and focus constraints explicit, the
model is given increasing flexibility in a dynamic situation where the current
focus and the user's assumed knowledge are continually changing.

4.3   The EDGE Discourse Planner

The EDGE discourse planner is based on two levels of planning. The first level is content planning. Here, prerequisite and 'subskill' relations between the concepts being explained are used to plan what to say given assumptions about the hearer's knowledge. Simple focus rules control ordering of goals/discourse segments where no stronger constraints apply. The second level is the discourse planning level. This level is concerned with planning the presentation (including the use of discourse markers and meta-comments) and the interaction with the user. The use of two levels of planning is similar to Litman's [1985] use of domain and discourse plans in discourse interpretation, and several curriculum planning systems such as [Murray 1989]. It may also be compared to McCoy's [1989] representation of both the communicative role and the content of utterances in her response schemas, though it is more powerful, as the communicative/discourse roles may apply to whole sections of the explanation, rather than single utterances.

The following sections will describe these two levels of planning in more detail, followed by a brief description of the user modelling component, and a summary of how far the criteria discussed above are satisfied by the system.

4.3.1   Planning communicative text

When planning how to present some complex information it is important to consider how that new information may be understood by the hearer. In many cases there may be prerequisite facts which must be known first, and there may be alternative ways of explaining something which will be more or less easy to understand by different hearers. For example, a task description may require (as a prerequisite) that the hearer can recognise the objects in the task description. If there are unfamiliar objects, they can be identified before they are referred to in the description. The task may also be described at different levels of detail depending on the knowledge of the hearer. The rest of this section will discuss how this type of reasoning is made possible in the EDGE content planner.

Deriving content plans

The EDGE content plans are based on an analysis of explanations of how simple electronic systems work. The initial analysis led to a schema-like description similar (but not identical) to Paris's PROCESS and CONSTITUENCY schemas [Paris 1988]. However, at the same time it was clear that many of the ordering constraints in the explanation (implicit in the schema) are due to prerequisite relations between the concepts being taught. For example, component de-

scriptions are given before causal explanations, and devices are identified and
given attributes before having their behaviour explained [Cox *et al.* 1988]. The
representation for content planning operators should therefore capture both
the alternative ways of describing or explaining considered to some extent by
Paris, and these prerequisite relationships between concepts.

A simple plan representation

Content planning operators may therefore have constraints,[4] prerequisites and
subgoals. The constraints are used for selecting alternative ways of explaining
something. The preconditions define things which need to be explained first if
unknown by the hearer, while the subgoals define how to explain the concept
in terms of subskills which must be explained. Unless specified, the subgoals
don't have a fixed order (though the given order acts as a default), so focus
rules may influence this ordering. However, preconditions must always be
satisfied before the main body (subgoals) of a goal.

A simplified set of high-level content plan operators are given in Figure 4.1.[5] The first definition is a plan operator to explain how a device (circuit)
works, applicable when there is a structural description available in the knowledge base. There is a prerequisite that the hearer understands the structure
of the device (which, by definition, includes the component behaviour) and
the plan involves first teaching the **process** (causal explanation) of the device
and then summarising its behaviour. The second definition uses a constraint
on the user's assumed knowledge to select an analogical description, if such
an analogical device exists and the user is familiar with the device. The third
structural/componential operator is used to identify and give the function
of the device (if not known) and to describe the components of the device.
Finally, the **identify** operator is used to identify the device as being of a
particular circuit type, if that information is available in the knowledge base
and the user knows what that circuit type is. The subgoal references a discourse plan (**dplan**) which involves an exchange with the user to convey some
given proposition; in later example plans this may be simplified to **inform**
(< *prop* >).

---

[4]These should not of course be confused with the general constraints on generating communicative text; they are simply part of the plan operator representation.

[5]The planning operators also have templates associated with them. These are used in
generating meta-comments on the plan being executed while a separate set of templates is
associated with each type of proposition in the explanation and is used for generating the
main propositional content of the text. The types of meta-comments which can be generated
are those which directly inform the user of what is about to be or has been said. Many other
types of meta-comments are used in discourse (discussed, for example, by Carbonell [1982]
and Sigurd [1987]), some of which have been used by Zuckerman and Pearl [1986] to improve
mathematical explanations.

```
(defplan how-it-works (device)
    :constraints ((getslot device 'structure))
    :preconditions ((structure (device)))
    :subgoals ((cplan process (device))
               (cplan behaviour (device)))
    :template ("how" (deviceref device) " works "))

(defplan structure (device)
    :constraints  ((getslot device #'device-analogy)
                   (understood 'structure
                       (list (getslot device #'device-analogy))))
    :subgoals ((cplan compare
                   (device
                       (getslot device #'device-analogy))))
    :template ("what" (deviceref device) "is like"))

(defplan structure (device)
    :preconditions ((identify (device))
                    (function (device)))
    :subgoals ((cplan components (device))))

(defplan identify (device)
    :constraints ((getslot device #'device-ctype)
                  (understood 'identify
                      (list (getslot device #'device-ctype))))
    :subgoals ((dplan teaching.exchange
                    ((list 'circuit-type device
                        (getslot device #'device-ctype)))))
    :template ("what type of circuit/component"
                  (deviceref device) "is"))
```

Figure 4.1: Example high-level operators to explain device behaviour

As mentioned before, as no fixed order is given for the subgoals, the two subgoals in the first definition may be in any order; explaining behaviour and then summarising it is the default, but it is also reasonable to give the behaviour, then explain how that behaviour arises from the structure of the device.

Subgoals of plan operators may be other content plans, discourse plans (including exchanges with the user to convey or check some information), or calls to LISP functions. These latter calls represent graphical actions or speech acts. Subgoals may also be called conditionally or iteratively on a set of objects (such as components). An example content plan involving graphical and discourse actions is given in Figure 4.2 along with the resulting textual and graphical output.

The plan representation is similar to using schemas, but defines the hierarchical decomposition of the explanation in terms of skills or concepts being taught, and allows prerequisites to be defined. It also provides the basis for a hierarchical discourse model based on the intentions of the speaker [Grosz and Sidner 1985] which may be used to decide on pronominalisation, meta-comments and discourse markers. The representation is a form of **skeletal** planning [Friedland and Iwasaki 1985] where prebuilt partial plans allow refinement or specialisation of plan goals, but it is extended to allow prerequisite relations.

Planning content

Having discussed the basic representation for plan operators, and given some examples, this section will show how these are used to plan the first few utterances of an explanation.

Initially, a high-level goal (or goals) is placed on an agenda. This agenda will always contain the remaining goals to be satisfied. Planning proceeds by selecting a goal from that agenda (using ordering relations to find valid next goals, and focus rules to choose among them); selecting a plan operator to use to expand that goal into subgoals (using constraints on the plan operators); and, depending on the knowledge of the user, placing new subgoals and prerequisite goals on the agenda. When there is a directly executable action in the plan this is immediately executed. Thus, planning proceeds incrementally, with only a partial representation of the future explanation plan.

Suppose, for example, the agenda initially contained the single content goal:

(1) ((cplan how-it-works (light-unit)))

The first plan operator would be selected, and if the system assumed that the user didn't already know the **structure** of the light-unit, it would place new

```
(defplan what-it-looks-like (device)
    :subgoals ((call pointat (device))
               (interaction teaching.exchange
                   ((list 'identify-diagram device))))
    :template ("what" (deviceref device) "looks like."))
```

This component here is a light dependent resistor.

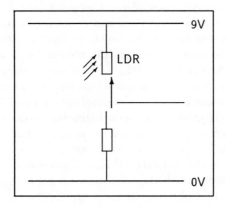

Figure 4.2: Identifying a component: plans and actions

items on the agenda so that it now contained the following goals:

(2) ((cplan structure (light-unit))
      (cplan process (light-unit))
      (cplan behaviour (light-unit)))

Ordering information would indicate that the precondition **structure** should be explained before the other two goals. This would therefore be the next goal to be expanded. If there were several possible next goals, then simple focus rules attempt to select between them. For example, if the system could either describe the resistor or the transistor next, but the user has just asked a question about the transistor, the system would choose to describe the transistor next.

As the goals are expanded, a representation of the discourse plan is built up. Each goal node in this representation has pointers to parent and subgoals, but also includes lists of any assumptions made about the user's knowledge (such as assuming that a concept was known when not putting a precondition on the agenda), and any alternative plan operators which could have been used to expand a goal. As Moore [1989b] points out, this type of information is useful when dealing with inarticulate follow-up questions (or interruptions), when it may be necessary to re-explain something in another way, or fill in missing information.

A simplified representation of a discourse plan is given in Figure 4.3, which illustrates how the first two utterances of the explanation arise, given a set of plan operators including the examples in Figure 4.1. At this point in the planning the agenda will contain the goals components, process and behaviour with the constraint that components should be described before the others.

Note that in the second utterance the pronoun *it* is used for the light detector circuit. Although this chapter does not consider the problem of sentence-level generation (EDGE simply selects templates depending on proposition type), it does use a simple pronominalisation algorithm. This is vital, if the user is to avoid inferring the wrong structure from the discourse (such as assuming that lack of pronominalisation indicated that a new topic was to begin). The algorithm is simply to use a pronoun for the principle focus of an utterance (marked in the templates) if that object was in the focus space of the preceding utterance *and* if the two utterances are both within a discourse segment which has that object in its focus space. The goal arguments (such as light-unit) provide a primitive model of focus. The second part of the rule avoids using a pronoun when a new topic begins which just happens to include an object in the last sentence of the previous topic.

Summary

The above description should be enough to show how prerequisites and constraints may be used to structure explanations which may involve both graphical and textual actions. Further details of the plans and device models used are given in [Cawsey 1989].

It is worthwhile at this point to compare the framework described so far with that developed by Moore and Paris [1989] (and discussed in [Hovy, this volume]). They have developed a text planner based on Rhetorical Structure Theory which may be used in the context of an interactive discourse. While the basic planning mechanism they use is very similar to that used here, they emphasise the rhetorical relations between discourse segments. The EDGE model uses only one such relation in the content plans: the PRECONDITION relation. This is similar to RST's BACKGROUND relation, but is used somewhat

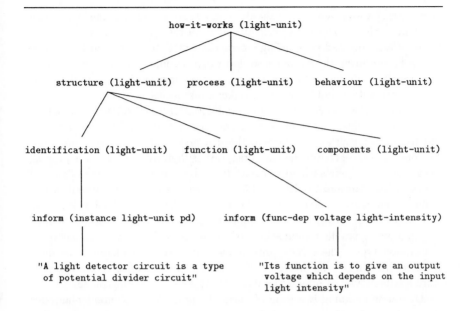

Figure 4.3: Example partially completed text content plan (simplified)

differently. However, the operators in the EDGE system used do not in general specify the relation between subgoals; the names of the operators correspond to the **effect** field of Moore and Paris's operators, where that effect could be something like

(3) (BEL ?hearer (CONCEPT (WHAT-IT-DOES LIGHT-UNIT)))

Most of the following discussion would also apply given a content planner such as the one described by Moore and Paris; however, where they were concerned with using the plan representation to provide context for dealing with follow-up questions, the EDGE system is more concerned with structuring an extended explanatory dialogue on some topic, and using the plan representation to deal appropriately with user interruptions.

4.3.2 Discourse planning

The content plans could be used alone to generate textual descriptions given assumptions about the knowledge of the hearer, as illustrated in the simple example above. However, two of the criteria for generating communicative text we discussed above were that it should be interactive, and that the intention of the speaker should be clearly recognisable from the text. The former requires a way of allowing and structuring interactions with the user, while the latter requires structuring the discourse so that the intentional structure is apparent. This involves adding meta-comments and discourse markers to indicate the discourse structure and hence the speaker's intentions.

Discourse plans then serve this double function: to structure interactions (using plans similar to the dialogue games used by Power [1974] and others) and to add appropriate markers to the discourse. They are concerned with the communicative role of the discourse, rather then with any specific propositional content. Their basic form comes from work on the structure of tutorial discourse [Sinclair and Coulthard 1975], who suggested that tutorial discourse could be analysed at five levels: the LESSON, the TRANSACTION (on some topic), the EXCHANGE, the MOVE and the LINGUISTIC ACT. Rules defined, for example, possible combinations of exchanges allowable for a particular transaction type. These rules provide an initial basis for planning discourse at these different levels. However, they have to be extended to allow for the more flexible styles of interaction desirable in explanatory discourse.

Discourse planning is a form of meta-planning. While content plan operators take domain objects as their arguments, discourse plan operators take content goals or propositions as their arguments. As mentioned before, the arguments of the plans provide a primitive model of discourse focus which may be used to decide on pronominalisation. Because some of these arguments are content goals, the system is able to pronominalise content goals themselves, such as saying *OK, I'll explain that*, rather than *OK, I'll explain how the light detector circuit works*.

Example plans

Some example discourse plan operators are given in Figure 4.4. The first, top level, operator (INFORMING TRANSACTION) is used to plan opening and closing exchanges at the beginnings and ends of topics. In this type of discourse (tutorial) opening exchanges consist of a framing move (essentially a topic opening discourse marker) and often a focusing move (meta-comment on future discourse), while closing exchanges negotiate the close of the topic with the hearer, allowing opportunity for follow-up questions. After the opening exchange is planned, the `plan-content` function will be used to pass control to the content planner, to determine the propositional content of the explanation. As soon as some proposition is planned, control passes back to the discourse planner, and the `teaching.exchange` plan operator is used to determine how to convey that proposition. If the proposition is believed *maybe* understood, the system questions the user to check her understanding. Otherwise, the system informs the user, then waits for acknowledgment that it was understood.

This acknowledgment is important. In the set of discourse plans currently used, the system will pause after expressing each proposition. As Moore [1989a] points out, this would not be desirable in general, and it would be better to reason about when best to pause. However, the EDGE system generates graphical/textual explanations where many pauses are required if the user is to see dynamic changes in the diagram. Also, most of the utterances are either part of crucial background information, or part of some sequence, where each step must be understood. Because of these two things, seeking an acknowledgement from the user after every utterance is acceptable. However, in other domains, an acknowledgement after each transaction on some topic or sub-topic might be more appropriate. Different dialogue styles such as this could be easily defined by changing the discourse plan operators appropriately.

When the system is waiting for an acknowledgement, the user has many options. These include asking the system to continue, asking a question, or signalling that she does not understand the explanation. Some of these are discussed further later in this chapter.

Planning explanatory dialogues

So, in the EDGE model, planning an explanatory dialogue is initiated by placing a goal such as the following on the agenda:

```
(4)  (dplan informing.transaction
          ((cplan how-it-works (light-unit))))
```

The first operator in Figure 4.4 is used to expand this goal, resulting in a new agenda as follows:

```
(5)  ((dplan boundary.exchange ((cplan...) open))
      (call plan-content ((cplan ...) close))
      (dplan boundary.exchange ((cplan ...) close)))
```

Discourse goals are always assumed to have a fixed order—you don't close a topic before opening it, or answer a question before it is asked—so the next goal to be expanded will be the opening boundary exchange. This will result in an opening marker and meta-comment, as illustrated at the beginning of Figure 4.6. The plan-content function will then start planning the content by putting the content goal (cplan how-it-works (light-unit)) on the agenda. As discussed in the previous section, this will lead to the next few utterances in the example, illustrated in the content plan in Figure 4.3. Figure 4.5 illustrates part of the plan structure resulting from the use of both discourse and content plans.

```
(defplan informing.transaction (teaching-goal)
   :subgoals ((dplan boundary.exchange (teaching-goal 'open))
              (call plan-content (teaching-goal))
              (dplan boundary.exchange (teaching-goal 'close))))

(defplan boundary.exchange (goal type)
   :constraints ((eql type 'open))
   :subgoals ((dplan framing.move (type))
              (dplan focussing.move (goal type))))

(defplan teaching.exchange (prop)
   :constraints
      ((maybe-understood prop)) ; if not sure user understands
   :subgoals                    ; ask a question to check
      ((dplan elicit.exchange (prop))))

(defplan teaching.exchange (prop) ; otherwise just inform user
   :subgoals ((dplan inform.exchange (prop))))

(defplan inform.exchange (prop)
   :subgoals ((dplan inform.move (prop))
              (dplan acknowledge.move (prop))))
```

Figure 4.4: High-level discourse plan

Figure 4.6 illustrates several types of exchange within the explanation.
The second column shows the type of exchange (in italics) and the relevant
proposition or content goal (in bold), while the first shows the actual text
generated.[6] In addition to the INFORMING exchange, where the system pauses
for acknowledgement,[7] there is an INFO-ELICIT exchange, where the system
checks whether the user knows some concept (needing this knowledge to decide
whether to explain this background information), and an ELICIT exchange,
where the system asks the user a more directed question to check that she does
know some proposition. Also, there are the two types of boundary exchange.

---

[6] Note that in these examples user input comes from menus.
[7] These acknowledgements, consisting of a simple mouse click, are not represented in the
example.

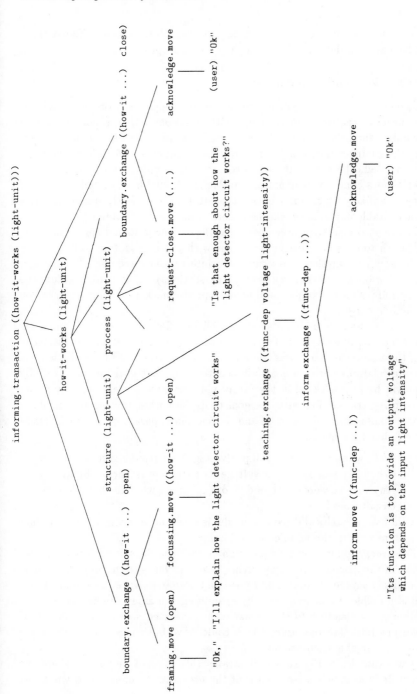

Figure 4.5: Simplified discourse plan

The discourse planner is responsible both for structuring these different types of exchange, and determining when they are appropriate.

Interruptions and remediation

Whenever the system is pausing for an acknowledgement, or for an answer to a question, the user can interrupt with questions. Also, when the system determines that the user has failed to understand something, it may 'interrupt' the main explanation with a remedial sequence. Whether system or user initiated, these REPAIR sequences are very important if the user is to understand a complex explanation. As Moore [1989a] has pointed out, a user model is unlikely to be sufficiently accurate that a perfectly understandable and acceptable explanation can be generated at the first attempt.

In order to deal with user questions, the discourse model (plan) must be used, both to guess at possible problems with the explanation so far, and to reason how (or whether) to resume the interrupted discourse. Special discourse plan operators (INTERRUPTING transactions) are used to structure the interruption by, for example, adding appropriate markers (e.g., *anyway*) when a topic is resumed.

Suppose the user interrupts with a well-specified question, such as asking what some component does. The system will first examine its future discourse plan, to reason whether it was going to say that anyway, and if so whether the ordering relations between goals allow it to bring that goal forward. Usually there will be no such goal in the future plan, and the system will initiate an interrupting transaction with the goal to explain what the component does. Using a combination of discourse and content plan operators, this might result in the following sequence:

(6)   Well, when it has a high input voltage its output resistance is low.
       When it has a low input voltage its output resistance is high.
       Anyway, we were in the middle of explaining what the heat detector
       circuit does.

Note that a hierarchical discourse model is essential in order to reason what the system was 'in the middle of' explaining.

However, suppose the user just signals that she doesn't understand some section of the discourse (e.g., by saying *What?*). The system must then guess at the likely source of trouble and possible alternative ways to explain things. This is possible, to some extent, by examining the assumptions made in expanding goals (leading to the explanation generated so far), and the alternative possible plan operators which could have been used. Both these are represented in the discourse model.

The example in Figure 4.7 illustrates this type of response, where the system finds that it has assumed that the user already understood what sort

Ok, Let's go through how a light detector unit works.	*Opening exchange* **How-it-works (light-unit)**
A light detector unit is a sort of potential divider circuit.	*Informing exchange* **Identification (light-unit)**
Its function is to provide an output voltage which depends on the input light-intensity.	*Informing exchange* **Function (light-unit)**
It consists of a light dependent resistor and a fixed resistor.	*Informing exchange* **Constituency (light-unit)**
This component here is a light dependent resistor.	*Informing exchange* **Component-identification (LDR)**
Do you know what it does?	*Info-elicit exchange* **What-it-does (LDR)**
— **I think so** Well, perhaps we better go over that and check. What do you think the output resistance is when it has a high input light intensity?	*Elicit exchange* **Particular-behaviour (LDR (light-intensity high))**
— **Low—fully conductive** No, not quite, it's actually quite low. . . .	
Ok, Is that enought about how the light detector works? — **Yes** Ok	*Closing Exchange* **How-it-works (light-unit)**

Figure 4.6: Structuring a simple explanation

User	What?
System	Did you not know what a light detector circuit is?
User	No.
System	OK, I'll explain that then. A light detector circuit is a type of potential divider circuit.
User	OK.
System	Anyway, I was going through how the light detector circuit works.

Figure 4.7: An interruption

of circuit a light detector was when explaining its behaviour. This is viewed, by the system, as an essential prerequisite to understanding the rest of the explanation, and a likely candidate causing the lack of understanding.

Interruptions such as these are not added to the main discourse model; the interrupting goal is added to the agenda, but pointers are not added to the main plan. It is therefore treated as a true interruption [Grosz and Sidner 1985], with separate focus and intentional structure. However, after an interruption, the items in focus in the interrupting sequence are used to determine the next goal selected from the agenda. This allows the system to attempt to follow on from the user's initiated topic, while still trying to satisfy its own goals.

The other type of interruption mentioned was the remediation sequence, initiated by the system. This is structured as an interruption (e.g., resuming the previous topic with *anyway*), but is added to the main discourse model as a complex type of response to an incorrectly answered question. Remediation plans are defined, based on work on tutorial dialogues (e.g., [Woolf and McDonald 1984; Collins and Stevens 1982]). For example, Figure 4.8 illustrates the discourse resulting from the strategy of 'give a helpful analogy and try asking again'.[8]

Conclusion

This section has shown how discourse planning operators may be used in conjunction with content planning operators to generate explanatory discourse. The interactions allowed in the discourse provide an important source of in-

---

[8]This is taken from an actual evaluation sessions where real (albeit computer-proficient) users explored the system to identify its problems and limitations and to provide a subjective view of the interaction.

1 Suppose the input heat intensity is high (hot).

2 What's the output voltage (V2) of the heat detector circuit going to be when the input heat intensity is high (hot)?

3 — **Low (0V).**

4 Wrong, not quite, Ok,

5 A heat detector circuit is much like a light detector circuit only:

6 • Its output voltage depends on the input light intensity.

7 • It has a thermistor instead of a light dependent resistor.

8 This component here is a thermistor.

9 Let's go through what a thermistor does.

10 When the input heat intensity (H1) of the thermistor is high (hot) the output resistance (R1) will be quite low.

11 When it is low (cold) the output resistance (R1) will be quite high.

12 So, what's the output voltage (V2) of the heat detector circuit going to be when the input heat intensity is high (hot)?

13 — **Quite high (towards 9V).**

14 Precisely, very good, it's quite high (towards 9V).

15 Anyway, we were in the middle of explaining how the low heat warning device works if it has the following inputs: heat intensity high.

Figure 4.8: Interrupting REMEDIATION sequence

formation about the user's knowledge which may be used in later planning decisions. The final part of the EDGE model is therefore a set of inference rules used to update the model of the user's knowledge as the dialogue progresses.

4.3.3 Updating assumptions about the user's knowledge

There are many possible sources of information about the user obtainable from dialogues such as the one above. Wahlster and Kobsa [1986] list five:

• default reasoning from stereotypes;

• initial models from previous sessions;

• explicit (direct) inference from the user's input;

• implicit (indirect) inference from the user's input; and

- what the system tells the user.

The EDGE user modelling component uses all these sources. Default reasoning uses **expertise level** stereotypes and the difficulty levels of the concepts [Chin 1988; Sleeman 1985]. Explicit inferences from the user's input includes inferring that a concept is probably not known if asked about; that a concept is maybe known if explained by the system; and that a concept is known if the user answers questions about that concept correctly. Implicit inferences include reasoning about whether related concepts are known given some knowledge of known or unknown concepts (such as assuming that prerequisites of a concept are probably known if the concept is known).

The basic representation of concepts in the model is based on the content planning operators rather than the underlying knowledge base. The operators define a hierarchy of concepts from the most general (how a device works) down to the most specific (what a component does given particular input values). For example, suppose the system has some direct evidence that the user knows a light-dependent resistor's behaviour when it is lit. This could be recorded as the following annotation to the plan operator `particular-behaviour`:

(7) `particular-behaviour (device input)`
     `        :understood (((LDR (light-intensity high)) yes))`

The annotations can obviously be extended to include any possible devices and input values. For example, the following would be used to indicate that there is evidence that the user does not know what the LDR does when it is dark, but she probably knows what a thermistor does when it is cold:

(8) `:understood (((thermistor (heat-intensity low)) maybe)`
     `             ((LDR (light-intensity low)) no)`
     `             ((LDR (light-intensity high)) yes))`

If there is evidence that the user knows all the subgoals of some plan, and hence the subskills and prerequisite skills of the concept defined by that plan, then the system has indirect evidence that the user understands that concept. For example, if the user knows the behaviour of a device for several possible input values, there is evidence that she knows the more abstract concept, i.e., the behaviour of the device in general. This conceptual hierarchy defined by the content planning operators allows the user model to be used both for high-level decisions which require general knowledge about the user, and detailed decisions which require more specific knowledge.

So, as the dialogue progresses, direct inference rules are used to update assumptions about the user's knowledge. When the system needs to know whether the user knows something, then indirect and stereotype reasoning can be used to infer this, given an absence of more certain knowledge. This includes reasoning whether the user understands the abstract concepts defined in high-level plans. The user's assumed knowledge may affect the content of the explanation, the remediation strategies selected, and the dialogue; for example, asking users questions about things they only *maybe* know, and asking users whether they understand things if this information is needed and there is no other source of information.

Without interaction, most of the direct inferences would be impossible. Without direct inferences, default (stereotype) and indirect inferences become more unreliable. Interaction therefore enables both better tailored explanations based on improved assumptions about the user's knowledge, and explanation repair if users still fail to understand the explanation.

4.3.4 Conclusion

The EDGE model as described above begins to satisfy many of the criteria for generating communicative text. It is planned from an underlying goal which is made clear in the discourse structure (**intentionality**) The content will depend on the prior knowledge of the hearer (**informativity**) but may use some standard domain-dependent and domain-independent conventions for structuring text (**intertextuality**). Cohesive relations may be maintained through use of pronouns (**cohesion**) while some **coherence** is maintained by allowing simple focus rules to select between partially ordered goals (and by the fact that items in focus in sub-plans must always be linked to items in focus in parent plans). The immediate discourse context (as defined by the discourse model) may be used to influence responses, and alternative discourse plans may be defined for different discourse situations such as teaching or giving help allowing the wider discourse context to influence the text (**situationality**). The explanations obviously are **interactiveinteractivity** and mix graphical and textual output.

The model does not satisfy the **acceptability** criterion, as there are not alternative plans appropriate for different underlying (hearer) goals. However, given knowledge of the hearer's goals it would be possible to use that in plan selection, if alternative ways of explaining the same thing were defined. The treatment of coherence is also over-simple, as it fails to give adequate consideration of the rhetorical relations used in structuring text, discussed by Hovy and others (e.g., [Hovy, this volume]).

4.4 Conclusion and Further Work

The EDGE discourse generator shows how a plan-based system can begin to satisfy many of the criteria which have to be satisfied in order to generate explanatory discourse, especially that of allowing interactive explanations where the user's understanding may be monitored and misunderstandings corrected. While each aspect of the system is very simple, and only begins to address the problems of generating this type of discourse, the overall framework seems to provide a promising approach for future explanation/discourse generators of this sort.

The main requirement for generating text in an interactive context is an explicit representation of the plans and goals of the system resulting in the generated text. This is a point made by Moore [1989a], and which should also be apparent from the EDGE model. This type of plan-based discourse model both allows better models of focus (allowing both improved pronominalisation and coherence between topics); an improved representation of the user's knowledge; and a representation of the immediate discourse context which may be used in explanation repair and the generation of meta-comments, for example. Using a partially ordered agenda of goals in the incremental generation of discourse allows the system to respond to user initiative by extending, re-ordering and developing the discourse plan in different ways depending on the local context.

The partial ordering of goals is important in allowing multiple constraints to influence the order of discourse segments. Currently, prerequisite constraints impose one type of ordering, while focus rules can overrule the default remaining ordering. Yet other constraints might include rhetorical relations (with their conventional ordering), and criteria such as to introduce the most important topic first. Also, the EDGE model does not address the problem of choosing when to include optional material, except where this can be decided based on the user's knowledge.

It is important to make these principles explicit, showing how the different options in generation depend on both the immediate and wider discourse context. In interactive discourse, the context (or the system's perception of it) may be continually changing. Text and discourse generators of the future should have the capability of monitoring and adapting to this changing situation, dynamically responding to the user's initiative.

Acknowledgements

This work was done while the author was supported by a studentship from the Science and Engineering Research Council. I would like to thank my reviewers for helpful comments on an early version of this chapter.

References

Black, J B and Wilensky, R [1979] An evaluation of story grammars. *Cognitive Science*, **3**, 213–230.

de Beaugrande, R and Dressler, W [1981] *Introduction to Text Linguistics*. London: Longman.

Carbonell, J G [1982] Meta-Language Utterances in Purposive Discourse. Technical Report CMU-CS-82-125, Department of Computer Science, Carnegie Mellon University.

Cawsey, A [1989] Generating Explanatory Discourse: A Plan-Based, Interactive Approach. PhD Thesis, Department of Artificial Intelligence, University of Edinburgh.

Chin, D [1988] Intelligent Agents as a Basis for Natural Language Interaction. PhD Thesis, Technical Report No. UCB/CSD 88/1396, Computer Science Division, University of California at Berkeley.

Collins, A and Stevens, A L [1982] Goal strategies of inquiry teachers. In R Glaser (ed), *Advances in Instructional Psychology*, Volume 2. Hillsdale, NJ: Lawrence Erlbaum Associates.

Cox, B, Jenkins, J and Pollitzer, E [1988] An explanation-driven, understanding-directed user model For intelligent tutoring systems. In *IEE Colloquium on Intelligent Tutoring Systems*, London, May 1988, pp4/1–4/3.

Dale, R [1990] Generating recipes: An overview of Epicure. This volume.

Draper, S W [1987] A user-centred concept of explanation. In *Proceedings of the Second Alvey Explanation Workshop*, Surrey, 8–9 January 1987, pp24–42.

Falkenheiner, B and Forbus, K D [1988] Setting up large-scale qualitative models. In *Proceedings of the 6th National Conference on Artificial Intelligence*, St Paul, Minnesota, 21–26 August 1988.

Forbus, K and Stevens, A [1981] Using Qualitative Simulations to Generate Explanations. Technical Report No. 4490, Bolt, Beranek and Newman.

Friedland, P E and Iwasaki, Y [1985] The concept and implementation of skeletal plans. *Journal of Automated Reasoning*, 1, 161–208.

Grosz, B J and Sidner, C L [1985] The Structures of Discourse Structure. Technical Report No. 6097, Bolt, Beranek and Newman.

Halliday, M A K and Hasan, R [1976] *Cohesion in English*. London: Longman.

Hovy, E H and McCoy, K F [1989] Focusing your RST: A step toward generating coherent multisentential text. In *Proceedings of the 11th Cognitive Science Conference*, Ann Arbor, August 1989, pp667–674. Also available as USC/Information Sciences Institute Research Report RS-89-246.

Hovy, E H [1985] Integrating text planning and production in generation. In *Proceedings of the 9th International Conference on Artificial Intelligence*, Los Angeles, Ca., 18–23 August 1985, pp848–851.

Hovy, E H [1988] Planning Coherent Multisentential Text. Technical Report RS-88-208, USC/Information Sciences Institute.

Hovy, E H [1990] Unresolved issues in paragraph planning. This volume.

Kieras, D E [1985] Thematic processes in the comprehension of technical prose. In B J Britton and J B Black (eds) *Understanding Expository Text : A Theoretical and Practical Handbook for Analyzing Explanatory Text*. Hillsdale, NJ: Lawrence Erlbaum Associates.

Litman, D L [1985] Plan Recognition and Discourse Analysis: An Integrated Approach for Understanding Dialogues. Technical Report No. 170, Department of Computer Science, University of Rochester.

McCoy, K F [1989] Generating context-sensitive responses to object related misconceptions. *Artificial Intelligence*, 41(2).

McCoy, K F and Cheng, J [1988] Focus of attention: Constraining what can be said next. In *Proceedings of the 4th International Workshop on Natural Language Generation*, Catalina Island.

McKeown, K R [1985] *Text Generation: Using discourse strategies and focus constraints to generate natural language text.* Cambridge: Cambridge University Press.

McKeown, K R, Wish, M and Matthews, K [1985] Tailoring explanations for the user. In *Proceedings of the 9th International Conference on Artificial Intelligence*, Los Angeles, Ca., 18–23 August 1985, pp794–798.

McKeown, K R [1988] Generating goal-oriented explanations. *International Journal of Expert Systems Research and Applications*, 4, 377–395.

Mann, W C and Moore, J A [1981] Computer generation of multiparagraph text. *American Journal of Computational Linguistics*, 7, 17–29.

Mann, W C and Thompson, S A [1987] Rhetorical Structure Theory: A Framework for the Analysis of Texts. Technical Report RS-87-190, USC/Information Sciences Institute.

Moore, J D [1989] Responding to 'Huh?': Answering vaguely articulated follow-up questions. In *Proceedings of the 1989 Conference on Human Factors in Computing Systems.*

Moore, J D and Paris, C [1989] Planning text for advisory dialogues. In *Proceedings of the 27th Annual Meeting of the Association for Computational Linguistics*, Vancouver, Canada, pp203–211.

Moore, J D [1990] A Reactive Approach to Explanation in Expert and Advice-Giving Systems. Technical Report RS-90-251, Information Sciences Institute, University of Southern California.

Paris, C [1988] Tailoring object descriptions to a user's level of expertise. *Computational Linguistics*, 14, 64–78.

Neal, J G, Dobes, Z, Bettinger, K and Byoun, J S [1988] Multi-modal references in human-computer dialogue. In *Proceedings of the 7th National Conference on Artificial Intelligence*, St Paul, Minnesota, 21–26 August 1988.

Murray, B [1989] Control for intelligent tutoring systems: A blackboard-based dynamic instructional planner. In D Bierman, J Breuker and J Sandberg (eds), *Artificial Intelligence and Education*, pp150–168. Amsterdam/Springfield VA: IOS.

Power, R [1974] A Computer Model of Conversation. Unpublished PhD Thesis, School of Artificial Intelligence, University of Edinburgh.

Pollack, M E, Hirschberg, J and Webber, B [1982] User participation in the reasoning processes of expert systems. In *Proceedings of the National Conference on Artificial Intelligence*, University of Pittsburgh, 18–20 August 1982, pp358–361.

Peachey, D R and McCalla, G I [1986] Using planning techniques in intelligent tutoring systems. *International Journal of Man-Machine Studies*, **24**, 77–98.

Rumelhart, D E [1975] Notes on a schema for stories. In D Bobrow and A Collins (eds), *Representation and Understanding*, pp211–238. New York: Academic Press.

Ringle, M H and Bruce, B C [1981] Conversation failure. In W G Lehnert and M H Ringle (eds), *Strategies for Natural Language Processing*. Hillsdale, NJ: Lawrence Earlbaum Associates.

Reithinger, N [1987] Generating pointing gestures and referring expressions. In G Kempen (ed), *Natural Language Generation*. Dordrecht: Martinus Nijhoff.

Sleeman, D [1985] UMFE: A user modelling front end subsystem. *International Journal of Man-Machine Studies*, **23**, 71–88.

Sinclair, J McH and Coulthard, R M [1975] *Towards an Analysis of Discourse: The English used by teachers and pupils*. Oxford: Oxford University Press.

Sigurd, B [1987] Meta-comments in text generation. In G Kempen (ed), *Natural Language Generation*. Dordrecht: Martinus Nijhoff.

Wahlster, W and Kobsa, A [1986] Dialog based user models. *IEE Special Issue on NL Processing*, pp948–960.

Wallis, J W and Shortliffe, E H [1984] Customised explanations using causal knowledge. In B G Buchanan and E H Shortliffe (eds) *Rule Based Expert Systems*, pp371–390. Reading, Mass.: Addison Wesley.

Weiner, J L [1980] BLAH, a system which explains its reasoning. *Artificial Intelligence*, **15**, 19–48.

Zuckerman, I and Pearl, J [1986] Comprehension-driven generation of meta-technical utterances in Math tutoring. In *Proceedings of the the 5th National Conference on Artificial Intelligence*, Philadelphia, Pa., 11-15 August 1986, pp606–611.

Woolf, B and McDonald, D D [1984] Context-dependent transitions in discourse. In *Proceedings of the National Conference on Artificial Intelligence*, University of Texas at Austin, 6–10 August 1984, pp355–361.

5 Natural Language Generation in COMET

Kathleen McKeown, Michael Elhadad, Yumiko Fukumoto, Jong Lim, Christine Lombardi, Jacques Robin, and Frank Smadja

Abstract

In this chapter we discuss the approach taken in the non-graphic modules of COMET (CoOrdinated Multimedia Explanation Testbed) using natural language generation techniques. Our focus is two-fold: (i) the derivation of new schemas from old for the content planner and (ii) the use of the Functional Unification Formalism (FUF) to allow for interaction across modules. Extensions that we have made to FUF allow it to be used as general purpose tool. We show how we are able to carry out non-grammatical tasks, such as lexical choice using FUF, as well as traditional grammatical realisation. The result is a cascaded series of grammars across which interaction can occur.

5.1 Introduction

Our overall focus in the development of COMET (CoOrdinated Multimedia Explanation Testbed) has been on producing explanations for equipment maintenance and repair in which text and graphics are fully integrated and coordinated [Feiner and McKeown 1989, 1990]. We have found that allowing for interaction between the various modules of the system is critical for achieving this goal. In this chapter, we discuss the approach we are taking in the non-graphic modules of COMET using natural language generation techniques and we show how this approach fosters possibilites for interaction. In particular, we provide an overview of COMET's content planner and of three other modules that have been implemented using the Functional Unification Formalism (FUF): the media coordinator, the lexical interface, and the sentence generator.

Extensions that we have made to FUF allow it to be used as a general purpose tool. We show how we are able to carry out non-grammatical tasks using the formalism, including lexical choice and the annotation of the content specification according to which concepts should be conveyed through graphics and which in text. We overview the FUF grammar used to produce sentences and show how it interacts with some decisions made earlier. This results in a series of cascaded grammars for three different tasks across which interaction can occur.

COMET's content planner produces a content specification for the multimedia explanation using a schema based approach. We show how we have been able to re-use a schema across domains, resulting in the beginnings of a hierarchical library of schemas that are more general than in previous work. Since the output of COMET's content planner specifies explanation content regardless of medium, the same explanation goals are used to influence both text and picture production.

5.2 System Overview

An overview of COMET's architecture is shown in Figure 5.1. On receiving a request for explanation (currently in internal notation), the **content planner** uses schemas to determine which information should be included from the underlying **knowledge sources** in the explanation. In this chapter, we restrict ourselves to discussion of explanation production from a static representation of the domain encoded in LOOM [MacGregor and Brill 1989], although we note that COMET also contains a detailed geometric knowledge base necessary for graphics generation [Seligmann and Feiner 1989] and two dynamic knowledge sources: a representation of the world as influenced by probabilistic plan execution [Baker 1989] and a rule-base learned over time [Danyluk 1989]. The content planner produces the full content for the explanation, represented as a hierarchy of logical forms (LFs) [Allen 1987], which are passed to the **media coordinator**. The media coordinator, which has been developed jointly with Feiner [Feiner and McKeown 1989; Elhadad *et al.* 1989], refines the LFs by adding directives indicating which portions are to be produced by the **text generator** and which by the **graphics generator** (developed by Seligmann and Feiner [1989]). These two generators each process the same LFs, producing text and graphics for the portions of the LFs that the media coordinator has directed them to realise. A **layout manager** is being developed by Feiner [1988] which will combine output from these two generators and format it on the display.

COMET is being developed for the domain of equipment maintenance and repair using the US Army AN/PRC-119 portable radio receiver-transmitter [Department of the Army 1986]. In this domain, COMET is required to produce instructions for carrying out certain maintenance or repair procedures. For example, if the user suspects that the radio has a loss of memory (i.e., transmitting frequencies are not retained from one usage of the radio to the next), the system would describe the procedure for troubleshooting loss of memory on request. In this chapter, we will use one step of this procedure (loading

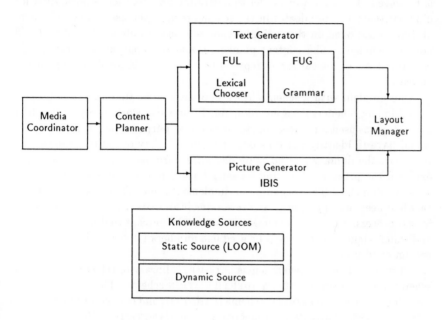

Figure 5.1: COMET's system architecture

frequency) to illustrate how COMET works. We will examine the components along the pipeline from content planner through text generator; see [Seligmann and Feiner 1989] for descriptions of the graphics generator and media layout components.

5.3   Content Planner

Once a user has entered a request for explanation (this could be either a procedure name or an object name), the content planner retrieves information from the knowledge base that is relevant in achieving the user's goal using a library of schemas and semantic predicates associated with each step in the schema. While the media coordinator and the surface generators are concerned with *how* to generate sentences, the content planner determines *what* to generate.

Depending on the input user goal (e.g., 'understand how to carry out a procedure'), the content planner selects a schema (e.g., the plan schema). The system selects information from the underlying knowledge base as the schema is traversed. It uses a user model to determine how to select information for different rhetorical predicates in the schema (e.g., if the user knows where an object is positioned on the radio, location information about the subpart will not be included). The content planner produces as output a hierarchically structured set of logical forms representing the propositional content of the answer.

One problem with a schema-based approach is the time-intensive process of developing schemas for a new domain. In previous work, every time a text generator was used for a new domain or new text purpose, one or more persons would have to identify patterns occurring in a variety of naturally occurring text from the domain for the same discourse purpose. For COMET, we have explored the process of re-using schemas for different discourse purposes and different domains. This began as an implementation effort, taking a schema that had been used previously and reworking it for COMET's domain. However, in the process, we found generalities that could be captured across domains and which suggest that it could be used in a number of different domains under certain conditions.

Currently there are two schemas in COMET's library of schemas: the PLAN schema and the CONSTITUENCY-IDENTIFICATION schema. These two schemas were derived from the PROCESS schema [Paris 1987] and CONSTITUENCY schema [McKeown 1985; Paris 1987], respectively, used in the TAILOR [Paris 1987] system. The PLAN schema is used in COMET to describe how to carry out an action for maintenance or repair (e.g., to describe how to load frequency), while the CONSTITUENCY-IDENTIFICATION schema is used to describe/identify an object for the user. In the remainder of this section, we will focus on how the PLAN schema is derived from the PROCESS schema.

The original PROCESS schema, shown in Figure 5.2, is represented using an Augmented Transition Network (ATN) formalism [Paris 1988]. Content is produced by traversing the graph and selecting a new proposition for each arc traversed. The PROCESS schema determines the content of an explanation describing how an object works. Thus, it dictates how to chain through cause-effect links in the knowledge base (the `main-link` arc). While chaining through the main links in the causal process, the PROCESS schema may decide to include information about a `side-link`, `attributive` information about an object involved in the cause-effect relation, or information about the `substeps` of a cause-effect link.

To derive the PLAN schema, shown in Figure 5.3, we noted that the steps of an action form a chain similar to the cause-effect chain. Thus, the `main-link` arc is mapped to the `main-step` arc which traces through the main steps of an action. The PLAN schema may need to make additional decisions about each step of the action; it can include `preconditions` of a step, `attributive` information about objects involved in a step, or `substeps` of a step. These

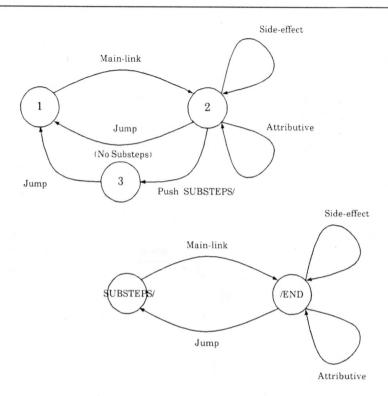

Figure 5.2: The PROCESS schema (from [Paris 1988])

correspond to the **side-effect**, **attributive**, and **substeps** of the process schema respectively. Tests on these arcs determine whether or not to include this information given the particular situation. For example, **attributive** information about an object (which in our domain means location or physical attributes such as size, since a person must be able to identify the object on the piece of equipment) is not included if it was included earlier in the text or the user is already knowledgeable about the object.

We can generalise from these two schemas to form a schema for any chaining relation in the knowledge base by mapping the **main-link** arc to the **main-step** in the new relation. The **attributive** arc remains in the generalised schema since **attributes** of any object mentioned in a relation may need to be included. If the relation is a hierarchical one, we would also retain an equivalent of the **substep** arc. Depending on the domain and relation,

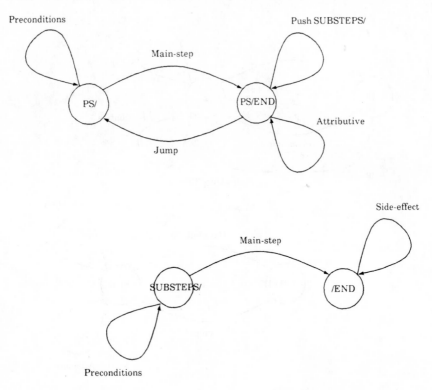

Figure 5.3: The PLAN schema

there may or may not be an equivalent of a **side-effect** or precondition. This generalised schema can be used as a skeleton when moving to a new domain.

Text produced using these two structurally similar schemas is quite different. Output produced by TAILOR [Paris 1987] using the PROCESS schema is shown in (1); text produced by COMET using the PLAN schema is shown in (2).

```
(defconcept load-freq-into-chan-1
             :is (:and load-freq :p
                       (:the substep1 turn-chan-knob-to-1)
                       (:the substep2 turn-mode-knob-to-sc)
                       (:the substep3 turn-fctn-knob-to-ld)
                       (:the substep4 enter-freq)))
```

Figure 5.4: LOOM knowledge base definition of the concept C-load-freq-into-chan-1

(1) A person speaking into the microphone causes the soundwaves to hit the diaphragm of the microphone. The diaphragm is aluminium and disc-shaped. The soundwaves hitting the diaphragm cause the diaphragm to vibrate. When the intensity of the soundwaves increases, the diaphragm springs forward. This causes the granules of the button to be compressed. The compression of the granules causes the resistance of the granules to decrease. This causes the current to increase. Then, when the intensity decreases, the diaphragm springs backward. This causes the granules to be decompressed. The decompression of the granules causes the resistance to increase. This causes the current to decrease. The vibration of the diaphragm causes the current to vary. The current varies like the intensity varies.

(2) Set the channel knob to position 1. Set the MODE knob to SC. Set the FCTN knob to LD. Now enter the frequency: first, press the FREQ button. This causes the display to show an arbitrary number. Next, in order to clear the display, press the CLR button. Next, enter the new frequency using the number buttons. Next, record this number in order to check it later. Finally, press Sto ENT. This causes the display to blink.

This text is produced in response to the menu request *How do I LOAD FRE-QUENCY?* The knowledge base concept from which content is selected is shown in Figure 5.4. The content planner produces an LF for each step in the plan. These may be complex LFs when the step has preconditions, attributes, or substeps. The logical form for the first step (eventually realised as *Set the channel knob to position 1*) is shown in Figure 5.5.

```
(((cat LF) (directive-act substeps)
  (substeps ((distinct
    ~(((process-concept c-turn)
       (process-type action)
       (speech-act directive)
       (roles ((medium ((object-concept c-channel-knob)
                        (quantification
                         ((definite yes) (countable yes)
                          (ref-obj 1) (ref-set 1)))
                        (location yes) (size yes)
                        (ref-mode description)))
               (to-loc ((object-concept c-position-1)
                        (location yes)
                        (ref-mode name)))))))))))))
```

Figure 5.5: A sample logical form produced by the process schema (the logical form for *Set the channel knob to position 1*)

5.3.1   Comparison and future directions

Content planners using schemas or using Rhetorical Structure Theory (RST) must include some ordering on the predicates or rhetorical relations used in generation. The work described here addresses an issue that must be faced by both approaches: how is a new ordering developed for a new domain? Thus, we expect our work to be applicable to both approaches by suggesting a methodology for deriving new orderings from old by developing a hierarchical knowledge base of schemas (or relations).

Other work that we are currently pursuing addresses the problem of allowing for more flexibility than is possible in a strict schema approach by using a new formalism, object-oriented rules, to represent strategies and by using a set of merging rules that merge and delete strategy output based on a model of the user [Wolz 1990].

5.4   Using FUF for Surface Realisation

Once COMET has determined what information should be expressed and how it is to be organised using a schema, the LF structure is passed to a media coordinator which determines which information should be realised in text and which in graphics, annotating the LFs according to its decisions. The annotated LF structure is then passed to both the text surface realisation component and to the graphics generator which realise their segments of the content in text and pictures respectively. The text surface realisation component includes both a lexical chooser and a grammar. With the exception of the graphics generator, IBIS [Seligmann and Feiner 1989], each of these components is implemented using the Functional Unification Formalism (FUF), an extended version of Functional Unification Grammar [Kay 1979; McKeown and Paris 1987; Elhadad 1989].

The use of a cascaded series of grammars for these tasks has a number of advantages: it allows for separate representation of constraints on a variety of decisions, it allows for interaction through unification between different stages of the generation process (including interaction with graphics through the media coordinator), and it allows us to use a common content description language that is gradually enriched with more information about the surface form. The media coordinator unifies the LF structure with its grammar to produce an LF structure annotated with directives about which media is to be used to realise a segment. The lexical chooser takes the annotated LF structure as input and unifies it with a Functional Unification Lexicon (FUL) to add words that will be used to the LF structure. Finally, the lexicalised LF is unified with a functional unification grammar (FUG) to build a surface structure and eventually linearise the resultant tree as a sentence. In this section, we describe FUF in detail, showing first how it has been used for the traditional grammatical realisation task. We then describe how we have used it for the media coordination task and for lexical choice.

5.4.1 The functional unification formalism and grammar

FUF is a general purpose functional unification tool implemented in Common Lisp and used throughout the COMET system. It is an extended implementation of the formalism introduced by Martin Kay [1979]. The extensions to the formalism introduced in FUF allow it to perform efficiently and to be used for other than purely syntactic tasks. In particular, we have added types, type-specific unification procedures, indexing, and the ability to perform general procedures difficult in unification alone through the use of a **test** facility [Elhadad 1989, 1990]. These additions allow it to be used for the media coordination task and for lexical choice.

In this section, we first describe the particular functional unification formalism used in COMET. We focus on its use for grammatical realisation, using examples from the grammar and input to FUG, as this has been the traditional use of FUFs in the past. We then describe input to FUG, a partial surface functional description (PSFD). Finally, we present COMET's grammar, describe how the grammar and input are unified, and give some examples of the types of decisions FUG is capable of making.

```
FD1={article:{definite:yes}, head:{lex:''cat''}}

FD2={article:{lex:''the''}, modifier:{lex:''black''}}

unify(FD1,FD2)={article:{definite:yes, lex:''the''},
                head:{lex:''cat''},
                modifier:{lex:''black''}}
```

Figure 5.6: A simple example of unification of two FDS

In functional unification, all objects are represented as functional descriptions (FDS). An FD describes a set of objects (most often linguistic entities) that satisfy certain properties. It is represented by a set of attribute-value pairs called features. The only operation defined on FDS is unification. The unification of two FDS produces a description which is compatible with both FDS. This process is very similar to set union. Basically, the input FD, the PSFD, is enriched with features from the grammar. Figure 5.6 illustrates the mechanism (the algorithm and the principles behind functional unification are presented in more detail in [Kay 1979; Elhadad 1989; McKeown 1985]).

The unification operation is, in general, non-deterministic because FDS can contain **alternations**. An alternation is a disjunction of features. Each disjunct is called a branch of the alternation. For example,

(3)   {size:small, color:{alt:{blue, white, red}}}

specifies that the colour of the object being described can be either red, blue or white. To unify a simple FD with an alternation, the unifier non-deterministically chooses one branch of the alternation.

Structure and function: constituents and categories

There are two approaches to the linguistic analysis of a sentence: structural and functional. In the structural analysis, substrings of the sentence are recognised as members of a certain class of constituents; different rules specify how the concatenation of segments of different categories can create larger constituents. For example, the concatenation of a string of category ARTICLE with a string of category NOUN could create a string of category NOUN PHRASE. The output of a structural analysis is a parse tree.

In contrast, the purpose of a functional analysis is to identify the *function* of each substring within a larger string of words. There is also a structural stage

```
((cat clause)
 (cset (agent medium process))
 (agent   ((cat np) (lex ''John'') (number singular)))
 (medium  ((cat np)
           (article ((cat determiner) (definite yes)))
           (head    ((cat noun) (lex ''knob'')))))
 (tense present)
 (mood  finite)
 (process ((cat verb) (lex ''turn''))))
```

Figure 5.7: The functional description representing *John turns the knob*

in a functional analysis, whose purpose is to identify the **constituents** of the sentence. A constituent is identified as such only if it plays a certain function with respect to the higher level constituent containing it. For example, in *John gives a book to Mary*, the group *a book* forms a constituent, of category NOUN GROUP, and it plays the role of the 'object upon which the action is performed' in the clause. (This role is often called the **medium** in functional grammars.)

As its name indicates, functional unification as a formalism is strongly geared to a functional type of analysis. The idea behind the definition of FDs is to represent the output of a functional analysis. In general, a constituent is represented as a set of features and is embedded in the FD under an attribute whose name reflects the function of the constituent. Figure 5.7 illustrates this point.

Note that this description contains both functional and structural indications. Structure is reflected by three devices: the embedding of features, the use of the special attribute **cat** which specifies the category of a constituent, and the special feature **cset** (**constituent set**) which identifies the constituents of an FD (this explains why **agent** is a constituent but **tense** is not).

Description of the surface functional description (PSFD)

FUF takes as input a fully lexicalised FD called a PSFD. PSFDs specify the meaning that must be expressed by the English text. They include both semantic and pragmatic constraints. The design of the PSFDs used in the COMET project has been influenced by the grammatical descriptions of the systemic school [Halliday 1985; Quirk *et al.* 1972; Winograd 1983].

Each PSFD corresponds to a single predicate-argument structure. The

Process types	Inherent roles	Circumstantial roles
action	agent, medium, benef	to-loc, from-loc
mental	processor, phenomenon	at-loc, cause
attributive	carrier, attribute	purpose, at-time
equative	identified, identifier	

Table 5.1: The roles used in COMET

predicate is called a **process** and the arguments are the **roles** of the process. There are two types of roles: **inherent** and **circumstantial**. Inherent roles are tightly bound to the process; they are the 'nuclear' participants of the event or action. Circumstantial roles are all optional.

To each process type corresponds a specific list of inherent roles. Circumstantial roles can be used with any type of process. Table 5.1 lists the roles currently used in COMET.

Each role is further decomposed into lower level descriptions. Certain roles are filled with other complete processes (e.g., **purpose** or **cause**); other roles are filled with object descriptions. Object descriptions contain the constituents shown in Table 5.2.

Attributes in the knowledge base can be realised in three different types of attributes in the PSFD: as **describers**, **qualifiers** or **classifiers**.

- Describers correspond to simple attributes, like colour and size. They are generally realised as simple adjectives, and in English occur before the head of a noun phrase, e.g., *a new battery*.

- Qualifiers correspond to more complex attributes. They can be realised by either prepositional phrases or relative clauses. They express complex relations between the object being referred to and other objects. Examples of qualifiers appear in *the dial which is on the right of the display* and *the battery which has been removed*. Qualifiers occur in English after the head of a noun phrase.

- Classifiers are used to specify the class of an object. For example, in *a science textbook*, *science* is used as a classifier for *textbook*. In the COMET domain, most of the classifiers are input to FUG in the head of the noun phrase, since they are generally derived by the lexical chooser from a concept in the knowledge base. There is, therefore, no real use of classifiers in the current version of the system. However, as we are planning on using lexical substitution as a cohesion device [Halliday and

Constituent	Features of the constituent
determiner	definite, distance, demonstrative, possessive
describer	a list of 'simple' attributes
head	lex, animate, person, number, gender
qualifier	a list of 'complex' attributes
classifier	a list of ancestors in an ISA hierarchy

Table 5.2: The constituents of object descriptions

Hasan 1976], it will become important to represent entities with their classifier specification. It will therefore be possible to refer to *a science textbook* as simply *the textbook* in subsequent references (cf. [Dale 1988] for the notion of subsequent references).

We have described so far the semantic description of the message to be conveyed. PSFDs can also include pragmatic features that constrain the way the message should be expressed, and control what effect it will have on the overall communication process with the user.

For example, the **mood** of the clause is specified in the PSFD. It is derived from the specification of the speech act in the LF. Thus, the mood imperative will often be used to realise a speech act of **action-query**. The focus of a sentence can also be specified in the PSFD. The focus can specify which role of the process is the one 'being talked about' (cf. [McKeown 1985] for an illustration of the use of focus information). A last example of pragmatic features is the `distance` feature in object descriptions. The `distance` feature indicates whether the object being referred to is presented as `far` or `near` from the speaker. The value of the `distance` feature constrains the way the determiner of the noun phrase is chosen by the grammar.

Figure 5.8 shows a PSFD as used in the system. Note that the lexical chooser has included in the PSFD all the required lexical items as well as the relevant morpho-syntactic features of the chosen words (for example, the feature `transitive-class` of the verb *to enter*). These features are stored along with each lexical item in the FUL (see Section 5.4.3 below).

The grammar in action: types of decisions made in FUF

We now illustrate how FUF operates on the input PSFDs and the type of decisions it is capable of making. A more complete exposition can be found in [McKeown and Elhadad 1990]. We illustrate the type of decisions made

```
((cat clause)
 (mood non-finite)
 (non-finite imperative)
 (tense present)
 (process-type action)
 (process ((lex 'enter')
           (voice-class non-middle)
           (transitive-class transitive)))
 (medium ((cat np)
          (head ((np-type common) (lex 'frequency')))
          (describer ((lex 'new')))
          (distance near)
          (definite yes)))
 (instrument ((cat np)
              (number plural)
              (prep ((lex 'using')))
              (head ((np-type common) (lex 'button')))
              (classifier ((lex 'number')))
              (definite yes)))
 (time-relater ((lex 'next'))))
```

Figure 5.8: PSFD for *Next, enter this new frequency using the number buttons*

by FUF through an example: we show how the structure of the output sentence is derived from the structure of the PSFD in the 'transitivity' part of the grammar.

Defining the structure of a sentence

One of the first decisions made in the grammar at the clause level is how to structure the sentence. It is important to notice that the structure of the input PSFD does not determine the structure of the sentence: the PSFD is structured in terms of semantic roles, following the predicate-argument structure of the content to be conveyed; the sentence is structured in terms of syntactic roles (for example, subject, verb, and complements) following grammatical constraints. There is no one-to-one mapping from this semantic structure to the syntactic structure.

In FUF, the syntactic structure is built from the underlying semantic structure. Semantic roles are mapped to the syntactic roles. The grammatical rules controlling this mapping are described as the **transitivity system** in [Halliday 1985]. The FUF treatment of this issue is simplified by the following assumption: the **process** of the PSFD is always mapped to the **verb** of the syntactic structure. This assumption reflects the belief that the process plays a central role in the semantic representation and that most often a verb is used to express this role. Unfortunately, this assumption is often too limiting: to express the PSFD

(4) ((process-type mental)
     (agent martin)
     (process dream))

a sentence of the form *Martin had a dream* is often preferable to *Martin dreamed*. The problem here is that the predicative element in a sentence is not always the verb; it can be a noun accompanied by a semantically empty verb. Danlos [1987] discusses this issue in more detail. We propose handling this problem through the processing of collocation information (see Section 5.4.4). In the COMET domain, however, which is task oriented, the assumption of 'verb-centrality' does not appear to be a strong limitation. Practically all the actions we have described so far are well described by a single semantically full verb.

The problem of determining syntactic structure is therefore to define a mapping from the semantic roles defined in the PSFD to the syntactic roles of a verb. The grammar processes this task in several stages: first, it determines whether the semantic roles will be realised by noun groups, by dependent clauses or by adverbial or prepositional groups. Then, in the **voice system**, it determines the final mapping of semantic to syntactic roles. Finally, it decides in what order the syntactic complements will be expressed in the text.

The mapping decision in the voice system is based on three types of considerations: what the voice of the sentence is (**active, passive** or **medium**[1]), whether the verb is transitive, intransitive or ditransitive (that is, how many inherent complements it can accept), and whether the semantic roles are specified in the input or not.

Note that we describe the voice of the sentence here as a constraint. In a more traditional approach, one would be tempted to describe the voice of the sentence as the output of the voice system: the purpose of the voice system is to determine the voice of the sentence. This is true in general, but we must also remember that the functional unification formalism is a **bidirectional** formalism: a constraint can be derived by the grammar, but it can also be given as input to the grammar. Thus, the grammar must behave correctly in both situations and propagate the consequences of a particular voice choice 'backwards'. Bidirectional processing also influences the effect of focus information on sentence structure.

---

[1]The **medium** voice is a term used in systemic grammars. It corresponds to a case where the medium of a process is realised as the subject of a verb, as in *the door opened*.

For example, the mapping

(5)   SUBJECT ← AGENT
      MEDIUM ← DIRECT-OBJECT

corresponds to the active voice of a transitive verb. This mapping will generate standard unmarked clauses like *Steve turns a knob*. If the agent is not specified in the input, the following mapping will be chosen:

(6)   SUBJECT ← MEDIUM

corresponding to *a knob is turned*. If the voice of the clause is specified in the input, the mapping will be made accordingly. Thus the mapping

(7)   SUBJECT ← MEDIUM
      BY-OBJECT ← AGENT

will be chosen if the passive voice is forced on the sentence.

Note that the unification formalism is particularly helpful in the implementation of the transitivity system. The mapping operation corresponds to a single unification operation (a conflation). Furthermore, the bidirectional types of influence we have mentioned are naturally handled by the formalism.

Figure 5.9 shows the fragment of the grammar that determines the mapping from semantic to syntactic roles. This segment is a complex alternation, specifying how the mapping must be done in each possible case. The first branch (not shown in the figure) is used for **middle** verbs (e.g., *to shine*). Middle verbs accept only one semantic case, the medium, which is realised as the subject of the clause (e.g., *the sun shines*). The second branch handles the normal case. It is itself broken into two sub-branches, corresponding roughly to the passive and the active voice. Note that, if the voice is specified in the input, then the choice between these two branches is not even considered; only one branch is tried (this is the meaning of the ⟨index on voice⟩ directive at the beginning of `alt non-middle-voice`). If the voice is not specified in the input, then one of the two branches is chosen non-deterministically. Once the voice is chosen, the actual mapping is performed. The precise mapping depends on the type of the process, since the set of inherent roles depends on the process type. For example, for action verbs at the active voice, the mapping[2] is

(8)   `(subject <↑ agent>)`
      `(object <↑ medium>)`
      `(iobject <↑ benef>)`

---

[2]The notation (a <↑ b >) means that the value of the feature a and b must be unified: this is called a **conflation**.

```
(alt voice (index on (verb voice-class))
 (  ...
    ;; Branch 2: non middle verbs only
    ((verb ((voice-class non-middle)))
     (alt non-middle-voice (index on voice)

      ;; Branch 2.1: Active voice.
      (((voice operative)
        (verb ((voice active)))
        ;; Map each syntactic role to corresp. semantic role
        (alt (index on process-type)
            (((process-type action)
              (subject <^  agent> )
              (object <^   medium> )
              (iobject <^  benef> ))
             ((process-type mental)
              (subject <^   processor> )
              (object <^   phenomenon> )
              (iobject none))
             ((process-type equative)
              (subject <^   identified> )
              (object <^   identifier> )
              (iobject none))
             ((process-type attributive)
              (subject <^   carrier> )
              (object <^   attribute> )
              (iobject none)))))

       ;; Branch 2.2: Passive voice.
       ((voice receptive)
        (alt (index process-type)
          (((process-type action)
            (by-obj ((np <^ agent> ))))))
          (alt
            ;; 'A book is given to mary by john'
            (((subject <^   medium> )
              (iobject <^  benef> ))
             ;; 'Mary is given a book by John'
             ((subject <^   benef> )
              (object <^   medium> )))))     ...)))))
```

Figure 5.9: Fragment of the grammar—transitivity system

5.4.2   The media coordinator

The media coordinator decides which parts of the final display layout are
to appear as graphics and which are to be displayed as text. The media
coordinator is implemented as a functional unification grammar (FUG). The
coordinator grammar is unified with the input logical form (LF) structure
produced by the content planner. Unification results in a logical form that is
identical to the input LF except that annotations have been added to the LF
to identify the information it contains as suitable for either text or graphics
display.

The coordinator works by first identifying each LF as one of the following
types: **simple actions**, which can be performed in one step; **compound actions**, which include more complicated actions and cause and effect sequences;
and **conditional actions**, or actions with an *if-then* relationship.

It then annotates the top level of the LF to mark it as one of these types.
The coordinator next checks the process-concepts and object-concepts within
the logical form. The following rules are applied to decide how each part of
the LF must be marked:

- process-concepts corresponding to simple actions are marked for display
  in both text and graphics;

- process-concepts which correspond to abstract actions, or actions which
  are not clearly shown in pictures, are marked for display in text only;

- object-concepts which show location information, such as the location
  of objects on the radio display panel, are marked for display as graphics
  only; and

- object-concepts showing attributive information, which includes colour,
  size and shape of objects, are marked for display as both graphics and
  text.

The annotated logical form produced by the media coordinator is passed as
input to both the lexical chooser and the graphics component. The markings
placed on the process-concepts and object-concepts can then be used directly
by each of these components to decide what to include in their displays. The
simple, compound and conditional markings on the logical forms can be used
by the lexical chooser and the graphics component to decide how to best
display the logical form. For example, it may be desirable to split a screen in
two to display a compound action, with half of the text appearing on one side
of the screen and the rest on the other side.

General description of the media coordinator

The **media coordinator** is implemented using a functional unification grammar which is unified with an input logical form. This unification results in a logical form in which attribute-value pairs have been used to mark each of the different information types. For convenience, we will call all of these newly added features **media markings**.

The media coordinator uses the constraint mechanism of F UGs to put a set of media markings at the appropriate location in an input LF. There are two cases to be considered: **process-concepts** and **object-concepts**.

Process level marking

The decisions about which actions are expressed in text, in graphics, or both, are made at the process-concept level. Based on the media coordinator experiment, decisions are made for each process-concept class. For instance, the process-concept **c-record** should be expressed only in text because it is a type of abstract action in the knowledge base; therefore the media markings selected for this process-concept are

(9) (MEDIA-GRAPHICS NO)
     (MEDIA-TEXT YES)

Hence, the grammar is structured as an alternation with one branch for each process-concept type. In each branch, the type of the input process concept is retrieved from the knowledge base using an extension of F UF. There is a separate branch for mental processes, actions, different types of attribution, and equative relations. Each branch enriches the input with the pairs of media markings suited to that process type.

An example of the part of the grammar which does this unification is shown in Figure 5.10. The effect which this part of the grammar has on an LF is illustrated in Figure 5.11.

Object level marking

The decisions about which media (text, graphics or both) are used to express the attributes of an object are made at the object-concept level. We would like information about the size, the colour and the location of an object to be expressed in graphics. Therefore, any FD whose object-concept value is **c-location**, **c-size**, or **c-color** is marked for display in graphics. Markings are placed on its subconstituents. Since information about size and location is represented at the object-concept level, the grammar traverses the object-concept FDs until it reaches this information. Figure 5.12 is the grammar for object level markings; Since the object-concept **c-model-knob** contains the

```
(ALT        ;; Find process type in knowledge base
(((control (member 'actions
              (loom::superconcepts <^ process-concept>)))
  (process-type action))
 ((control (member 'mental
              (loom::superconcepts <^ process-concept>)))
  (process-type mental))
 ((control (member 'attributive
                  (loom::superconcepts <^ process-concept>)))
  (process-type attributive))
 ((control (member 'equative
                  (loom::superconcepts <^ process-concept>)))
  (process-type equative))))

(alt process-concept
  (((process-concept none))
    ((alt
        (index on process-concept) ;; branches for each process-type
        (((process-type action)    ;; BRANCH 1
          (MEDIA-GRAPHICS YES)     ;; put media markings
          (MEDIA-TEXT YES)         ;; put media markings
          ...))
         ((process-type mental)    ;;BRANCH 2
          (MEDIA-GRAPHICS NO)
          (MEDIA-TEXT YES)
          ...)))))
```

Figure 5.10: Example grammar (process level)

Abstract Action: *Record this number in order to check it later.*

```
INPUT:    ((cat LF)
          (directive-act substeps) ...
          (substeps ((distinct
            ˉ(((process-concept c-record)
               (speech-act directive)  ...  ))))))
OUTPUT:   ((cat LF)
          (directive-act substeps) ...
          (substeps ((distinct
            ˉ(((process-concept c-record)
               (speech-act directive) ...
               (MEDIA-TEXT YES)
               (MEDIA-GRAPHICS NO)))))))
```

Figure 5.11: Example input/output (process level)

---

object-concepts `c-location` and `c-size` at its subconstituents level, media markings are added at that level.

Advantages of FUG for the implementation of the media coordinator

The media coordinator is implemented as a FUG which takes as input a semantic description of a communicative goal which is to be realised in text or graphics. The input to the coordinator is a group of FDs and the output is a group of FDs with more refined directives added to satisfy the goal. Hence, the coordinator acts as a filter which enhances the description of a communicative goal. The use of the unification formalism allows the coordinator to receive as input and output structures expressed in the same formalism. In fact, by using this formalism, it is easy for any component of the system to add annotations to the LFs. As a result, generality is postulated for the entire process.

The functional description formalism used in the media coordinator grammar enables the coordinator to analyse the input information precisely by checking the value of pairs at any level. Media constraints can then be placed at very small segments of the input FDs. This concise analysis allows the input to the graphics and text components to be closely integrated, with very small portions of a proposition appearing in graphics only and the remainder in both, or *vice versa*.

```
((cat object-role)
 (alt (...
       ((object-concept c-color);; object-concept is c-color
        (MEDIA-TEXT NO)              ;; put media markings
        (MEDIA-GRAPHICS YES))   ;; put media markings
       ((object-concept c-size)
        (MEDIA-TEXT NO)
        (MEDIA-GRAPHICS YES))
       ...
```

Figure 5.12: Example grammar (object level)

5.4.3   The lexical chooser

In COMET, the lexical chooser (LC) is the module responsible for two natural language generation subtasks: lexicalisation and semantic grammaticalisation.[3] The LC is part of the text surface generator. It receives its input from the media coordinator and passes its output to FUG (refer back to Figure 5.1 to see how the LC fits into COMET's overall architecture). The LC achieves its task using a modified version of unification.

As input, the LC is given the annotated LF structure. A single LF includes both pragmatic and semantic features; a feature can have as its value either an atom or, recursively, an LF. The pragmatic features (e.g. speech-act, mood, aspect, tense, etc.) encode the communicative goals behind the utterance to be generated; the semantic features are used to specify the content of the utterance to be generated. This content has been filtered from the knowledge base by the content planner. There are three major types of knowledge base entities: compound processes, elementary processes and objects. Since we work in a task-oriented domain, compound processes are represented as plans. Thus a top-level LF is a plan, whose preconditions, substeps, goal and effects can be of the following types:

- an **action**, i.e., a partial description of an elementary knowledge base process: this action contains a description of the process and its semantic roles, which in turn contain object descriptions;

---

[3]Conceptually, the grammaticalisation task of a natural language generator can be decomposed into two subtasks: (i) the expression of semantic content by grammatical devices (e.g., expression of a request by use of the interrogative mood), which we call semantic grammaticalisation; and (ii) the enforcement of syntax (e.g. subject-verb agreement) and building of syntactic structure. The first task is carried out in the lexical chooser and the second task in FUG.

- an **attribution**, i.e., the expression of the value of a role of an elementary knowledge base entity (elementary process or object);
- an **equation**, i.e., the expression of the identity between the role values of two elementary knowledge base entities; or
- recursively, a plan.

The LC chooses different sentence structures depending on the structure of the input plan; for example, it maps plans with preconditions and substeps onto conditional sentence structure (*If . . . then . . .*), plans with substeps and effect onto causal sentence structures (*. . . causes . . .* or *. . . because . . .*). This mapping of various types of compound processes onto various types of sentence structures is an example of the semantic grammaticalisation task carried out by the LC.

As output, the LC produces a list of PSFDs which are passed as input to FUG. Each member of this list is subsequently completed by enrichment when unified with COMET's grammar. Thus, the features of a PSFD are those the grammar needs as specification (see Section 5.4.1). The task of the LC is to map lists of LFs onto lists of PSFDs. It thus consists of mapping semantic and pragmatic features specifying the content and situation of enunciation of an utterance respectively, onto systemic features specifying the lexical items (using the special feature lex) and the overall grammatical form of that utterance (e.g., declarative). This task involves both complete lexical choices and partial grammatical choices. In the design of COMET's LC our main concern has been lexical choice, for the two following reasons:

- since COMET's grammar is very semantically oriented, it can handle all final choices of closed-class items (e.g., articles, determiners, pronouns, etc.) allowing the LC to concentrate on choosing open-class items (i.e., verbs, nouns, adjectives and adverbs); and
- most construction of grammatical form is handled in FUG.

In the general case, the mapping between a LF and a PSFD works as follows: each elementary action description in the LF is mapped onto a clause of the PSFD, and each object description in the LF onto a nominal (i.e., noun phrase, pronoun or proper noun) of the PSFD. Both mappings are made by unifying the description with the FUL. As in a FUG, there are two kinds of pairs in a FUL: **keys** and **enrichments**. Keys are pairs that are expected to be in the input LF. They are used as tests. Enrichments are pairs that are added to the input LF when the corresponding key is found. Also, as in a FUG, a FUL is structured as a large alternation of FDs. However, while unification with a FUG is performed top-down, unification with a FUL is performed bottom-up, starting with the most embedded sub-LFs. It is performed this way because

LF of the sentence *Set the channel knob to position 1*:

```
((process-concept c-turn)
 (process-type action)
 (speech-act directive)
 (roles ((medium ((object-concept c-channel-knob)
                  (quantification
                   ((definite yes)  (countable yes)
                    (ref-obj 1)  (ref-set 1)))
                  (ref-mode description)))
         (to-loc ((object-concept c-position-1)
                  (ref-mode name))))))
```

LF of the sentence *Turn the radio onto the front panel*:

```
((process-concept c-turn)
 (process-type action)
 (speech-act directive)
 (roles ((medium ((object-concept c-radio-transmitter)
                  (quantification
                   ((definite yes) (countable yes)
                    (ref-obj 1) (ref-set 1)))
                  (ref-mode description)))
         (on-loc ((object-concept c-front-panel)
                  (quantification
                   ((definite yes) (countable yes)
                    (ref-obj singular) (ref-set singular)))
                  (ref-mode description))))))
```

Figure 5.13: Two LFs of the same concept with different role values

PSFD of the sentence *Set the channel knob to position 1*:

```
((mood non-finite)
 (non-finite imperative)
 (medium  ((number singular) (countable yes)
           (definite yes)  (np-type common)
           (cat np)
           (head ((cat noun) (lex 'knob')))
           (classifier ((cat noun) (lex 'channel')))))
 (to-loc ((np-type proper) (cat np) (lex 'position 1')))
 (cat clause)
 (process-type action)
 (verb  ((lex 'turn') (voice-class non-middle)
         (transitive-class transitive)))))
```

PSFD of the sentence *Turn the radio onto the front panel*:

```
((mood non-finite)
 (non-finite imperative)
 (medium ((number singular) (countable yes)
          (definite yes) (np-type common)
          (cat np) (lex 'radio')))
 (on-loc ((number plural) (countable yes)
          (definite yes) (np-type common)
          (cat np)
          (head ((cat noun) (lex 'panel')))
          (classifier ((cat noun) (lex 'front')))))
 (cat clause)
 (process-type action)
 (verb ((lex 'turn') (on-loc-prep 'onto')
        (voice-class non-middle)
        (transitive-class transitive))))
```

Figure 5.14: PSFDs corresponding to the LFs of the previous figure

Part of the FUL used to map the LFs of Figure 5.13 onto the PSFDs of Figure 5.14:

```
((ALT
  (((concept-type process)                      ;;key
    (cat clause)                                ;;enrichment
    (ALT (((speech-act directive)               ;;key
      (mood non-finite) (non-finite imperative) ;;enrichments
      (ALT  (((process-type action)             ;;key
              (medium <^ roles medium> )        ;;enrichments
              (to-loc <^ roles to-loc> )
        (ALT (index on process-concept)
          (((process-concept c-turn)
            (ALT                 ;; Is medium a type of discrete-knob?
              (((control                         ;;key
                ((member   'discrete-knob
                 (loom::superconcepts
                          <^ roles medium object-concept>)]
              (verb ((lex 'set')             ;;enrichment 1
                (voice-class non-middle)
                (transitive-class transitive)))))
            ((verb ((lex 'turn')            ;;enrichment 2
              (on-loc-prep 'onto')
              (voice-class non-middle)
              (transitive-class transitive))]
```

Figure 5.15: Part of the FUL encoding the choice between two verbs

the lexicalisations of process roles sometimes constrain the possible lexicalisations of the process itself. Collocations, discussed in the next section, are one example of a linguistic phenomenon inducing such constraints. Another example of the need for this bottom-up unification-based lexical choice is presented in Figures 5.13, 5.14 and 5.15.

Figure 5.13 presents two LFs of the concept c-turn, with c-channel-knob and c-radio-transmitter as the respective mediums. Figure 5.14 presents the two corresponding PSFDs produced by the LC.[4] Figure 5.15 presents the part of the FUL used to map the LFs of Figure 5.13 onto the PSFDs of Fig-

[4]Since unification is monotonous, all the features of the LF of a sentence will be in the PSFD of that sentence. In order to clarify the import of the unification process, the PSFDs above have been stripped from the features of the corresponding LF and only enrichments from the FUL have been kept. However, in the real PSFDs produced by the unifier, all the features of the LF are present in the corresponding PSFD.

ure 5.14. For each example, the lexicon is first accessed to lexicalise the object-concepts embedded in the roles of the top-level LF: c-channel-knob by *channel knob*, c-radio-transmitter by *radio*, c-position-1 by *position 1* and c-front-panel by *front-panel*. It is then accessed again to lexicalise the process-concept of the top-level LF: c-turn by *to set* in the first example where c-channel-knob is the medium, and by *to turn* in the second example where c-radio-transmitter is the medium. The motivation for such choices is that *to set* is more appropriate when there is a discrete set of possible positions for the medium. As illustrated in Figure 5.15, this lexical choice is implemented by a CONTROL special feature in the FUL entry for the concept c-turn. CONTROL is one of the extended features of FUF: it allows invocation of an arbitrary LISP predicate, specified as the value of the feature, during the unification process. Only if this predicate is satisfied will unification of the FD containing the CONTROL pair succeed. In this example, CONTROL is used to have FUL directly querying the knowledge base for additional information about the medium of c-turn. If the medium is an instance of discrete-knob, the verb *to set* is chosen; otherwise, *to turn* is chosen. Note that this use of CONTROL introduces a backward loop in the otherwise linear flow of control of the generator. It allows FUL to relieve the schema traverser from producing all the information the LC will need to perform its choice. COMET's LC can also choose between words based on context: for example, it will choose the verb *re-install* or *return* in place of *install* when it instructs the user to install an object that it has previously instructed the user to remove.

The use of the unification algorithm for lexical choice is a totally novel approach. It has a number of advantages:

- It allows for the integration of various types of constraints in a uniform formalism (e.g., in COMET, the choice of verb for a process has been constrained simultaneously by its location in the domain hierarchy, by the semantic features of its role, by the contextual features of the previous discourse, and by collocational constraints: see the next section).

- Since functional unification is bidirectional, constraints can be either given as input to the LC or specified in the FUL, wherever is appropriate for the particular constraint. The bidirectional nature of unification ensures that whatever the source, the constraints will be accounted for in the output.

- The FUL is modular and declarative and thus easily extensible and modifiable, something of paramount importance for a generation lexicon. In the development of the COMET prototype, people with little expertise of how lexical choice is performed have been able to satisfactorily enter new entries in the FUL.

- Having a uniform formalism for both the LC and the grammar lays the ground for a system where feedback and backtracking is allowed between the two. Although such a feedback is not yet part of COMET, the fact that both modules are unification-based minimises the potential difficulties of such an implementation: for example, a certain amount of interaction can occur by simply combining the two grammars.

- Control information need not be specified by the lexicon builder; it is provided by the unification scheme. Thus the lexicon builder does not need to specify how constraints interact.

Using unification for lexical choice in this way does have some problems, however. Unlike morpho-syntactic grammaticalisation, which is fundamentally a monotonous process of *enriching* a partial representation (the PSFD) by additional features, lexicalisation and semantic grammaticalisation are fundamentally a process of *rewriting* a representation (the LF) into another (the PSFD). Thus, an implementation using enrichment means the PSFD contains some irrelevant features. We are currently working on extending the lexical chooser to include a rewriting system as in [Dale 1988]. We plan to implement such a rewriting system using FUF.

5.4.4   Including collocational constraints in the lexicon

The use of a FUL for lexical choice gives us the flexibility of a word-based lexicon. After single words are selected, they can be combined in complex and various ways through the syntactic grammar; this is in contrast to most previous work on lexical choice (see, for example, PAULINE [Hovy 1987], Danlos' generator [Danlos 1987], PHRED [Jacobs 1985], ANA [Kukich 1983]) which relies on phrasal lexicons. However, there are also cases in our domain where the presence of one word automatically requires the selection of one or more other words. To allow for the selection of such flexible word pairs and phrases, we are incorporating collocational constraints as part of the lexicon. Consider the following examples:

(10)   a   Eight single channels and six frequency hopping channels may be loaded.

      b   The amplifier provides 50 watts of power.

      c   Do not allow the lithium battery to become short circuited.

The fact that one *loads a battery*, that an amplifier *provides some power*, and that *short circuit* functions as a description is part of the lexical knowledge necessary for surface generation. Similarly, compounds such as *lithium battery*, *maintenance battery*, *main battery*, *holding battery*, *mounting base*, and *cardiopulmonary resuscitation* need to be specifically entered into COMET's lexicon, since they are the lexicalisations of important concepts in the knowledge base. These verb-noun, noun-noun or noun-adjective pairs are called **co-occurrence relations** or **idiosyncratic collocations**. To correctly understand or produce natural language, such lexical relations need to be specifically encoded in the lexicon.

Most previous work handled this problem by hand encoding the knowledge in the lexicon. Providing this knowledge manually is both tedious and likely to be incomplete. In contrast, we provide XTRACT [Smadja 1989; Smadja, to appear], a tool which automatically acquires co-occurrence knowledge from the statistical analysis of large textual corpora. An idiosyncratic collocation is reflected in the language by a correlation of common appearance of several items.[5] XTRACT identifies lexical relations in a large sample of natural language data by making statistical observations, and retrieves different forms of lexical relations. Currently, XTRACT acquires multiple-words compounds, predicative relations (verb-noun, verb-particle, verb-adverb, and noun-adjective) and phrasal templates. Such collocations represent meaningful lexical entities in the considered domain, and require specific entries in the lexicon. Of course, a large sample of textual data is necessary, and the corpus must contain text as close as possible to the application, in terms of the domain and style. For COMET, such a corpus has not yet been made available, although we are pursuing the acquisition of a collection of online equipment manuals for equipment maintenance and repair. In this section, we show how this can be used in the framework of COMET. This enrichment of the COMET lexicon is carried out in two stages: first, word associations are acquired from textual corpora; then, these are interpreted and entered in the lexicon in a form useful for COMET. We describe here the two stages in turn.

First phase: acquiring lexical relations from corpora

The acquisition of information from large textual corpora has already been addressed in the past [Choueka 1989; Church 1989] but with different methods and goals. Choueka only retrieved uninterrupted sequences of words, and he was more interested in retrieving frequently used idiomatic expressions than idiosyncratic collocations. Church does retrieve interrupted sequences, but he is more interested in descriptive than functional aspects of co-occurrence knowledge.

In the first phase, XTRACT takes as input a corpus and produces a list of tuples of the form

(11)   <LR, cook-info>

---

[5]That is, within a single syntactic unit, such as a noun phrase or verb phrase.

word 1	word 2	type	strength	spread
stock	market	noun-noun	47.018	3230.17
stock	prices	noun-noun	12.1118	744.351
stock	index	noun-noun	9.16489	398.062
stock	futures	noun-noun	5.37002	243.978
stock	share	noun-noun	5.19129	173.443
stock	percent	noun-noun	3.4996	95.6964
stock	crash	noun-noun	3.42894	165.778
stock	company	noun-noun	3.22943	116.829
stock	bond	noun-noun	2.91769	126.468
stock	exchange	noun-noun	2.39398	141.06
stock	collapse	noun-noun	2.24019	67.3291
stock	options	noun-noun	2.06977	44.2949
stock	investors	noun-noun	1.60009	26.3327
stock	traders	noun-noun	1.59178	58.3823
stock	value	noun-noun	1.36733	35.2819
stock	plunge	noun-noun	1.3507	39.1179

Table 5.3: Collocates for the word *stock*

where LR is a lexical relation between two open-class words and `cook-info` is
a set of statistical figures representing the lexical relation within the distribution of the collocates. For example, `cook-info` contains an evaluation of the
correlation factor of LR and additional information on the relative positions of
the two words in the corpus. `cook-info` is used to filter out irrelevant associations and to retrieve global syntactic information. A more detailed description
of XTRACT can be found in [Smadja 1989].

This first stage of XTRACT has been tested on a two million word corpus
taken from *The Jerusalem Post* archives. It has retrieved several hundred
lexical relations such as:

- *to clamp* with *curfew*, as in *the authorities clamped a curfew* ...;
- *to plant* with *bomb*, as in *the terrorists planted a bomb in* ...;
- *violent* with *clash*, as in *there has been a violent clash today* ...

An experiment using this first stage of XTRACT for software re-use is described
in [Maarek and Smadja 1989].

The full implementation of XTRACT has been used on a 10 million word corpus consisting of stock market reports.[6] Figure 5.3 gives partial results in the stock market domain for the word *stock*. cook-info contains an evaluation of the correlation factor of w_1 and w_2 (**strength** in Figure 5.3), and additional information on their relative positions in the corpus (**spread** in Figure 5.3). The larger the strength, the more strongly the two words are related, and the larger the spread, the more rigidly they are used in combination with one another. Church [1989] produces similar results to those in Figure 5.3 without the last column (the spread attribute). Once a table like this has been compiled, XTRACT needs to analyse the word associations and produce syntactic phrases directly usable by COMET.

Compiling syntactic frames

Before being able to use lexical relations, we need to have more information on their syntactic relations. This is the role of the second phase, **syntactic interpretation**. If we are dealing with a noun and a verb, for example, we need to know if the noun is the actor or the object of the verb before using the relation for generation. Syntactic interpretation consists of producing lexical frames for collocational phrases. More precisely, from a pair of words retrieved by XTRACT, we produce a syntactic phrase that would represent the lexical relations at the structural level. This should not be confused with corpus parsing or tagging (as described, for example, in [Garside 1987]): we are not interested in retrieving the syntactic relation between two words in a given sentence, but rather in retrieving properties of a recurring syntactic structure in which those two words repeatedly appear in a large corpus. This analysis is carried out by examining the concordances of a given pair of words and the information contained in cook-info. This produces three different kinds of phrases depending on the part of speech of the words involved and their use in the corpus.

In the case of noun-noun or noun-adjective relations, the problem is relatively simple since, in most cases they appear in uninterrupted sequences of words. For example, in the context of COMET, this involves such pairs as *main battery, lithium battery, cardiopulmonary resuscitation*, etc. In the stock market corpus, we retrieved compounds such as: *bear market, bull market, stock market, interest rates, trade deficit, tender offer, foreign exchange, New York Stock Exchange*, and *The Dow Jones average of 30 industrials*.

For noun-verb and verb-adjective relations the situation is more complex. These lexical relations are harder to identify since they correspond to inter-

---

[6]This corpus is taken from the Associated Press newswire; all the work done with this corpus has been carried out in collaboration with Bell Communication Research, 445 South Street, Morristown, NJ 07960-1910.

rupted word sequences in the corpus. In these cases, we want to retrieve the syntactic role played by the words. `cook-info` provides information on the most frequent structural pattern in which the two words co-appear; for example, a noun and a verb will belong to this category of collocations if they are always used together with the noun as the object of the verb. Our method is based on the simple observation that when a noun is the deep or semantic agent of a verb, it is principally used before the verb; similarly, when it is the semantic object of a verb, it is principally used after it. Some complications might arise due to passive constructs and/or embedded relative clauses. To reduce the ambiguities, we are currently using a bottom-up parser which takes as input an incomplete sentence substructure and returns all possible parses. In the stock market domain, this analysis allowed us to retrieve such associations as *trade ... actively, mix ... narrowly, use ... widely, watch ... closely, stock ... rose, fell, closed, jumped, continued, declined, crashed* and so on.[7] More details and results can be found in [Smadja 1989].

Finally, in some cases, XTRACT encounters phrases that are used very frequently in a relatively frozen way. In these cases XTRACT captures this information in phrasal templates containing one or more empty slots. Examples of such entries are:

(12)   a   The NYSE's composite index of all its listed common stocks rose *number* to *number*.

   b   On the American Stock Exchange, the market value index was up *number* at *number*.

   c   The Dow Jones average of 30 industrials fell *number* points to *number*.

   d   The closely watched index had been down about *number* points in the first hour of trading.

   e   The average finished the week with a net loss of *number*.

Their usage for language generation gives an impression of fluency that cannot be equalled with compositional sentences, since their structure is slightly idiosyncratic and even sometimes hard to understand for non-specialists. In this case what remains to be done for generation is template filling. XTRACT retrieves several hundred such templates.

At the end of this stage, XTRACT produces a list of syntactic phrases like the following:

---

[7]The ellipses here represent a gap of zero or more words in the corpus; the words need not be adjacent.

$$
\left[
\begin{array}{ll}
\text{subject} & = \left[
\begin{array}{ll}
\text{cat} & = \quad NP \\
\text{head} & = \left[
\begin{array}{ll}
\text{cat} & = \quad N \\
\text{lex} & = \quad \text{``stock''}
\end{array}
\right]
\end{array}
\right] \\[6em]
\text{action} & = \left\{
\begin{array}{l}
\left[
\begin{array}{ll}
\text{type} & = \quad \text{co-occurrence knowledge} \\
\text{cat} & = \quad V \\
\text{lex} & = \quad \text{``rise''} \\
\text{sem} & = \quad \text{pointer to the knowledge base}
\end{array}
\right] \\[3.5em]
\left[
\begin{array}{ll}
\text{type} & = \quad \text{co-occurrence knowledge} \\
\text{cat} & = \quad V \\
\text{lex} & = \quad \text{``fall''} \\
\text{sem} & = \quad \text{pointer to the knowledge base}
\end{array}
\right] \\[3.5em]
\left[
\begin{array}{ll}
\text{type} & = \quad \text{co-occurrence knowledge} \\
\text{cat} & = \quad V \\
\text{lex} & = \quad \text{``jump''} \\
\text{sem} & = \quad \text{pointer to the knowledge base}
\end{array}
\right] \\[1em]
\dots
\end{array}
\right\}
\end{array}
\right]
$$

Figure 5.16: An example lexical entry for the word *stock*, part of the collocational zone

(13) a   X <V <head <V "load">> <NP <head <N "channel" >>>
  b   X <V <head <V "short circuit">>> Y
  c   <N "lithium battery">
  d   <N "main battery">
  e   <N "cardiopulmonary resuscitation">

These syntactic phrases are then represented in a FUL as shown in Figure 5.16. Note that the lexicon builder must determine what concept in the knowledge base each of these phrases point to, and enter this as the feature sem. The advantage of using FUF for representing and manipulating collocations is that several collocations can be used in the same sentence, and unification will handle interactions between the two. Similarly, unification is used to merge a word-pair collocation where the words are separated by arbitrary distance with other words in the sentence.

5.5   Conclusions

We have provided an overview of the natural language techniques used in
COMET, focusing on the re-use of schemas across domains for the content
planner and the use of FUF for three components of the system: the media
coordinator, the lexical interface, and the grammatical realisation component,
FUG. We have shown how schemas can be derived for a new domain by generalising schemas used in another domain. Developing ordering constraints on
content is a problem that must be considered whether using an RST approach
(see [Hovy, this volume; Scott and Souza, this volume]) or a schema based approach. The techniques we have described could be applied to either schema
predicates or RST relations.

We have also described FUF, an extended implementation of functional
unification grammar, and shown how it can be used for non-grammatical tasks
as well as traditional syntactic processing. COMET uses a series of cascaded
grammars in the non-graphics components of the system. The use of the
unification formalism for these tasks has several benefits:

1. It results in a declarative representation of constraints on a variety of
   decisions. This declarative representation is easily modified.

2. It will allow for interaction among decisions made in the different components. While the unifier is currently called separately for each of the
   grammars, combining the separate grammars into one would allow for
   interaction across boundaries. This would mean, for example, that a
   syntactic decision might influence a decision made by the media coordinator, which would ultimately influence choices made in the graphics
   component. Similarly, syntactic constraints could also influence decisions made by the lexical chooser.

3. Finally, the use of FUF allows for complex interaction between constraints
   within a module. This has proved useful for the generation of collocations
   within a sentence, allowing for flexibility in how they can be merged with
   other collocations and words of the sentence.

Our current research directions include extending the use of FUF to the content planner as well. We plan to use FUF to represent local constraints on
organisation of content. This will extend interaction across the boundaries of
the text surface generator and the content planner.

References

Allen, J [1987] *Natural Language Understanding*. Menlo Park, Ca.: Benjamin Cummings Publishing Company, Inc.

Department of the Army [1986] *TM 11-5820-890-20-1 Technical Manual: Unit Maintenance for Radio Sets AN/PRC-119, ...* Headquarters, US Dept of the Army.

Baker, M [1989] Probabilistic analogical inference in human and expert systems. Technical Report, Columbia University, February 1989.

Booher, H R [1975] Relative comprehensibility of pictorial information and printed words in proceduralized instructions. *Human Factors*, 266–277.

Choueka, Y [1989] Looking for needles in a haystack. In *Proceedings of RIAO*, 1989.

Church, K and Hanks, K [1989] Word association norms, mutual information, and lexicography. In *Proceedings of the 27th Annual Meeting of the Association for Computational Linguistics*, Vancouver, Canada, 1989, pp76–83.

Dale, R [1988] Generating Referring Expressions in a Domain of Objects and Processes. PhD thesis, Centre for Cognitive Science, University of Edinburgh.

Danlos, L [1987] *The Linguistic Basis of Text Generation*. Cambridge: Cambridge University Press.

Danyluk, A [1989] Finding new rules for incomplete theories: Explicit biases for induction with contextual information. In *Proceedings of the Sixth International Workshop on Machine Learning*, Ithaca, NY, June 1989, pp34–36.

Elhadad, M [1989] Extended functional unification programmars. Technical Report No. CUC-420-89, Department of Computer Science, columbia University.

Elhadad, M [1990] Types in functional unification grammars. In *Proceedings of the 28th Annual Meeting of the Association for Computational Linguistics*, Pittsburgh, 6–10 June 1990.

Elhadad, M, Seligmann, D D, Feiner, S and McKeown, K [1989] A common intention description language for interactive multi-media systems. In *A New Generation of Intelligent Interfaces: Proceedings of IJCAI89 Workshop on Intelligent Interfaces*, Detroit, 22 August 1989, pp46–52.

Feiner, S [1988] A grid-based approach to automating display layout. In *Proceedings of Graphics Interface '88*, Edmonton, June 1988, pp192–197.

Feiner, S and McKeown, K R [1989] Coordinating text and graphics in explanation generation. In *Proceedings of the DARPA workshop on Natural Language and Speech*, Harwich, Mass., October 1989.

Feiner, S and McKeown, K R [1990] Generating coordinated multimedia explanations. In *CAIA 90: Proceedings of the IEEE conference on AI applications*, IEEE, March 1990.

Garside, R [1987] *The Computational Analysis of English: a Corpus Based Approach*. New York: Longman.

Halliday, M A K [1985] *An Introduction to Functional Grammar*. London: Edward Arnold.

Halliday, M A K and Hasan, R [1976] *Cohesion in English*. London: Longman.

Hovy, E H [1987] *Generating Natural Language under Pragmatic Constraints*. PhD thesis, Yale University.

Hovy, E H [1990] Unresolved issues in paragraph planning. This volume.

Jacobs, P S [1985] *A knowledge-based approach to language production*. PhD Thesis, University of California at Berkeley.

Kay, M [1979] Functional grammar. In *Proceedings of the 5th Annual Meeting of the Berkeley Linguistics Society*, Berkeley, Ca., 17–19 February 1979, pp142–158.

Kukich, K [1983] Design of a knowledge based text generator. In *Proceedings of the 21st Annual Meeting of the Association for Computational Linguistics*, Massachusetts Institute of Technology, Cambridge, Mass., 15–17 June 1983, pp145–150.

Maarek, Y and Smadja, F [1989] Full text indexing based on lexical relations, an application: Software libraries. In *Proceedings of ACM SIGIR*, Cambridge, 1989, pp198–206.

MacGregor, R and Brill, D [1989] Loom reference manual. Technical report, USC/Information Sciences Institute, Marina del Rey, Ca.

McKeown, K and Elhadad, M [1990] A contrastive evaluation of functional unification grammar for surface language generators: A case study in choice of connectives. In C L Paris, W R Swartout, and W C Mann (eds), *Natural Language in Artificial Intelligence and Computational Linguistics*, to appear.

McKeown, K [1985] *Text Generation: Using Discourse Strategies and Focus Constraints to Generate Natural Language Text*. Cambridge: Cambridge University Press.

McKeown, K R and Paris, C L [1987] Functional unification grammar revisited. In *Proceedings of the 25th Annual Meeting of the Association for Computational Linguistics*, Stanford University, 6–9 July 1987, pp97–103.

Paris, C L [1987] The Use of Explicit User models in Text Generation: Tailoring to a User's Level of Expertise. PhD Thesis, Columbia University.

Paris, C L [1988] Tailoring object descriptions to a user's level of expertise. *Computational Linguistics*, **14** (3), 64–78.

Pavio, A [1971] *Imagery and Verbal Processes*. New York: Holt, Rinehart and Winston.

Quirk, R, Greenbaum, S, Leech, G and Svartvik, J [1972] *A Grammar of Contemporary English*. London: Longman.

Scott, D and Souza, C S [1990] Getting the message across in RST-based text generation. This volume.

Seligmann, D D and Feiner, S [1989] Specifying composite illustrations with communicative goals. In *Proceedings of the ACM Symposium on User Interface Software and Technology*, Williamsburg, VA, November 13–15, 1989.

Smadja, F [1989] Microcoding the lexicon with co-occurrence knowledge. In *Proceedings of the First International Workshop on Lexical Acquisition*, Detroit, August 1989.

Smadja, F [1990] Lexical co-occurrence, the missing link. *Journal of Literary and Linguistic Computing*, to appear.

Winograd, T [1983] *Language as a Cognitive Process.* Reading, Mass.: Addison-Wesley.

Wolz, U [1990] Extending User Expertise in Interactive Environments. PhD Thesis, Columbia University.

6 An Overview of Head-driven Bottom-up Generation

Gertjan van Noord

Abstract

In this chapter I discuss the properties of a tactical generation approach that has recently become popular: head-driven bottom-up generation.

It is assumed that bidirectional grammars written in some unification-based or logic-based formalism define relations between strings and some representation, usually called **logical form**. The task for a generator is to generate for a given logical form the strings that are related to this logical form by the grammar.

I show that the early approaches to this conception of the generation problem such as [Shieber 1988], [Wedekind 1988] and [Dymetman and Isabelle 1988] are not entirely satisfactory for general purposes. Furthermore, I define a simple bottom-up generator, called BUG1 for reference, as prototypical for the head-driven bottom-up approach as defended by, for example, [van Noord 1989; Calder, Reape and Zeevat 1989; Shieber *et al.* 1989; Shieber *et al.* 1990]. I will argue that head-driven bottom-up generation is to be preferred because the order of processing is directed by the input logical form and the information available in lexical entries; moreover, the algorithm puts fewer restrictions on grammars than some other generators.

6.1 Introduction

For a number of years, several authors have been working on the tactical generation problem in logic-based or unification-based grammar formalisms such as DCG [Pereira and Warren 1980] and PATR II [Shieber *et al.* 1983] (or linguistic theories that use similar formalisms such as LFG [Bresnan 1982], UCG [Zeevat, Klein and Calder 1987] and CUG [Uszkoreit 1986]). In most natural language generation systems, there are two distinct components: the **strategic** part, concerned with deciding 'what to say', and the **tactical** part, concerned with 'how to say it'. For a discussion of this division of labour see for example [Appelt 1987; McKeown 1985; Thompson 1977].

A bidirectional unification grammar defines relations between strings and an abstract representation that is sometimes called the **logical form**. The parsing problem is to determine the corresponding logical form(s) for a given string; similarly, the (tactical) generation problem is to determine the corresponding string(s) for a given logical form. This conception of the generation problem is different from the approaches of Busemann [1989] and Saint-Dizier [1989]: in these two works, the generation method relies on the parsing of a control structure by a specialised grammar in order to construct a syntactic representation. Moreover, it is different from the approach of De Smedt [this volume] in that I assume a clear distinction between the declarative definition of the relation between strings and logical forms (the grammar), and the different processes that are used to compute this relation (the parser and/or the generator).

None of the early approaches to the tactical generation problem in this context (such as [Shieber 1988], [Wedekind 1988] and [Dymetman and Isabelle 1988]) were entirely satisfactory for general purposes. In Section 6.2 I will summarise some of the criticisms.

Because of these criticisms other approaches were investigated, some of which turned out to be very similar in nature. For example, the work reported in [van Noord 1989; Calder, Reape and Zeevat 1989; Shieber *et al.* 1989][1] can be seen as variations on one theme: the head-driven bottom-up approach. In this approach, the order of processing is geared towards the logical form of the input (head-driven) and the information available in lexical entries (bottom-up). In Section 6.3.1 I will define a simple version of such a generator, BUG1, to explain the properties of head-driven bottom-up generation. The shortcomings of BUG1 are discussed together with some possible extensions. Furthermore, I clarify the relation between BUG1 and the simple left-corner parser as described in [Pereira and Shieber 1987].

Throughout this chapter I will define examples and algorithms using the programming language Prolog. I thus assume that readers have some knowledge of Prolog; excellent introductions within the NLP context are [Gazdar and Mellish 1989; Pereira and Shieber 1987].

In this chapter I will hardly touch upon lexical issues; in fact, I will assume that a lexical entry is just a unification grammar rule, accidentally without any daughters. For a more realistic approach, see, for example, [Isabelle, Dymetman, and Macklovitch 1988] and [Shieber *et al.* 1990]. I will assume that such approaches can be incorporated in the framework described here.

6.2   Problems with Early Approaches

This section gives an overview of some of the problems that led to the head-driven bottom-up approach.

---

[1] Martin Kay presented a similar generator at the MT workshop *Into the Nineties*, Manchester, August 1989.

Problems that a generator can face are divided in two types.

The first type of problem is the following. It is quite easy to define grammar rules which most known generators will fail to handle (e.g., a DCG rule such as vp --> [to], vp). In fact, the generation problem in (unrestricted) unification grammars can easily be proved to be undecidable. Therefore, each generator is usually restricted to a particular class of grammars for which it is useful, although this class is not always clearly defined. I am interested in a generator that will work for linguistically relevant unification grammars, thus I prefer some generator over another if it handles some linguistically motivated grammar whereas the other does not.

It is clear that people may disagree on the notion 'linguistically relevant'. Consequently, implementations of different linguistic theories may use different generation algorithms. In this chapter I am interested in the family of **lexical** and **sign-based** linguistic theories, for example theories such as HPSG [Pollard and Sag 1987], and unification-based versions of categorial grammar [Zeevat, Klein and Calder 1987; Uszkoreit 1986].

The second type of problem is simply the performance of the generator. Although it is hard to give any complexity results for generation from a unification grammar (for example, because the problem is undecidable), it seems to be possible to prefer generators that are more **goal-directed** than others, resulting in dramatic differences in performance.

First I will describe the principal problem for top-down generators such as Wedekind's [1988] LFG-generator and Dymetman and Isabelle's [1988] generator for DCGs. Then I will discuss the Shieber's [1988] chart-based bottom-up generator.

6.2.1   Top-down generators and left recursion

To illustrate the principal problem for top-down generators, I will define a very simple top-down generator in Prolog. Assume that grammars are defined as Prolog clauses of the form

(1)   `Node ---> Nodes`

where `Node` is a term of the form

(2)   `node(Syn/LF, P0-PN)`

and `Nodes` is a Prolog list of such nodes. `LF` represents the logical form; `P0-PN` is a difference-list representation of the string, and `Syn` can be any Prolog term representing syntactic information. As an example, consider the grammar in Figure 6.1.[2] A suitable parser for this simple grammar will instantiate `LF` in the call

---

[2]For the sake of simplicity the sample grammars will define very simplistic logical forms.

```
node(s/LF,P0-PN) --->                    % s rule
    [ node(Np,P0-P1),
      node(vp(Np,[])/LF,P1-PN) ].

node(vp(Subj,T)/LF,P0-PN) --->           % vp complementation
    [ node(vp(Subj,[Obj|T])/LF,P0-P1),
      node(Obj,P1-PN) ].

node(np/LF,P0-PN) --->                    % np rule
    [ node(det/LF,P0-P1),
      node(n/LF,P1-PN) ].

node(np/john,[john|X]-X) --->
    [].                                   % john
node(np/mary,[mary|X]-X) --->
    [].                                   % mary
node(n/boy,[boy|X]-X) --->
    [].                                   % boy
node(n/girl,[girl|X]-X) --->
    [].                                   % girl
node(det/_,[the|X]-X) --->
    [].                                   % the

node(vp(np/Np,[])/sleep(Np),             % to sleep
    [sleeps|X]-X) ---> [].

node(vp(np/Np,[np/Np2])/                  % to kiss
    kisses(Np,Np2),[kisses|X]-X) ---> [].

node(vp(np/Np,[np/Np2,p/up])/             % to call up
    call_up(Np,Np2),[calls|X]-X) ---> [].

node(p/up,[up|X]-X) ---> [].              % up
```

Figure 6.1: A grammar for a fragment of English

```
generate(LF,String) :-
    gen(node(_/LF,String-[])).

gen(Node) :-
    ( Node ---> Nodes ),
    gen_ds(Nodes).

gen_ds([]).
gen_ds([Node|Nodes]) :-
    gen(Node),
    gen_ds(Nodes).
```

Figure 6.2: A naive top-down generator

(3) `parse(node(s/LF,[john,kisses,the,boy]-[]))`

to `kisses(john,boy)`. Note that, in this grammar, a lot of interesting feature percolations are defined in the lexical entries. Now consider the naive top-down generation algorithm in Figure 6.2. The algorithm simply matches a node with the mother node of some rule and recursively generates the daughters of this rule. Because of Prolog's left-to-right search strategy, this algorithm will not terminate if we give it the semantics `sleeps(boy)`, because when it applies rule **s**, it will try to generate a node with an unknown logical form and an unknown syntactic category. The algorithm thus will apply rule **s** for this node, and will go into an infinite loop because each time it chooses rule **s** for the first daughter of rule **s**.

Therefore, the order in which nonterminals are expanded is very important, as was noted in [Dymetman and Isabelle 1988] and [Wedekind 1988]. If, in the foregoing example, the generator first tries to generate the second daughter, then the first daughter can be generated without problems afterwards. In Dymetman and Isabelle's [1988] approach, the order of generation is defined by the rule-writer by annotating DCG rules. In Wedekind's [1988] approach, this ordering is achieved automatically by essentially a version of the goal-freezing technique [Colmerauer 1982]. Put simply, the generator only generates a node if its logical form is instantiated; otherwise the generator will try to generate other nodes first.

A specific version of the first approach is an approach where one of the daughters has a privileged status. This daughter, which we might call the **head** of the rule, will always be generated first. The notion **head** may be defined by the rule writer or by some other method. I will simply assume that

for all rules the first daughter of the list of daughters represents the head.[3]
For example, the **vp complementation** rule will now look as follows:

```
(4)  node(vp(Subj,T)/LF,P0-PN) ---> % vp complementation
       [ node(vp(Subj,[Obj|T])/LF,P0-P1),
         node(Obj,P1-PN) ].
```

Now, without any modification to the original definition of **gen_ds**, this change
will imply that heads are generated first.

The resulting simple top-down generation algorithm is equivalent to the
approaches of [Dymetman and Isabelle 1988] and [Wedekind 1988] with respect
to one major problem: the left-recursion problem.

Suppose this generator tries to generate a sentence for the logical form
sleeps(boy). The generator will first try to generate a verb phrase after the
selection of rule **s**, assuming that the second daughter is appropriately chosen
as the head. However, to generate this verb phrase the generator will try
to apply the **vp complementation** rule. For this rule to apply it will try
to apply the same rule for its first daughter. Each time the same rule can
be applied (predicting longer and longer lists of complements), resulting in
non-termination, because of left recursion.

Now the question is whether this problem is a linguistically relevant problem. According to Klaus Netter (personal communication), the foregoing type
of rules can not be written in LFG, and therefore Wedekind's generator has
been used without any problems for LFG-grammars. I want to argue that at
least for linguistic theories such as UCG, other versions of unification-based
categorial grammars and some versions of HPSG, left-recursive rules such as
the **vp complementation** rule occur very frequently. Moreover, in [Shieber
et al. 1989; van Noord 1989] we have argued at length that the problem can
not be solved by an *ad hoc* restriction on the length of this list of complements.
Several Germanic languages require rules where this list of complements can
grow during a derivation (in case of cross-serial dependencies) without a linguistically motivated upper bound. The conclusion of this section, therefore,
is that top-down generators have problems with some linguistically motivated
left-recursive analyses.[4]

---

[3] Note that this does not imply that this daughter is the leftmost daughter; the information
about the left-ro-right order of daughters is represented by the difference-list representation
of strings in each node. Moreover, note that this particular representation may be the result
of some compilation step from a representation that is more convenient for the rule writer.

[4] It is not necessarily the case that this left recursion is caused by the leftmost daughter
of a rule; the left recursion is caused by the node that is generated first. Thus the German
and Dutch equivalents of the **vp complementation** rule, where the order of the head and
the argument is switched, present exactly the same problem.

6.2.2 Shieber's chart-based generator

Shieber [1988] proposes a chart-based generator where rules are applied in a bottom-up fashion. Results are kept on an Earley-type chart. To make this process goal driven, there is only one restriction: the logical form of every subphrase that is found must subsume some part of the input logical form. This restriction results in the **semantic monotonicity** requirement on grammars; this restriction requires that the logical form of each daughter of a rule subsumes part of the logical form of the mother node of that rule. An example will clarify the strategy. Assume we want to generate a string for the logical form

(5) `kisses(boy,girl)`

with the grammar in Figure 6.1. As the generator starts, it will try to select rules without any daughters (as the chart is still empty) whose logical form subsumes part of the input logical form.

First, it can apply the rules `boy`, `girl`, `kisses` and `the`. After entering these entries on the chart, the noun phrases *the girl* and *the boy* can be built. Now a VP dominating *kisses* and *the girl* will be constructed as well, resulting in a VP with the logical form

(6) `kisses(_,girl)`

Finally, a rule applies that combines the NP dominating *the boy* and the VP dominating *kisses the girl*, resulting in the sentence *the boy kisses the girl* with the required logical form. Note that no other rules can apply, because their resulting logical form does not subsume part of the original logical form.

The requirement that every rule application yields a logical form that subsumes part of the input only results in a complete generator if the grammar is semantically monotonic. Shieber himself admits that this requirement is too strong:

> Perhaps the most immediate problem raised by the methodology for generation introduced in this chapter is the strong requirement of semantic monotonicity. ... Finding a weaker constraint on grammars that still allows efficient processing is thus an important research objective.
>
> [Shieber 1988, Section 7]

In fact, the grammar in Figure 6.1 is not semantically monotonic, because it can assign the logical form

(7) `call_up(boy,girl)`

to the sentence *the boy calls the girl up*. Note that the logical form of the
particle *up* does not subsume any part of the resulting logical form (`call_up` is
an identifier without any internal structure). Other examples where semantic
monotonicity is not obeyed are cases where semantically empty words such
as *there* and *it* are syntactically necessary, and prepositional verbs such as
count on. Furthermore, analyses of idioms will usually be semantically nonmonotonic. As an example, consider the case where a sentence like *John kicks
the bucket* has a logical form `kick_bucket(john)`.

Another disadvantage of this generator is the nondeterministic style of processing. The requirement that we can only apply rules in which the logical form
subsumes some part of the input logical form does not direct the generation
process very much. Furthermore, subsumption checks (for example, to check
whether a result already is present in the chart) lead to a considerable processing overhead. These efficiency considerations also led to the head-driven
bottom-up family of generators to be discussed in the next section.

In summary, the principal problem of top-down generators is left recursion.
This problem is solved in a chart-based bottom-up generator at the cost of
severe restrictions on possible grammars, and rather inefficient processing.

6.3   Head-driven Bottom-up Generation

In this section, I want to discuss the merits of the family of head-driven
bottom-up generators. In the first section I will define BUG1, a simple member of this family. In the second section I will argue why the head-driven
bottom-up approach is favourable. The third section discusses some problems with BUG1 and discusses some extensions. The fourth section shows how
parsing and generation can be incorporated in a general architecture. In the
fifth section I will give some more ambitious examples and some experimental
results.

6.3.1   BUG1: a head-driven bottom-up generator

In this section I will present a simple variant of a head-driven, bottom-up generator, called BUG1, which I use as prototypical for the approaches presented in
[van Noord 1989; Calder, Reape and Zeevat 1989; Shieber *et al.* 1989; Shieber
et al. 1990].

As a simplifying assumption, I will require for the moment that rules have
a head (unless of course a rule does not have any daughters). Moreover, the
logical form of this head must be *identical* to the logical form of the mother
node; i.e., the mother node and the head share their logical form. Note that
for each rule in the grammar in Figure 6.1, it is possible to choose a head that
will fulfill this requirement.

```
bug1(Node):-
    predict_word(Node,Small),
    connect(Small,Node).

connect(Node,Node).
connect(Small,Big) :-
    predict_rule(Small,Middle,Others,Big),
    gen_ds(Others),
    connect(Middle,Big).

gen_ds([]).
gen_ds([Node|Nodes]):-
    bug1(Node),
    gen_ds(Nodes).

predict_word(node(_/LF,_),node(S/LF,P)):-
    ( node(S/LF,P) ---> [] ).

predict_rule(Head,Mother,Others,_):-
    ( Mother ---> [Head|Others] ).
```

Figure 6.3: The Prolog definition of BUG1

The algorithm consists of two parts. The **prediction** part predicts a lexical entry. The **connection** part tries to build a parse tree matching the top goal and starting from this lexical entry. The algorithm BUG1 proceeds as follows. Its input will be some node N with some logical form LF. First BUG1 tries to find the **pivot**, a lexical entry whose logical form unifies with LF (the **prediction** step). Note that the logical form of this lexical entry will be instantiated by the prediction step. Now BUG1 is going to build from this pivot larger entities as follows. It selects a rule whose head unifies with the pivot. The other daughters of this rule are generated recursively. For the mother node of this rule this procedure will be repeated: selecting a rule whose head unifies with the current node, generate the daughters of this rule and connect the mother node. This part of the algorithm, called the **connection** part, will end if a mother node has been found that unifies with the original node N. In Prolog this can be defined as in Figure 6.3. As an example, consider what happens if this algorithm is activated by the query

(8) bug1(node(s/kisses(mary,john),String-[]))

First the clause predict_word will select the pivot, a lexical entry with a logical form that can unify with kisses(mary,john). The definition for kisses is a possible candidate. This results in a node

(9)   Small = node(vp(np/mary,[np/john])/kisses(mary,john),
            [kisses|X]-X)

This node is going to be connected to the original node by the connect clauses. To be able to connect the VP to (ultimately) the s, a rule will be selected of which the VP can be the head. The **vp complementation** rule is a possible candidate. If this rule is selected, the following instantiations are obtained:

(10) Others = [node(np/john,X-PN)]
      Middle = node(vp(np/mary,[])/kisses(mary,john),
            [kisses|X]-PN)

The list Others is generated recursively, instantiating X-PN into [john|Y]-Y; so, the next task is to connect

(11) Middle = node(vp(np/mary,[])/kisses(mary,john),
            [kisses,john|Y]-Y)

This node can be unified with the head of rule s, thereby instantiating the logical form of the NP. This NP again is generated recursively and the Middle node of the s rule will become:

(12) node(s/kisses(mary,john),[mary,kisses,john|Y]-Y)

This node can easily be connected to the s by the first clause for connect, because it can be unified with the s node; the variable String in the query will be instantiated into [mary,kisses,john].

As another example, consider the case where the logical form is built in a semantically nonmonotonic way:

(13) bug1(node(s/call_up(mary,john),String-[]))

The predictor step will select the lexical entry for *calls*, after which the generator will try to connect this VP to the s node, as in the foregoing example. After the generation of the first element of the complement list, john, the first entry of the complement list of the dominating VP is fully instantiated, so the particle can be generated without problem. In the connect step the s rule can be applied after which the connect step terminates, instantiating String as [mary,calls,john,up]. In Section 6.3.5 I will give some more interesting examples.

6.3.2 Why head-driven bottom-up generation?

Here I will argue why head-driven generation is to be preferred.

First note that the order of processing is not left-to-right, but always starts with the head of a rule. The logical form of this head is always known by the prediction step. This constitutes the top-down information of the algorithm. Apart from the top-down logical form information, the algorithm is directed by the information of the lexicon because the order of processing is bottom-up. Head-driven bottom-up generators are thus geared towards the semantic content of the input on the one hand and lexical information on the other hand. Of course this is especially useful for grammars that are written in the spirit of *lexical* linguistic theories. These two sources of directedness yield generators with acceptable performance.

Apart from considerations of efficiency, the major reason for constructing bottom-up generators has been the left-recursion problem summarised in Section 6.2. If the base case of the recursion resides in the lexicon, the bottom-up approach does not face these problems. Typically, in grammars that are based on theories such as HPSG, UCG and CUG, these cases occur frequently, but are handled by BUG1 without any problems.

6.3.3 Problems and extensions

Of course, the simple architecture of BUG1 faces a number of problems. However, several extensions to BUG1 can be and have been proposed to deal with some of them.

Restrictions on heads

The assumption that heads always share their logical form with the mother node will be too restrictive for several linguistic or semantic theories. Some extensions to BUG1 are possible that handle more sophisticated grammars. For example, it is possible, as proposed in [van Noord 1989], to enlarge the power of the prediction step. By inspection of the grammar, it may be possible to precompile possible relations between the logical form of some top node and the logical form of the pivot of that node.

Another extension is the architecture advocated in [Shieber *et al.* 1989; Shieber *et al.* 1990], where rules are divided into two types. The first type of rules are the ones where the head indeed shares its logical form with the mother node. In the second type of rule there is no such node. The algorithm does not necessarily predict a lexical entry, but it predicts a rule of the second type, or a lexical entry. The daughters of this rule are then generated in a top-down fashion, after which the mother node of the rule is connected to the top node bottom-up, as in BUG1. If all rules of a grammar are of the first type,

the algorithm behaves similar to BUG1. If no rules have a head, the algorithm
reduces to a top-down generator.

In the generator for UCG [Calder, Reape and Zeevat 1989] it is also assumed
that heads share their logical form with the mother node ('all logical forms are
projected from the lexicon'); as an extension to this, a special arrangement is
made to allow for type raising as well.

Nodes which share their logical form

Another problem is posed by rules where the logical form of the head is shared
with the logical form of some other daughter. In fact, the NP rule of Figure 6.1
is such a rule:

```
(14)  node(np/LF,PO-PN) --->          % np rule
          [ node(n/LF,P1-PN),node(det/LF,PO-P1) ].
```

In principle, this situation can lead to non-termination of the algorithm. A
simple (partial) solution to the problem is to augment the algorithm as follows. In BUG1 only semantic top-down information is used (in the prediction
step). The prediction step can easily be augmented to use some syntactic information as well. Assuming that the predicate link(SynMoth,SynHead) is a
precompiled table of the transitive closure of possible syntactic links between
mothers and heads, similar to the link predicate in the BUP parser [Mat-
sumoto *et al.* 1983] between mothers and left-most daughters, the definition
of select_word and select_rule can be changed as follows:

```
(15)  select_word(node(M/LF,_),node(S/LF,P)):-
          ( node(S/LF,P) ---> [] ),
          link(M,S).
      select_rule(Head,node(M/S,P),Others,node(Syn/_,_)):-
          ( node(M/S,P) ---> [Head|Ds] ),
          link(Syn,M).
```

In most practical cases this technique solves the problem.

Delayed evaluation of nodes

Although I have argued that the 'heads first' approach usually implies that
the logical form of a node is instantiated at the time this node has to be generated, it is possible to write reasonable grammars where this is not the case.
For example, **raising-to-object** constructions can be analysed in a way that
is problematic for BUG1. Assume that the logical form for the sentence *John
believes Mary to kiss the boy* will be believes(john,kiss(mary,boy)). Furthermore, assume that *Mary* is the syntactic object of *believes*. A reasonable

definition of the lexical entry *believes* in the spirit of Figure 6.1 is then the following:

```
(16)  node(vp( np/Np,
              [ np/Np2, vp(np/Np2,[])/Vp ])/believes(Np,Vp),
          [believes|X]-X) ---> [].
```

This lexical entry has two complements, a noun phrase and a verb phrase. Furthermore, it is stated that the logical form of this noun phrase is identical to the logical form of the subject of the embedded verb phrase.

Such an analysis can be defended as follows. Assume that passive is accounted for by some lexical rule that, intuitively speaking, takes the object from the SUBCAT list and makes it the subject (such as in LFG). Now if *believes* is defined as above, then this passive rule will also naturally account for sentences such as *Mary is believed to kiss the boy*.

Now, as the generator proceeds bottom-up, it will try to generate the object noun phrase *before* the embedded verb phrase has been generated, i.e., before the link between the embedded subject and the object is found. As a result, the logical form of the object is not yet instantiated, and therefore BUG1 will not terminate in this case. Assuming that the analysis of raising-to-object is correct then it might be necessary to augment BUG1 with some version of **goal freezing**. If the generator comes across a uninstantiated logical form, then the execution of that node is suspended until the logical form is instantiated. In the case of *believes*, this will imply that the embedded verb phrase will be generated first, after which the object can be generated. An implementation of this technique is reported in [van Hemel 1989].

Verb second

BUG1 can correctly handle analyses that make use of empty elements such as in cases of **gap threading** analyses of *wh*-movement, topicalisation and relativisation [Pereira 1981]. In such cases a possible pivot for, say, a noun phrase can be the empty noun phrase whose semantics obviously unifies with the input; this pivot can easily be connected to the noun phrase goal. As usual, the threading of information will check whether the gap is properly related to an antecedent. In Section 6.3.5 I will give some experimental results of a grammar that includes topicalisation.

If the *head* has been 'moved', however, there will be a problem for BUG1. Consider the analysis of **verb second** phenomena in Dutch and German. In most traditional analyses, it is assumed that the verb in root sentences has been 'moved' from the final position to the second position. Koster [1975] convincingly argues for this analysis of Dutch. Thus a simple root sentence in German and Dutch usually is analysed as in the following examples:

(17)   Vandaag kust$_i$ de man de vrouw ϵ_i.
       Today kisses the man the woman.

(18)   Vandaag heeft$_i$ de man de vrouw ϵ_i gekust.
       Today has the man the woman kissed.

(19)   Vandaag [ziet en hoort]$_i$ de man de vrouw ϵ_i.
       Today sees and hears the man the woman.

In DCGs, such an analysis can easily be defined, by percolating the information of the verb second position to some empty verb in the final position. Consider the simple grammar for Dutch in Figure 6.4; in this grammar, a special empty element is defined for the empty verb. All information of the verb in the second position is percolated through the rules to this empty verb. Therefore, the definition of the several VP-rules is valid for both root and subordinate clauses. This grammar does not handle topicalisation, but assumes that all root sentences start with the subject. In the appendix to this chapter, a more realistic grammar for Dutch is presented that handles topicalisation. There is some freedom in choosing the head of rule **s**. If it is the case that the verb is always the semantic head of **s**, then BUG1 can be made to work properly if the prediction step includes information about the verb second position that is percolated via the other rules. In general, however, the verb will not be the semantic head of the sentence, as is the case in this grammar. Because of the **vp_mod** rule, the verb can have a different logical form compared to the logical form of the **s**. This poses a problem for BUG1. The problem comes about because BUG1 can (and must) at some point predict the empty verb as the pivot of the construction. However, in the definition of this empty verb, no information (such as the list of complements) will become instantiated (unlike the usual case of lexical entries). Therefore the **vp complement** rule can be applied an unbounded number of times. The length of the lists of complements now is not known in advance, and BUG1 will not terminate.

In [van Noord 1989], an *ad hoc* solution is proposed. This solution assumes that the empty verb is an inflectional variant of a verb. Moreover, inflection rules are only applied after the generation process is finished (and has yielded a list of lexical entries). During the generation process the generator acts as if the empty verb is an ordinary verb, thereby circumventing the problem. However, this solution only works if the head that is displaced is always a lexical entry. This is not true in general. In Dutch the verb second position can not only be filled by (lexical) verbs but also by a conjunction of verbs. Moreover, it seems to be the case that some constructions in Spanish are best analysed by assuming the 'movement' of complex verbal constructions to the second position (VP second): for example, **V-preposing** [Torrego 1984] and **predicate raising** ([Bordelois 1988] and references cited there; but see also [Groos and Bok-Bennema 1986]).

```
node( s/Sem, P0-PN) --->                    % s -> Subj, v, vp
    [ node(vp(Np,[],V)/Sem,P2-PN),
      node(Np,P0-P1),
      node(V,P1-P2)].

node( vp(Subj,T,V)/LF, P0-PN) --->          % vp complement
    [ node(vp(Subj,[H|T],V)/LF, P1-PN),
      node(H,P0-P1) ].

node( vp(A,B,C)/D, String) --->             % vp_v
    [ node(v(A,B,C)/D, String)].

node( vp(A,B,C)/Sem, P0-PN) --->            % vp_mod
    [ node(adv(Arg)/Sem,P0-P1),
      node(vp(A,B,C)/Arg,P1-PN) ].

node( v(A,B,node(vp(A,B,_)/Sem,String)/
    Sem, P-P) ---> [].                       % empty verb

node( np/john,[john|X]-X) --->
    [].                                      % john
node( np/mary,[mary|X]-X) --->
    [].                                      % mary
node(adv(Arg)/today(Arg),
    [vandaag|X]-X) ---> [].                  % vandaag (today)
node( v(np/S,[np/O],nil)/
    kisses(S,O), [kust|X]-X) ---> [].        % kust (kisses)
```

Figure 6.4: A grammar for a fragment of Dutch

Here I will propose a more general solution that requires some cooperation of the rule writer. In this solution, it is assumed that there is a relation between the empty head of a construction and some other construction (in the case of verb second the verb second constituent). However, the relation is usually implicit in a grammar; it comes about by percolating the information through different rules from the verb second position to the verb final position. I propose to make this relation explicit by defining an empty head as a Prolog clause with two arguments as in:

(20) gap(node(v(A,B,nil)/Sem, String),
          node(v(A,B,node(v(A,B,nil)/Sem,String))/Sem,P-P)).

This definition can be understood intuitively as follows: once you have found some node A (the first argument of **gap**), then there could just as well have been the (gap) node B (the second argument of **gap**). Note that a lot of information is shared between the two nodes, thereby making the relation between the antecedent and the empty verb explicit.[5] Another way to understand this is by writing the gap declaration as an ordinary definite clause:

(21) node(v(A,B,node(v(A,B,nil)/Sem,String))/Sem,P-P) :-
          node(v(A,B,nil)/Sem, String).

The use of such rules can be incorporated in BUG1 by adding the following clause for **connect**:

(22) connect(Small,Big) :-
          gap(Small,Gap), connect(Gap,Big).

Note that the problem is now solved because the rule for the gap will only be selected after its antecedent has been built. Some parts of this antecedent are then unified with some parts of the gap; the SUBCAT list, for example, will thus be instantiated in time.

Other extensions

The generator defined so far will generate sentences with logical forms that are **compatible** with the input logical form. It is possible to define a stricter generator that will only generate sentences whose logical form subsumes the input logical form (**coherence**) and is subsumed by the input logical form (**completeness**). For a discussion, see [Wedekind 1988; van Noord 1989; Shieber *et al.* 1989].

---

[5]This may suggest that the relation between the antecedent and gap is now fully accounted for by this definition (as in, for example, **extraposition grammars** [Pereira 1981]); however, in this solution the rule writer is still responsible for the percolation of the verb second information in each rule.

```
prove(Call) :-
    predict_unit(SubCall,Call),
    connect(SubCall,Call).

connect(Call,Call).
connect(Child,Ancestor):-
    predict_rule(Child,Ancestor,Parent,Siblings),
    prove_ds(Siblings),
    connect(Parent,Ancestor).

prove_ds([]).
prove_ds([H|T]):-
    prove(H),
    prove_ds(T).
```

Figure 6.5: A general proof procedure

The generator as it stands may be rather non-deterministic with respect to the particular choice of the inflectional form of lexical entries. For example, the agreement features of a verb may only be known after the generation of the subject. Some uninteresting non-determinism can be eliminated by postponing this choice to a postprocess. Instead of yielding a string, the generator will yield a list of lexical entries for which inflectional rules select the appropriate form. For more details see [Shieber *et al.* 1990].

It is also possible to allow for extra Prolog predicates in DCG rules. For example, in [Shieber *et al.* 1989] this possibility is used to implement quantifier storage. In general, there may be some problems with this technique as the order of selection of literals is unlike that in the usual top-down DCG case. Again, delayed evaluation techniques will prove useful here.

6.3.4   A uniform architecture

Shieber [1988] argues for a uniform architecture for parsing and generation. I will argue that BUG1 and a simple version of a left-corner parser [Pereira and Shieber 1987] can be regarded as two instantiations of a simple general proof procedure for Horn clauses. Such a general procedure can be defined as in Figure 6.5. In this definition the two clauses predict_unit and predict_rule are parameterised for a specific task such as parsing or generation. In the case of parsing, predict_unit simply finds a representation of the first word of the sentence; in the case of generation, it finds a representation of the pivot

of the sentence. The clauses for `predict_rule` are similarly parameterised to
define different orders of selection of the literals of the clause. For parsing,
a left-to-right selection is useful; for generation, a head-first selection. Thus,
the above general proof procedure constitutes a bottom-up proof procedure
where top-down filtering is defined via the `predict_unit` and `predict_rule`
predicates. In [Ruessink and van Noord 1989] a generalised version of this
proof procedure is defined, where `predict_unit` is replaced by a predicate
that predicts a non-chain rule.

6.3.5   Some experimental results

In this section we will give some experimental results achieved with a specific
version of the generation algorithm described here. This version is implemented in SICstus Prolog by Herbert Ruessink and the author, and runs on a
DEC RISC 3100 workstation. In the appendix, a DCG grammar for a fragment
of Dutch is defined. This grammar is compiled into a bottom-up parser and a
head-driven bottom-up generator. The small grammar handles the following
types of construction:

- topicalisation
- verb second
- subcategorisation
- cross serial dependencies
- subject and object control verbs
- auxiliaries
- some idioms
- extraposition

The time taken to generate some sentences from their corresponding logical
forms is given in Appendix 1.

   The algorithm is also in use in a more elaborate system: the MiMo2 research MT system. Usual generation times for this system, which contains
grammars for Dutch, English and Spanish with a much broader coverage and
larger lexicon, are satisfactory. However, generation times can increase dra-
matically if analyses are defined where the logical form is built in a non-
compositional way.

6.4   Summary

In this chapter I have given an overview of algorithms for tactical generation
within unification-based formalisms. I have argued that head-driven bottom-

up generators are useful for two reasons. First, the order of processing is geared towards the semantic content of the input and the information in the lexicon. This results in goal-directed algorithms with reasonable performance in practice. Second, this order of processing puts less restrictions on grammars than top-down generators and Shieber's chart-based bottom-up generator. Head-driven bottom-up generators are especially useful for grammars written in the spirit of lexical, sign-based linguistic theories.

Appendix 1: Generation times for a DCG grammar for Dutch

The first line for each entry is the input logical form, then follows a sentence that is generated, with its English translation. The fourth line for each entry gives the time in CPU seconds to generate the first sentence and the total time to compute all possible sentences. Most multiple results arise because different topicalisations are possible according to the grammar; also, different attachments are possible for extraposed constituents (these do not correspond to any differences in logical form according to this grammar).

(23) `perf(try(jane,kiss(jane,tarzan)))`
Jane heeft Tarzan proberen te kussen.
Jane has tried to kiss Tarzan.
1 sec. — 4 sec. (4 results)

(24) `perf(see(pl(man),help(tarzan,kiss(sg(vrouw),jane))))`
De mannen hebben Tarzan de vrouw Jane zien helpen kussen.
The men have seen Tarzan help the woman to kiss Jane.
1 sec. — 2 sec. (8 results)

(25) `fut(perf(try(tarzan,catch(tarzan,jane))))`
Tarzan zal Jane op hebben proberen te vangen.
Tarzan will have tried to catch Jane.
1 sec. — 4 sec. (4 results)

(26) `perf(say(pl(man),see(jane,in_trouble(pl(woman)))))`
De mannen hebben gezegd dat Jane de vrouwen in de puree ziet zitten.
The men have said that Jane sees the women are in trouble.
4 sec. — 13 sec. (8 results)

(27) `force(pl(men),jane,see(jane,help(tarzan,kiss(pl(woman),`
                                            `pl(mary)))))`
De mannen dwingen Jane om Tarzan de vrouwen Mary te zien helpen kussen.
The men force Jane to see Tarzan help the women to kiss Mary.
10 sec. — 35 sec. (24 results)

Appendix 2: A simple DCG for Dutch

Each node is a term x(Cat/LF, Topic, Verb2, Deriv) where Topic is used for a gap-threading analysis of topicalisation; Verb2 percolates information on verb second; and Deriv is a simple derivation tree. Category is a term representing syntactic information and LF represents the argument structure, input for generation.

Arguments of partial_ex are predicates that are executed during compilation. Thus some of these rules will become 'metarules', in case these executable calls have several solutions. The 'object' grammar is thus somewhat larger.

```
partial_ex( extra/2 ).   partial_ex( verb/4 ).
partial_ex( aux/5 ).     partial_ex( member/2 ).
partial_ex( topicalizable/1) .

% main -> topic v0 s
x(main/LF,X-X,nil,main(T,V,S)) -->
  x(Topic, Y-Y, nil, T), { topicalizable(Topic) },
  x(v0(VT,fin,B,C)/VS,Z-Z,nil,V),
  x(s(fin)/LF,Topic-nil,v0(VT,fin,B,C)/VS,S).

topicalizable(np(_)/_).   topicalizable(pp/_).

% sbar -> comp s
x(sbar(fin)/LF,I-I,nil,sbar(C,S)) -->
  x(comp(fin,SS)/LF,O-O,nil,C),
  x(s(fin)/SS,P-P,nil,S).

x(sbar(infin,Sj)/LF,I-I,nil,sbar(C,S)) -->
  x(comp(infin,SS)/LF,O-O,nil,C),
  x(vp(te,Sj,[])/SS,P-P,nil,S).

% s -> np vp
x(s(VF)/LF,I-O,Verb,s(SS,VV)) -->
  x(np(Agr)/Sj,I-O2,nil,SS),
  x(vp(VF,np(Agr)/Sj,[])/LF,O2-O,Verb,VV).

% vp -> compl vp
x(vp(VF,S,T)/LF,I-O,V,vp(C,VP)) -->
  x(H,I-O2,nil,C),  { extra(H,no) },
  x(vp(VF,S,[H|T])/LF,O2-O,V,VP).

% vp -> vp compl (extraposition)
x(vp(VF,S,T)/LF,I-O,V,vp(VP,C)) -->
  x(vp(VF,S,[H|T])/LF,O2-O,V,VP),
  x(H,I-O2,nil,C),    { extra(H,yes) }.
```

```
extra(sbar(_)/_,yes).    extra(sbar(_,_)/_,yes). % must be extraposed
extra(np(_)/_,no).       extra(part/_,no).        % may not
extra(pp/_,_).                                     % can be extraposed

% vp -> v1
x(vp(VF,Sj,Sc)/LF,I-0,V,vp(VV)) -->
   x(v(VF,Sj,Sc-[])/LF,I-0,V,VV).

% v1 -> v0
x(v(VF,Sj,Sc)/LF,I-0,V,v(VV)) -->
   x(v0(main,VF,Sj,Sc)/LF,I-0,V,VV).

% v1 -> aux v1
x(v(F,Sj,Sc)/LF,I-0,V,v(A,B)) -->
   x(v0(aux,F,Sj,v(_A,_B,_C)/_S+Sc)/LF,I-I2,V,A),
   x(v(_A,_B,_C)/_S,I2-0,nil,B).

% gap -> v0
gap(x(v0(VT,fin,Sj,Sc)/LF,_,nil,Tree),
   x(v0(VT,fin,Sj,Sc)/LF,X-X,v0(VT,fin,Sj,Sc)/LF,vgap)).

% np -> det n
x(np(Nm)/LF,I-I,nil,np(Det,N)) -->
   x(det(Ns,Nm)/LF,nil-nil,nil,Det),
   x(n(Nm)/Ns,nil-nil,nil,N).

% pp -> p np
x(pp/LF,I-I,nil,pp(P,NP)) -->
   x(p(Np)/LF,J-J,nil,P),
   x(np(_)/Np,0-0,nil,NP).

% topic ->
x(Topic,Topic-nil,nil,topic_gap) -->
   { topicalizable( Topic ) }.

x(np(sg)/john,I-I,nil,np(john)) --> [jan].
x(np(sg)/mary,I-I,nil,np(mary)) --> [marie].
x(np(sg)/jane,I-I,nil,np(jane)) --> [jane].
x(np(sg)/tarzan,I-I,nil,np(tarzan)) --> [tarzan].
x(n(sg)/sg(man),I-I,nil,n(man)) --> [man].
x(n(pl)/pl(man),I-I,nil,n(mannen)) --> [mannen].
x(n(sg)/sg(woman),I-I,nil,n(vrouw)) --> [vrouw].
x(n(pl)/pl(woman),I-I,nil,n(vrouwen)) --> [vrouwen].
x(n(sg)/sg(mashed_potatoes),I-I,nil,n(puree)) --> [puree].
x(det(Ns,_)/Ns,I-I,nil,det(de)) --> [de].
x(det(Ns,pl)/Ns,I-I,nil,det(e)) --> [].
x(p(Np)/naar(Np),I-I,nil,p(naar)) --> [naar].
```

```
x(p(Np)/in(Np),I-I,nil,p(in)) --> [in].
x(p(Np)/van(Np),I-I,nil,p(van)) --> [van].
x(p(Np)/aan(Np),I-I,nil,p(aan)) --> [aan].
x(part/op,I-I,nil,part(op)) --> [op].
x(comp(fin,S)/dat(S),0-0,nil,comp(dat)) --> [dat].
x(comp(fin,S)/because(S),0-0,nil,comp(dat)) --> [omdat].
x(comp(infin,S)/S,0-0,nil,comp(om)) --> [om].
x(comp(infin,S)/S,0-0,nil,comp(om)) --> [].

% verbs and auxes pick out an inflectional variant:
x(v0(main,Fin,np(Agr)/A1,Sc)/LF,I-I,nil,v0(Form)) -->
  [ Form ],    { verb(LF,np(Agr)/A1,Sc,List),
  member(Fin/Agr/Form,List) }.

x(v0(aux,Fin,np(Agr)/A1,Verb+Sc)/LF,I-I,nil,aux(Form)) -->
  [ Form ],     { aux(LF,Verb,Sc,np(Agr)/A1,List),
  member(Fin/Agr/Form,List) }.

verb(sleep(A1),_/A1,X-X,
  [fin/sg/slaapt,fin/pl/slapen,infin/_/slapen,part/_/geslapen]).

verb(catch(A1,A2),_/A1,[part/op,np(_)/A2|X]-X,    %particle verb
  [fin/sg/vangt,fin/pl/vangen,infin/_/vangen,part/_/gevangen]).

verb(in_trouble(A1),_/A1,[pp/in(sg(mashed_potatoes))|X]-X, %idiom
  [fin/sg/zit,fin/pl/zitten,infin/_/zitten,part/_/gezeten]).

verb(kiss(A1,A2),_/A1,[np(_)/A2|X]-X,
  [fin/sg/kust,fin/pl/kussen,infin/_/kussen,part/_/gekust]).

verb(say(A1,A2),_/A1,[sbar(fin)/dat(A2)|X]-X,
  [fin/sg/zegt,fin/pl/zeggen,infin/_/zeggen,part/_/gezegd]).

% object control
verb(force(A1,A2,A3),Sj/A1,[sbar(infin,Sj/A1)/A3,np(_)/A2|X]-X,
  [fin/sg/dwingt,fin/pl/dwingen,infin/_/dwingen,part/_/gedwongen]).

verb(try(A1,A2),Sj/A1,[sbar(infin,Sj/A1)/A2|X]-X,  % subject control
  [fin/sg/probeert,fin/pl/proberen,infin/_/proberen,
  part/_/geprobeerd]).

verb(give(A1,A2,A3),_/A1,[np(_)/A2,np(_)/A3|X]-X,
  [fin/sg/geeft,fin/pl/geven,infin/_/geven,part/_/gegeven]).

verb(give(A1,A2,A3),_/A1,[pp/aan(A3),np(_)/A2|X]-X,
  [fin/sg/geeft,fin/pl/geven,infin/_/geven,part/_/gegeven]).

aux(perf(X),v(part,np(Agr)/A1,Sc)/X,Sc,np(Agr)/A1,
```

```
[ fin/sg/heeft,fin/pl/hebben,infin/_/hebben, part/_/gehad]).

aux(fut(X),v(infin,np(Agr)/A1,Sc)/X,Sc,np(Agr)/A1,
  [ fin/sg/zal,fin/pl/zullen,infin/_/zullen ]).

aux(X,v(infin,Sj,Sc)/X,Sc,Sj,[ te/_/te ] ).

aux(try(A1,A2),v(te,_/A1,Sc)/A2,Sc,np(Agr)/A1, %raising
  [ fin/sg/probeert,fin/pl/proberen,infin/_/proberen,
    part/_/proberen ] ).

aux(see(A1,A2),v(infin,Sj,A-[Sj|E])/A2,A-E,np(Agr)/A1, % aci raising
  [ fin/sg/ziet, fin/pl/zien, infin/_/zien,part/_/zien ] ).

aux(help(A1,A2),v(infin,Sj,A-[Sj|E])/A2,A-E,np(Agr)/A1, % aci raising
  [ fin/sg/helpt, fin/pl/helpen,infin/_/helpen,part/_/helpen ] ).
```

Acknowledgements

It is clear that this report bears heavily on work by and discussions with the authors of [Shieber *et al.* 1989; Wedekind 1988; Dymetman and Isabelle 1988; Calder, Reape and Zeevat 1989; and Shieber 1988]. I would also like to thank my colleagues on the MiMo2 project, a machine translation research project involving some members of Eurotra-Utrecht. While carrying out the work described here, I was supported by the European Community and the NBBI through the Eurotra project.

References

Appelt, D E [1987] Bidirectional grammars and the design of natural language generation systems. In *Theoretical Issues in Natural Language Processing 3*, New Mexico State University, 7–9 January 1987, pp206–212.

Bordelois, I [1988] Causatives: from lexicon to syntax. *Natural Language and Linguistic Theory*, 6, 57–93.

Bresnan, J (ed) [1982] *The Mental Representation of Grammatical Relations*. Cambridge, Mass.: MIT Press.

Busemann, S [1989] Generation strategies for GPSG. In *Extended Abstracts of the Second European Natural Language Generation Workshop*, University of Edinburgh, 6–8 April 1989.

Calder, J, Reape, M and Zeevat, H [1989] An algorithm for generation in unification categorial grammar. In *Proceedings of the Fourth Conference of the European Chapter of the Association for Computational Linguistics*, University of Manchester Institute of Science and Technology, Manchester, UK, 10–12 April 1989, pp233-240.

Colmerauer, A [1982] *PROLOG II: Manuel de référence et modèle théorique.* Groupe d'Intelligence Artificielle, Faculté des Sciences de Luminy.

Dymetman, M and Isabelle, P [1988] Reversible logic grammars for machine translation. In *Proceedings of the Second International Conference on Theoretical and Methodological issues in Machine Translation of Natural Languages,* Center for Machine Translation, Carnegie Mellon University, Pittsburgh, 12–14 June 1988.

Gazdar, G and Mellish, C S [1989] *Natural Language Processing in Prolog: an Introduction to Computational Linguistics.* Reading, Mass.: Addison Wesley.

Groos, A and Bok-Bennema, R [1986] The structure of the sentence in Spanish. In I Bordelois, H Contreras, and K Zagona (eds) *Generative Studies in Spanish Syntax,* pp 67–80. Dordrecht: Foris.

Grosz, B, Sparck Jones, K and Webber, B L (eds) [1986] *Readings in Natural Language Processing.* Los Altos: Morgan Kaufmann.

Isabelle, P, Dymetman, M and Macklovitch, E [1988] CRITTER: a translation system for agricultural market reports. In *Proceedings of the 12th International Conference on Computational Linguistics,* Budapest, 22–27 August 1988, pp261–266.

Koster, J [1975] Dutch as an SOV language. *Linguistic Analysis,* 1, 111–136.

Matsumoto, Y, Tanaka, H, Hirakawa, H, Miyoshi, H and Yasukawa, H [1983] BUP: a bottom up parser embedded in Prolog. *New Generation Computing,* 1(2), 145–158.

McKeown, K R [1985] *Text Generation.* Cambridge: Cambridge University Press.

Pereira, F C N [1981] Extraposition grammars. *Computational Linguistics,* 7(4), 243–256.

Pereira, F C N and Shieber, S M [1987] *Prolog and Natural Language Analysis.* Stanford: Center for the Study of Language and Information.

Pereira, F C N and Warren, D [1980] Definite clause grammars for language analysis: a survey of the formalism and a comparison with augmented transition networks. *Artificial Intelligence,* 13, 231–278.

Pollard, C and Sag, I [1987] *Information Based Syntax and Semantics.* Stanford: Center for the Study of Language and Information.

Ruessink, H and van Noord, G [1989] Remarks on the bottom-up generation algorithm. Technical report, Department of Linguistics, OTS RUU Utrecht.

Saint-Dizier, P [1989] A generation method based on principles of government and binding theory. In *Extended Abstracts of the Second European Natural Language Generation Workshop,* University of Edinburgh, 6–8 April 1989.

Shieber, S M [1988] A uniform architecture for parsing and generation. In *Proceedings of the 12th International Conference on Computational Linguistics,* Budapest, 22–27 August 1988, pp614–619.

Shieber, S M, Uszkoreit, H, Pereira, F C N, Robinson, J and Tyson, J [1983] The formalism and implementation of PATR II. In B J Grosz and M E Stickel (eds) *Research on Interactive Acquisition and Use of Knowledge,* pp39–79. Menlo Park: SRI International.

Shieber, S M, van Noord, G, Moore, R C and Pereira, F C N [1989] A semantic-head-driven generation algorithm for unification based formalisms. In *Proceedings of the 27th Annual Meeting of the Association for Computational Linguistics*, Vancouver, Canada, pp7–17.

Shieber, S M, van Noord, G, Moore, R C and Pereira, F C N [1990] Semantic-head-driven generation. *Computational Linguistics*, to appear.

De Smedt, K J M J [1990] IPF: an incremental parallel formulator. This volume.

Thompson, H [1977] Strategy and tactics in language production. In W A Beach, S E Fox, S Philosoph (eds.) *Papers from the Thirteenth Regional Meeting of the Chicago Linguistics Society*, Chicago, 14–16 April 1977.

Torrego, E [1984] On inversion in spanish and some of its effects. *Linguistic Inquiry*, **15**, 103–129.

Uszkoreit, H [1986] Categorial unification grammar. In *Proceedings of the 11th International Conference on Computational Linguistics*, Bonn, August 1986, pp187–194.

van Hemel, M A J [1989] A delayed generation strategy for a semantic-head-driven generation algorithm. Technical report, Department of Linguistics, OTS RUU Utrecht.

van Noord, G [1989] BUG: A directed bottom-up generator for unification based formalisms. *Working Papers in Natural Language Processing, Katholieke Universiteit Leuven, Stichting Taaltechnologie Utrecht*, **4**.

Wedekind, J [1988] Generation as structure driven derivation. In *Proceedings of the 12th International Conference on Computational Linguistics*, Budapest, 22–27 August 1988, pp732–737.

Zeevat, H, Klein, E and Calder, J [1987] Unification categorial grammar. In N Haddock, E Klein and G Morrill (eds) *Categorial Grammar, Unification Grammar and Parsing*, pp195–222. Working Papers Volume 1, Centre for Cognitive Science, University of Edinburgh.

7 IPF: An Incremental Parallel Formulator

Koenraad J. M. J. De Smedt

Abstract

We present a computer simulation model of the human speaker which generates sentences in a piecemeal way. The module responsible for grammatical encoding (the tactical component) is discussed in detail. Generation is conceptually and lexically guided and may proceed from the bottom of the syntactic structure upwards as well as from the top downwards. The construction of syntactic structures is based on unification of so-called **syntactic segments**.

7.1 Introduction

Introspection, speech errors and psycholinguistic experiments suggest that natural sentence generation is planned in distinct stages and proceeds in a piecemeal fashion. It is now generally accepted that two main modules can be distinguished in a generation system: a **conceptualiser**, which determines the content of the message, and a **formulator**, which builds the necessary grammatical structures for each message [Levelt 1989; Garrett 1980]. The output of this linguistic module is then articulated by the **articulator**, a motor component. Table 7.1 gives an overview of these modules and presents the formulator in more detail.

Although the modules operate in sequence, there is no need to process only units corresponding to whole sentences on each level. Therefore, it is suggested that these modules can operate independently and in parallel on different fragments of an utterance [Kempen and Hoenkamp 1987; De Smedt and Kempen 1987]. For example, while the formulator is constructing the syntactic form of one conceptual fragment, the conceptualiser can simultaneously plan the next message. Moreover, there may be parallelism *within* the formulator itself; in particular, the syntactic tree formation process does not necessarily proceed in a linear fashion. Sister branches of a syntactic structure may be worked out in parallel by separate processes. Some speech errors of the exchange type [Garrett 1975] reflect this form of computational simultaneity. Figure 7.1 illustrates the global operation of incremental parallel generation.

A natural language generation system which operates according to these assumptions must be supported not only by an incremental and parallel gener-

A	**conceptualiser** (What to say?)
B	**formulator** (How to say it?)
B.1	Grammatical Encoder (preverbal messages to surface structures) –lexicalisation (lemma selection) –formation of syntactic structures (functional and surface structures)
B.2	Phonological Encoder (surface structures to phonetic plans) –selection of lexical forms (internal composition of words) –prosodic planning (intonation contour, metrical structure)
C	**articulator** (Say it!)

Table 7.1: The components of the natural language generation process

ation strategy, but also by a grammar formalism which is designed to meet the constraints imposed by an incremental mode of generation. In previous work, the following three requirements have been put forward to allow maximally incremental sentence generation [Kempen 1987]:

1. Because it cannot be assumed that conceptual fragments which are input to the formulator are chronologically ordered in a particular way, it must be possible to expand syntactic structures *upwards* as well as *downwards* (cf. also De Smedt and Kempen [1987]).

2. Because the size of each conceptual fragment is not guaranteed to cover a full clause or even a full phrase, it must be possible to attach *individual* branches to existing syntactic structures.

3. Because the chronological order in which conceptual fragments are attached to the syntactic structure does not necessarily correspond to the linear precedence in the resulting utterance, the language generation process should exploit variations in word order as they are made necessary by the partial utterance, but observing language-particular restrictions on word order.

In order to meet these criteria, Kempen [1987] proposes a formalism based on **syntactic segments**. This grammar, which was later called **Segment Grammar** (sg), is further developed by [De Smedt and Kempen, forthcoming; De Smedt 1990]. After a brief overview of sg, we will show how a formulator can exploit this grammar formalism to generate sentences in an incremental and parallel mode. A computer simulation program called IPF (Incremental

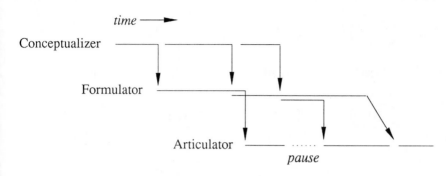

Figure 7.1: Parallelism in sentence generation indicated by means of overlapping lines

Parallel Formulator) has been implemented on the basis of SG for a small but interesting subset of the Dutch grammar and lexicon.

7.2 Segment Grammar

In order to meet the demands of incremental sentence generation mentioned above, Kempen [1987] proposes a formalism for constructing syntactic structures out of so-called syntactic **segments** which each represent one immediate dominance (ID) relation. A segment consists of two nodes representing grammatical categories, and an arc representing a grammatical function. They are graphically represented in vertical orientation, where the top node is called the **root** and the bottom node the **foot**. The syntactic structure shown in Figure 7.2 consists of four segments.

Syntactic structures in SG are composed by means of an elementary operation which I will call **local unification** of nodes. This operation is applicable in two situations:

1. When the root of one segment unifies with the foot of another, the two segments are **concatenated**, causing the syntactic structure to grow in depth.

2. When two roots unify, the segments are **furcated**, causing the structure to grow in breadth only. Furcation is not possible in other formalisms such as Tree Adjoining Grammars (TAGs) [Joshi 1987] or phrase structure grammars; hence SG differs from these other formalisms in that sister nodes can be incrementally added.

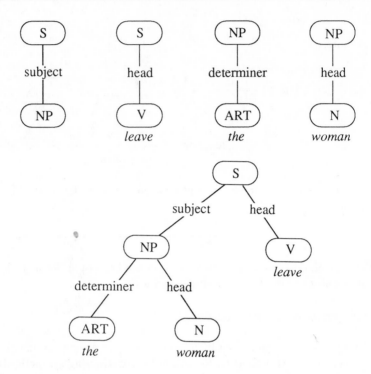

Figure 7.2: Syntactic segments and syntactic structure for the sentence *The woman left*

Agreement is enforced by specifying which features are shared between the root and the foot of a segment. This sharing relation is the same as **re-entrancy** in other unification-based grammars [Shieber 1986]. The unification of nodes which share features causes 'feature transport' in the syntactic structure. In fact, shared features are not transported but unified. Subsequent unifications may eventually cause many nodes in the structure to share the same features. Segments and their components are modeled on a computer as objects in the object-oriented language CommonORBIT, an extension of Common LISP [De Smedt 1987, 1989, 1990]. The **aspects** (or **slots**) of an object representing a node are interpreted as features. Aspects may also contain procedural knowledge. Thus, feature structures are represented as active computational objects rather than passive stores of information. This allows the generation algorithm itself to be be distributed over a number of objects. The incremental addition of constituents to a syntactic structure suggests that knowledge about the linear precedence (LP) of constituents is kept separate from knowledge about immediate dominance (ID). An SG assigns two distinct representations to a sentence, an **f-structure** (or **functional structure**) representing functional relationships between constituents, and a **c-structure** (or **constituent structure**) which represents left-to-right order of constituents.

7.3   An Overview of IPF

We will now be concerned mainly with **grammatical encoding**, which is that part of the formulator which is responsible for the construction of syntactic structures expressing a speaker's intention. Little attention will be given to the origin of the semantic structures which are input[1] to this module. To demarcate the scope of the computer model, it will be assumed that three types of semantic information enter the formulator:

1. **Semantic concepts**: these are references to entities, events, etc., in the domain of discourse which are to be referred to in the utterance.

2. **Semantic roles**: these are deep case relations between concepts. There is no special meaning attached to the case labels; they simply serve to distinguish which concept has which case.

3. **Features**: for simplicity, it is assumed that these are prepared by the conceptualiser in a rather language-specific form and can thus readily be used as syntactic features. Examples are DEFINITENESS, NUMBER, etc.

On the output side, the details concerning the realisation of surface structures as phonologically specified strings will not be dealt with here. The output of the grammatical encoder consists of c-structures which are taken as input by the phonological encoder, presumably in a left-to-right fashion. C-structures contain syntactically specified words in order and are incrementally derived from f-structures. During generation they are provided with a constellation of features which allow the phonological encoder to produce phonologically specified strings in order. A schematic overview of the formulation process is given in Figure 7.3.

7.4   The Generation of F-Structures

The grammatical encoder first creates f-structures, which reflect grammatical relations between constituents. Meaning elements are encoded as syntactically

---

[1] Discourse structures are also input to the formulator; however, since IPF at present handles only individual sentences, discourse information is not taken into account here, except in the disguise of features such as DEFINITENESS.

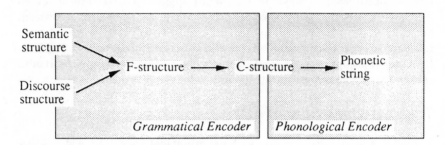

Figure 7.3: The generation of subsequent linguistic descriptions during the formulation stage

categorised lexical elements, syntactic relations and syntactic features. These are incrementally added to form a syntactically coherent functional structure.

7.4.1   Lexical guidance

If syntactic structures have a conceptual origin, then the subcategorisation properties of lexical items rendering those concepts in the input must clearly be taken into account [Kempen and Hoenkamp 1987]. For example, the similarly structured conceptual representations underlying (1a) and (1b) result in different syntactic structures due to the differing subcategorisation properties of *know* and *want*. Constructing a complete syntactic frame before selecting lexical items could result in ungrammaticality, as in (1c); therefore, generation must be conceptually and lexically driven.

(1)   a   John knew he hit Peter.

     b   John wanted to hit Peter.

     c   *John wanted he hit Peter.

On the other hand, lexical items to be incrementally incorporated in a partially constructed sentence are subject to categorial restrictions imposed by the syntactic structure which has been built up to that point. For example, suppose that in (1b) the verb *hit* is chosen first; a subsequent lexicalisation of its direct object is restricted to an NP. Incremental generation is also partially syntax-driven in this sense.

Moreover, IPF does not assume any particular order in which conceptual material is input into the formulator. Consequently, it is very well possible that the direct object NP is created first; a subsequent 'upward expansion' of the syntactic structure may then cause the NP to obtain a role in an S which

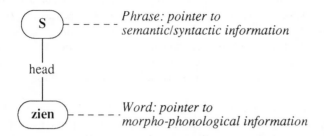

Figure 7.4: The distribution of information in a lexical segment

has been created at a later stage. Thus, subcategorisation restrictions do not always propagate from the top of the tree downward; in the case of upward expansion, restrictions propagate upward as well.

7.4.2 The lexicon

Lexical entries in SG are not simple strings, but are instead structured objects. It will not be surprising that the basic building block of the lexicon is modelled as a segment. A **lexical segment** is a segment where the foot is a word. Content words are modelled as lexical segments where the arc is **head**, whereas function words have different grammatical relations. As in X-bar theory, the category of the phrasal node is determined by that of its head, e.g. NP-head-NOUN, S-head-VERB, PP-head-PREPOSITION, etc. Examples of the English lexicon are NP-head-CITY (a nominal lexical segment) and S-head-TRY (a verbal lexical segment). The representation of lexical entries as lexical segments allows a clear separation of two kinds of information traditionally assigned to words, as schematically represented in Figure 7.4:

1. **Syntactic/semantic** information: syntactic category and valence (in the form of a subcategorisation frame), as well as the meaning content of the lexical entry, are assigned to the roots of lexical segments (the phrases). This part of a lexical entry is sometimes called the **lemma** [Kempen and Huijbers 1983].

2. **Morpho-phonological** information: morphological class associated with a categorial label (part of speech), as well as the phonological sound form, are associated with the feet of lexical segments (the words).

Since meaning is associated with the root of the segment, the segment is always accessed through the root in generation (whereas in parsing it could be accessed via the lexeme on the foot). An SG further contains a set of lexical segments for functorisation and a set of non-lexical segments for **intercalation** (see below). Since these segments have, in principle, the same form as the segments in the lexicon, there is no true distinction between the grammar and the lexicon. All language-specific knowledge is contained in a broad lexicon of segments. Hence an SG is a **lexicalised grammar** [Schabes, Abeillé and Joshi 1988].

Because lexical segments always link a word to a phrase, the lexicon is thus essentially a **phrasal** lexicon. In such a lexicon, it is straightforward to include multi-word phrases in the form of ready-made furcations of segments. In this way, idioms and frequently used syntactic fragments can readily be stored. Idioms and other multi-word phrases are thus more or less fully speci-fied syntactic structures[2] comparable to the trees proposed in TAG by Abeillé and Schabes [1989].

We will now explain in detail what happens when a conceptual message enters the formulator. Recall that there are three kinds of input messages to the formulator: semantic concepts, semantic roles, and features. To explore incremental production in a fine-grained way, each input message is processed individually. Each conceptual fragment will spawn its own parallel formulation process which may overlap with other processes.

7.4.3 Lexicalisation

The first kind of message is a request to formulate a semantic **concept**. For each such input, a linguistic **sign** is created with the semantic concept as its referent. An example input (in LISP notation) is the following:

```
(2)  (FORMULATE (A SIGN
                 (CONCEPT (AN APPLE))))
```

This sign is actually nothing else than a generic, empty syntactic category, to be refined to a more specific category by the formulator. In contrast to Steels and De Smedt [1983], who use the inheritance hierarchy to refine a linguistic sign, this kind of refinement is performed by an independent lexicalisation process, which selects lexical entries and subsequently unifies the sign with one of these entries. We will not be concerned here with the semantic aspects of lexicalisation, but only with the syntactic aspects. The process of lexical selection can be controlled by means of different architectures, e.g., parallel or sequential. It is likely that the human speaker accesses lexical entries in parallel [Levelt 1989], so IPF selects an entry from competing parallel processes. However, since the sign to be refined can only unify with one entry at a time,

---

[2]For ease of storage, the current implementation stores multi-segment expressions as a collection of individual segments which are not composed until they are activated.

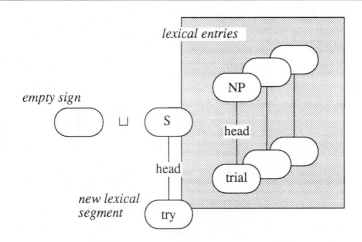

Figure 7.5: Refinement by unification

lexicalisation proceeds in a largely sequential mode anyway. If the sign to be lexicalised is unrelated to any other sign, then obviously the first refinement by unification will succeed. This is exemplified in Figure 7.5.

However, if the sign expressing the concept is already syntactically related to another one in the current sentence, its lexicalisation may be subject to subcategorisation restrictions. Thus, unification may fail; if so, another lexical entry is tried, and so on. If no lexical entries succeed in the unification process, a syntactic dead end is signalled and perhaps a repair or restart occurs. Figure 7.6 illustrates this selection process.

SG is a lexicalist grammar in the sense that the lexicon is an autonomous component where lexical entries are generated by lexical rules. These processes include, e.g., passivisation (the relation between an active lexical entry and a passive one), nominalisation (the relation between a verbal and a nominal lexical entry) and other derivational processes. Indeed, all lexically governed, bounded, structure-preserving processes are treated lexically [Bresnan 1978, 1982]. Thus, SG disavows structure-changing transformations in favour of having just one level of f-structure. When needed, the lexical selection process will generate new lexical entries by means of lexical rules.

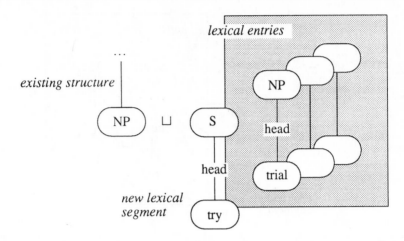

Figure 7.6: Subcategorisation affects lexicalisation: when the verbal lexical entry *try* has been rejected, the nominal lexical entry *trial* will unify with the existing N P

7.4.4   Case, grammatical function, and intercalation

The formulator may receive a request to formulate a case relation between two signs. Case relations signal which roles are filled by semantic concepts in other concepts. An example input is the following:

```
(3)  (LET ((SIGN1 (A SIGN
                   (CONCEPT 'OTTO)))
           (SIGN2 (A SIGN
                   (CONCEPT (AN EAT)))))
       (DEFINE-CASE SIGN1 'AGENT :IN SIGN2))
```

The bridge between descriptions of situations and syntactic structure is provided by means of a **case frame** which assigns syntactic roles to particular participants in the situation represented by the sentence. Since lexical entries in SG are phrasal categories, it is logical to attach case frames to the roots of lexical segments rather than to the feet. A case frame is represented as an association list, where with each case a syntactic function is associated. Sometimes more information may be associated with the function, e.g. categorial restrictions, a 'surface' case marker in the form of a preposition, and an indication of whether this function is optional (marked by a '0') or obligatory. Furthermore, a case frame includes not only 'pure cases' (Tesnière's [1959] 'actants'), but also modifiers or adjuncts, i.e., Tesnière's 'circonstants'). An example of a Dutch case frame is the following:

```
(4)  ((AGENT (SUBJECT))
      (THEME
        (DIRECT-OBJECT NP))       ;categorial restriction
      (LOCATION
        (MODIFIER IN-LEMMA) O)   ;prep = surface case marker
      (DIRECTION (MODIFIER NAAR-LEMMA) O))  ;O = optional
```

When the formulator receives a request to formulate a semantic role between two linguistic signs, this role is looked up in the case frame of the superior sign. This, of course, presupposes that this constituent has already been lexicalised, for otherwise no case frame is available. If necessary, the formulator process waits until lexicalisation has occurred. The second step consists of looking up the grammatical relation associated with the semantic role. This will yield corresponding segments, e.g., an S-subject-NP segment. Such segments are called **intercalating** segments, because they relate one phrase to another. Thus, the lexicon directly constrains the choice of intercalating segments to be incorporated in an f-structure, e.g., the choice between S-subject-NP or S-subject-S. When more than one intercalating segment is possible, they are tried one after the other until one fits between the two phrases. If the foot has not been lexicalised yet—which is quite possible—then clearly the first intercalation will succeed; this must be considered a random guess. The occurrence of a lexicalisation later on in the context of an existing intercalating segment may invalidate this choice, and backtracking should occur. The intercalation mechanism is schematically shown in Figure 7.7.

7.4.5   Features and functorisation

Features (e.g., PLURAL or DEFINITE), are formulated by simply assigning them to a node. Certainly such semantico-syntactic features are derivable from other semantic or discourse information, but this will not concern us here. Thus the formulator may receive, for example, the following request:

```
(5)  (LET ((SIGN1 (A SIGN
                    (CONCEPT (AN APPLE)))))
      (DEFINE-FEATURES SIGN1 '(DEFINITE + PLURAL -)))
```

It will be assumed that this attachment of features to linguistic signs occurs *before* they are lexicalised. This is because they may actually restrict lexicalisation, for they play a role in the unification with lexical segments. Attachment *after* lexicalisation is not guaranteed to be successful and might require backtracking. The main role of features is that they guide various **functorisation**

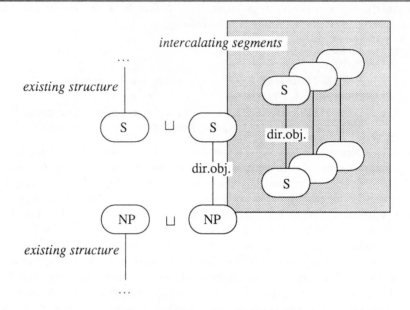

Figure 7.7: The intercalation process

processes, e.g. the addition of function words or inflections. The manner
in which features trigger functorisation is language dependent. For example,
when a sentence in Dutch gets the value '+' for the feature PERFECT, an
auxiliary is added. Other languages such as Latin, for example. share the feature PERFECT between S and the finite verb, which undergoes an inflectional
change. Features which trigger inflectional change may simply be shared. On
the other hand, features which surface as function words will give rise to the
addition of one or more segments, which are called **functor** segments. These
segments are associated with categories: for example, determiners are associated with the NP, and auxiliaries are associated with the S. Unification is used
as a general mechanism to choose among various possible functor segments.
In Dutch, for example, one of several articles can be added, depending on the
definiteness, gender and number of the NP.[3] Unification will try to unify the
roots of all these functor segments with the NP until one succeeds. In principle,
this could be a parallel operation, except that the NP cannot be involved in

---

[3]It must be added that functorisation of the NP is slightly simplified here, for it deals
only with articles, and does not account for quantifiers and other elements which may occur
in conjunction with—or in replacement of—articles.

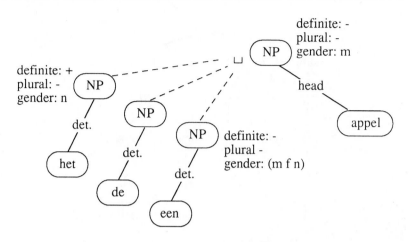

Figure 7.8: Functorisation of the NP in Dutch

more than one unification at the same time. The addition of articles by means of functorisation in the NP is schematically represented in Figure 7.8.

On the S level, functorisation may result in the addition of auxiliaries. This is performed in a fashion similar to functorisation in the NP. In addition, it is decided which verb (main or auxiliary) shares with S the feature FINITE. A finite verb agrees with its matrix sentence, in the sense that features like PERSON and PLURAL are shared between them.[4]

7.5 The Generation of C-Structures

F-structures, as constructed by the process explained above, express ID relations but do not express any left-to-right order of constituents. By way of example, the f-structure in Figure 7.9 is assigned to the Dutch sentences (6a)–(6d). F-structures are complete when the head and other obligatory segments (according to the valence information in the phrasal nodes) have been incorporated and when the functorisation process has taken place. The assignment of left-to-right positions to constituents is modeled as the piecemeal derivation of a different kind of structure, a c-structure. Somewhat like ID/LP format for phrase structure rules, SG handles ID and LP separately. However, there are two crucial differences. First, whereas a phrase structure based system

---

[4]Following a classical transformational generative grammar approach, this could also be modeled as the addition of a segment with as its foot a constituent +INFL.

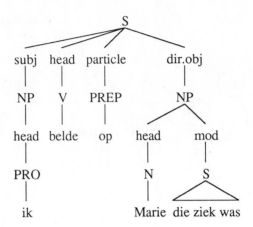

Figure 7.9: F-structure of (2a-d)

specifies a relative ordering of sister nodes, SG assigns a position to a constituent independently of its sisters; therefore, a system of *absolute* positions is used. Second, the assignment of LP in SG may be attended by a revision of ID relations. Consequently, the ID relations in the f-structure and those in the c-structure for a sentence may not be isomorphic; for example, the c-structure Figure 7.10 is assigned to (6a). For clarity, the internal details of the relative clause are left out.

(6) a Ik belde Marie op, die ziek was.
        I called up Mary, who was ill.

     b Ik belde Marie, die ziek was, op.

     c Mariĕ, die ziek was, belde ik op.

     d Marie belde ik op, die ziek was.

7.5.1 Destinations

The procedure which assigns left-to-right positions works in a bottom-up fashion: the foot node of a segment is attached in the c-structure directly under its **destination**, which is normally the root of the segment. The destination of a constituent is determined by its mother in the f-structure, i.e., the node which is root of the segment where the constituent is the foot. Normally, the address which the matrix constituent assigns as destination of its dependents is the

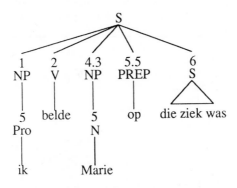

Figure 7.10: C-structure of (2a)

matrix constituent itself, i.e., ID relations in the c-structure are by default the same as those in the corresponding f-structure. Figure 7.11 is a schematic representation of the destination procedure.

Such indirect determination of the destination may seem complicated, but it guarantees that the root node of a segment in f-structure exerts control over the ID relation of the foot node. This will prove useful in the treatment of constructions where nodes go to higher-level destinations, e.g. the extraposed relative clause in (6c). C-structures which are non-isomorphic to the corresponding f-structures may account for discontinuous constituency. This is discussed more fully in De Smedt and Kempen [1990].

7.5.2 Holders

Since f-structures are constructed in a piecemeal fashion, it is natural to assign word order incrementally as well. As soon as a node has been lexicalised and attached to its mother in the f-structure, IPF attempts to assign it a left-to-right position in the corresponding c-structure. Because not all constituents are available at the same time, it is difficult to encode word order relative to other constituents. Therefore, SG prefers an *absolute* order of constituents. For this purpose, a **holder** is associated with each phrase. A holder is a vector of numbered slots that can be 'filled' by constituents. Figure 7.12 shows some holders associated with the c-structure in Figure 7.10.

The foot node of each segment in the grammar has a feature **positions** which lists all possible positions that the node can occupy in its destination. These possibilities can be seen as language-specific constraints on word order

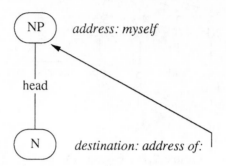

Figure 7.11: Finding the destination of a node via the address of its mother

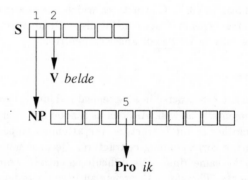

Figure 7.12: Diagram showing some holders for the structure in Figure 7.10; the first and second positions of the S have just been occupied

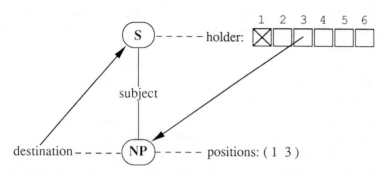

Figure 7.13: Destination and linearisation processes: assign NP to the third slot in the holder of its destination because the first slot is already taken

variation. Constituents will try to occupy the first available slot. For example, the subject NP in Dutch may occur either in sentence-initial or third position (cf. example (6a) *vs* (6c)). In the grammar for Dutch, this is specified so that the foot of an `S-subject-NP` segment may go to holder slots 1 or 3. When a subject NP is assigned a position in the holder of its destination, it will first attempt to occupy position 1. Suppose that position 1 has already been occupied by another constituent, due to earlier conceptual input, it will attempt to go to position 3. A schematic overview of such a situation is given in Figure 7.13.

Such a situation may give rise to a word order variation like that in (6c) and (6d), where *ik* takes third position rather than first. If the utterance has proceeded beyond the point where a constituent can be added, a syntactic dead end occurs and a self-correction or restart may be necessary. Alternatively, the constituent may end up somewhere else; for example, the final slot in the S is a 'dump' for late material (**right dislocation**). The relative clause in (6a) and (6d) is an instance of such a construction. In order to utter partial sentences, it must be possible to determine the word order of those constituents to be uttered independently of any constituents which are to be incorporated in the utterance at a later stage. For example, it must be possible to determine the word order of fragment (7a) correctly, avoiding, for example, the ungrammatical order in (7b):

(7) a Yesterday, I ...

  b ∗I, yesterday ...

Although human speakers do not always make perfect sentences, and sometimes produce clear ordering errors, it seems generally possible, at least in languages like English and Dutch, to determine the order of single fragments one after the other during incremental production. In fact, we might hypothesise the following:

> Incremental production is only possible if for the assignment of left-to-right position to a constituent, the simultaneous presence of other constituents of the phrase is not required.

If this empirical claim is true, the necessary knowledge to determine word order can be encoded locally on the level of single segments, as is done in SG. The number of holder slots in a Dutch clause is substantial. In order to keep an overview, positions *within* positions are sometimes used. The Dutch sentence can be divided into six main parts, each having its own internal ordering. Decimal notation is used to represent such slots: for example, '3.2' is the second slot in the third main slot. Some holder slots can be occupied by a single constituent only; others may be occupied by an unspecified number of constituents (for example, an indefinitely long list of APs in front of a noun).

7.5.3 Topicalisation, accessibility and word order variation

In IPF, there is no explicit feature signalling what is to be topic of an utterance. Rather, what is topic is implicitly coded in the order in which the conceptualiser passes concepts to the formulator. We assume that pragmatic notions such as topic/focus strongly correlate with conceptual accessibility, i.e., the topic in the discourse may be conceptually more accessible and hence tends to be realised sooner (cf. Bock and Warren [1985]). Similarly, constituents which are long or complex and hence consume more processing time in the grammatical encoder will tend to move toward the end of the utterance, because earlier positions are likely to have been taken up by other constituents. Thus, the tendency of such constituents to occur at the end of the sentence is not a hard rule of linguistic structure, but an emerging property of the generation process as it is proposed here. Experience with the implementation of IPF/SG shows that these timing factors can be simulated in a program. Alternative orderings of the same conceptual input stimuli into the formulator can indeed result in word order variations on the surface level. For example, the utterances in (8) were generated by IPF under circumstances which differed solely by the fact that in (8a) the concept underlying *Otto* was given sooner than in (8b); while in (8b), the concept underlying *appel* (apple) was given sooner.

(8)   a   Otto ...heeft een appel gegeten.
           Otto has eaten an apple.

     b   Een appel ...heeft Otto gegeten.
           [As before, but with a variation in word order.]

Similarly, in SVO languages like English, passivisation can be triggered by conceptual accessibility. If a constituent which would be the object in an active sentence is fronted, it becomes a likely candidate for the subject function; hence a passive lemma is appropriate. In summary, if there is indeed a strong link between fronting, topicalisation and conceptual accessibility [Bock 1987; Bock and Warren 1985; Levelt 1989] then topicalisation by fronting (and by means of other mechanisms like passivisation) is an important emerging property of the generation strategy. This is not to say that accessibility is the *only* factor determining the order in which conceptual fragments are input into the formulator; it seems that certain rhetorical effects unrelated to accessibility may affect word order as well. Kolk's [1987] adaptation theory suggests that the conceptual input to the formulator can be subject to manipulation which is learned by the speaker. Thus, it is certainly possible that some factors determining word order are coded in terms of an order imposed on conceptual elements as they enter the formulator. Although experiments with IPF show that conceptual accessibility can indeed account for variations in word order, the timing of the parallel processes in grammatical encoding is not very sophisticated, since the current implementation gives all parallel processes the same priority; they are therefore capable of carrying out roughly the same proportion of processing in the same period of time. In a multiprocessing environment it is often possible to allot more computational resources to one process than to another. This would be another way to affect word order by means of timing in the generation process.

7.5.4 A small example

In order to make the foregoing mechanisms more concrete, we now present a small example of grammatical encoding. The example will involve the choice between (8a) and (8b). The input consists of the following LISP expression:

```
(DEFUN S-TEST ()
  "Test for: Otto heeft een appel gegeten."
  (LET ((SIGN1 (A SIGN (SEMANTIC-REFERENT (THE-OBJECT 'OTTO))))
        (SIGN2 (A SIGN (SEMANTIC-REFERENT (AN EAT))))
        (SIGN3 (A SIGN (SEMANTIC-REFERENT (AN APPLE)))))
    ;; first define features; these could be computed
    (DEFINE-FEATURES SIGN1 '(DEFINITE + PLURAL -))
    (DEFINE-FEATURES SIGN2
      '(INTERROGATIVE - PERFECT + FUTURE - PAST - FINITE +))
    (DEFINE-FEATURES SIGN3 '(DEFINITE - PLURAL -))
    (FORMULATE SIGN1)     ;; Otto...
    (SLEEP 5)
```

```
(FORMULATE SIGN2)      ;; heeft gegeten ...
(SLEEP 5)
(DEFINE-CASE SIGN1 'AGENT :IN SIGN2)
;; Otto heeft gegeten ... = upward expansion
(SLEEP 5)
(FORMULATE SIGN3)      ;; een appel
(SLEEP 5)
(DEFINE-CASE SIGN3 'THEME :IN SIGN2)
;; Otto heeft een appel gegeten ... = downward expansion
))
```

Note that, apart from the DEFINE-FEATURES commands, there are five commands to the formulator, three involving FORMULATE and two involving DEFINE-CASE. They are spaced in the time dimension by means of SLEEP commands which each cause the system to be dormant for approximately 5 seconds of real time. Shorter periods of time between the commands to the formulator cause more competition between parallel processes, as will be indicated below. Each command to the formulator results in an independent grammatical encoding process which runs in parallel to everything else going on in the system. Figures 7.14 and 7.15 present two snapshots of the generation process; f-structures are shown in the upper window while c-structures are shown in the lower window. Figure 7.15 shows how the sign for the concept *Otto* has stayed ahead of the sign for *apple* and occupies a position earlier in the sentence. This results in a c-structure corresponding to sentence (8a).

If the timing in the test input is changed so that there are shorter periods of time between the various inputs, then their computation overlaps more. The chance that the constituents of the sentence occupy alternative left-to-right positions in the c-structure therefore increases. Figure 7.16 shows how the sign for *Otto* is 'overtaken' by that for *apple* and ends up in holder slot 3 of the s. This results in a c-structure corresponding to sentence (8b).

7.6   Concluding Remarks

IPF is a computer model for incremental grammatical encoding which exploits the representation of grammatical and lexical knowledge in terms of syntactic segments. It allows the piecemeal input of conceptual material and can construct functional structures not only from the top down, but also from the bottom up. Surface structures (c-structures) are derived in an equally piecemeal fashion. Conceptual fragments are small, although 'chunking' of conceptual material can be achieved by a number of simultaneous inputs.

A lexically guided system is proposed, in the sense that meaning is directly responsible for the choice of appropriate lexical items, which in turn are associ-

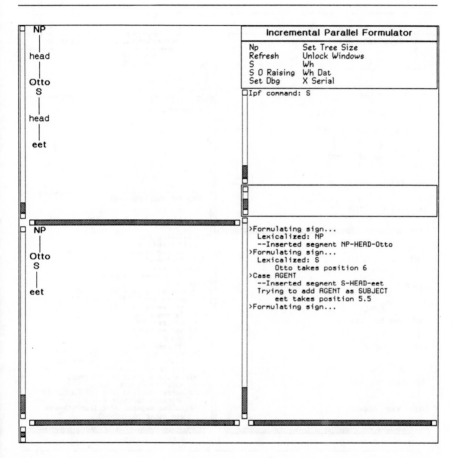

Figure 7.14: Snapshot of the first few seconds of the generation of example (8a)

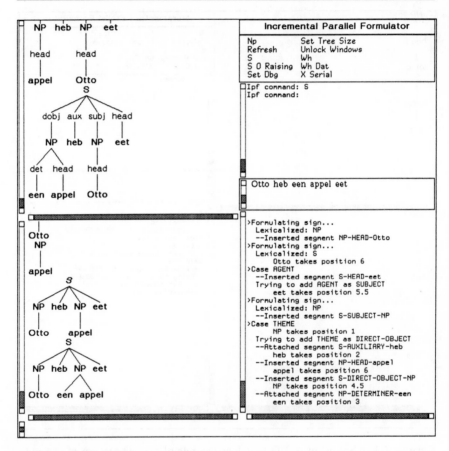

Figure 7.15: Snapshot of the completion of the generation of example (8a)

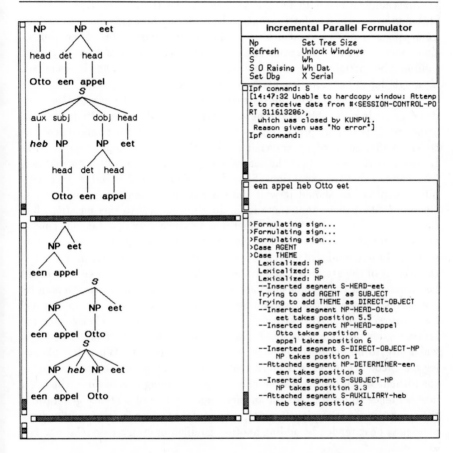

Figure 7.16: A snapshot of a generation of example (8b)

ated with possible categories. Possible words and categories are filtered by the current syntactic context. Although conceptual changes other than addition of new concepts are currently not implemented in IPF, they are, in principle, possible (cf. De Smedt and Kempen [1987]). Conceptual replacement or deletion of concepts, semantic roles or features could be modeled either by undoing previous unifications with functor segments or by the construction of a new sentence structure. The latter seems to be preferred because undoing previous unifications involves a great deal of bookkeeping of past states of the unification space. When a conceptual change invalidates a piece of currently built (and maybe partially uttered) structure, the structure as a whole is discarded, although dependent constituents may be re-used.

Within the formulator, the c-structure produced by the grammatical encoder is made accessible to the next substage, the phonological encoder. In principle, left-to-right processing of the c-structure by the phonological encoder can be achieved by traversing this structure in a depth-first fashion. However, it is possible that the sentence is generated in a bottom-up fashion by means of upward expansion. Should the phonological encoder start with bits and pieces or should it wait until a reasonable sentence structure has emerged? We believe that there is no absolute answer to this question, but that both are possible. People sometimes produce very spontaneous speech and sometimes very careful and deliberate speech. It seems that a main determinant of these modes of speech is how the phonological encoder interfaces to the output of the grammatical encoder. In the case of careful speech, it could be assumed that the phonological encoder applies certain heuristics to plan its processing. Certainly there should be a mechanism to prevent 'skipping over' the position of required constituents, e.g., the finite verb of a clause. One solution to this problem consists of marking the positional slots in c-structures which are to be occupied by such required constituents. When the phonological encoder finds such a marker, it waits until the position is filled by a constituent which overwrites the marker. A remaining question is: when is a new sentence to be started? In an incremental mode of sentence generation, the answer is not so straightforward, for a sentence which is, in principle, complete may be extended by adding another modifier or even a case relation. For example:

(9)   a   He came to my house ... at about ten o'clock ... because he needed money.

       b   I already told you ... that she got married.

A new sentence seems to be triggered by at least two kinds of conceptual addition:

1. When a new concept is not related to anything in the sentence; or

2. When a new concept is related to the current utterance, but does not fit into the syntactic structure, because the utterance has proceeded beyond the point where the new constituent can be added (as discussed ·above).

In that case, either the sentence is already complete, and a new one is started, or the current structure is abandoned and a restart is attempted.

References

Abeillé, A and Schabes, Y [1989] Parsing idioms in lexicalized TAGs. In *Proceedings of Fourth Conference of the European Chapter of the Association for Computational Linguistics*, University of Manchester Institute of Science and Technology, Manchester, UK, 10–12 April 1989, pp1–9.

Bock, J K and Warren, R [1985] Conceptual accessibility and syntactic structure in sentence formulation. *Cognition*, **21**, 47–67.

Bock, J K [1987] Exploring levels of processing in sentence production. In G Kempen (ed) *Natural language generation: New results in Artificial Intelligence, psychology and linguistics*, pp351-363. Dordrecht: Martinus Nijhoff Publishers.

Bresnan, J (ed) [1982] *The Mental Representation of Grammatical Relations*. Cambridge, Mass.: MIT Press.

De Smedt, K [1990] Incremental sentence generation: a computer model of grammatical encoding. PhD Thesis, NICI TR No. 90–01, Nijmegen Institute of Cognition Research and Information Technology, 1990.

De Smedt, K and Kempen, G [forthcoming] Segment Grammar: a formalism for incremental sentence generation. In *Proceedings of the 4th International Workshop on Natural Language Generation*, Santa Catalina Island, 17–21 July 1988.

De Smedt, K and Kempen, G [1990] Discontinuous constituency in Segment Grammar. In *Proceedings of the Symposium on Discontinuous Constituency*, ITK, Tilburg, 25–27 January 1990, pp97–111.

De Smedt, K and Kempen, G [1987] Incremental sentence production, self-correction and coordination. In G Kempen (ed) *Natural language generation: new results in Artificial Intelligence, psychology and linguistics*, pp365-376. Dordrecht: Martinus Nijhoff Publishers.

De Smedt, K [1987] Object-oriented programming in Flavors and CommonORBIT. In R Hawley (ed) *Artificial Intelligence programming environments*, pp 157–176. Chichester: Ellis Horwood.

De Smedt, K [1989] Object-oriented knowledge representation in CommonORBIT. Internal report 89-NICI-01, Nijmegen Institute for Cognition Research and Information Technology, University of Nijmegen.

Garrett, M [1975] The analysis of sentence production. In G Bower (ed) *The Psychology of Learning and Motivation*, Volume 9, pp133–177. New York: Academic Press.

Garrett, M [1980] Levels of processing in sentence production. In B Butterworth (ed) *Language Production*, Volume 1: *Speech and Talk*, pp177–219. New York: Academic Press.

Joshi, A [1987] The relevance of tree adjoining grammar to generation. In G Kempen (ed) *Natural language generation: New results in Artificial Intelligence, psychology and linguistics*, pp233–252. Dordrecht: Martinus Nijhoff Publishers.

Kempen, G and Hoenkamp, E [1987] An incremental procedural grammar for sentence formulation. *Cognitive Science*, **11**, 201–258.

Kempen, G and Huijbers, P [1983] The lexicalization process in sentence production and naming: indirect election of words. *Cognition*, **14**, 185–209.

Kempen, G [1987] A framework for incremental syntactic tree formation. In *Proceedings of the Tenth International Joint Conference on Artificial Intelligence*, Milan, Italy, 23–28 August 1987, pp655–660. Los Altos: Morgan Kaufmann.

Kolk, H [1987] A theory of grammatical impairment in aphasia. In G Kempen (ed) *Natural language generation: New results in Artificial Intelligence, psychology and linguistics*, pp377–391. Dordrecht: Martinus Nijhoff Publishers.

Levelt, W [1989] *Speaking: from intention to articulation*. Cambridge, Mass.: MIT Press.

Schabes, Y, Abeillé, A and Joshi, A K [1988] Parsing strategies with 'lexicalized' grammars: application to Tree Adjoining Grammars. In *Proceedings of the 12th International Conference on Computational Linguistics*, Budapest, 22–27 August 1988, pp578–583.

Shieber, S M [1986] *An Introduction to Unification-Based Approaches to Grammar*. CSLI Lecture Notes No. 4. Stanford: Center for the Study of Language and Information.

Steels, L and De Smedt, K [1983] Some examples of frame-based syntactic processing. In Fr Daems and L Goossens (eds) *Een spyeghel voor G. Jo Steenbergen*, pp293–305. Leuven: Acco.

Tesnière, L [1959] *Eléments de syntaxe structurale*. Paris: Klincksieck.

8 The Architecture of a Generation Component in a Complete Natural Language Dialogue System

Helmut Horacek

Abstract

This chapter[1] describes a generator which includes two essentially new components, enabling the generator to exhibit exceptional capabilities: one of them performs meaning preserving transformations on a purely conceptual level, and the other performs mappings of predicates used on this level onto lexemes and grammatical functions (which may involve considerable structural changes). When the generator is part of a complete natural language dialogue system (the system WISBER, in our case), these components are urgently needed because of the increased task area which is due to requirements of the other components and influences of the dialogue.

8.1 Introduction

In the last decade a significant number of natural language (NL) generation systems have been designed and implemented. A significant proportion of these, however, are more or less stand-alone systems mainly featuring a selected set of subtasks specific to NL generation. Despite the fact that there are many powerful approaches among them, this situation leaves unanswered some important questions concerning the design of NL generation systems:

- Typically, a few strong but somewhat narrowly designed subsystems are created under the assumption that they contribute to a larger system that covers all aspects of the generation task. To what extent can all relevant phenomena be covered by a candidate component when pursuing this approach? We suspect that there might be a tendency towards

---

[1]The work described in this chapter is part of the joint project WISBER, which is supported by the German Federal Ministry for Research and Technology under grant ITW 8502. The partners in the project are: Nixdorf Computer AGENT, SCS Orbit GmbH, Siemens AG, the University of Hamburg and the University of Saarbrücken.

covering some easily treatable phenomena by several components, while leaving some difficult ones aside.

- What would be an adequate control structure that combines subsystems in a sufficiently transparent but, nevertheless, at least moderately efficient way?

- How can a generator be successfully integrated into a complete NL system? How do the techniques used relate to those applied in the analysis and discourse components?

Our own work concerns a generation component which is integrated into a complete system (the NL consultation system WISBER [Horacek *et al.* 1988]), which also includes NL analysis and is able to behave coherently over a sequence of utterances in a dialogue of reasonable complexity. By presenting the methods applied in this generator, we hope to give at least partial answers to the above questions. Moreover, in an environment like ours, some particular aspects, which we feel to be widely neglected in the field of NL generation, require urgent consideration:

- The initial specification from which an utterance is to be generated must be expected to be oriented primarily to the needs of the system's dialogue and evaluation components, rather than being particularly accommodated to the purposes of generation.

- The interrelations to the process of (prior and subsequent) analysis augment the basis for choosing among alternatives, in particular with respect to referring expressions.

Before describing our generator, we outline the environment provided by the complete system.

8.2   The Embedding System WISBER

WISBER is a fully implemented German NL consultation system. It covers the whole spectrum of NL processing tasks including analysis, response determination, and generation. The chosen domain of application is financial investment. Consultation dialogues have special characteristics which we had to take into account when designing WISBER (the following characteristics mainly have an impact on the generation part of the system):

- The communication behaviour of a system designed for consultation dialogues must be very flexible. In particular, this comprises mastering an extended coverage of speech acts including, e.g., recommendations.

- The dialogue partner's command of domain dependent terminological knowledge is not necessarily identical to that of the system. Therefore, WISBER is able to paraphrase terminology which the user would probably not understand.

- When expressing wants and beliefs, modal verbs are quite frequently used. They are therefore also included in WISBER's generation capabilities.

- In our domain (as in many others) measurements (in this case, money and percentages) play an important role. For that reason, we have developed a general way of representing and processing measurements, including the flexible generation of referring expressions.

A sample dialogue, which will be referred to subsequently in this chapter, is given in Figure 8.1.

Figure 8.2 shows WISBER's processing modules and knowledge sources. C-structures and F-structures are constituent and functional structures in an LFG-like formalism [Kaplan and Bresnan 1982]; D-structure is a discourse structure as in Kamp's Discourse Representation Theory [Kamp 1981]. In this chapter we will concentrate on semantic-pragmatic (i.e., strategic) generation. In our view, this aspect of generation is confronted with more difficult problems than the tactical stage, and there is still little agreement about the design and the suitability of methods applied in strategic generation.

The knowledge used by the semantic-pragmatic components (including the generation components discussed in this chapter) is split into a terminological and an assertional part (each manipulated by a dedicated component), and a formalism dedicated to represent the meaning of utterances:

- QUIRK (QUIck Reimplementation of KL-ONE) provides the means to construct a terminological knowledge base (TBox) of concept and role definitions with limited reasoning facilities [Bergmann and Gerlach 1986].

- QUARK [Poesio 1988] is used to store and manipulate the assertional knowledge base (ABox) including facts about the user and the domain as well as wants and beliefs of the conversants.

- IRS (Interne RepräsentationsSprache) [Bergmann *et al.* 1987] is used by the components of WISBER at all levels of semantic-pragmatic analysis and generation.

QUIRK is a KL-ONE-like [Brachman and Schmolze 1985] representation system that provides a terminological representation language based on the syntax and semantics of NIKL [Schmolze 1985], reasoning capabilities (e.g., classification), as well as program and user interfaces. With respect to generation it is mainly used for performing terminological transformations on IRS formulas, e.g., for

1	WISBER:	Guten Tag, hier ist WISBER.
		Hello, this is WISBER.
2	USER:	Ich habe 40000 DM geerbt und möchte diesen Betrag anlegen.
		I have inherited 40000 DM and want to invest this sum.
3	WISBER:	Welche Laufzeit soll die Anlage haben?
		What term should the investment have?
4	USER:	Die Laufzeit der Anlage soll acht Jahre betragen.
		The term of the investment should be eight years.
5	WISBER:	Besitzen Sie ein Sparbuch mit mehr als zwei Nettomonatseinkommen?
		Do you have a savings account with more than two net months income?
6	USER:	Ich habe fünf Nettomonatseinkommen auf mehreren Sparbüchern.
		I have five net months income in several savings accounts.
7	WISBER:	Möchten Sie während der Laufzeit auf den Betrag zurückgreifen können?
		Do you want to be able to have access to your money during the term of the investment?
8	USER:	Nein.
		No.
9	WISBER:	Dann empfehle ich Ihnen Pfandbriefe. Sie haben eine Rendite von 7%.
		Then I recommend bonds to you. They have an interest rate of 7%.
10	USER:	Gibt es Anlagen mit einer höheren Rendite als 7%?
		Are there investment forms with an interest rate higher than 7%?
11	WISBER:	Nein.
		No.

Figure 8.1: A sample dialogue

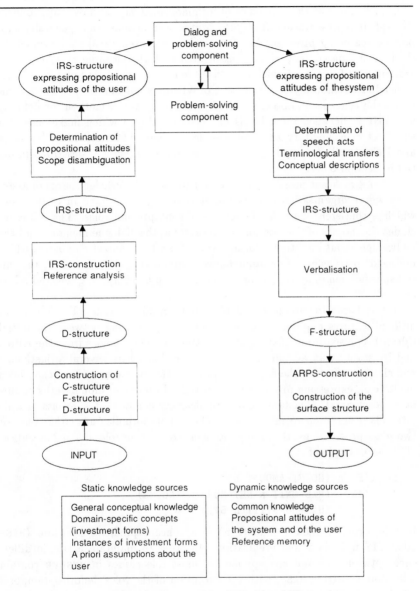

Figure 8.2: WISBER's architecture

paraphrasing (see Section 8.3.2). The design of the ontology follows certain principles aimed at the avoidance of terminological gaps and overlaps to yield an explicit representation of objects, states, and actions, thus generally supporting reasoning processes (as described in [Horacek 1989]). Consequently, the information content which is associated with the meaning of lexemes and grammatical functions (which comprise the lexical, syntactic-functional level) is distributed unevenly over the parts of WISBER's domain model (which comprises the conceptual, object-oriented level). However, a method for defining a transition between these levels has been developed which makes use of a small set of elementary and composable correspondence schemata [Horacek and Pyka 1988]. Its application to the generation process is described in detail in Section 8.3.4.

QUARK makes it possible to build and consult a knowledge source of assertions whose organisation reflects the epistemology embedded in QUIRK, and which is consistent with the definitions of concepts and roles. The ABox includes the models of the user and of the system, the dialogue memory, and the knowledge about investment forms. Apart from these knowledge bases, which are used to transfer information between different system modules, the initial specification of system utterances is built up by composing selected ABox entries.

IRS is based on predicate calculus, but contains a rich collection of additional features required by different levels of processing between the initial ('deep') representation of the system's utterance which comes from the ABox, and its state at an advanced stage of generation where several adjustments and changes effecting the final appearance of the utterance have already been made (e.g., expressing propositional attitudes in terms of modal verbs or surface speech acts). Constants and variables may denote states, events or time intervals in addition to individuals. The atomic formulas are either one- or two-place predications, the predicates being concepts or roles defined in QUIRK. (1) is an example of IRS:

(1)   ((E- n (MONEY-AMOUNT n))
       (AND (HAS-UNIT n NET-MONTHS-INCOME)
             (HAS-QUANTITY n 5)))

In this formula, (MONEY-AMOUNT n) is a concept predication, while (HAS-QUANTITY n 5) is a role predication. In order to maintain a simple difference between role and concept names, most role names in WISBER contain a heading substring HAS-, with the exception of the roles denoting temporal relations like BEFORE, DURING, AFTER, OCCURS, HOLDS, MEETS and OVERLAPS. In addition to the standard quantifiers **exist** $\exists$ and **forall** $\forall$, vague quantifiers (*a few*, *several*) or quantities (*two to three*, *less than five*, *only three*) can also be represented. Vague quantifiers can be evaluated by the ABox mechanism, but they do not belong to the system's generation competence. Indefinite and definite descriptions (*the man with a grey beard*) are also handled as quantifiers (i.e., they have a scope). The determiner E- in the previous formula is used for indefinite descriptions; the determiner DS is used for definite descriptions. Quantifications are always restricted by a VARIABLE RANGE (i.e. a semantic restrictor, such as (MONEY-AMOUNT n) in the above formula). IRS also provides means for representing propositional attitudes.

8.3   The Generation Component

The design of the architecture for WISBER's generation component is substantially influenced by the representation facilities of the embedding system and by the principles underlying the ontology of the domain model. Hence, the coverage of the domain model is pretty much dependent on (and, to some extent, limited by) the accuracy exhibited in the analysis of the underlying domain. However, meeting the strict ontological requirements in expressing the relevant domain aspects guarantees the availability of verbalisations for all parts of the model, even though a straightforward composition usually does not lead to fluent text.

The flexibility of IRS supports an approach enabling many slight and stepwise changes when processing at the semantic-pragmatic level is performed. Thus, progress in the generation procedure is characterised by a continuous development up to a certain point. However, when approaching the choice of words and associated decisions, the significant ontological differences between the conceptual and lexical levels demand a ridge in the overall process in order to obtain a specification in syntactic-functional terms. Once this level of representation is reached, several methods are known which are capable of producing adequate surface structures and, finally, the required sentences.

In order to obtain transparency in the internal development of transferring and modifying the initial specifications of system utterances, we have partitioned the entire generation process into several sequentially connected modules, and appropriate interfaces have been specified *a priori*. In the overall process, some exceptional capabilities are needed because of the ontological differences between the conceptual and lexical levels: operations on the conceptual level are of major importance and the repertoire of lexical choices must be rather powerful. Consequently, the entire generation process in WISBER, which is partitioned into six subtasks, includes the two essentially new ones: terminological transformations on the conceptual level (Section 8.3.2), and the verbalisation task responsible for the transition to the lexical level (Section 8.3.4). More traditional subtasks are the subsequent phases, involving surface transformations and syntactic realisation (Section 8.3.5). This set is completed by the starting phase devoted to text organisation (Section 8.3.1) and the task responsible for generating conceptual descriptions (Section 8.3.3), which work on the same level as the terminological transformations.

The structure that represents the initial specification for generation is produced by the central system component dedicated to dialogue control [Gerlach and Horacek 1989]. It results from one of the dialogue rules which are responsible for creating communicative system goals. This structure consists of a small set of propositional attitudes (as defined in [Sprenger and Gerlach 1988]) expressing wants of the system effecting the knowledge of the other conversant. Hence, the representation level of the initial structure for the generation side is identical to the level of the final structure produced by the analysis component. In the current version of the system, only a single want is selected as a communicative goal because the text organisation module is still in its preliminary stage. In particular, the treatment of belief discrepancies which may result from, e.g., the discovery of presupposition failures (see [Bergmann and Gerlach 1987]), is not yet elaborated and included in the dialogue component. Given an initial specification in the terms described above the goal of the generation component is to produce an utterance or a sequence of utterances which is considered to be the best choice among the system's repertoire of actions to achieve the intended purpose. The following sections describe in detail the creation of utterances and the effect of the overall context on the vast number of decisions involved in this process.

8.3.1   Text organisation

The first step of the generation process consists in appropriately associating speech acts with the relevant system wants and grouping them into a specific order. WISBER can deal with the speech acts ASK, ASSERT, and RECOMMEND. The propositional content which is created by the domain-dependent problem solving component [Busche and Schachter-Radig 1988] is still simple at this stage. It is either a role associated with the investment under discussion, or a specific investment form and (some of) its property values. Nevertheless, the original structure is subject to significant changes and enhancements in the course of the subsequent processing phases.

Occasionally, the system needs to acquire some additional information in order to achieve progress in its consultation and reasoning processes (i.e., the system wants to know something). Whenever there is sufficient indication that the user might be a promising candidate to collect that information from, she is asked about this information. Hence, the speech act ASK is generated. These indications may go back to default assumptions, or the required information may simply refer to a mutually known user want. The speech act ASSERT is chosen if the associated proposition is part of or can be derived from the factual knowledge of the system (according to the reasoning capabilities of the ABox) and there is an actual purpose to communicate it (i.e., the system wants the user to know something). The standard example is a reply to a request for information, as in utterance [11] in Figure 8.1. Other purposes are the adjustment of incorrect user beliefs, and repair measures to remove presupposition failures.

In the cases treated so far, only a single speech act is generated. If, however, the system wants to communicate a proposition which, usually in a less precise form, belongs to the user's want context, a **recommendation** is the appropriate speech act. In consultation situations, the creation of this goal is based on the prior existence of a user want either specified by the user herself, or derived in the course of the reasoning processes initiated by the dialogue control component. The recommendation is followed by an assertion which puts the emphasis on a particular feature of the consultation object which is expected to be of particular interest to the user (see Section 8.3.3). In the current version of the system, only a single feature (to which the highest plausibility of being interesting is attributed) is selected to be mentioned. Achieving more flexibility in this respect would be a useful area for future work.

In an extended version of the system, we plan to use rhetorical predicates to organise the content of speech acts. This will help, for instance, in describing and comparing closely competing alternatives in an early, imprecise recommendation. In such cases, the application of the 'compare and contrast' strategy (as it has been identified in [McKeown 1982]) would be an appropriate method. However, its original texture would have to undergo some modifications due to the peculiarities of consultation situations. When proposing two or three investment forms as candidates for investing someone's money, the emphasis lies significantly more on the presentation of their differences than on their common properties. Hence, the common properties have been the basis on which the selected investment forms have been chosen among all available ones to meet the user's requirements most closely (so the user should be familiar with them). Because the consultation process must go on by increasing the concreteness of the proposal, the distinctive properties have to be described with special care in order to incline the user to utter appropriate judgements about the proposed alternatives and to express her preferences more clearly.

8.3.2 Terminological transformations

Once appropriate speech acts have been determined, their associated propositional content is subject to further modification. The contribution here of terminological transformations, an essentially new task in a generator, consists in selecting an appropriate level of granularity on a purely conceptual basis by performing terminological equivalence operations, if required. The aim is to choose a concise, but still comprehensible, alternative according to the known and/or assumed experience of the user.

The method is realised by a tool called FTRANSLATE [Bergmann 1987] which works very similar to the algorithm described in [Stallard 1986] for NIKL expressions. It consists of two procedures with inverse functionality: CONTRACT and EXPAND. For our purposes, only EXPAND is of relevance, because, by convention, the dialogue component creates always the most compact expression when alternatives are available. EXPAND takes a formula and recursively substitutes subexpressions for selected concepts or roles according to relevant QUIRK definitions. The expansion stops when no more concepts (and roles) flagged for the purpose of being substituted are encountered. The resulting structure can be built by methods known from classification, and it is logically equivalent to the original one as long as only defined concepts are involved.

For purposes of generation, it is sometimes preferable to relax the strict requirement of logical equivalence in favour of producing simpler and, therefore, more easily comprehensible expressions even though the results may occasionally represent overgeneralisations or may contain inaccuracies when compared to the original specifications. Moreover, when a concept is a specialisation of more than one superconcept, EXPAND can choose how to continue the terminological expansion and how to associate additional roles with either of the superconcepts.

However, FTRANSLATE does not consider these cases at the current stage of development.

When applying FTRANSLATE to the generation process, a specialised concept can be alternatively expressed by a more general one which must be augmented by additional roles and appropriately restricted fillers to maintain terminological equivalence. The choice of which alternative is preferred in a concrete discourse situation is guided by pursuing two partially conflicting Gricean maxims:

- the resulting utterance should be as concise as possible, but still contain the necessary information (including, in particular, co-operative overanswering); and

- all parts of the utterance should be comprehensible for the other conversant.

Consequently, the most concise expression is always the preferred one, unless there is evidence for the fact that some of its parts do not fall into the dialogue partner's command of terminological knowledge. While the second criterion constitutes the necessary condition for communicative adequacy, the first one aims at achieving possible improvements. The associated procedures, however, work exactly in the opposite order. The most concise alternative is produced in the first way and modifications (i.e., expansions) are made later according to concrete demands derivable from the dialogue partner model. This approach helps to keep the overall effort as low as possible because the most compact alternative is best suited for reasoning processes. The requirements of presentation, however, may cause a change in the suitability of alternatives.

The quality achievable in producing alternative expressions depends heavily on the accuracy exhibited in the design of the appropriate terminological definitions. Hence, it is a very delicate and difficult task to express features of a particular fact in an explicit way by defining terminologically equivalent structures. However, this is also a requirement of the principles of ontology on which the design of the domain model is based. The difficulty is even more severe when confronted with the restricted expressiveness that is common to most knowledge representation formalisms but necessary in order to achieve sufficient manageability. Either the power of the knowledge representation formalism is not sufficient to express the necessary relations or a crucial language element is not taken into account by the associated reasoning component (like structural descriptions (SD) in KL-ONE based classifiers and reasoners). We accept the first case as a hard limitation of our approach (i.e., the content of our model is as complex only as we are able to represent its parts explicitly). In the second case, we add special purpose reasoners to overcome the shortcomings of the generally applicable facilities.

Moreover, the attainment of sensitive assumptions about the user's experience by inferring them from the course of the dialogue is also far from easy. Still, we are able to perform some terminological transformations based on simple *a priori* assumptions. For instance, in WISBER's domain model, a *Notgroschen* (money set aside for a rainy day) is defined to be fully equivalent to a savings account of (at least) two net months income (see the formal definitions in Figure 8.3). According to these definitions, the meaning of the special notion *Notgroschen* can be alternatively expressed by a more general one (*savings account*), accompanied by the more precise value restriction (VR) which is associated with the definition of *Notgroschen*. Assuming that the user is unfamiliar with the term *Notgroschen*, the production of utterance [5] in Figure 8.1 resulting from the expansion of *Notgroschen* to *a savings account* together with the restrictive attribute *with more than two net months income* is preferred.

Just as for concepts, it is also possible to replace the appearances of certain roles in IRS-formulas. This is the case for roles which are associated with a complex meaning and can be defined more explicitly in terms of possibly rather complex conceptual structures consisting of concepts and roles associated with less complex meanings. The terminological equivalence is expressed by transformation rules, which have the same expressive power as structural

```
(DEFCONCEPT NOTGROSCHEN
    (SPECIALIZES SAVINGS-ACCOUNT)
    (ROLE HAS-VALUE (VR AMOUNT-OF-NOTGROSCHEN)))

(DEFCONCEPT AMOUNT-OF-NOTGROSCHEN
    (SPECIALIZES AMOUNT-OF-MONEY)
    (ROLE HAS-QUANTITY (VR (CONSTANTS 2)))
    (ROLE HAS-UNIT     (VR (CONSTANTS NET-MONTHS-INCOME)))))
```

Figure 8.3: Terminological definitions

descriptions. For reasons of an efficient application of terminological replacements, these rules are preferred to equivalent Tbox definitions because they
are easier to access.

In KL-ONE, structural description allows us to express how roles of a concept interrelate in terms of other concepts. Structural descriptions are usually
applied to express the meaning attributed to a specialised concept with respect
to (one of) its generalisations. Our application deviates from this usage insofar
as we consider only cases where the meaning of the specialisation manifests
itself merely in an additional role or in a role restriction (hence, the specialised
concept must not be marked as primitive). Consequently, the meaning associated with this role (or with the restriction) can alternatively be expressed by
the structural description, which is exactly what we want.

To get access to the concepts involved in a structural description without
changing their meaning, we need to make an embedded 'call' to each of these
concepts, and to bind the formal parameters of the called concept to the actual
arguments to be used in the context of this call. The structural description
(the box labelled SD in Figure 8.5) has associated with it a version of another
concept. The structure of this internal version is isomorphic to the regular
generic version. The interrelations between the roles are expressed by a set of
pairs of role chains (the double-bordered boxes in Figure 8.5). In each pair of
role chains, the paths obtained by following these chains must lead to the same
concept. Occasionally, a filler may be restricted to a certain subtype of the
value restriction (via VRDIFF, the value restriction difference). The empty path
is also feasible, which is represented by the predicate SELF. In our mechanism,
a pair of role chains is expressed by an equation which operates on the two
role chains.

As an example, Figure 8.4 shows a rule which explicates the meaning

```
(DEFCONCEPT  INVESTMENT
  (ROLE HAS-LIQUIDITY      (VR (CONSTANTS HIGH))))


                    ====>


  (DEFCONCEPT
    (SD POSSIBILITY
      (= (HAS-EXPERIENCER) (HAS-POSSESSOR))               ; [1]
      (= ((VRDIFF HAS-EXPERIENCEE CONVERT) HAS-AGENT)  ; [2]
         (HAS-POSSESSOR))
      (= (HAS-EXPERIENCEE HAS-SOURCE) SELF)              ; [3]
      (= (HAS-EXPERIENCEE OCCURS DURING) (HAS-TERM)))) ; [4]
```

Figure 8.4: A terminological transformation rule

of the role called HAS-LIQUIDITY—to be more precise, *high liquidity*—which represents the liquidity associated with an investment. If an investment is associated with high liquidity then it must be possible for the owner of the investment to convert the investment into money again during its term. This is expressed by a POSSIBILITY which refers to this investment, its owner (reached via HAS-POSSESSOR) and the term of the investment (the time interval reached via HAS-TERM). By means of the associated role chains shown in Figure 8.4, some relations are defined which express that:

- the possibility is at the disposal of the owner of the investment (equation [1]): the EXPERIENCER of the POSSIBILITY must be the same as the POSSESSOR of the INVESTMENT;

- its owner is also the agent of the conversion action (equation [2]): the EXPERIENCEE of the POSSIBILITY must be a CONVERT action due to a value restriction: its AGENT must be the POSSESSOR of the investment;

- the object which suffers the conversion is the investment itself (equation [3]): the EXPERIENCEE of the POSSIBILITY must also have a SOURCE which is required to be the INVESTMENT itself; and

- the possibility of conversion occurs during the term of the investment (equation [4]): the EXPERIENCEE of the POSSIBILITY (CONVERT) takes place (OCCURS) at a certain time interval which holds DURING the time interval that is associated with the TERM of the INVESTMENT.

The corresponding KL-ONE structure is presented in the graph in Figure 8.5. Thus, *high liquidity associated with an investment* can be paraphrased by *the possibility of its owner to have access to the money during the term of investment.* Again, the relevance of this rule for a concrete discourse situation is determined by an *a priori* assumption, i.e., that the user is assumed to be unfamiliar with the meaning of a certain notion (in this case, the liquidity of an investment, represented by the role HAS-LIQUIDITY).

When applying the rule in Figure 8.4 to the formula in Figure 8.6 which contains a reference to the role to be re-expressed, the state (s) representing this role (HAS-LIQUIDITY) is first replaced by a subformula denoting the concept copy attached to the structural description (i.e. the POSSIBILITY). Thereafter, the content of the equations is transduced into logic formulas and appended to the newly inserted subformula. This is a rather straightforward process in those cases which we are able to handle (no problems of scoping arise due to a restriction to singular objects in the transformations): variables and the semantic restrictors (denoting the concepts they are instances of) are inserted for each concept which occurs on a path of any of the role chains. Moreover, role predications are generated for each part of the role chains (excluding multiple occurrences) and they are inserted in a suitable place in the formula (according to the scope of the variables referred to in the role predications).

Figure 8.7 illustrates the effect of the rule in Figure 8.4 when being applied to the subexpression that is to be expanded in expression Figure 8.6, which is the IRS-formula representing the system utterance at the stage of processing before the terminological transformations are applied. The formula in Figure 8.6 can be paraphrased as *Do you want to have an investment with high liquidity?* when addressing the user (the speech act is **ask**). Figure 8.7 no longer contains a term the user is not familiar with; thus, utterance [7] in Figure 8.1 is the preferred form of asking the user whether she wants the investment to be associated with high liquidity.

8.3.3   Generating conceptual descriptions

The intermediate result obtained so far is a single speech act or a sequence of speech acts that bear slots for IRS-formulas representing the associated contents. These formulas, however, may still contain expressions that denote entities in an ambiguous way. In order to make the entities referred to easily identifiable for the hearer, further descriptive and distinctive properties (a conceptual specialisation or, in most cases, further roles) are added.

First of all, the values of the features specifying definiteness or indefiniteness are determined for those variables which have been inserted in the formula as a result of the terminological transformations. Such a feature yields

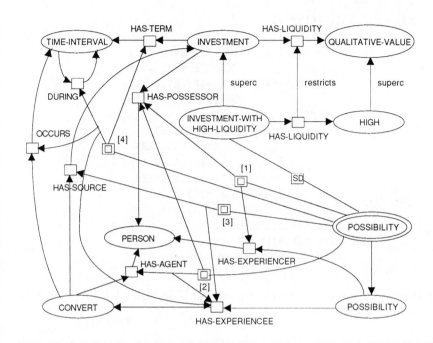

Figure 8.5: The structural description attached to `INVESTMENT-WITH-HIGH-LIQUIDITY`

```
((E- w (WANT w))
 ((E- s
      (STATE s
           ((DS x (INVESTMENT x))
            (HAS-LIQUIDITY x HIGH))))
   (AND (HAS-EXPERIENCEE w s)
        (HAS-EXPERIENCER w USER)))))
```

Figure 8.6: IRS-representation of utterance [7] in Figure 8.1 before the terminological transformation

```
((E- w (WANT w))
  ((E- y (POSSIBILITY y))
    ((E- f (CONVERT f))
      (AND ((E- ti1 (AND (TIME-INTERVAL ti1)
                         (OCCURS f ti1)))
            ((DS ti2 (AND (TIME-INTERVAL ti2)
                          (DURING ti1 ti2)))
             ((DS x (INVESTMENT x))
              (AND (DS p (AND (PERSON p)
                              (HAS-POSSESSOR x p)
                              (HAS-AGENT f p)
                              (HAS-EXPERIENCER y p)))
                   (HAS-TERM x ti2)
                   (HAS-SOURCE f x)))))
           (HAS-EXPERIENCEE y f))
      (AND (HAS-EXPERIENCEE w y)
           (HAS-EXPERIENCER w USER)))))
```

Figure 8.7: IRS-representation of utterance [7] in Figure 8.1 after the terminological transformation

---

the value INDEFINITE if the referred entity has not been mentioned earlier in the dialogue and if there exist more entities of the same type in the domain of discourse; otherwise, it yields the value DEFINITE. Because of context, some of the definite descriptions can be replaced by constants. In the formula in Figure 8.7, this applies to the expression referring to the possessor of the investment (referred to by the variable p, which is in turn replaced by the constant USER).

Our generator is also able to create a pragmatic anaphor to denote a particular object, if an action involving this object but not explicitly mentioning it has been uttered previously. For instance, the selection of the determiner *the* in utterance [3] in Figure 8.1 (*Which term should the investment have?*) is justified by the reference to an investing action in utterance [2], the preceding user utterance (*I want to invest 40000* DM). We think that significant psychological justifications are present for the assignment of definiteness in this instance. In pursuing the task of consultation, the system's dialogue component has made an attempt to increase the degree of precision concerning the specification of the user's desire to invest her money. Thereby, the object of the investing action has been involved in the associated reasoning process (in fact, it is the dominant object in this process). Consequently, its inclusion in the focus of attention, which is the usual criterion to assign the referring NP a feature indicating definiteness, seems to be perfectly adequate.

Next, the selection of additional characteristic properties for expanding entity descriptions is performed. In the case of an indefinite description a combination of property values is determined which uniquely identifies the entity denoted by the description. For definite descriptions, the selected properties and their values must be recognisably distinct from those of potentially confusable objects according to the features established as being mutually known in the course of the dialogue. In the representation obtained so far (shown in Figure 8.7), the investment x, if not characterised more precisely, might still be confused with the savings account introduced in utterance [5] in Figure 8.1. Thus, the HAS-VALUE role (and its filler, *40000* DM) is chosen to assist the hearer in distinguishing clearly among the candidate referents (the set of assets referred to in the dialogue), thus excluding for sure the savings account with its known value of five net months income. Hence, the investment is uniquely identified by the HAS-VALUE role. Therefore, the role predication (HAS-POSSESSOR x USER), which expresses a known fact, can be removed. The resulting formula representing utterance [7] at the actual processing stage is shown in the formula in Figure 8.8.

The selection of appropriate features for a conveniently identifiable entity description is based on the content of the dialogue memory and on domain-dependent preference lists expressing the relative importance and the salience of competing properties. For an asset, its value, which is expressed by the associated amount of money, has been given the highest priority (this property qualifies best as uniquely identifying because of the wide range of possible values) followed by the interest rate (because of its high degree of importance for the investor).

Moreover, all variables (which denote concepts) and all roles in the formula which refer to discourse entities or relations already mentioned in the dialogue so far are flagged to indicate their reference to mutually known discourse objects. These flags are used during the verbalisation phase to indicate optionality in expressing mutually known entities and relations. Therefore, the expansion of a conceptual description does not necessarily have effects on the final appearance of the utterance on the surface. It is up to the verbalisation phase whether and how the parts of the conceptual description are lexically expressed. In the instance under discussion, *der Betrag (the sum)* is the chosen expression referring to the investment. Taken on its own, it is still referentially ambiguous; however, because the term of the investment (which has been introduced in utterance [3] as a property of this investment) is mentioned again, we consider the reference to be conveniently resolvable

```
((E- w (WANT w))
  ((E- y (POSSIBILITY y))
    ((E- f (CONVERT f))
      (AND ((E- ti1 (AND (TIME-INTERVAL ti1)
                          (OCCURS f ti1)))
            ((DS ti2 (AND (TIME-INTERVAL ti2)
                          (DURING ti1 ti2)))
              ((DS x (INVESTMENT x))
                (AND (DS m (AND (MONEY-AMOUNT m)
                                (HAS-QUANTITY m 40000)
                                (HAS-UNIT m DM)
                                (HAS-VALUE x m)))
                     (HAS-TERM x ti2)
                     (HAS-SOURCE f x)))))
            (HAS-EXPERIENCEE y f)
            (HAS-EXPERIENCER y USER)
            (HAS-AGENT f USER))
      (AND (HAS-EXPERIENCEE w y)
           (HAS-EXPERIENCER w USER)))))
```

Figure 8.8: IRS-representation of utterance [7] before the verbalisation phase

for the user in the overall context. However, it should be noted that neither the check for a potential ambiguity nor a verification of the contextual resolvability reflecting the above considerations is performed by the verbalisation component.

8.3.4   Verbalisation

At this stage the content of a speech act is completely specified, so the verbalisation process can now be applied. It is preceded by a small procedure that determines whether the speech act itself is to be verbalised explicitly (e.g., for a recommendation) or it is to be expressed implicitly by selecting an appropriate surface speech act. In the latter case, only the propositional content (the experiencee of the speech act) is subject to further treatment by the verbalisation procedure; otherwise the entire IRS-expression is considered.

Moreover, decisions concerning the generation of modal verbs are also made prior to the proper verbalisation process because of the significance of the addressee of the speech act for the feasibility of the selection (this refers, in particular, to the choice between *möchten* (*want*) and *sollen* (*should*)). If the dialogue partner is supposed to clarify a certain intention, she may be asked by *Do you want that (if)* ... ? or, more concisely by *Should* ... ? In the latter case the use of *should* is only feasible because the addressee of the utterance is identical to, or in some relation with, the person whose intention is referred to by the modal verb *should*. This effect of the speech act on the admissibility of the word choice is not captured by the correspondence schemata applied in the verbalisation procedure. Therefore, some restructuring is performed first (still on the level of the IRS) which results in changing WANT to SOLLEN (*should*) and in removing the subexpression which refers to the experiencer of the propositional attitude. In our reference dialogue, the selection of *soll* (*should*) proves to be necessary because an alternative sentence with *möchten* (*want*) would be stylistically awkward.

The verbalisation process is responsible for finding a suitable selection of predicates on the lexical level (attributed to lexemes and grammatical functions) that express appropriately the information content associated with the predicates on the conceptual level (attributed to concepts and roles). This task is, in fact, an inverted lexeme interpretation which is essentially new in this particular form. This transition involves considerable restructuring because the (relevant) meanings of lexemes and grammatical functions may be related unevenly to the information content associated with the predicates used in our domain model.

Consequently, structures on the conceptual level can be expanded or contracted to yield suitable correspondences on the lexical level. A set of elementary schemata, called ZOOM schemata, serves the purpose of defining correspondences between the atomic elements on both representation levels: concept and role nodes and connecting links on the conceptual level, and lexemes and grammatical functions on the lexical level. This includes simple one-to-one mappings expressed by MICRO ZOOM schemata as well as operations which involve more complex structures on the conceptual level. Also the 'empty lexeme' (a word with an uninstantiated PRED feature) is a valid mapping result which is most suitably chosen for expressing major categories like *person*, *object*, and *time interval* in a given context. Later, an F-structure representing an empty lexeme yields a pronoun on the surface, unless the PRED feature is instantiated as the result of another mapping operation (i.e., the empty lexeme is effectively overwritten).

Because the lexical level is identified as the basic and original one (as it reflects the structure of the language itself), ZOOM schemata always cover exactly one lexical element. In addition to the (basic) MICRO ZOOM schema, more complex schemata may cover any of the following (connected) structures on the conceptual level:

- a role node and both its adjacent links (this is the STANDARD ZOOM schema);
- a concept node, a role node, and a link connecting them (the MIX ZOOM schema); or
- two roles, all their adjacent links, and a concept which establishes a connection between the roles via two of these links (the MACRO ZOOM schema).

The MICRO ZOOM schema maps any type of node (a concept or a role node) onto a noun, a verb, an adjective, or a feature value. Complex noun phrases and complete sentences are built by composing nouns with the aid of suitable auxiliary verbs and grammatical functions (the genitive attribute, in particular) which are possible mapping results of the connecting links. By these compositions, phrases like *the name of the project*, *the name is* WISBER, *the project has a name*, *the name* WISBER are produced from a structure on the conceptual level which consists of two concepts, PROJECT and STRING (its instance is WISBER in this example), and the connecting role HAS-NAME. These clauses can be joined adequately to yield coherent sentences. Moreover, function verbs may also be specified as correspondences instead of auxiliaries: Thus, the creation of *the project bears a name* is also possible.

Methods leading to results similar to those of the STANDARD ZOOM schema are also found in other approaches. These schemata map role nodes (together with both their adjacent links) onto grammatical functions. The results can be combined with verbs and nouns derived by MICRO ZOOM schemata. For instance, a structure consisting of an OWNING state and its associated entities, the fillers of the EXPERIENCER and EXPERIENCEE roles, is mapped onto the verb *besitzen* (*to own*) where the subject and object slots bear the NPs derived from the entities.

The MIX ZOOM schema covers nominalisations derived from verbs denoting processes or states (referring to their agent and theme or, experiencer and experiencee, respectively). Thus, the conceptual structure corresponding to the noun *leader* does not only comprise the concept called LEADING (as the conceptual structure mapped onto the verb *leading* would), but it includes also the associated role HAS-AGENT and the link connecting them. Consequently, the link connecting the HAS-AGENT role and its filler may be mapped onto the auxiliary *to be* by means of a MICRO ZOOM schema, thus contributing to the phrase *x is a leader*.

By applying the MACRO ZOOM schema, a large conceptual construct can be expressed by a single element on the lexical level (typically by a genitive attribute). For instance, the most concise way to express the relation between bonds and the bank issuing these bonds is by means of a genitive attribute. Hence, the MACRO ZOOM schema comprises a concept (ISSUING), two roles

(HAS-AGENT and HAS-THEME) and all links to form a bridge between both their role fillers (the bank as the issuer and the bonds as the thing being issued). Whereas the meaning of the relation between the bank and the bonds is still obvious in this case, ambiguities may arise in other instances due to the conciseness with which the underlying fact is expressed: in *Miller's project*, the person referred to may be either the leader of the project or simply a person working on it (hence, the concept being in the center of the construct covered by the MACRO ZOOM schema is either LEADING or WORKING). Thus, application of a suitable combination of correspondence schemata may yield *Bill leads the project, Bill is the leader of the project*, and *Bill's project* as alternative verbalisations for the same conceptual structure differing only in the degree of explicitness.

Moreover, relations represented explicitly on the conceptual level for purposes of reasoning can be expressed implicitly on the lexical level. This is done by the application of SUBSTITUTION schemata which enable the production of concise utterances as well as the generation of some kinds of paraphrases. This facility is a feature not yet observed in other approaches. Its effect is always the unification of two syntactic-functional structures derived from conceptual nodes. SUBSTITUTION schemata occur in companion with MICRO ZOOM and MIX ZOOM schemata. A SUBSTITUTION schema may refer to a role node and to the concept filling this role (a SUBSTITUTION schema of type 1). For instance, the combined meaning of the role named HAS-TITLE and its filler, the concept STRING, can be expressed by *title* or by, for example, WISBER, if either of the conceptual units has been mapped onto the empty lexeme so that the unification of the associated F-structures succeeds.

Moreover, any of the phrases *the leader, a leader*, or *(the) leaders* may be obtained when mapping the conceptual construct consisting of the concept PERSON and the link by which this concept is attached to the role HAS-AGENT, which is, together with the concept LEADING and the link connecting them covered by a MIX ZOOM schema (see left side of Figure 8.9). Furthermore, a SUBSTITUTION schema may refer to two concept nodes, thereby also covering the joining role and both its adjacent links (a SUBSTITUTION schema of type 2). A typical example is an expression referring to a person by her name without expressing the category *(person)* explicitly. In this case, the empty lexeme is the selected mapping result for the concept PERSON so that a unification with the lexeme denoting her name succeeds (see the right side of Figure 8.9). Unification may also fail due to a feature other than PRED; for example, SPEC or NUMBER may result in a clash under certain circumstances.

The ZOOM and SUBSTITUTION schemata provide a way of achieving significant flexibility in expressing the content of conceptual structures. This is particularly the case for the verbalisation of objects which are quantifiable by measurements. Two substitutions are usually involved to produce refer-

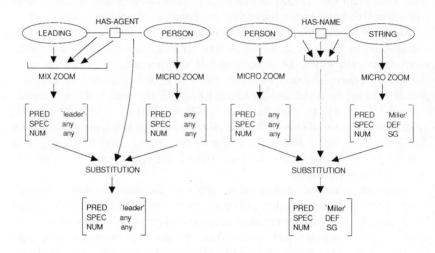

Figure 8.9: SUBSTITUTION schemata of type 1 (left side) and type 2 (right side)

---

ring expressions which are composed of a quantity (an integer, the filler of a HAS-QUANTITY role) and a unit (a unit denomination, the filler of a HAS-UNIT role), thus identifying the measurement. If an object is typically identifiable by some quantifiable property, an adequate referring expression may be produced by a series of substitutions. First, a measurement is referred to by means of its quantity and its unit, and the resulting expression is used again to refer to the object that is quantified by this measurement. A typical example in our domain is the identification of an asset by the amount of money denoting its value, simply yielding, for example, *40000* DM. Furthermore, the role HAS-VALUE may be expressed by a grammatical function (a prepositional attribute in this case): *Pfandbriefe um 40000* DM (*bonds by 40000* DM), which is derived by applying a STANDARD ZOOM schema. Finally, this relation can be expressed explicitly by *Pfandbriefe in der Höhe von 40000* DM (*bonds at a value of 40000* DM) or, in an inverse form, *40000* DM *in Form von Pfandbriefen* (*40000* DM *in form of bonds*). Both expressions are derived by MICRO ZOOM schemata.

It seems to us that our representation of measurements is more general, but less richly elaborated than Dale's representation [Dale, this volume]. Moreover, the flexibility of our verbalisation mechanism enables us to produce a greater variety of surface expressions. In any case, both approaches could profit from elements of the other.

In order to express comparisons in a compact way we have introduced the element cmp(op, a, b) into IRS, where op (operation) denotes a comparison operator and a and b stand for variables denoting measurements (this construct has no counterpart in QUIRK). In preparation for the verbalisation phase this expression is transformed so that the comparison operator can be handled like a role node to which two links are attached for connecting the measurements appropriately.

From that, phrases like *with more than* and *is greater than* can be produced by applying MICRO ZOOM schemata. Moreover, it is also possible to generate tense features for expressing the information provided by time intervals (associated with states and events) which are related in a way proposed by Allen (this is described in [Horacek and Pyka 1988] in detail).

A collection of some typical mapping schemata is presented in Table 8.1. However, this table contains some simplifications: for instance, in order to map the role HAS-AGENT onto the grammatical function SUBJECT, the involved action and the corresponding verb must fit properly. This information is specified in the corresponding mapping schema, but is omitted in Table 8.1 for the sake of readability.

When the schemata are suitably defined, the application of local mappings and the composition of the results lead, by means of unification, to a consistent functional structure. This is done in the following way: for each conceptual element in an IRS expression, specifications of all locally legal mappings are generated and ordered according to stylistic preference criteria explained later. According to this ordering, those elements which are newly introduced in the dialogue and, therefore, must be expressed unconditionally, precede the others which have been flagged to indicate that they refer to mutually known entities or relations.

The production of (partial) F-structures derived from (single) mappings and the attempt to compose several of them is done by selecting the available alternatives in a depth-first fashion. Starting from the formula shown in Figure 8.8, WANT, POSSIBILITY, and CONVERT are mapped onto verbs by means of the MICRO ZOOM schema. Moreover, the roles borne by these concepts are mapped onto appropriate case slots, which is done by the STANDARD ZOOM schema. Most of their slots are easily filled (either by a structure resulting from the mapping of one of these concepts or by an NP obtained after mapping the constant USER). In Figure 8.10, the creation of the partial F-structure corresponding to *Möchten Sie zurückgreifen ... ? (Do you want to have access to ... ?)* is presented. The order in which the operations are applied does not really matter. The expansion of this F-structure by mapping CONVERT and its roles follows the same lines.

Note that the generation of an F-structure for a lexical unit that requires

Schema Class	Type of Schema		Schema Instances	
STANDARD ZOOM	concept	⇔ lexeme	BUYING	⇔ kaufen (to buy)
			BOND	⇔ Wertpapier (bond)
			RECOMMEND	⇔ empfehlenswert (recommendable)
			TIME-INTERVAL	⇔ empty lexeme
	role	⇔ grammatical function	HAS-AGENT	⇔ SUBJECT
			DURING	⇔ ADJUNCT + während (during)
MICRO ZOOM	role	⇔ lexeme	HAS-TERM	⇔ Laufzeit (term)
	link	⇔ auxiliary	INVESTMENT/HAS-TERM	⇔ haben (to have)
			HAS-TERM/MEASUREMENT	⇔ sein (to be)
	link	⇔ grammatical function	HAS-TERM/ INVESTMENT	⇔ GENITIVE-ATTRIBUTE
MIX ZOOM	concept role	⇔ lexeme	LEADING, HAS-AGENT	⇔ Leiter (leader)
MACRO ZOOM	concept roles	⇔ grammatical function	LEADING, HAS-AGENT, HAS-THEME	⇔ GENITIVE-ATTRIBUTE
SUBSTITUTION	link	⇔ —	INTEREST-RATE/MEASUREMENT	⇔ —
	role	⇔ —	HAS-VALUE	⇔ —

Table 8.1: A collection of mapping schemata

some dependent structure(s) (like obligatory case roles) also involves the creation of features for these fillers (NUMBER, SPEC, and INF in Figure 8.10). If a new partial result clashes with the functional structures produced so far (a **lexical** clash), backtracking is invoked. This is also the case if a conceptual element covered by an already completed mapping operation is referred to once again by the actual mapping specification (a **conceptual** clash). For instance, generating *leader* for the concept LEADING, and SUBJECT for the attached role HAS-AGENT, produces a conceptual clash because both mappings comprise the role HAS-AGENT (and, of course, a lexical clash, too).

So far, all parts of the formula in Figure 8.8 outside of the scope of time interval ti1 have been consumed. The time interval itself is then mapped onto the empty lexeme and the result is integrated into the F-structure containing *zurückgreifen* by means of a SUBSTITUTION of type 2 (via the OCCURS role) so that the structures produced for ti1 and f are unified (this does not modify the intermediate result). Furthermore, the role HAS-TERM is mapped onto the noun *Laufzeit* (*term*) via a MICRO ZOOM schema. Thereafter it is attached to *zurückgreifen* via a STANDARD ZOOM schema which creates an adjunct (ADJ) including a PCASE feature, thus linking ti1 and ti2 (see the upper part of Figure 8.11).

The search process stops when all (obligatory) conceptual elements are covered and the resulting F-structure is complete (i.e. there is a single F-structure comprising all partial mapping results, and this structure does not contain an uninstantiated obligatory slot). If the resulting F-structure is not complete, the process is continued by mapping the optional elements until a complete F-structure covering at least the obligatory elements is produced (if this is not possible, backtracking is invoked to try alternate mappings). At the end, a suitable function verb may be inserted if a noun phrase has been produced instead of a complete sentence.

In our example, all obligatory elements are already mapped (the investment x and its value are known), but the theme of *zurückgreifen* is still uninstantiated. Hence, an NP is generated for x which could simply be *the investment*. However, because x is marked to be known, an empty lexeme is the preferred mapping result, for which the NP *der Betrag* (*the sum*) resulting from (MONEY-AMOUNT m) via a MICRO ZOOM schema is substituted as a prepositional object (POBJ) by a SUBSTITUTION schema of type 2 via the role HAS-VALUE (see the lower part of Figure 8.11). Hence, the amount of money has been included to avoid empty lexemes in the final result. As the F-structure is now complete, the verbalisation process stops.

The verbalisation process involves choices between alternative mappings which raise conditions on the resulting structure, thus restricting the applicability of further mappings. Decisions are made implicitly by favouring what is considered to be the locally best choice (according to the ordering) and by

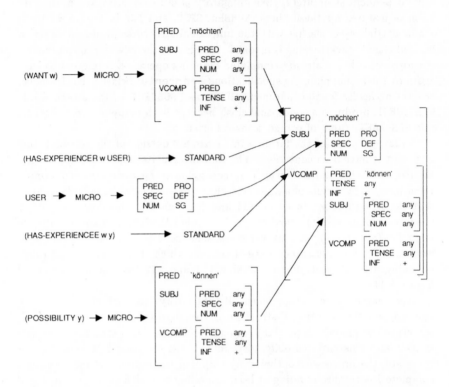

Figure 8.10: Unification of partial mappings via MICRO ZOOM and STANDARD ZOOM schemata

accepting the first legal solution. This simple mechanism has turned out to be reasonable in examples of the complexity treated so far. The ordering is based on stylistic criteria as well as on the exploitation of contextual information obtained from the dialogue memory. Stylistic criteria comprise the avoidance of indefinite pronouns if possible, the production of complete sentences, and a preference for concise verbalisations (unless they contain parts to be focussed in an implicit form only). This preference is mainly influenced by the common knowledge established so far in the discourse. The question of whether or not to verbalise entities and relations which are mutually known is the reason for omitting the syntactically optional attribute *of the investment* in sentence (7), because the investment and its term have been introduced previously in the dialogue.

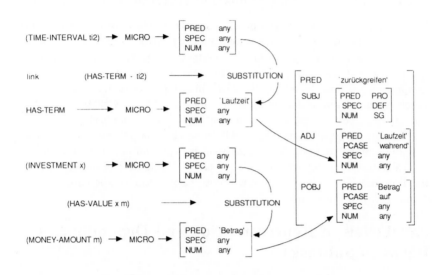

Figure 8.11: Unification of partial mappings via SUBSTITUTION schemata

The relations with quantification and scoping have been elaborated for simple cases only. Determiners in IRS-formulas are mapped onto SPEC and NUMBER features in a straightforward way. The conditions for a forced topicalisation identified in [Horacek 1987] have not been integrated into our generator. So far, the only place where scoping is relevant concerns the determination of main and subordinate clauses when the creation of relative clauses is performed.

Once the level of functional descriptions is reached, the creation of certain syntactic reductions justified by contextual dialogue information can be achieved more easily than by the mapping schemata just introduced. As an alternative to utterance [9] in Figure 8.1, the recommendation can also be expressed by *Pfandbriefe sind empfehlenswert* (*Bonds are recommendable*). The (intermediate) result after applying the correspondence schemata is the functional structure corresponding to the sentence *Es ist empfehlenswert Pfandbriefe zu kaufen* (*It is advisable to buy bonds*). The existence of the indefinite pronoun in the subject location triggers its replacement by the subject of the infinitive group. The omission of the infinitive *to buy*, which is necessary in order to ensure grammaticality, is justified by the fact that the connection between the involved action (BUYING) and the bonds is known to the other conversant.

8.3.5   Surface transformations and syntactic realisation

Components of comparable competence are also found in other systems (e.g., SUTRA [Busemann 1983] in the system HAM-ANS [Hoeppner *et al.* 1983]). In WISBER, these tasks are performed by the tactical generator NUGGET [Jablonski, Rau and Ritzke 1987]. The F-structures produced by the verbalisation component are transduced to structures in the propositional language ARPS which represent the initial specifications for NUGGET. The tactical generator consists of a specific syntactic component, a structure simplifying component and a morphological component. All these components work with a functionally augmented DCG. The theoretical background of NUGGET as well as its realisation and implementation are already described elsewhere [Jablonski, Rau and Ritzke 1988], so we will not describe this component in a more detailed way in this chapter.

8.4   Levels of Representation and Dependencies Between Subtasks

The flow of control in our generation module is a purely sequential one. In our experience, this approach seems to be perfectly adequate to check the design of a complex and fairly intertwined process by testing more complex examples in a simply verifiable environment. However, in an extended, fully elaborated system, a more sophisticated control mechanism will earn increasing interest (preferably a cascaded approach like [Reithinger 1987]) because the likely gain in efficiency may be necessary. When a significant number of choices is available in all phases of the generation process, the resulting combinatorial explosion must be drastically reduced by pruning less promising alternatives; this can be done more easily when information from several levels is available at an early stage.

   The sequence of processes consisting of the subtasks presented in the previous section follows almost exactly the classical partition into a strategic component (concerned with 'what to say') and into a tactical component (concerned with 'how to say it'). In this respect, only the status of terminological transformations is not entirely clear: they may equally well be counted as a contribution to the tactical part. On one hand, the variants at disposal are terminologically equivalent, which is an indication that it is merely the question of *how* to express a certain fact. On the other hand, different levels of granularity refer to different details of the global fact to be expressed, which is more on the level of *what* is to be included in a message. In any case, we believe that both views are plausible ones, so a strict distinction between 'what to say' and 'how to say it' does not seem to be possible in all instances, as is the case for terminological transformations.

Phase/Subtask	Level of Representation	Decisions to be made/Choices involved
text organisation	QUARK ↓ IRS	selection of speech acts, their order and contents (choice of rhetorical predicates)
terminological transformations	IRS	alternative conceptual descriptions accommodated to the user's knowledge
conceptual descriptions	IRS	augmenting ambiguous descriptions choice of additional attributes
verbalisation	IRS ↓ F-structure	expressing speech acts, word choice modal verb generation, feature selection suppressing or including optional parts
surface transformations	F-structure/ARPS	generating anaphora and gapping
syntactic realisation	ARPS ↓ strings	word order, inflections

Table 8.2: The phases of the generation process

In the whole process four different levels of representation are recognisable. The initial structures (the wants of the system) are entries in QUARK. After the transition to speech acts, IRS takes care of the representation. Expressions in this language are modified until the verbalisation phase is reached. At this stage the transition to functional descriptions is performed followed by a further restructuring phase and a transition to surface strings. Thus, the number of representation levels is the same as in Dale's system EPICURE [Dale, this volume]. Whereas our F-structure resembles closely to the abstract syntactic structure used in that approach, QUARK and IRS representations are much different from the knowledge base and recoverable semantic structures used in EPICURE. This is mainly due to the ontological differences between the cognitive and lexical levels which are typical for our approach.

The subtasks in WISBER's generator almost form a pattern consisting of a repeating sequence of transitions and structure modifying tasks. The exception to this regular structure manifests itself in the adjacent tasks concerned with terminological transformations and with the generation of conceptual descriptions. When increasing the repertoire of choices for each subtask, the sequential order of processes is particularly problematic at this point, because the results produced by both of these tasks influence each other. For purposes of illustration, the phases of generation and the levels of representation together with the associated decisions are presented in Table 8.2.

8.5   Comparison with Other Systems

In contrast to WISBER, the system KAMP [Appelt 1985] presents an integrated approach using what is effectively a continuum of conditions and decisions, rather than a sequence of subtasks. However, the flexibility in lexical realisations in that system is rather poor; hence, we suspect that significant extensions of the system's lexical coverage will cause severe problems in its control structure.

Only one of the three restructuring tasks described here (surface transformations, on the lexical level) is well established in other approaches. The other two tasks (terminological transformations on the conceptual level, and the verbalisation process as the transition from the conceptual to the lexical level) are the novel subtasks in the present approach. Their integration has proved to be necessary because of the significant ontological differences between predicates on the conceptual and on the lexical level, which is a characteristic feature of our approach. In other generators (for instance, MUMBLE [McDonald 1983] and KING [Jacobs 1987]) there are also restructuring operations which approach some of the potential of ours, but their conceptual status seems to be much less clear.

Our approach to generating conceptual descriptions can be considered as a supplement to Dale's method, which is based on a measurement called **discriminatory power** [Dale, this volume]. Whereas this measurement is useful in obtaining the shortest possible descriptions on a formal basis, our method may be used to select between several of them by means of pragmatic criteria. Occasionally, this may lead to a slightly larger description than the minimal one. However, we believe that such a description may be preferable in some instances (for example, the colour and the size of an object may be preferable to a single, but less salient feature, at least under certain circumstances).

Whereas in other systems (e.g., HAM-ANS [Hoeppner *et al.* 1983; Jameson and Wahlster 1982]) the task of generating conceptual descriptions is usually called NP generation, its status is, in principle, more general in our approach. This is because the relevant level of representation is a purely conceptual one where syntactic structures like an NP cannot yet be identified. Hence, our method can also be used to establish a unique reference to a specific event, if each one out of a set of events of the same type may be a possible referent. This is done in just the way as it has been demonstrated for (physical) objects. However, the suitability of properties to enable a unique identification must be determined for these cases: hence, the temporal relations associated with events are the most appropriate discrimination criteria.

Another very interesting approach to the generation of descriptions, which focuses on conversational implicature, has been undertaken by Reiter [this volume]. Whereas WISBER could also generate some of the examples he presents (by means of FTRANSLATE), most of the implicatures, which are implicitly present in the knowledge representation formalism, cannot be exploited by our generator.

8.6 Conclusion

In summarising our approach at this stage, it is appropriate to return to the questions raised in the first section. According to the partition into subcomponents pursued in our approach, the association of phenomena (as it has been presented) follows quite naturally for some of them, whereas others fall into the competence area of several components. In such cases a specification of preferences is determined to a certain extent in terms of parameters, leaving their evaluation and final decisions to the last component involved in respective issues. This refers, in particular, to the contributions of the component responsible for the generation of conceptual descriptions and to the verbalisation component in the task of generating referring expressions (in fact, the first one creates options to be exploited by the second).

In order to combine these components to build a system that covers all areas of generation, three aspects have proved to be decisively important in our approach:

- first and foremost, the representation of utterances in terms of IRS-expressions at the cognitive level has helped us to maintain adequate connections between adjacent modules in all phases of generation;

- moreover, the ontology provided by the QUIRK definitions has proved to be a very important orientation. Thus, not only are the syntax and conventions associated with the IRS the same for all generation components, but so is the content of IRS formulas in terms of the predicates used; and

- finally, explicit definitions of correspondences between elements of cognitive and lexical representation levels are necessary, which are composable and enable some restructuring on the transition between the representation levels.

At the current stage of development we cannot provide much evidence for the suitability of control structures. In our sequential approach, the overhead caused by first generating optional parts and then possibly leaving them without further elaboration is necessary (because neither of the involved components has sufficient competence to recognise early enough the suitability or unsuitability of optional parts on its own). If the flow of control can go back and forth between subcomponents, superfluous operations can be reduced as a result of the improved communication between the modules. Moreover, if a particular decision cannot be delayed by creating optional elements in the produced specifications, some alternatives must be pruned at an early stage of processing. Thus, the locally best choice made by some component is expected to be the best one in the subsequent components, too; this has been the case in the examples we have treated so far. However, in a more elaborated version, we envisage a combination of a cascaded approach (as in [Reithinger 1987]), the pursuit of a small set of promising alternatives in parallel, and some kind of 'forward pruning', which is the only technique currently used.

As for the position of the generator in a complete NL system, there is an obvious symmetry concerning the initial and goal structures of generation and analysis (in inverse order). With respect to processing, however, some tasks which are quite crucial in analysis are of minor importance in generation (such as, for instance, scope analysis), whereas the tasks devoted to terminological transformations and the generation of conceptual descriptions do not have obvious counterparts on the analysis side. To some extent, reference resolution and inferences in the evaluation process itself can be considered as associated tasks. Moreover, both parts of processing update and access common knowledge sources (the dialogue memory and the partner model). In our generator, information from these knowledge sources is exploited frequently (mainly for choices between alternatives) irrespective of whether the information has been provided by analysis or generation modules.

Of course, the architecture chosen for our system is not the only way of organising the task of generation in a complete NL system; however, we believe that it is a convincing approach, because:

- its coverage includes many interesting and, to some extent, exceptional features (e.g., terminological transformations and flexibility in the transition from the conceptual to the lexical level, also including modal verb generation); and

- the course of a dialogue in a complete NL system feeds coherent specifications to the generation component, which influence its decisions more justifiably than externally specified parameters.

In any case, it is important to pursue a holistic approach in order to learn how the treatment of certain phenomena may suitably be organised in a complete natural language system.

Acknowledgements

I would like to thank all my colleagues in the WISBER project for their assistance in the design and implementation of the generator and of the embedding system, and for fruitful discussions in all phases of the work. Special thanks are due to Henning Bergmann, who designed and implemented the tool called FTRANSLATE, and to Heinz Marburger who contributed the component dedicated to the generation of conceptual descriptions.

References

Appelt, D [1985] *Planning English Sentences*. Cambridge: Cambridge University Press.

Bergmann, H and Gerlach, M [1987] *Semantisch-pragmatische Verarbeitung von Äußerungen im natürlichsprachlichen Beratungssystem* WISBER. In W Brauer and W Wahlster (eds), *Wissensbasierte Systeme: GI-Kongreß 1987*, pp318–327. Berlin: Springer. Also available as WISBER Report No. 15, Department of Computer Science, University of Hamburg.

Bergmann, H [1987] Short Description of FTRANSLATE. WISBER Memo No. 30, Department of Computer Science, University of Hamburg.

Bergmann, H, Fliegner, M, Gerlach, M, Marburger, H and Poesio, M [1987] IRS: The Internal Representation Language. WISBER Report No. 14, Department of Computer Science, University of Hamburg.

Bergmann, H, and Gerlach, M [1986] QUIRK: Implementierung einer TBox zur Repräsentation begrifflichen Wissens. WISBER Memo No. 11, Department of Computer Science, University of Hamburg.

Brachman, R and Schmolze, J [1985] An overview of the KL-ONE knowledge representation system. *Cognitive Science*, **9**, 171–216.

Busche, R and Schachter-Radig, M-J [1988] INFERENCE: Implementation eines Inferenzmechanismus: Spezifikation und Architektur des Regelinterpreters. WISBER Memo No. 20, SCS GmbH, Hamburg, 1988.

Busemann, S [1983] Oberflächentransformationen bei der automatischen Generierung geschriebener deutscher Sprache. Thesis, Department of Computer Science, University of Hamburg.

Dale, R [1990] Generating recipes: An overview of Epicure. This volume.

Gerlach, M and Horacek, H [1989] Dialog control in a natural language system. In *Proceedings of the 4th Conference of the European Chapter of the Association for Computational Linguistics*, University of Manchester Institute of Science and Technology, Manchester, 10–12 April 1989, pp27–34.

Hoeppner *et al.*[1983] Beyond domain-independence: experience with the development of a German language access system to highly diverse background systems. In *Proceedings of the Eighth International Joint Conference on Artificial Intelligence*, Karlsruhe, West Germany, 8–12 August 1983, pp588-594..

Horacek, H [1987] The choice of words in the generation process of a natural language interface. *Applied Artificial Intelligence*, **1**, 117-132.

Horacek, H, Bergmann, H, Block, R, Fliegner, M, Gerlach, M, Poesio, M and Sprenger, M [1988] From meaning to meaning: a walk through WISBER's semantic-pragmatic processing. In W Hoeppner (ed) *Künstliche Intelligenz: GWAI-88*, pp118–129. Berlin: Springer. Also available as WISBER Report No. 30, Department of Computer Science, University of Hamburg.

Horacek, H and Pyka, C [1988] Towards bridging two levels of representation: Linking syntactic-functional and object-oriented paradigms. In J-L Lassez and F Chin (eds) *International Computer Science Conference '88—Artificial Intelligence: Theory and Applications*, Hong Kong, pp281–288. Also available as WISBER Report No. 32, Department of Computer Science, University of Hamburg.

Horacek, H [1989] Towards principles of ontology. In D Metzing (ed), *GWAI-89*, pp323–330. Berlin: Springer.

Jablonski, K, Rau, A and Ritzke, J [1987] Konzeption und Architektur des taktischen Textgenerierungssystems NUGGET. WISBER Memo No. 12, Nixdorf Computer AG.

Jablonski, K, Rau, A and Ritzke, J [1988] NUGGET: Ein DCG-basiertes Textgenerierungssystem. WISBER Report No. 27, Nixdorf Computer AG.

Jameson, A and Wahlster, W [1982] User modelling in anaphora generation: Ellipsis and definite descriptions. In *Proceedings of ECAI-82*, pp222–227.

Jacobs, P [1987] Knowledge-intensive natural language generation. *Artificial Intelligence*, **33**, 325–378.

Kamp, H [1981] A theory of truth and semantic representation. In J Groenendijk, T Janssen and M Stockhof (eds), *Formal Methods in the Study of Language*, Volume 136, pp277–322. Amsterdam: Mathematical Centre Tracts.

Kaplan, R and Bresnan, J [1982] Lexical-Functional Grammar. In J Bresnan (ed) *The Mental Representation of Grammatical Relations*, pp173–281. Cambridge, Mass.: MIT Press.

McDonald, D D [1983] Natural language generation as a computational problem: An introduction. In M Brady and C Berwick (eds), *Computational Models of Discourse*. Cambridge, Mass.: MIT Press.

McKeown, K [1982] Generating Natural Language Text in Response to Questions about Database Structure. PhD Thesis, Department of Computer and Information Science, University of Pennsylvania.

Poesio, M [1988] The QUARK Reference Manual. WISBER Memo No. 22, Department of Computer Science, University of Hamburg.

Reiter, E [1990] Generating descriptions that exploit a user's domain knowledge. This volume.

Reithinger, N [1987] Ein erster Blick auf POPEL: Wie wird was gesagt? In K Morik (ed), *GWAI-87: 11th German Workshop on Artificial Intelligence*, pp315–319. Berlin: Springer.

Schmolze, J [1985] The Language and Semantics of NIKL. Draft paper, Bolt Beranek and Newman Inc.

Sprenger, M and Gerlach, M [1988] Expectations and propositional attitudes: Pragmatic issues in WISBER. In J-L Lassez and F Chin (eds), *International Computer Science Conference '88—Artificial Intelligence: Theory and Applications*, Hong Kong, pp327–334. Also available as WISBER Report No. 28, Department of Computer Science, University of Hamburg.

Stallard, D [1986] A terminological simplification transformation for natural language question-answering systems. In *Proceedings of the 24th Annual Meeting of the Association for Computational Linguistics*, Columbia University, pp241–246.

9 Generating Recipes: An Overview of Epicure

Robert Dale

Abstract

EPICURE is a natural language generation system whose principal concern is the generation of referring expressions which pick out complex entities in connected discourse. This chapter provides an overview of the system, showing how the various components of its architecture contribute to the achievement of this goal, and highlights two important features of the system: its sophisticated underlying ontology, which permits the representation of non-singular entities, and its use of a notion of **discriminatory power**, to determine what properties should be used in describing an entity.

9.1 Introduction

EPICURE is a natural language generation system whose principal concern is the generation of referring expressions which pick out complex entities in connected discourse: in particular, the system generates natural language descriptions of cookery recipes. This chapter has three purposes:

- to describe the overall architecture and operation of the system, showing how, given the goal of telling a user how to carry out a particular recipe, the various components of the system contribute to the achievement of this goal;

- to describe the underlying ontology and corresponding representation language used in the system; and

- to describe the mechanisms the system uses in order to generate a variety of appropriate referring expressions in discourse.

Figure 9.1 shows an example of the kind of recipe generated by EPICURE, given the following inputs:

- a top level goal, which we can characterise in this case as *make butterbean soup*;

- a set of data structures corresponding to the ingredients required; and

229

four ounces of butter beans
a large onion
a medium potato
two carrots
two sticks of celery
one ounce of butter
1.5 pints of unsalted stock
0.5 pints of milk
four tablespoons of cream
some sea salt
some freshly ground black pepper
some grated nutmeg

Soak, drain and rinse the butter beans. Peel and chop the onion. Peel and chop the potato. Scrape and chop the carrots. Slice the celery. Melt the butter. Add the vegetables. Saute them. Add the butter beans, the stock and the milk. Simmer. Liquidise the soup. Stir in the cream. Add the seasonings. Reheat.

Figure 9.1: An example recipe produced by EPICURE

- some specification of the actions the hearer is assumed to understand how to carry out.

In Section 9.3, we describe how these inputs together result in the generation of a recipe; and in Section 9.4, we look in detail at the mechanisms involved in the generation of appropriate referring expressions within recipes. As a prerequisite, however, Section 9.2 below describes the representational language used to describe entities like those that appear in the recipe in Figure 9.1.

9.2   The Representation of Ingredients

9.2.1   The problem

We take the view that there are two kinds of entities in the world: informally, **things** and **events**. Within EPICURE, we are first and foremost concerned with the representation of things, although, as we will see below, the representation language adopted also encompasses events, drawing out some parallels that are worth further investigation.

In most natural language systems, it is assumed that all the entities in the domain of discourse are singular individuals. In more complex domains, such as recipes, this simplification is of limited value, since a large proportion of the objects we find are masses or sets, such as those described by the following two noun phrases respectively:

(1)   a   two ounces of salt

        b   three pounds of carrots

We need a representation language which permits us to represent non-singular entities like these, just as easily as it permits representation of simpler objects. Given the task in hand, the representation must meet two particular requirements:

1. Since the domain we are dealing with is an essentially dynamic one, the representation should make it straightforward to model changes of state as a recipe proceeds.

2. The representation should capture all the information that is required for the generation of appropriate referring expressions.

9.2.2   Generalised physical objects

As a solution to this problem, EPICURE makes use of a notion of generalised physical object or **physobj**, defined as follows:

(2)   A generalised physical object is any (not necessarily contiguous) collection of contiguous regions of space occupied by matter.

This permits a consistent representation of entities irrespective of whether they are viewed as individuals, masses or sets, by representing each as a **knowledge base entity** (KBE) with an appropriate STRUCTURE attribute. This attribute specifies whether the object is to be viewed as an individual, a set or a mass.

Things are simplest, as one might expect, in the case of singular individuals. The knowledge base entity corresponding to *a carrot* is shown in Figure 9.2. This data structure can be read as saying that *a carrot* is a carrot-shaped package of carrot-matter. Although this might appear to be a rather long-winded way of specifying the required information, for our purposes it provides just the right separation between information about the kind of matter the object consists in, and information about the way in which that matter is bounded (this is essentially a distinction between necessary and contingent properties of the entity).

Note how the same style of representation encompasses more complex entities: the knowledge base entity corresponding to *three pounds of carrots*, for example, is that shown in Figure 9.3.

$$
\text{KBE} = \begin{bmatrix}
index = x_0 \\
state = s_0 \\
spec = \begin{bmatrix}
structure = individual \\
substance = carrot \\
packaging = \begin{bmatrix}
shape = carrot \\
size = regular
\end{bmatrix}
\end{bmatrix}
\end{bmatrix}
$$

Figure 9.2: The knowledge base entity corresponding to *a carrot*

$$
\text{KBE} = \begin{bmatrix}
index = x_1 \\
state = s_0 \\
spec = \begin{bmatrix}
structure = set \\
quantity = \begin{bmatrix}
unit = pound \\
number = 3
\end{bmatrix} \\
element = \begin{bmatrix}
structure = individual \\
substance = carrot \\
packaging = \begin{bmatrix}
shape = carrot \\
size = regular
\end{bmatrix}
\end{bmatrix}
\end{bmatrix}
\end{bmatrix}
$$

Figure 9.3: The knowledge base entity corresponding to *three pounds of carrots*

$$
\text{KBE} = \left[\begin{array}{l} index = x_1 \\ state = s_1 \\ spec = \left[\begin{array}{l} structure = mass \\ quantity = \left[\begin{array}{l} unit = pound \\ number = 3 \end{array} \right] \\ substance = carrot \\ grated = + \end{array} \right] \end{array} \right]
$$

Figure 9.4: The knowledge base entity corresponding to *three pounds of grated carrot*

9.2.3 Modelling changes of state

We mentioned above that we required a representation which makes it straightforward to model changes of state as a recipe proceeds. To see that our representation satisfies this demand, notice that a knowledge base entity models a physobj in a particular **state**: in each of the two examples above, the data structures shown describe entities in state s_0. An entity may change during the course of a recipe, as processes are applied to it: in particular, apart from gaining new properties such as being peeled, chopped, etc., an ingredient's STRUCTURE may change, for example, from set to mass. Each change of state results in the creation of a new knowledge base entity. Suppose, for example, a grating event is applied to our three pounds of carrots between states s_0 and s_1: the entity shown in Figure 9.3 will then become a mass of grated carrot, represented in state s_1 by the KBE shown in Figure 9.4.

9.2.4 Representing eventualities

Objects do not exist in a vacuum: they participate in relations which we may informally call states and events. In the ontology developed here, any collection of objects and the state or event in which they participate is referred to as an **eventuality**.

It has often been noted that strong parallels can be drawn between the logic of objects and the logic of events (see, for example, Mayo [1961] and Zemach [1979]). Just as in the case of objects, we represent each eventuality by an index, and then predicate properties of that index as a means of repre-

$$
\text{KBE} = \begin{bmatrix} index = e_0 \\[4pt] occurs = \begin{bmatrix} begin = s_0 \\ end = s_1 \end{bmatrix} \\[10pt] spec = \begin{bmatrix} substance = grating \\ structure = event \\[6pt] participants = \begin{bmatrix} in = \begin{bmatrix} agent = j \\ object = x_0 \end{bmatrix} \\[10pt] out = \begin{bmatrix} agent = j \\ object = x_0 \end{bmatrix} \end{bmatrix} \end{bmatrix} \end{bmatrix}
$$

Figure 9.5: The knowledge base entity corresponding to a particular grating event

senting information about the eventuality in question. Just as a physobj has a specification of SUBSTANCE, so too does each eventuality; and just as a physobj has a structure, so does an eventuality. The substance of an eventuality is the 'process stuff' that it consists in; the structure is the perspective from which the eventuality is viewed.[1] Figure 9.5 shows the representation of a particular *grating* event.

Note the use of the distinct IN and OUT participants here. The IN participants are those entities which exist in the BEGIN state of the event, and the OUT participants are those which exist in the END state of the event. Although this is not the case in the present example, some events, by means of their EFFECTS, can bring new entities into existence, or destroy existing entities: the usefulness of this aspect of the representation will be demonstrated below.

9.3   Generating the Recipe

Given a top level goal, EPICURE first decomposes that goal recursively to produce a plan consisting of operations at a level of detail commensurate with the assumed knowledge of the hearer. This plan is then used to produce a

---

[1] Readers familiar with Bach's [1986] work will recognise similarities here with his attempts to apply Link's [1983] work on objects to the domain of eventualities.

discourse whose structure mirrors that of the plan itself. During the course of a recipe, ingredients take on new properties: and so, in order to describe the recipe, EPICURE therefore has to model the recipe's execution, so that the processes which produce referring expressions always have access to a representation of the ingredients in the state they are in at the time at which they are to be described.

This section describes the various components of the system implicated in the above description of what EPICURE does.

9.3.1 The overall architecture of the system

The architecture of the EPICURE is shown in Figure 9.6.[2] Conceptually, the system comprises four distinct processing modules (the discourse planner, the discourse generator, the clause generator and the domain modeller), and six distinct knowledge sources (the plan library, the hearer model, the discourse model, the world model, the lexicon and the grammar).

Given a top level goal, which we might gloss in the case of the recipe in Figure 9.1 as *make butterbean soup*,[3] EPICURE requires three primary inputs in order to generate an appropriate recipe: a set of data structures that represent the ingredients to be used (as described in Section 9.2 above), a library of planning operators that define actions available in the domain, and a model of the hearer's capabilities. EPICURE then uses a number of planning axioms to determine to what extent the event corresponding to the top level goal should be decomposed to accommodate the hearer's particular capabilities.

9.3.2 The plan library

EPICURE starts out with a particular goal to be achieved: in the present context, this is the goal of having produced the result of a particular recipe. In order to do this, EPICURE has to know what actions are necessary to achieve this goal. In line with standard approaches in the planning literature (see, for example, [Tate 1985]), these actions (or **operators**) are defined in terms of their preconditions and effects. In addition, if the action is a macro-operator rather than a primitive action, the definition contains a body which specifies the subactions that make up that action. From the point of view of the macro-operator, these subactions are primitives; however, each subaction may also be defined in terms of its subactions, and so on. Thus, in principle, any

---

[2]The following conventions are used in this diagram: data structures are represented by long flat boxes, whereas process modules are represented by the more squat boxes. An arrow pointing from box *A* to box *B* is intended to show that data flows from *A* to *B*.

[3]Since, in the current model at least, EPICURE has no physical capabilities whatsoever, the goal of carrying out some action reduces to the goal of describing to someone else how to carry out that action.

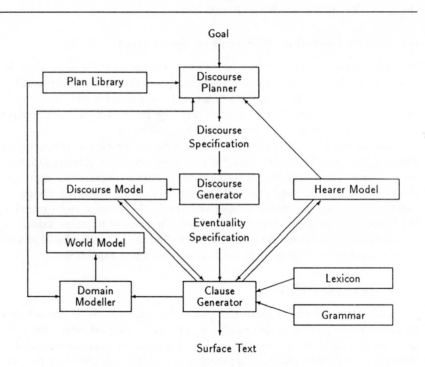

Goal

Plan Library

Discourse Planner

Discourse Specification

Discourse Model

Discourse Generator

Hearer Model

Eventuality Specification

World Model

Lexicon

Domain Modeller

Clause Generator

Grammar

Surface Text

Figure 9.6: The overall structure of EPICURE.

action may be decomposed into lower-level actions. Within EPICURE, each planning operator is represented as an underspecified event, such that when the PARTICIPANTS in the event and the BEGIN and END states of the event are instantiated, the result is an instance of the kind of action corresponding to the planning operator.

The collection of operator definitions known to EPICURE resides in the **plan library**. The information held in operator definitions is used by EPICURE in two ways. First, in conjunction with knowledge of the hearer's capabilities (as maintained in the hearer model, described below), information about the expansion of an operator is used by the discourse planner in order to determine just how much detail is required in the description of a plan of action (the basic idea here is very similar to that proposed by Sacerdoti [1977]). Second, the effects information is used by the domain modeller to update the world model so that its state is consistent with the effects of the operations described.

9.3.3 The hearer model

The hearer model maintained by EPICURE contains various kinds of information:

- For each action in the domain, if the hearer is assumed to know how to carry out that action, this fact is specified in the hearer model. The discourse planner makes use of this knowledge in determining the level of detail at which a plan should be described.

- For each entity in the domain, if the hearer has any knowledge of that entity apart from that gained from the discourse, then this information is specified in the discourse model. In the current version of the system, this information is minimal: the hearer is assumed to know that both herself and the speaker are present in the domain.

- The hearer is assumed to know the information maintained in a taxonomy of substances, so that, for example, a superordinate term such as *seasoning* can be used to describe an ingredient whose substance is *salt*.

Thus, the hearer model plays two distinct roles in the current system: it provides EPICURE with the means to determine the level of detail necessary to describe the plan; and it provides the system with the justification for using particular kinds of noun phrases to refer to entities in the domain.

9.3.4 Building the discourse specification

The discourse planner is that component of EPICURE which determines 'what to say' at the topmost level: that is, it determines which particular actions

should be described. This is done using the information stored in the plan
library and the hearer model, as described above.

The result of this process is a tree-structured discourse specification, which
corresponds to the hierarchical decomposition of the plan it describes. Given
the hearer's capabilities assumed in the recipe in Figure 9.1, applying this
mechanism to the top level goal results in the plan structure shown in Figure 9.7; the key provides an English gloss of each node in the plan, with those
nodes which are not explicitly described in the output surrounded by square
brackets.

Some discourse-level optimisation is then carried out on this structure,
primarily for the purposes of making the resulting text more fluent (this is
similar in some respects to the **message optimisation** phase described in
Mellish [1988]). This process involves massaging the structure to enable the
use of ellipsis and conjunction in the linguistic description of the plan: thus,
for example, the three actions which might be described one after the other
as

   (3)   Soak the beans.
          Drain the beans.
          Rinse the beans.

can be described together by the sentence

   (4)   Soak, drain and rinse the beans.

The discourse specification which results from the optimisation phase is shown
in Figure 9.8.

Once the optimised discourse specification has been constructed, it is
passed to the discourse generator. This component has two responsibilities,
which it fulfills in an interleaved fashion as it walks around the discourse
specification in a left-to-right, depth-first fashion: the discourse model is constructed as a hierarchy of focus spaces which matches the structure of the discourse specification itself; and the eventuality specifications which constitute
the leaf nodes of the discourse specification are passed to the clause generator
for realisation.

9.3.5   Domain modelling and clause generation

Domain modelling

Before deciding on the semantic content of the description of an event, the
clause generator first passes the eventuality specification in question to the
domain modeller. The domain modeller retrieves the operator definition
corresponding to the eventuality from the plan library, and uses the information about the effects of the operator to update the world model appropriately.

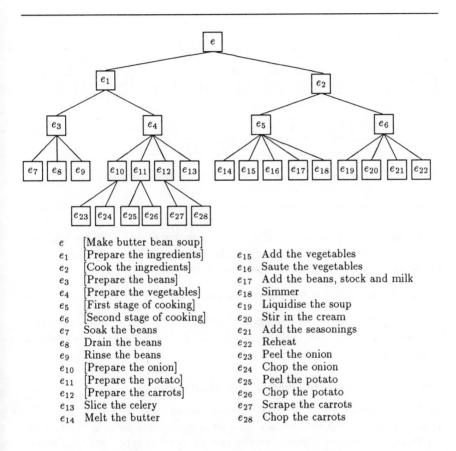

e	[Make butter bean soup]
e_1	[Prepare the ingredients]
e_2	[Cook the ingredients]
e_3	[Prepare the beans]
e_4	[Prepare the vegetables]
e_5	[First stage of cooking]
e_6	[Second stage of cooking]
e_7	Soak the beans
e_8	Drain the beans
e_9	Rinse the beans
e_{10}	[Prepare the onion]
e_{11}	[Prepare the potato]
e_{12}	[Prepare the carrots]
e_{13}	Slice the celery
e_{14}	Melt the butter
e_{15}	Add the vegetables
e_{16}	Saute the vegetables
e_{17}	Add the beans, stock and milk
e_{18}	Simmer
e_{19}	Liquidise the soup
e_{20}	Stir in the cream
e_{21}	Add the seasonings
e_{22}	Reheat
e_{23}	Peel the onion
e_{24}	Chop the onion
e_{25}	Peel the potato
e_{26}	Chop the potato
e_{27}	Scrape the carrots
e_{28}	Chop the carrots

Figure 9.7: The butter bean soup plan

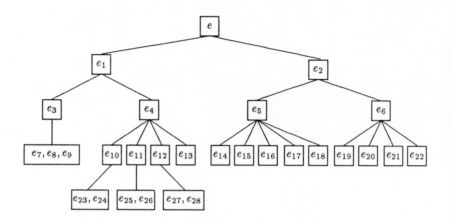

Figure 9.8: The optimised butter bean soup plan

Doing this *before* generating a clause means that the generator can have access to information about the state of the world as it will be *after* the event in question has taken place: for example, in the sentence

(5)   Remove the skin from the avocado.

the parts of the avocado do not figure as individual entities in the domain until *after* the event described has taken place. We will examine how this works in more detail below.

The two intermediate levels of representation

As has often been noted in the generation literature, a representational formalism that is useful for one task may be inappropriate for other tasks (see, for example, Swartout [1983]). In the case of EPICURE, the particular structures which are useful for modelling the domain for the purposes of planning are not the most appropriate for the generation of text. More particularly, an eventuality specification as provided by the discourse generator, since it consists of an instantiated plan operator, may include information that is not required in the description of that eventuality: in this sense, the structure is over-specified. In another respect, the structure may be under-specified: in particular, the participants in the eventuality are specified by means of their indices alone, with no associated information attached.

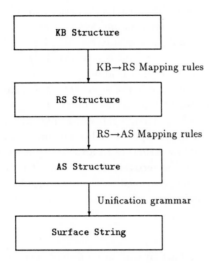

Figure 9.9: The levels of representation in clause generation

Within EPICURE, the clause generation process consists of a series of trans-
ducers, as shown in Figure 9.9. These levels could be compiled together, but
it is conceptually simpler to deal with them as distinct processes. Thus, given
an eventuality specification, the clause generator uses a set of **mapping rules**
to build a **recoverable semantic structure**. This specifies the underlying
semantic content of the utterance to be generated. In this structure, the indices of objects are replaced by structures which describe the semantic content
of the noun phrases that will describe these objects; and any participants and
other information in the eventuality which are not to be described will have
been omitted. Thus, the mechanism used to build the recoverable semantic
structure represents the bridge between knowledge representation and semantic representation, where the latter is a linguistically-motivated construct. The
semantic representation is intended to be domain-independent: the particular
mechanism used by EPICURE to construct the recoverable semantic structure
in the current domain could be replaced by a different mechanism to permit
it to generate text for other applications which use quite different knowledge
representation formalisms.

As the name suggests, the recoverable semantic structure corresponding
to an event to be described represents the semantic content which should be

recoverable from the utterance by the hearer: this does not mean that all of this semantic content need be explicitly *realised* by the clause generator. So, for example, the use of *one*-anaphora and verb phrase ellipsis is not represented at the level of recoverable semantic structure; for related reasons, it is the recoverable semantic structure that is integrated into the discourse model.

A second set of mapping rules is applied to the recoverable semantic structure, resulting in the construction of an **abstract syntactic structure**. This structure is much closer to the surface syntax of the linguistic form that will eventually be produced: it incorporates ordering information, and takes account of the scope for *one*-anaphora and other forms of ellipsis. The mapping from recoverable semantic structure to abstract syntactic structure is one-to-many: so, for example, the recoverable semantic structure will specify which illocutionary act is to be performed by the utterance being generated, but will not specify which particular surface form is to be used to realise this act.

Generating a clause

In order to choose the participants to be described in a given event, for each SUBSTANCE we have a verb **case frame**[4] (see, for example, [Fillmore 1968]) which specifies the correspondences between participants in the knowledge base structure and participants in the recoverable semantic structure. The frame for **peel**, for example, is as follows:

(6)   **Peel**   **Verb case role**   **Eventuality participant**
       OBJECT [oblig +]   IN:OBJECT

This states that the OBJECT in the recoverable semantic structure is the value of ⟨IN OBJECT⟩ in the knowledge base structure.[5] Verb case roles are marked as to whether they are **obligatory**: non-obligatory elements may, under circumstances to be described later, result in null NP constituents.

Since the participants to be included in the recoverable semantic structure may be drawn from either the ⟨PARTICIPANTS IN⟩ or ⟨PARTICIPANTS OUT⟩ features of the event to be described, the verb case frames thus also determine whether an entity is to be described as it was before or after the event in question takes place. This permits us to generate sentences like *Remove the skin from the avocado*: the corresponding verb case frame in this case is

---

[4]In EPICURE, there is a simple one-to-one mapping from eventuality types to lexical items; thus, in its present form, the system is incapable of describing an **exchange-money** event, for example, by choosing between the verbs *buy* and *sell*.

[5]In the notation used here, given a structure F, the path ⟨F A B⟩ picks out the value of the feature b in the structure which is the value of the feature a in the structure F.

(7)   remove   **Verb case role**   **Eventuality participant**
                 OBJECT [oblig +]   OUT:REMAINDER
                 INDOBJECT [oblig −]   IN:OBJECT

The EFFECTS of the **remove** operator create two new entities from the entity addressed as ⟨IN OBJECT⟩: in this case, the avocado minus its skin (subsequently accessed as ⟨OUT RESULT⟩) and the skin itself (accessed as ⟨OUT REMAINDER⟩).

9.4   Generating Referring Expressions

To construct a referring expression corresponding to a knowledge base entity, we first build a recoverable semantic structure which specifies the semantic content of the noun phrase to be generated. As described above, an abstract syntactic structure is then constructed from the recoverable semantic structure. Unlike the recoverable semantic structure, this closely matches the syntactic structure of the resulting noun phrase, and is suitable for passing directly to a PATR II-like unification grammar (see, for example, Shieber [1986]). It is at the level of abstract syntactic structure that processes such as elision and *one*-anaphora take place.

9.4.1   Pronominalisation

When an entity is to be referred to, we first check to see if pronominalisation is possible. Some previous approaches to the **pronominalisation decision** have taken into account a large number of contextual factors (see, for example, McDonald [1980:218–220]). The approach taken here is relatively simple. EPICURE makes use of a discourse model which distinguishes two principal components, corresponding to Grosz's [1977] distinction between local focus and global focus. We call that part of the discourse model corresponding to the local focus **cache memory**: this contains the lexical, syntactic and semantic detail of the current utterance being generated, and the same detail for the previous utterance. Corresponding to global focus, the discourse model consists of a number of hierarchically-arranged **focus spaces**, mirroring the structure of the recipe being described. These focus spaces record the semantic content, but not the syntactic or lexical detail, of the remainder of the preceding discourse. In addition, we make use of a notion of **discourse centre**: this is intuitively similar to the notion of centering suggested by Grosz, Joshi and Weinstein [1983], and corresponds to the focus of attention in the discourse. In recipes, we take the centre to be the RESULT of the previous operation described. Thus, after an utterance like

(8)   Soak the butterbeans.

the centre is the entity described by the noun phrase *the butterbeans*. Subsequent references to the centre can be pronominalised, so that the next instruction in the recipe might then be

(9) Drain and rinse them.

Following Grosz, Joshi and Weinstein [1983], references to other entities present in cache memory may also be pronominalised, provided the centre is pronominalised.[6]

If the intended referent is the current centre, then this is marked as part of the STATUS information in the recoverable semantic structure being constructed, and a null value is specified for the structure's descriptive content, addressed as ⟨SPEC TYPE⟩. In addition, the verb case frame used to construct the utterance specifies whether or not the linguistic realisation of the entity filling each case role is obligatory: as we will see below, this allows us to model a common linguistic phenomenon in recipes (**recipe context empty objects**, after Massam and Roberge [1989]). For a case role whose surface realisation is obligatory, the resulting recoverable semantic structure is then as follows:

$$(10) \quad \text{RS} = \begin{bmatrix} index = x \\ sem = \begin{bmatrix} status = \begin{bmatrix} given = + \\ centre = + \\ oblig = + \end{bmatrix} \\ spec = \begin{bmatrix} type = \phi \end{bmatrix} \end{bmatrix} \end{bmatrix}$$

This will be realised as either a pronoun or an elided NP, generated from an abstract syntactic structure which is constructed in accordance with the following rules:

- If the STATUS includes the features [*centre*, +] and [*oblig*, +], then there should be a corresponding element in the abstract syntactic structure, with a null value specified for the descriptive content of the noun phrase to be generated;

---

[6]We do not permit pronominal reference to entities last mentioned before the previous utterance: support for this restriction comes from a study by Hobbs, who, in a sample of one hundred consecutive examples of pronouns from each of three very different texts, found that 98% of antecedents were either in the same or previous sentence [Hobbs 1978:322–323]. However, see Dale [1988a, 1988b] for a suggestion as to how the few instances of long-distance pronominalisation that do exist might be explained by means of a theory of discourse structure like that suggested by Grosz and Sidner [1986].

- If the STATUS includes the features [*centre*, +] and [*oblig*, −], then this participant should be omitted from the abstract syntactic structure altogether.

In the former case, this will result in a pronominal reference as in

(11)   Remove <u>them</u>.

where the abstract syntactic structure corresponding to the pronominal form is as follows:

$$
(12) \quad \text{AS} = \begin{bmatrix} index = x \\ sem = \begin{bmatrix} status = \begin{bmatrix} given = + \\ centre = + \\ oblig = + \end{bmatrix} \\ spec = \begin{bmatrix} agr = \begin{bmatrix} num = pl \\ case = acc \end{bmatrix} \\ desc = \phi \end{bmatrix} \end{bmatrix} \end{bmatrix}
$$

However, if the participant is marked as non-obligatory, then reference to the entity is omitted, as in the following:

(13)   Fry the onions.
       Add the garlic ϕ.

Here, the case frame for **add** specifies that the indirect object is non-obligatory; since the entity which fills this case role is also the centre, the complete prepositional phrase *to the onions* can be elided. Note, however, that the entity corresponding to *the onions* still figures in the recoverable semantic structure; thus, it is integrated into the discourse model, and is deemed to be part of the semantic content recoverable by the hearer.

9.4.2   Full definite noun phrase reference

If pronominalisation is ruled out, we have to build an appropriate description of the intended referent. In EPICURE, the process of constructing a description is driven by two principles, very like Gricean conversational maxims [Grice 1975]. The **principle of adequacy** requires that a referring expression should identify the intended referent unambiguously, and provide sufficient information to serve the purpose of the reference; and the **principle of efficiency**, pulling in the opposite direction, requires that the referring expression used must not contain more information than is necessary for the task at hand.[7]

These principles are implemented in EPICURE by means of a notion of **discriminatory power**. Suppose that we have a set of entities U such that

(14) $U = \{x_1, x_2, \ldots, x_n\}$

and that we wish to distinguish one of these entities, x_i, from all the others. Suppose, also, that the domain includes a number of attributes (a_1, a_2, and so on), and that each attribute has a number of permissible values (v_{n_1}, v_{n_2}, and so on); and that each entity is described by a set of attribute-value pairs. In order to distinguish x_i from the other entities in U, we need to find some set of attribute-value pairs which are together true of x_i, but of no other entity in U. This set of attribute-value pairs constitutes a **distinguishing description** of x_i with respect to the context U. A **minimal distinguishing description** is then a set of such attribute-value pairs, where the cardinality of that set is such that there are no other sets of attribute-value pairs of lesser cardinality which are sufficient to distinguish the intended referent.

We find a minimal distinguishing description by observing that different attribute-value pairs differ in the effectiveness with which they distinguish an entity from a set of entities. Suppose U has N elements, where $N > 1$. Then, any attribute-value pair true of the intended referent x_i will be true of n entities in this set, where $n \geq 1$. For any attribute-value pair $<a,v>$ that is true of the intended referent, we can compute the discriminatory power (notated here as F) of that attribute-value pair with respect to U as follows:

(15) $F(<a,v>, U) = \dfrac{N-n}{N-1}$ $1 \leq n \leq N$

F thus has as its range the real number interval $[0,1]$, where a value of 1 for a given attribute-value pair indicates that the attribute-value pair singles out the intended referent from the context, and a value of 0 indicates that the attribute-value pair is of no assistance in singling out the intended referent.

Given an intended referent and a set of entities from which the intended referent must be distinguished, this notion is used to determine which set of properties should be used in building a description which is both adequate and efficient.[8] The sum of the system's knowledge of any given object in the current domain is relatively impoverished (i.e., only a very small number of

---

[7]Similar considerations are discussed by Appelt [1982, 1986].

[8]Strictly speaking, this mechanism is only applicable in the form described here to those properties of an entity which are realisable by what are known as **absolute** (or **intersective** or **predicative**) adjectives (see, for example, Kamp [1975], Keenan and Faltz [1978]). This is acceptable in the current domain, where many of the adjectives used are derived from the verbs used to describe processes applied to entities.

properties are known to be true of any given object). This has the result that it is usually straightforward to build a distinguishing description. However, in domains where knowledge about objects is denser in this respect, some additional criteria are likely to be required in order to choose between equally concise descriptions, such as the stylistic preference criteria discussed by Horacek [this volume]. An additional problem disguised by this lack of density of knowledge is that the process of finding a minimal distinguishing description is, in fact, computationally intractable in the general case: Reiter [this volume] points out that it is equivalent to the greedy heuristic for minimal set cover.

There remains the question of how the constituency of the set U of entities is determined: in the present work, we take the context always to consist of the **working set**. This is the set of distinguishable entities in the domain at any given point in time: the constituency of this set changes as a recipe proceeds, since entities may be created or destroyed.[9]

Suppose, for example, we determine that we must identify a given object as being a set of olives which have been pitted (in a context, for example, where there are also olives which have not been pitted); the corresponding recoverable semantic structure is then as in Figure 9.10.

Note that this recoverable semantic structure can be realised in at least two ways: as either *the olives which have been pitted* or *the pitted olives*. Both forms are possible, although they correspond to different abstract syntactic structures. Thus, the generation algorithm is non-deterministic in this respect (one might imagine there are other factors which determine which of the two realisations is preferable in a given context; however, EPICURE is not capable of such sophistication). The abstract syntactic structure for the simpler of the two noun phrase structures is as shown in Figure 9.11.

9.4.3   One anaphora

The algorithms employed in EPICURE also permit the generation of *one*-anaphora, as in

(16)   Slice the large green capsicum.
       Now remove the top of <u>the small red one</u>.

The recoverable semantic structure corresponding to the noun phrase *the small red one* is as shown in Figure 9.12: note that the *one*-anaphoric process has not yet taken place.

---

[9]A slightly more sophisticated approach would be to restrict U to exclude those entities which are, in Grosz and Sidner's [1986] terms, only present in closed focus spaces. However, the benefit gained from doing this (if indeed it is a valid thing to do) is minimal in the current context because of the small number of entities we are dealing with.

$$
\text{RS} = \left[\begin{array}{l} index = x \\[2ex] sem = \left[\begin{array}{l} status = \left[\begin{array}{l} given = + \\ unique = + \end{array} \right] \\[3ex] spec = \left[\begin{array}{l} agr = \left[\begin{array}{l} countable = + \\ number = pl \end{array} \right] \\[3ex] type = \left[\begin{array}{l} category = olive \\[2ex] props = \left[\begin{array}{l} size = regular \\ pitted = + \end{array} \right] \end{array} \right] \end{array} \right] \end{array} \right] \right]
$$

Figure 9.10: The recoverable semantic structure corresponding to *the pitted olives*

$$
\text{AS} = \left[\begin{array}{l} index = x \\[2ex] sem = \left[\begin{array}{l} status = \left[\begin{array}{l} given = + \\ unique = + \end{array} \right] \\[3ex] spec = \left[\begin{array}{l} agr = \left[\begin{array}{l} countable = + \\ number = pl \end{array} \right] \\[3ex] desc = \left[\begin{array}{l} head = olive \\[2ex] mod = \left[\begin{array}{l} head = pitted \end{array} \right] \end{array} \right] \end{array} \right] \end{array} \right] \right]
$$

Figure 9.11: The abstract syntactic structure corresponding to *the pitted olives*

$$
\text{RS} = \begin{bmatrix} index = x_2 \\ sem = \begin{bmatrix} status = \begin{bmatrix} given = + \\ unique = + \end{bmatrix} \\ spec = \begin{bmatrix} agr = \begin{bmatrix} number = sg \\ countable = + \end{bmatrix} \\ type = \begin{bmatrix} category = capsicum \\ properties = \begin{bmatrix} colour = red \\ size = small \end{bmatrix} \end{bmatrix} \end{bmatrix} \end{bmatrix} \end{bmatrix}
$$

Figure 9.12: The recoverable semantic structure corresponding to *the small red capsicum*

The mechanisms which construct the abstract syntactic structure determine whether *one*-anaphora is possible by comparing the recoverable semantic structure corresponding to the previous utterance with that corresponding to the current utterance, to identify any elements they have in common. The two distinct levels of representation play an important role here: in the recoverable semantic structure, only the basic semantic category of the description has special status (this is similar to Webber's [1979] use of restricted quantification), whereas the embedding of the abstract syntactic structure's DESC feature closely matches that of the noun phrase to be generated. For *one*-anaphora to be possible, the two recoverable semantic structures being compared must have the same value for the feature addressed by the path ⟨SEM SPEC TYPE CATEGORY⟩. Rules which specify the relative ordering of adjectives in the surface form are then used to build an appropriately nested abstract syntactic structure which, when unified with the grammar, will result in the required *one*-anaphoric noun phrase. In the present example, this results in the abstract syntactic structure in Figure 9.13.

9.4.4 Pseudo-partitive noun phrases

Partitive and pseudo-partitive noun phrases, exemplified by *half of the carrots* and *three pounds of carrots* respectively, are very common in recipes; EPICURE

$$
\begin{bmatrix}
index = x_2 \\[2pt]
sem = \begin{bmatrix}
status = \begin{bmatrix} given = + \\ unique = + \end{bmatrix} \\[4pt]
spec = \begin{bmatrix}
agr = \begin{bmatrix} number = sg \\ countable = + \end{bmatrix} \\[6pt]
desc = \begin{bmatrix}
head = \begin{bmatrix} mod = \begin{bmatrix} head = red \end{bmatrix} \\ head = \phi \end{bmatrix} \\[6pt]
mod = \begin{bmatrix} head = small \end{bmatrix}
\end{bmatrix}
\end{bmatrix}
\end{bmatrix}
\end{bmatrix}
$$

Figure 9.13: The abstract syntactic structure corresponding to *the small red one*

$$\text{RS} = \begin{bmatrix} index = x \\[2pt] sem = \begin{bmatrix} status = \begin{bmatrix} given = - \end{bmatrix} \\[4pt] spec = \begin{bmatrix} agr = \begin{bmatrix} number = pl \\ countable = + \end{bmatrix} \\[6pt] quant = \begin{bmatrix} agr = \begin{bmatrix} number = 3 \\ countable = + \end{bmatrix} \\[6pt] type = \begin{bmatrix} category = pound \end{bmatrix} \end{bmatrix} \\[10pt] subst = \begin{bmatrix} agr = \begin{bmatrix} number = pl \\ countable = + \end{bmatrix} \\[6pt] type = \begin{bmatrix} category = carrot \end{bmatrix} \end{bmatrix} \end{bmatrix} \end{bmatrix}$$

Figure 9.14: The recoverable semantic structure corresponding to *three pounds of carrots*

is capable of generating both. So, for example, the pseudo-partitive noun phrase *three pounds of carrots* (as represented by the knowledge base entity shown in Figure 9.3) is generated from the recoverable semantic structure shown in Figure 9.14 via the abstract syntactic structure shown in Figure 9.15.

The generation of partitive noun phrases is explained in detail in Dale [1988b].

9.4.5   The unification grammar

Once the required abstract syntactic structure has been constructed, this is passed to a unification grammar. In EPICURE, the grammar consists of phrase structure rules annotated with path equations which determine the relationships between abstract syntactic units and surface syntactic units: the path equations specify arbitrary constituents (either complex or atomic) of feature structures.

$$
\begin{bmatrix}
index = x \\
sem = \begin{bmatrix}
status = \begin{bmatrix} given = - \end{bmatrix} \\
spec = \begin{bmatrix}
agr = \begin{bmatrix} countable = + \\ number = 3 \end{bmatrix} \\
desc = \begin{bmatrix}
spec_1 = \begin{bmatrix} agr = \begin{bmatrix} countable = + \\ number = 3 \end{bmatrix} \\ desc = \begin{bmatrix} head = pound \end{bmatrix} \end{bmatrix} \\
spec_2 = \begin{bmatrix} agr = \begin{bmatrix} countable = + \end{bmatrix} \\ desc = \begin{bmatrix} head = carrot \end{bmatrix} \end{bmatrix}
\end{bmatrix}
\end{bmatrix}
\end{bmatrix}
$$

Figure 9.15: The abstract syntactic structure corresponding to *three pounds of carrots*

There is insufficient space here to show the entire NP grammar, but we provide some representative rules in Figure 9.16 (although these rules are expressed here in a PATR-like formalism, within EPICURE they are encoded as Prolog Definite Clause Grammar (DCG) rules [Clocksin and Mellish 1981]). Applying these rules to the abstract syntactic structures described above results in the generation of the appropriate surface linguistic strings.

9.5 Conclusion

In this chapter, we have described the overall operation of EPICURE, the underlying representation of entities that it uses, and the particular mechanisms it uses to produce noun phrase referring expressions. The overall architecture is particularly appropriate to a generation system whose purpose is to generate a structured discourse in a dynamically changing context. The underlying representation used provides a flexible representation for a wide range of en-

$$NP \rightarrow Det\ N1$$

$<Det\ sem>$	$=$	$<NP\ sem\ status>$
$<NP\ syn\ agr>$	$=$	$<NP\ sem\ spec\ agr>$
$<N1\ syn\ agr>$	$=$	$<NP\ syn\ agr>$
$<Det\ syn\ agr>$	$=$	$<N1\ syn\ agr>$
$<N1\ sem>$	$=$	$<NP\ sem\ spec\ desc>$

$$N1 \rightarrow N$$

$<N\ sem>$	$=$	$<N1\ sem\ head>$

$$N1_1 \rightarrow AP\ N1_2$$

$<AP\ sem>$	$=$	$<N1_1\ sem\ mod>$
$<N1_2\ sem\ head>$	$=$	$<N1_1\ sem\ head>$

$$NP_1 \rightarrow NP_2\ N1[+of]$$

$<NP_2\ sem>$	$=$	$<NP_1\ sem\ spec\ desc\ spec_1>$
$<N1\ sem>$	$=$	$<NP_1\ sem\ spec\ desc\ spec_2>$
$<N1\ syn\ agr>$	$=$	$<NP_1\ sem\ spec\ agr>$
$<NP_2\ sem\ status>$	$=$	$<NP_1\ sem\ status>$

$$NP_1 \rightarrow NP_2\ PP[+of]$$

$<NP_2\ sem\ status>$	$=$	$<NP_1\ sem\ status>$
$<NP_2\ sem>$	$=$	$<NP_1\ sem\ spec\ desc\ spec>$
$<PP\ sem>$	$=$	$<NP_1\ sem\ spec\ desc\ set>$

Figure 9.16: A fragment of the noun phrase grammar

tities in the particular domain of application, both singular and non-singular; and the mechanisms used for generating appropriate referring expressions in discourse, which permit the generation of a wide range of pronominal forms, *one*-anaphoric forms and noun phrase structures, have much wider applicability than that exercised here.

EPICURE is implemented in C-Prolog running under UNIX.

References

Appelt, D E [1982] Planning Natural-Language Utterances to Satisfy Multiple Goals. Technical Note No. 259, SRI International, Menlo Park, Ca., March, 1982.

Appelt, D E [1986] *Planning English Sentences.* Cambridge: Cambridge University Press.

Bach, E [1986] The algebra of events. *Linguistics and Philosophy,* 9, 5–16.

Clocksin, W F and Mellish, C S [1981] *Programming in Prolog.* Berlin: Springer-Verlag.

Dale, R [1988a] The generation of subsequent referring expressions in structured discourses. Chapter 4 in M Zock and G Sabah (eds) *Advances in Natural Language Generation: An Interdisciplinary Perspective,* Volume 2, pp58–75. London: Pinter Publishers Ltd.

Dale, R [1988b] Generating Referring Expressions in a Domain of Objects and Processes. PhD Thesis, Centre for Cognitive Science, University of Edinburgh.

Fillmore, C [1968] The case for case. In E Bach and R T Harms (eds) *Universals in Linguistic Theory.* New York: Holt, Rinehart and Winston.

Grice, H P [1975] Logic and conversation. In P Cole and J L Morgan (eds) *Syntax and Semantics,* Volume 3: *Speech Acts,* pp41–58. New York: Academic Press.

Grosz, B J [1977] The Representation and Use of Focus in Dialogue. Technical Note No. 151, SRI International, Menlo Park, Ca., July, 1977.

Grosz, B J, Joshi, A K and Weinstein, S [1983] Providing a unified account of definite noun phrases in discourse. In *Proceedings of the 21st Annual Meeting of the Association for Computational Linguistics,* Massachusetts Institute of Technology, Cambridge, Mass., 15–17 June 1983, pp44–49.

Grosz, B J and Sidner, C L [1985] Discourse structure and the proper treatment of interruptions. In *Proceedings of the Ninth International Joint Conference on Artificial Intelligence,* University of California at Los Angeles, Los Angeles, Ca., 18–23 August 1985, pp832–839.

Grosz, B J and Sidner, C L [1986] Attention, intentions, and the structure of discourse. *Computational Linguistics,* 12, 175–204.

Hobbs, J R [1978] Resolving pronoun references. *Lingua,* 44, 311–338.

Horacek, H [1990] The architecture of a generation component in a complete natural language dialogue system. This volume.

Kamp, H [1975] Two theories about adjectives. In E L Keenan (ed) *Formal Semantics of Natural Language: Papers from a colloquium sponsored by King's College Research Centre, Cambridge*, pp123–155. Cambridge: Cambridge University Press.

Keenan, E L and Faltz, L M [1978] *Logical Types for Natural Language*. UCLA Occasional Papers in Linguistics, No. 3.

Link, G [1983] The logical analysis of plurals and mass terms: a lattice-theoretical approach. In R Bauerle, C Schwarze and A von Stechow (eds) *Meaning, Use and Interpretation of Language*, pp302–323. Berlin: de Gruyter.

Massam, D and Roberge, Y [1989] Recipe context null objects in English. *Linguistic Inquiry*, **20**, 134–139.

Mayo, B [1961] Objects, events, and complementarity. *Philosophical Review*, **LXX**, 340–361.

Mellish, C [1988] Natural language generation from plans. Chapter 7 in M Zock and G Sabah (eds) *Advances in Natural Language Generation: An Interdisciplinary Perspective*, Volume 1, pp131–145. London: Pinter Publishers Ltd.

McDonald, D D [1980] Natural Language Generation as a Process of Decision-Making under Constraints. PhD Thesis, Department of Computer Science and Electrical Engineering, MIT.

Reiter, E [1990] Generating descriptions that exploit a user's domain knowledge. This volume.

Sacerdoti, E D [1977] *A Structure for Plans and Behavior*. New York: North Holland.

Shieber, S M [1986] *An Introduction to Unification-based Approaches to Grammar*. Chicago, Illinois: The University of Chicago Press.

Swartout, W R [1983] XPLAIN: A System for Creating and Explaining Expert Consulting Programs. ISI Reprint Series No. RS-83-4, USC Information Sciences Institute, Marina Del Rey, Ca., July, 1983.

Tate, A [1985] A Review of Knowledge-based Planning Techniques. Technical Report No. AIAI-TR-9, Artificial Intelligence Applications Institute, University of Edinburgh, 1985.

Webber, B L [1979] *A Formal Approach to Discourse Anaphora*. London: Garland Publishing.

Zemach, E [1979] Four ontologies. In F J Pelletier (ed) *Mass Terms: Some Philosophical Problems*, pp63–80.

10 Generating Descriptions that Exploit a User's Domain Knowledge

Ehud Reiter

Abstract

Natural language generation systems should customise object descriptions according to the extent of their users' domain and lexical knowledge. The task of generating customised descriptions is formalised as a task of finding descriptions that are **accurate** (truthful), **valid** (fulfill the speaker's communicative goal), and **free of false implicatures** (do not give rise to unintended conversational implicatures) with respect to the current user model. An algorithm that generates descriptions that meet these constraints is described, and the computational complexity of the generation problem is discussed.

10.1 Introduction

10.1.1 The problem

When a person hears an utterance, she usually uses her domain knowledge to expand on the literal semantic content of the utterance. Suppose, for example, a hearer heard the utterance

(1)   There is a shark in the water

The knowledgeable hearer would not just record the information that a member of a certain fish species was present in the water. Instead, she would access her domain knowledge about sharks, recall that they were large, carnivorous, and possibly dangerous fish, and then perhaps make further inferences, such as the fact that swimming in the area was not advisable.

The text, then, serves as a trigger or index into the reader's domain knowledge, and thus communicates far more than its literal content. This process is so natural and automatic in humans that we tend to take it for granted, except when it fails. Failure typically occurs when the hearer does not have the expected domain knowledge. For example, someone who knew nothing about sharks would not make the above inferences, and might decide that it was in fact okay to go swimming in the area. For such a naive hearer, a more explicit utterance such as (2) would be better:

(2)   There is a dangerous fish in the water

Utterance (2), though, would sound odd to the knowledgeable hearer. In fact, such a hearer would probably draw the **conversational implicature** [Grice 1975] that the animal in question *could not* be a shark. For, the hearer would reason, if the object had been a shark, then the speaker, knowing that her hearer was knowledgeable, would have used the short description *shark*, instead of the longer description *dangerous fish*.

Thus, utterance (1) is appropriate for the knowledgeable hearer, but inappropriate for the naive hearer (because she may fail to make the inference that swimming is not advisable). On the other hand, utterance (2) is appropriate for the naive hearer, but inappropriate for the knowledgeable hearer (because she may draw the incorrect and unintended conversational implicature that the animal is not a shark). A computer natural language (NL) generation system should be able to produce (1) for the knowledgeable hearer, and (2) for the naive hearer. The question discussed in this chapter is how such a system can be constructed, and what principles underlie the choice of (1) for the knowledgeable hearer, and (2) for the naive hearer.

More formally, we identify three constraints that utterances must satisfy:

- **accuracy**: the utterance should be truthful;
- **validity**: the utterance should trigger the desired inferences in the hearer; and
- **freedom from false implicatures**: the utterance should not lead the hearer to draw incorrect conversational implicatures.

Utterance (1) fails for the naive hearer because it is not valid (she does not draw the inference that swimming is a bad idea), while (2) fails for the knowledgeable hearer because it is not free of false implicatures (she draws the incorrect implicature that the animal is not a shark). This chapter presents a model of the above constraints, within the context of the task of generating object descriptions that are intended to inform the user that an individual object is a member of a KL-ONE class [Brachman and Schmolze 1985]. So, in the above examples, both *shark* and *dangerous fish* are ways of communicating that the object belongs to the class `Dangerous Animal`.

Horacek's FTRANSLATE terminological transfer system [Horacek, this volume] performs the related task of communicating a KL-ONE class definition to the user. Dale's EPICURE system [Dale, this volume], in contrast, has the much different communicative task of generating **referring expressions** that identify a particular object in the current discourse context. Other related work includes Paris's [1988] TAILOR system, which generates descriptions of classes of objects (e.g., encyclopaedia articles). Paris was interested in customising descriptions for different users, but she focused on the problem of selecting appropriate **rhetorical structures** [McKeown 1985], while the focus here is on selecting appropriate content words.

The rest of the introductory section briefly describes the FN system, which generates informational descriptions of objects. Section 10.2 presents a formalisation of the object description problem and of the accuracy, validity, and freedom-from-false-implicatures constraints. Section 10.3 gives a computational analysis of the description generation problem. It describes in some detail the generation algorithm used by the FN system, and it also discusses some formal NP-hardness results that apply to the description generation problem. Section 10.4 briefly discusses some possibilities for future work.

10.1.2   The FN system

The object description procedure described in this chapter has been incorporated into the FN system. FN is an NLG system that helps users decide whether they wish to use a particular object in a plan. FN might, for example, help a user decide if she wants to take a particular airline flight on a business trip, or use a particular computer system to write a report. FN determines which object attributes the user should be informed of, creates a description that communicates these attributes, and then generates a surface form for the description.

FN's input is the user's plan, and the object the user is considering using in her plan. The plan is always an instantiation of a **recipe** [Pollack 1990][1] in FN's recipe library, and contains annotations that indicate which object attributes affect the desirability of using that recipe with a particular object. For example, the `fly-on-business-trip` recipe might signal that the departure and arrival times of a flight affected the flight's desirability, but the cost of the flight did not (because business travelers usually do not care about cost). The `word-processing` recipe might mark the available text processors and the quality of attached printers as attributes that affected the desirability of using a particular computer for word processing.

When FN is given a plan, it uses the annotations to build a set of attributes that should be communicated to the user. It then determines what information the description should explicitly mention in order to successfully communicate this set of attributes. This is called the **content determination** problem, and is the topic of this chapter. Finally, FN calls a surface-form generation system to produce the textual form of the description.

The content determination process involves making decisions such as the following:

---

[1] A recipe is essentially a plan outline, and is similar to the **operator schemata** of STRIPS [Fikes and Nilsson 1971].

- If the system wishes to inform the user that a flight lands at LaGuardia airport, should it say this explicitly, and call the flight a *flight to La-Guardia*; or, can it instead just call the flight a *shuttle*, and rely on the user to know that *shuttles* to New York typically land at LaGuardia?

- If the system wishes to communicate that the computer in question runs the EDT text editor and the RUNOFF text formatter, should it say this explicitly, and describe the computer as a *computer that runs* EDT *and* RUNOFF; or, can it instead just describe the computer as a VMS VAX, and rely on the user to have the domain knowledge that such machines usually run EDT and RUNOFF?

Making such choices requires a good model of the user's domain and lexical knowledge, and a formal theory of what constraints descriptions should obey.

FN has been implemented, and an annotated trace of the content determination portion of an example run is shown in Figure 10.1 (the generation algorithm is described in Section 10.3.1). In this example, a computer, HUC1, is described to a system manager who wants to do word processing as

(3)   ... a BSD microVAX that has a LaserWriter, and runs LaTeX ...

The same computer would be described (in the same word processing context) to a less-knowledgeable engineer as

(4)   ... a Unix computer that has a laser printer, and runs *nroff, emacs,* and LaTeX ...

The differences between the two descriptions are a result of the engineer having less domain knowledge, and different **basic level** classes (see Section 10.2.4). For example, while the engineer must explicitly be told that the computer runs the *nroff* text processor, the system manager is assumed to be able to infer this from the fact that the computer runs the BSD operating system.

10.2 Object Descriptions

10.2.1 Knowledge representation

FN uses a simplified version of KL-ONE [Brachman and Schmolze 1985] as its knowledge representation language. An initial set of **roles** and **primitive classes**[2] is specified, and from these new classes can be defined by taking the intersection of existing classes, or by applying **value restrictions** (vrs) to the roles of existing classes. The more complex class formation operators of KL-ONE, such as role differentiation, are not supported.

---

[2]KL-ONE categories are referred to in this chapter as **classes**. This differs from Brachman and Schmolze, who use the term **concept** for KL-ONE categories.

```
; describe Huc1 to a system manager who wants to create a document
; The initial description is just the list of attributes to be communicated to the user
Initial description:
(COMPUTER (AVAILABLE-PERIPHERAL PRINTER
                    (PRINT-QUALITY HIGH))   ; High-quality printer available
          (AVAILABLE-SOFTWARE LATEX)        ; LaTeX text formatter available
          (AVAILABLE-SOFTWARE TEX)          ; TeX text formatter available
          (AVAILABLE-SOFTWARE NROFF)        ; nroff text formatter available
          (AVAILABLE-SOFTWARE VI)           ; vi text editor available
          (AVAILABLE-SOFTWARE EMACS)        ; emacs text editor available
          (AVAILABLE-SOFTWARE CSH)          ; csh command processor available
          (AVAILABLE-SOFTWARE SH))          ; sh command processor available
```

```
; (AVAILABLE-SOFTWARE TEX) is removed because it is implied by
; (AVAILABLE-SOFTWARE LATEX)
After find-minimal-s-simplification:
```

```
(COMPUTER (AVAILABLE-PERIPHERAL PRINTER (PRINT-QUALITY HIGH))
          (AVAILABLE-SOFTWARE LATEX) (AVAILABLE-SOFTWARE NROFF)
          (AVAILABLE-SOFTWARE VI) (AVAILABLE-SOFTWARE EMACS)
          (AVAILABLE-SOFTWARE CSH) (AVAILABLE-SOFTWARE SH))
```

```
; COMPUTER and PRINTER are replaced by the basic-level classes MICROVAX and LASERWRITER
After find-ns-simplifications:
```

```
(MICROVAX (AVAILABLE-PERIPHERAL LASERWRITER (PRINT-QUALITY HIGH))
          (AVAILABLE-SOFTWARE LATEX) (AVAILABLE-SOFTWARE NROFF)
          (AVAILABLE-SOFTWARE VI) (AVAILABLE-SOFTWARE EMACS)
          (AVAILABLE-SOFTWARE CSH) (AVAILABLE-SOFTWARE SH))
```

```
; PRINT-QUALITY:HIGH is removed because it is implied by LASERWRITER
After find-minimal-s-simplification:
```

```
(MICROVAX (AVAILABLE-PERIPHERAL LASERWRITER)
          (AVAILABLE-SOFTWARE LATEX) (AVAILABLE-SOFTWARE NROFF)
          (AVAILABLE-SOFTWARE VI) (AVAILABLE-SOFTWARE EMACS)
          (AVAILABLE-SOFTWARE CSH) (AVAILABLE-SOFTWARE SH))
```

```
; Most of the AVAILABLE-SOFTWARE attributes are replaced by (RUNS-OS BSD), which implies
; them
After check-local-brevity:
```

```
(MICROVAX (RUNS-OS BSD)
          (AVAILABLE-PERIPHERAL LASERWRITER)
          (AVAILABLE-SOFTWARE LATEX))
```

Description realisation is: *a* BSD *microvax that has a LaserWriter, and runs* LaTeX

Figure 10.1: A sample run of FN

FN also has a set of **user models**. These specify the domain and lexical knowledge of different users. They contain three kinds of information: **default role fillers** for classes; **realisations** for classes and roles; and a list of which classes are **basic-level** (see Section 10.2.4).[3] A **default role filler** is a role filler that is usually, but not always, present in members of a class. Default role fillers are inherited, and the defaults of subsumed classes take precedence over the defaults of subsuming classes.[4]

A **lexical realisation** is simply a word (or sequence of words) that may be used to denote a class. The user model only specifies realisations that are **lexical units** (i.e., dictionary entries. See Zgusta [1971; Section 3.3]). A class that can be realised with a lexical unit is called a **lexical class**. Roles can also have realisations, and roles with realisations are called **realisable roles**. A class definition that is stated solely in terms of lexical classes and realisable roles is called a **realisable definition**,[5] and any class that has such a definition is called a **realisable class**. Note that a realisable class can potentially have several realisable definitions.

We define the **default expansion** of a class C to be the class formed by combining C's definition with C's inherited defaults. For example, if class C inherits the default role fillers R1:V1 and R2:V2, then the default expansion of C would be the class (C with role value restrictions R1:V1 and R2:V2). Note that a class can have different default expansions in different user models.

An example knowledge base (with no user model) is shown in Figure 10.2. Primitive classes include Shark and Cetacean. Water Animal is an example of a non-primitive class, and is defined by placing the value restriction Habitat: Water on the class Animal. Object-1 represents a particular individual, who belongs to the primitive class Great White Shark and has role fillers Habitat:Water and Dangerous:True.

The same knowledge base with a superimposed user model is shown in Figure 10.3. Default role fillers are noted in parentheses, and include Habitat: Land for Mammals, and Dangerous:True for Sharks. Figure 10.3 also shows the default expansions of Shark and Dolphin. The default expansion of Shark is (Shark with VR Dangerous:True), and the default expansion of Dolphin is (Dolphin with VR Dangerous:False). Note that the default expansion of Dolphin does not include Habitat:Land (potentially inherited from Mammal)

---

[3]The user model cannot represent a user who has a different subsumption taxonomy; for example, someone who believes that Dolphins are a type of Fish, or that Dogs are Water Animals (see McCoy [1988]).

[4]If a class inherits conflicting defaults from different parents, and the conflict cannot be resolved according to the subsumed-class-takes-precedence rule, then the conflicting defaults are ignored, and no default filler is assumed for the role in question. This is similar to Kautz and Selman's [1989] **skeptical reasoning**.

[5]The FN system contains a simple generation grammar that can generate a text surface form from any realisable definition.

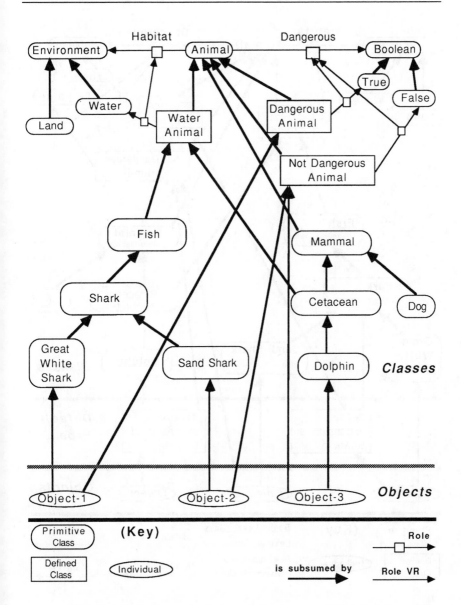

Figure 10.2: An example knowledge base (no user model)

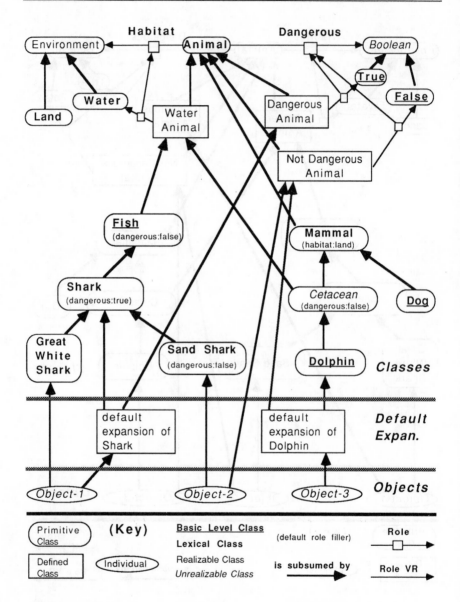

Figure 10.3: The knowledge base with a user model superimposed

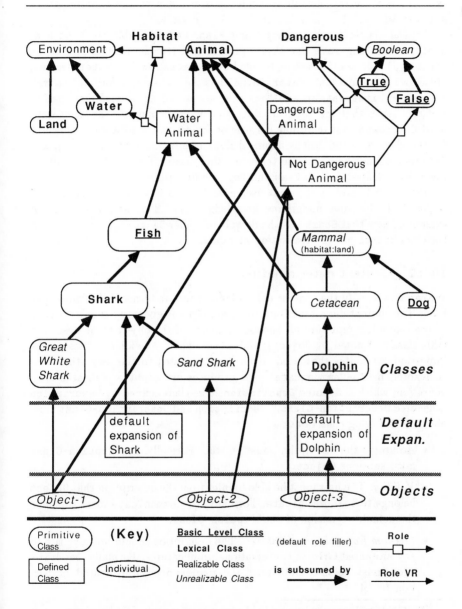

Figure 10.4: The knowledge base with a different user model

as a VR, because this default role filler is overridden by the definitional VR
Habitat:Water, which is inherited from Water Animal.

Lexical classes, such as Shark and Fish, and realisable roles, such as
Habitat and Dangerous, are shown in bold font (the actual realisations are
not shown). Classes that are realisable but not lexical, such as Water Animal,
are shown in normal font. Water Animal has the realisable definition (Animal
with VR Habitat:Water), and thus can be realised as *animal that lives in
water*. Classes that are not realisable, such as Cetacean, are shown in italic
font. Cetacean is not realisable because no lexical unit realisation is specified
for the class (i.e. the user is assumed not to know the word *cetacean*), and
Cetacean cannot be defined in terms of other classes, because it is primitive.
Basic-level classes, such as Fish and Dog, are underlined.

Figure 10.4 shows a different user model (for a less knowledgeable user)
imposed on the same underlying knowledge base. This user does not, for
example, know that Shark has the default role filler Dangerous:True, or that
the class Mammal has the realisation *mammal*.

10.2.2   Content determination

We can now specify the content determination task in terms of the knowledge
base. The content determination subsystem of FN is given two inputs: a class
whose role fillers represent all known attributes of the object to be described
(this class is denoted by Object); and a class whose role fillers represent the
important attributes that need to be communicated to the user (this class
is denoted by To-Communicate). FN produces as output a realisable class
definition, which is denoted Description. The class defined by Description
is denoted Description-Class.[6] Description and Description-Class must
obey the following constraints:

- *Accuracy*: the description must be true. Formally, Description-Class
  must subsume Object.

- *Validity*: The user must be able to infer from the description that Object
  belongs to To-Communicate. Formally, To-Communicate must subsume
  the default expansion of Description-Class.

- *Freedom from false implicatures*: The description should not give rise to
  any unwanted Gricean conversational implicatures. Formally, Description must be maximal under the **preference rules** stated in Section 10.2.4.

---

[6]Description-Class is not required to be a pre-existing member of the knowledge base; it
can be any class that is definable from the primitive classes and roles. In KL-ONE terminology,
Description-Class can be any member of the **virtual lattice** of classes.

Intuitively, Description is valid if every attribute the system wishes to communicate is equal to (or subsumes) a parent class, a defining VR, or an inherited default role filler of Description-Class; and Description is free of false implicatures if there is no preferred utterance that would constitute an accurate and valid description.

For example, suppose Object was Object-1, and To-Communicate was Dangerous Animal. With the user model given in Figure 10.3, FN would return a Description of Shark, since it meets the above constraints.

- *Accuracy*: Shark subsumes Object-1.

- *Validity*: Dangerous Animal subsumes the default expansion of Shark.

- *Freedom from false implicatures*: Shark is maximal under the preference rules of Section 10.2.4.

If the user model was changed to the one in Figure 10.4, then Shark would no longer be a valid description, because its default expansion is not subsumed by Dangerous Animal under this user model. Given this user model, FN would return the description Dangerous Fish (Fish with VR Dangerous:True). This description is accurate, valid, and free of false implicatures under the Figure 10.4 user model (it is not free of false implicatures under the Figure 10.3 user model).

10.2.3   The importance of defaults

The role and handling of defaults in FN deserves some elaboration. The basic assumption is that lexical classes (i.e., nouns and adjectives) represent mental categories in the hearer's mind, and that these categories can have both 'typical' and 'necessary' attributes. Default role fillers are intended to represent typical attributes, and defining VRs are intended to represent necessary attributes. In this context, it is interesting to note that current psychological thinking tends to reject the idea that most lexical categories are defined through necessary and sufficient attributes, and instead has stressed prototypical and exemplar models of mental categories [Smith and Medin 1981]. Accordingly, it is likely that FN's lexical classes will almost all be primitive, and have few (if any) definitional role fillers, but many default role fillers.

Most of FN's power then, comes from taking advantage of default role fillers. The proper representation and handling of these defaults is thus extremely important. Basically, FN treats default role fillers as KL-ONE IDatas, except that it implements the following conflict-resolution rule among defaults: if class A is subsumed by class B, then the defaults associated with A will take precedence over the defaults associated with B (standard KL-ONE systems inherit all IDatas, and do not perform any conflict resolution). All defaults must be inheritable—there is no equivalent to KL-ONE's non-inherited Data properties.

A user model can attach default role fillers to any class, and not just to lexical classes. In other words, the assumption is that humans can have mental categories for, and associate defaults with, categories that are not realisable as lexical units. This is supported by various psychological results, for example by Osherson and Smith's [1981] finding that the prototypical attributes people associated with a *pet fish* were quite different from the prototypical properties that people associated with either *pets* or *fish*. However, it turns out that complete freedom to attach defaults to any class makes it computationally intractable to generate descriptions that meet the above constraints. This is discussed in Section 10.3.2.

10.2.4   Avoiding unwanted conversational implicatures

Grice [1975] proposed that four **maxims of conversation** (Quality, Quantity, Relevance, and Manner) underlie the way people use language. Grice further suggested that if a speaker uttered an utterance that did not obey these maxims, and therefore seemed long, unwieldy, or irrelevant, then the hearer would assume that the speaker could do no better, because there was no shorter and more manageable utterance that would fulfill the speaker's communicative goals. For example, suppose a speaker, A, actually uttered (5) to a knowledgeable hearer, B:

(5)   There is a dangerous fish in the water

B would then assume that A *could not* have used a shorter utterance such as *there is a shark in the water*, or *there is a piranha in the water*. That is, B would assume that either the animal was not a shark, piranha, or other kind of commonly known dangerous fish; or that A did not know what kind of fish was present. If this was incorrect, because the animal was a shark and A knew this, then B would have drawn an incorrect conversational implicature.

An NL generation system, then, must be careful to avoid generating text that violates the Gricean maxims and thus leads the reader to draw incorrect conversational implicatures. Descriptions that do not carry incorrect conversational implicatures are called **free of false implicatures**.

For the analysis below, it is useful to define **components** of descriptions. A description component is any lexical class that is mentioned in the description's realisable definition, together with any roles in which that class is embedded. For example, the realisable definition (Animal with VR Habitat:Water) has the components Animal and Habitat:Water; and the realisable definition (Man with VRs Hair-Color:Grey and Pet:(Shark with VR Dangerous:False)) has the components Man, Hair-Color:Grey, Pet:Shark, and Pet:(Dangerous:False).

The Gricean maxims of conversational implicature are interpreted as follows:

Quality: the maxim of quality is interpreted to mean that a description must be **accurate**, i.e., that `Description-Class` must subsume `Object`.

Quantity: within the context of generating object descriptions, the most natural interpretation of this maxim seems to be that descriptions should not contain any unnecessary open class words.[7] Unfortunately, it is very difficult, from a computational point of view, to implement this rule, due to the fact that an individual word may occur in the realisations of several lexical classes.[8]

Therefore, the maxim of quantity is instead interpreted to mean that a description cannot contain any components that could be eliminated or **reduced**. **Reducing** a component means replacing the component's lexical class by a new lexical class, whose realisation uses a subset of the open-class words used by the original class. For example, `Shark` (realisation *shark*) is a reduction of `Sand Shark` (realisation *sand shark*).

Relevance: the maxim of relevance is interpreted similarly to the maxim of quantity.

Manner: Grice's maxim of manner has several submaxims. The only one investigated here is the submaxim of **brevity**.

The most desirable interpretation of the brevity submaxim would probably be that the chosen description should have a surface realisation that uses as few open-class words as possible. However, unless severe limitations are placed on the contents of the knowledge base, finding the valid description that has the fewest open-class words is computationally intractable (it can be shown to be NP-hard via a straightforward reduction from the **minimal set cover** problem). Therefore, the brevity submaxim is instead interpreted to mean that a description is unacceptable if a valid description with fewer open-class words can be formed through one particular mechanism, namely replacing one or more existing description components by a single new description component. This is called the **local brevity** rule. The local brevity rule tells us, for example, that `Shark` is a better description than `Dangerous Fish`, and thus `Dangerous Fish` is unacceptable as a description if `Shark` could be used instead.

---

[7]Very roughly, an open class word is any noun, verb, adjective, or adverb. See Cruse [1986] or Clark and Clark [1977] for a more precise definition.

[8]More precisely, it is NP-hard to determine if a description has unnecessary open class words, even if the restrictions suggested in Section 10.3.2 are imposed.

Note that both Dale [this volume] and Horacek [this volume] base some
of their system's operation on the brevity maxim. Dale's goal is to find
the referring expression with the fewest number of attributes (not fewest
number of open-class words), and he uses a heuristic algorithm that usually, but not always, finds this description. Horacek has a similar goal,
which he achieves by assuming knowledge base restrictions that are similar in spirit to the **full brevity** constraints discussed in Section 10.3.2.

Basic Levels: Cruse [1977] has proposed an additional source of Gricean conversational implicatures, and that is the failure to use basic level [Rosch
1978] classes in a description.[9] Accordingly, a description is deemed
unacceptable if it has components that use non-basic-level classes, and
some of these classes could be replaced by basic-level classes without
making the description invalid. For example, `Dog` is a better description
than `Mammal`, because `Dog` is a basic-level class, and thus `Mammal` is an
unacceptable description if `Dog` could be used instead.

It is convenient to restate the above rules in terms of a requiring a description to be a maximal element, under a set of preference rules, of the set of
accurate and valid descriptions. That is, if S is the set of accurate and valid
descriptions, then we will say that $A \in S$ is **free of false implicatures** if
there is no $B \in S$ such that B is preferred over A under one of the preference
rules. The preference rule formalisation is similar to the partially-ordered sets
that Hirschberg [1985] used to formalise scalar implicatures.

The preference rules are as follows.

Unnecessary components: description A is preferred over description B if
A's components are a subset of B's components.

Lexical preference: description A is preferred over description B if A's components use the same roles as B, and A's lexical classes are equal to or
lexically preferred over B's lexical classes. A lexical class A is lexically preferred over a lexical class B if A is basic-level and B is not, or
if A is a reduction of B.

Local brevity: description A is preferred over description B if A's realisation
uses fewer open class words than B's realisation, and A can be formed
from B by replacing one or more of B's components by a single new
component.

The lexical-preference ordering for the lexical classes of Figure 10.3 is shown
in Figure 10.5. The basic level classes `Fish`, `Dolphin`, and `Dog` are preferred

---

[9]The basic level hypothesis of psychology [Rosch 1978] says that certain classes, called
basic level classes, are special and in some sense cognitively preferred by humans. Among
other things, they are the classes children learn first; the classes people react fastest to in
reaction-time experiments; and the classes people usually use in null-context descriptions.

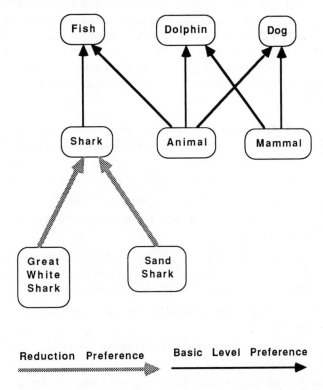

Figure 10.5: The lexical class preference hierarchy

over all other classes, and the class Shark is preferred over Sand Shark and Great White Shark because of the reduction rule (assuming that these classes have the realisations *shark*, *sand shark*, and *great white shark*). Remember that descriptions must first of all be accurate, which means, for example, that Dolphin could not replace Animal in a description of Object-1, even though Dolphin is lexically preferred over Animal.

The assumption will be made in this chapter that the above rules do not conflict. This means, in particular, that if lexical class A is preferred over lexical class B, then A's realisation must not contain more open-class words than B's realisation (if this is violated, the lexical preference and local brevity rules may conflict). This can be supported by psychological and linguistic findings that basic level classes are almost always realised with single words (Rosch [1978]; Berlin, Breedlove, and Raven [1973]). However, there are a few exceptions to this rule, i.e., there do exist a small number of basic level categories that have realisations that require more than one open class word. For example, `Savings-Account` is a basic level class for some people, and it has a realisation that uses two open class words. This leads to a conflict of the type mentioned above: basic level `Savings-Account` is preferred over non-basic-level `Asset`, but `Savings-Account`'s realisation contains more open-class words than `Asset`'s.

To illustrate the preference rules, suppose the generation system was told to describe `Object-1` under a `To-Communicate` of `Dangerous-Animal`. Consider the following potential descriptions:

(6)   a   *great white shark* (`Great White Shark`)

       b   *dangerous fish* (`Fish` with VR `Dangerous:True`)

       c   *dangerous shark* (`Shark` with VR `Dangerous:True`)

       d   *shark* (`Shark`)

All of the above accurately describe `Object-1`. Under the user model shown in Figure 10.3, all of the above are also valid. However, only (6d) is maximal under the preference rules and hence free of false implicatures. For,

- (6a) is not maximal, because (6d) is preferred over (6a) by the Lexical Preference rule;

- (6b) is not maximal, because (6d) is preferred over (6b) by the Local Brevity rule; and

- (6c) is not maximal, because (6d) is preferred over (6c) by the Unnecessary Components rule.

If the user model shown in Figure 10.4 were used, then (6a) would no longer be a realisable definition, and (6d) would no longer be valid, so only (6b) and (6c) would be accurate and valid descriptions. Only (6b) would be free of false implicatures, however, because (6b) is preferred over (6c) by the Lexical Preference rule (since basic level `Fish` is lexically preferred over `Shark`).

10.3   Algorithm and Complexity Analysis

10.3.1   Generation algorithm

This section describes an algorithm that generates descriptions that are accurate, valid, and free of false implicatures. The algorithm starts with an initial description that is accurate and valid, and checks if this description is maximal under the preference rules. If so, it is returned. If not, the description is replaced by a preferred description, and the process is repeated.

The following terminology is used in the description of the algorithm:

- A description $D1$ is a **simplification** of a description $D2$ if $D1$ can be formed by removing components from $D2$, and/or by replacing some of $D2$'s lexical classes by preferred lexical classes. For example, under the knowledge base and user model shown in Figure 10.3, `Fish` is a simplification of `Animal`, `Water-Animal`, `Shark`, `Sand Shark`, and `Great White Shark`.

  A description satisfies the Unnecessary Components and Lexical Preference rules if and only if it does not have a simplification that is accurate and valid.

- A description $D1$ is an **s-simplification** of a description $D2$ if $D1$ is a simplification of $D2$, and the class defined by $D1$ subsumes the class defined by D2. $D1$ is an **ns-simplification** of $D2$ if it is a simplification of $D2$, but not a subsumer of $D2$. For example, `Fish` is an s-simplification of `Shark` and `Sand Shark`, but an ns-simplification of `Animal`.

- A description $D1$ is a **minimal s-simplification** of a description $D2$ if $D1$ is an s-simplification of $D2$, and there is no intermediate description $D3$, such that $D3$ is an s-simplification of $D2$, and $D1$ is an s-simplification of $D3$. `Fish`, for example, is a not a minimal s-simplification of `Sand Shark`, because there is an intermediate description, namely `Shark`, that is an s-simplification of `Sand Shark`, and that has `Fish` as its own s-simplification. `Fish` is, however, a minimal s-simplification of `Shark`, since there is no intermediate description between `Fish` and `Shark`.

The generation algorithm can now be defined in terms of the following subroutines:

`Find-Minimal-S-Simplifications`: this routine takes as input an accurate and valid description `Input`, and checks `Input`'s minimal s-simplifications to see if any of them are valid. If a valid minimal s-simplification is found, the routine returns it.

`Find-Valid-S-Simplification`: this routine takes as input an *invalid* description `Input`, and checks to see if a valid description can be formed from `Input` by making a series of s-simplifications. This can only happen when a class that subsumes `Input` has a default role filler that specifies a correct value for a role of `To-Communicate`, but this correct value is cancelled or overridden by a default role filler from a different class. `Find-Valid-S-Simplification` looks for such cases, and, if it finds one, applies the minimal possible set of s-simplifications to `Input` that will insure that the correct default is no longer cancelled. If this results in a valid description, `Find-Valid-S-Simplification` succeeds. Otherwise, it recurses with the simplified version of `Input`.

Find-Non-Minimal-S-Simplifications: this routine handles cases where the Input description is valid, and no single minimal s-simplification of the Input description results in a valid description, but a non-minimal set of s-simplifications will nonetheless produce a valid simplified description. This can only happen when a correct default is overridden or cancelled by an incorrect default (as in Find-Valid-S-Simplification), but the incorrect default is itself overridden by another correct default. If Find-Non-Minimal-S-Simplification detects such a case, it applies the minimum possible set of s-simplifications to Input that will insure that the incorrect default no longer applies. If this results in a valid description, Find-Non-Minimal-S-Simplification returns successfully. Otherwise, Find-Valid-S-Simplification is called to see if a valid description can be formed by further simplifying the description.

For example, using the knowledge base and user model of Figure 10.3, suppose To-Communicate was Not-Dangerous Animal, and Object was Object-2. Then, Sand Shark would be an example of a valid description whose minimal s-simplification (Shark) was not valid, but that nevertheless did possess a valid simplification, namely Fish. This is the situation mentioned above, where a correct default (Dangerous:False from Sand Shark) overrides an incorrect default (Dangerous:True from Shark), which itself overrides a correct default (Dangerous:False from Fish).

Find-NS-Simplifications: this routine looks for ns-simplifications, i.e., simplifications that are not subsumers. It first finds all cases where the lexical preference ordering suggests replacing an existing lexical class by a preferred lexical class that does not subsume the existing lexical class (e.g. replacing Animal by Fish). The routine applies all of these replacements, and checks if this results in a valid description. If so, Find-NS-Simplification reports success. If not, a modified form of Find-Valid-S-Simplification is called to see if undoing some (but not all) of the replacements will lead to a valid description.

The generation system repeatedly calls Find-Minimal-S-Simplifications, Find-Non-Minimal-S-Simplifications, and Find-NS-Simplifications, until none of the routines can make any further changes in the description. When this happens, the current description cannot be simplified in any way, and therefore must be maximal under the Unnecessary Components and Lexical Preference rules.

The generation system has two additional subroutines:

Check-Local-Brevity: this routine tries replacing existing description components by new components. If such a replacement results in a valid description, the new description is simplified with the above routines, and then compared against the input description to see if its realisation uses fewer open class words.

`Check-Local-Brevity` uses a list of potential description components in order to run more efficiently. These are possible description components that are accurate, potentially of some use in communicating components of `To-Communicate`, and not clearly inferior to other possible description components. The generation system calculates this list once for each description task.

`Make-Initial-Description`: this routine first checks if `To-Communicate` does in fact subsume `Object`. If it does not, an error is signalled. Otherwise, `Make-Initial-Description` checks if `To-Communicate` is itself a realisable class. If so, `To-Communicate` is returned as the initial description.

If the above fails because `To-Communicate` is not realisable, `Make-Initial-Description` forms a description that includes all of the potential description components (see `Check-Local-Brevity`). If this description is valid, it is returned as the initial description. Otherwise, `Find-Valid-S-Simplification` is called to see if this description has a valid s-simplification. If so, this s-simplification is returned. Otherwise, `Make-Initial-Description` signals that it is impossible to construct a valid, accurate, and realisable description.

Figure 10.6 gives a trace of the generation algorithm running on the `Shark` example, and Figure 10.7 shows a flow-chart of the algorithm.

10.3.2 The computational complexity of generating descriptions

Generating descriptions that are accurate, valid, and free of false implicatures is generally an NP-hard task (NP-hard in the number of attributes in `To-Communicate`). In the algorithm, the potential exponential blow-up occurs in `Find-Valid-S-Simplification` and `Find-NS-Simplification`. In `Find-Valid-S-Simplification`, the problem is that there can be several sets of minimal s-simplifications that cause a correct default to no longer be overridden. `Find-Valid-S-Simplification` must try each one, and may need to recurse on each one as well. Because the recursion can potentially go as deep as the number of components in the description, the result is that exponential time may be needed to check if there are any valid subsumers of `Input`. The problem in `Find-NS-Simplifications` is similar: it may be that each lexical class in the description has several possible replacements (i.e., there is more than one preferred class that does not subsume the original class), and an exhaustive search is needed to determine if some combination of the possible

Knowledge Base and User Model (as shown in Figure 10.3):

Input: `Object = Object-1`
     `To-Communicate = Dangerous-Animal`

Steps:

1. `Make-Initial-Description` notes that `To-Communicate` is itself accurate and realisable. Therefore, the initial `Description` is set to the value of `To-Communicate`, namely `Dangerous Animal`.

2. `Find-NS-Simplifications` notes that `Dangerous Fish` is an ns-simplification of `Dangerous Animal`, since `Fish` is preferred over `Animal`. Since `Dangerous Fish` is accurate and valid, it is returned as the new `Description`.

3. `Check-Local-Brevity` notes that the single component `Shark` can replace the two components `Fish` and `Dangerous:True` of `Dangerous Fish`. Since the resultant description, `Shark`, is accurate, valid, and uses fewer open class words in its realisation, it is returned as the new `Description`. This step would not be executed if the user model shown in Figure 10.4 was in use.

4. `Find-Minimal-S-Simplifications`,
   `Find-Non-Minimal-S-Simplifications`, `Find-NS-Simplifications`, and `Check-Local-Brevity` all fail to find a better description than `Shark`. Therefore, the generation procedure algorithm terminates.

Output Description: `Shark`

Figure 10.6: A simple trace of the generation algorithm

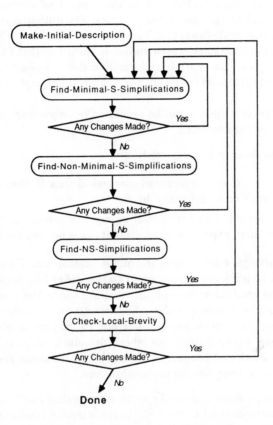

Figure 10.7: The generation flow chart

replacements can lead to a valid description.

It should be emphasised that the above problem is not just an artifact of the particular algorithm used, but rather is a fundamental aspect of the description generation problem. Checking if a description has a valid simplification is provably NP-hard. A partial proof of this is given in Section 10.3.3.

If the above problems did not occur, then the generation algorithm would run in polynomial time (polynomial in the number of components in To-Communicate, and in the number of potential description components considered by Check-Local-Brevity). Therefore, the algorithm will run in polynomial time if the knowledge representation is limited so that Find-Valid-S-Simplification only has one minimal simplification to examine at each stage, and Find-NS-Simplifications only has to look at one replacement for each lexical class.

In particular, descriptions can be generated in polynomial time if the following restrictions are enforced:

1. Lexical preference hierarchy restrictions:

   (a) If lexical class *A* is preferred over lexical class *B*, then *A* must either subsume or be subsumed by *B*.

   (b) If a lexical class has several immediate parents in the hierarchy, then these parents must be disjoint (have no members in common).

2. Default-role-filler-attachment restriction: default role fillers can only be attached to primitive classes, or to classes defined by applying a single role value restriction to a primitive class, where the restriction value must itself be a primitive class. So, defaults can be attached to Water Animal or Dangerous Animal, but not to Dangerous Water Animal. Dangerous Water Animal can inherit defaults from its subsumers (e.g. Water Animal and Dangerous Animal), but it cannot specify new defaults that are not present in its subsumers.

The first lexical preference hierarchy restriction requires the lexical preference hierarchy to have some connection with the subsumption taxonomy; the second requires the portion of the lexical preference hierarchy that is applicable to any individual object to be a tree. The default-role-filler-attachment restriction limits the classes that can have defaults attached to them. Note that the knowledge base and user models shown in Figures 10.2, 10.3, and 10.4 obey all of the above restrictions.

Roughly speaking, if any of the above restrictions are removed, then detecting if a description has a valid simplification (and thus generating valid free-of-false-implicatures descriptions) becomes an NP-hard problem. It is interesting to note that the above restrictions do seem to be obeyed by people most of the time. Almost all of the descriptions in a corpus of human-generated descriptions,[10] for example, can be generated with a knowledge base that fits the restrictions. The few exceptions occurred when a default was associated with a class that was defined by applying a single value restriction to a primitive class, but where the restriction value was not itself a primitive class.

There are many other restrictions that could be imposed on the knowledge base, including:

No default role fillers: if default role fillers are not allowed, then descriptions can be generated in polynomial time if the lexical preference hierarchy restrictions are met (the default-role-filler-attachment restrictions are no longer needed).

Full brevity: it is possible to find, in polynomial time, the accurate and valid description whose realisation has the fewest possible number of open class words, if the following restrictions are enforced:

- Default role fillers can only be specified for primitive classes (although other classes can inherit defaults from primitive classes). Note that the Osherson and Smith finding discussed in Section 10.2.3 suggests that people do not obey this restriction.

- Primitive classes cannot overlap: if a primitive class A neither subsumes nor is subsumed by a primitive class B, then no object can belong to both A and B.

- To-Communicate does not contain any value restrictions embedded within other value restrictions (for example, (Man with VR Pet:(Shark with VR Dangerous:False)) is forbidden).

In the other direction, generalising the knowledge representation tends to make the description generation problem even more intractable:

Richer subset of KL-ONE: if the knowledge representation system is expanded to allow additional class-formation operators, and this expansion makes subsumption calculation NP-hard [Nebel 1988], then it will be NP-hard to determine if a description class is valid (let alone free of false implicatures), even if the above restrictions are imposed.

Default logic: if default attributes are expressed through **default logic** [Reiter 1980] formulas, instead of as KL-ONE IDatas, then determining if a description class is valid becomes at least NP-hard, and perhaps undecidable. Even using a severely weakened form of default logic can cause validity detection to become intractable [Kautz and Selman 1989].

---

[10] Approximately 100 human-generated descriptions of computers were examined. They were taken from newspaper and trade-journal articles, and USENET bulletin-board postings.

10.3.3   An NP-hardness proof

If defaults can be attached to arbitrary classes, then detecting if a description class has a valid simplification is an NP-hard problem. A proof is presented below of the central lemma of this argument, which is that Find-Valid-S-Simplification's task is NP-hard in this case (a complete proof that the generation problem is NP-hard is given in Reiter [1990]).

Lemma: If default role fillers can be attached to arbitrary classes, then it is NP-hard to determine if an invalid description class has a valid simplification.

Proof: A reduction is made from the **satisfiability** problem, which is known to be NP-hard [Garey and Johnson 1979].
  Satisfiability: Given a boolean formula in conjunctive normal form (a conjunction of disjuncts), determine if there is any value of the variables that will make the formula true.
  Example: $(X_1)(X_1 + X_2)$ is satisfiable, by making both X_1 and $X2$ *true.*
  Example: $(X_1)(\neg X_1)$ is not satisfiable, because this formula is always *false,* no matter what value X_1 has.

The reduction works as follows. Given a satisfiability problem, we create the following knowledge base:

- We create a primitive lexical class C, and a realisable role OK.

- For each term $Term_j$ in the satisfiability problem, we create a realisable role PTerm$_j$.

- For each variable X_i in the satisfiability formula, we create two realisable roles, TX$_i$ and FX$_i$. The intention is that the presence of TX$_i$:true in a description indicates that variable X_i should have the value *true,* and the presence of FX$_i$:true in a description indicates that variable X_i should have the value *false.*

- For every term $Term_j$, for every non-negated variable X_i contained in that term, we associate the default role filler (PTerm$_j$:true) with the class (C with value restriction TX$_i$:true).

- For every term $Term_j$, for every negated variable $\neg X_i$ contained in that term, we associate the default role filler (PTerm$_j$:true) with the class (C with VR FX$_i$:true).

- For every X_i, we associate the default role filler (OK:false) with the class (C with VRs TX$_i$:true and FX$_i$:true).

- We associate the default (OK:true) with the class C.

With the above knowledge base, we then set:

- Object to be class C with the role fillers OK:true, PTerm$_j$:true (for every *PTerm$_j$*), TX$_i$:true (for every TX$_i$), and FX$_i$:true (for every FX$_i$);

- To-Communicate to be class C with role fillers OK:true, and PTerm$_j$:true (for every PTerm$_j$); and

- Input to be class C with role fillers TX$_i$:true (for every TX$_i$), and FX$_i$:true (for every FX$_i$).

With the above setup, Input is itself an invalid description (because OK:false can be inferred from it). Now, suppose the original satisfiability problem has a solution X_{sat}. Then, it is easy to see that a valid simplification D$_{val}$ for Input can be constructed according to the mapping suggested above: for every X_i, let D$_{val}$ contain VR TX$_i$:true if X_i is *true* in X_{sat}, and VR FX$_i$:true if X_i is *false* in X_{sat}.

Conversely, suppose Input has a valid simplification D$_{val}$. Then, let X_{sat} be the variable assignment constructed as follows: X_i is *true* if TX$_i$:true is a VR in D$_{val}$, *false* if FX$_i$:true is a VR in D$_{val}$, and either *true* or *false* if neither TX$_i$:true or FX$_i$:true are VRs in D$_{val}$. Note that TX$_i$:true and FX$_i$:true cannot both be VRs in D$_{val}$, for then D$_{val}$ would inherit the incorrect default OK:false, and thus be invalid. Now, because D$_{val}$ is valid, for every term $Term_j$, the corresponding PTerm$_j$:true must be inferable from D$_{val}$, which means that either $Term_j$ contains a non-negated X_i whose corresponding TX$_i$:true is a VR in D$_{val}$ (and therefore this X_i is *true* in X_{sat}); or, $Term_j$ contains a negated $\neg X_i$ whose corresponding FX$_i$:false is a VR in D$_{val}$ (and therefore this X_i is *false* in X_{sat}). In either case, $Term_j$ will be satisfied by the variable assignment X_{sat}. Thus, X_{sat} is a solution to the original satisfiability problem.

Thus, a solution to the original satisfiability problem exists if and only if Input has a valid simplification. Therefore, an algorithm that could determine if an arbitrary Input has a valid simplification can solve an arbitrary satisfiability problem. Thus, determining if an invalid description has a valid simplification is an NP-hard problem. See Figure 10.8 for an example of the above reduction.

If the Find-Valid-S-Simplification algorithm discussed in Section 10.3.1 was applied to the above problem, it would note that each TX$_i$:true and FX$_i$:true pair generated an incorrect default OK:false, and that this default overrode a correct default, OK:true, that came from class C. Each of these defaults could be removed in one of two ways: by eliminating TX$_i$:true from the description, or by eliminating FX$_i$:true from the description. Find-Valid-S-Simplification would, in the worst case, have to investigate all possible combinations of ways of removing the defaults (in effect, all possible value assignments to the X_is), and check if any of these resulted in a valid description.

Satisfiability problem:

$$(X_1 + \neg X_2)(\neg X_3)(\neg X_1 + X_2)$$

Roles:

PTerm$_1$ (corresponds to term $(X_1 + \neg X_2)$)
PTerm$_2$ (corresponds to term $(\neg X_3)$)
PTerm$_3$ (corresponds to term $(\neg X_1 + X_2)$)
TX$_1$ and FX$_1$ (correspond to variable X_1)
TX$_2$ and FX$_2$ (correspond to variable X_2)
TX$_3$ and FX$_3$ (correspond to variable X_3)

Default role fillers:

(C with VR TX$_1$:true) implies PTerm$_1$:true (because X_1 is in $(X_1 + \neg X_2)$)
(C with VR FX$_2$:true) implies PTerm$_1$:true (because $\neg X_2$ is in $(X_1 + \neg X_2)$)
(C with VR FX$_3$:true) implies PTerm$_2$:true (because $\neg X_3$ is in $(\neg X_3)$)
(C with VR FX$_1$:true) implies PTerm$_3$:true (because $\neg X_1$ is in $(\neg X_1 + X_2)$)
(C with VR TX$_2$:true) implies PTerm$_3$:true (because X_2 is in $(\neg X_1 + X_2)$)
(C with VRs TX$_1$:true and FX$_1$:true) implies OK:false
(C with VRs TX$_2$:true and FX$_2$:true) implies OK:false
(C with VRs TX$_3$:true and FX$_3$:true) implies OK:false
C implies OK:true

Description Problem:

To-Communicate = (C with VRs PTerm$_1$:true, PTerm$_2$:true, PTerm$_3$:true, and OK:true)

Object = (C with VRs PTerm$_1$:true, PTerm$_2$:true, PTerm$_3$:true, TX$_1$:true, FX$_1$:true, TX$_2$:true, FX$_2$:true, TX$_3$:true, FX$_3$:true, and OK:true)

Input = (C with VRs TX$_1$:true, FX$_1$:true, TX$_2$:true, FX$_2$:true, TX$_3$:true, and FX$_3$:true)

Solution: Input has a valid simplification, namely C with VRs TX$_1$:true, TX$_2$:true, and FX$_3$:true. This corresponds to

$X_1 = true$ because TX$_1$:true is in the solution
$X_2 = true$ because TX$_2$:true is in the solution
$X_3 = false$ because FX$_3$:true is in the solution

Figure 10.8: Encoding satisfiability as a description problem

---

10.4   Future Work

Among the many possibilities for future work are the following.

10.4.1   Other kinds of descriptions

The FN system only produces informational descriptions of individual objects. It would be interesting to investigate other tasks, such as generating referring expressions [Dale, this volume], or generating informational descriptions of classes [Paris 1988], to see if these tasks could also be formalised in terms of finding a description that is accurate, valid, and free of false implicatures. It would certainly be necessary to change the definition of the validity constraint to reflect the new communicative goals, but would it also be necessary to change the definition of the freedom-from-false-implicatures constraint? Ideally, a single set of preference rules could be found that applied to all description tasks, and perhaps to other NL generation tasks as well.

10.4.2   Linear-time generation

This chapter has investigated what restrictions are necessary to insure that descriptions can be generated in polynomial time. McDonald (personal communication) has suggested that any cognitively realistic generation system must run in *linear* time, and it would be interesting to look at what knowledge base and user model constraints would be required, and what preference rules would be acceptable, in a linear time generation system.

Acknowledgements

Many thanks to Cecile Balkanski, Barbara Grosz, Joe Marks, Warren Plath, Candy Sidner, Va-on Tam, Bill Woods, and the anonymous reviewers for their help and suggestions. This work was partially supported by a National Science Foundation Graduate Fellowship, an IBM Graduate Fellowship, and a contract from U S WEST Advanced Technologies. Any opinions, findings, conclusions, or recommendations are those of the author and do not necessarily reflect the views of the National Science Foundation, IBM, or U S WEST Advanced Technologies. UNIX is a trademark of ATT Bell Laboratories; MicroVAX, VAX, and VMS are trademarks of Digital Equipment Corporation.

References

Berlin, B, Breedlove, D and Raven, P [1973] General principles of classification and nomenclature in folk biology. *American Anthropologist*, **75**, 214–242.

Brachman, R and Schmolze, J [1985] An overview of the KL-ONE knowledge representation system. *Cognitive Science*, 9, 171–216.

Clark, H and Clark, E [1977] *Psychology and Language: an Introduction to Psycholinguistics*. New York: Harcourt Brace Jovanovich.

Cruse, D [1977] The pragmatics of lexical specificity. *Journal of Linguistics*, 13, 153–164.

Cruse, D [1986] *Lexical Semantics*. Cambridge: Cambridge University Press.

Dale, R [1990] Generating recipes: An overview of Epicure. This volume.

Fikes, R and Nilsson, N [1971] Strips: a new approach to the application of theorem proving to problem solving. *Artificial Intelligence*, 2, 189–208.

Garey, M and Johnson, D [1979] *Computers and Intractability: a Guide to the Theory of NP-Completeness*. San Francisco, Ca.: W H Freeman.

Grice, H [1975] Logic and conversation. In P Cole and J Morgan (Eds), *Syntax and Semantics*: Volume 3, *Speech Acts*, pp43–58. New York: Academic Press.

Hirschberg, J [1985] *A Theory of Scalar Implicature*. Report MS-CIS-85-56, LINC LAB 21, Department of Computer and Information Science, University of Pennsylvania,

Horacek, H [1990] The architecture of a generation component in a complete natural language dialogue system. This volume.

Kautz, H and Selman, B [1989] Hard problems for simple default logics. *Proceedings of the First International Conference on Knowledge Representation and Reasoning*, Toronto, May 1989, pp189–197.

McCoy, K [1988] Reasoning on a highlighted user model to respond to misconceptions. *Computational Linguistics*, 14, 52–63.

McKeown, K R [1985] *Text Generation: Using Discourse Strategies and Focus Constraints to Generate Natural Language Text*. Cambridge: Cambridge University Press.

Nebel, B [1988] Computational complexity of reasoning in BACK. *Artificial Intelligence*, 34, 371–383.

Osherson, D and Smith, E [1981] On the adequacy of prototype theory as a theory of concepts. *Cognition*, 9, 35–58.

Paris, C [1988] Tailoring object descriptions to a user's level of expertise. *Computational Linguistics*, 14, 64–78.

Pollack, M [1990] Plans as complex mental attitudes. To appear in P Cohen, J Morgan, and M Pollack (eds), *Intentions in Communication*. Cambridge, Mass.: MIT Press.

Reiter, E [1990] Generating Appropriate Natural Language Object Descriptions. PhD thesis, Aiken Computation Lab, Harvard University.

Reiter, R [1980] A logic for default reasoning. *Artificial Intelligence*, 13, 81–132.

Rosch, E [1978] Principles of categorization. In E Rosch and B Lloyd (eds), *Cognition and Categorization*, pp27–48. Hillsdale, NJ: Lawrence Erlbaum Associates.

Smith, E and Medin, D [1981] *Categories and Concepts*. Cambridge, Mass.: Harvard University Press.

Zgusta, L [1971] *Manual of Lexicography*. Prague: Academia Press.

11 The Problem of Serial Order: A Neural Network Model of Sequence Learning and Recall

George Houghton

Abstract

This chapter describes a neural network model (the **competitive queuing** model) of sequence learning and recall applied to the problem of learning and recalling English words. The model is an example of the class of **interactive activation** models and it is claimed that the model constitutes a significant development of these models, providing solutions to problems in earlier linguistic work in this paradigm. It is argued that the form of recall provides a principled basis for understanding certain psycholinguistic data and the prevalence of co-articulation in speech production.

11.1 Introduction

In recent years, significant advances in the study of language generation have been made using symbolic computational models which draw on ideas from AI and theoretical linguistics, and which employ the same discrete mathematical formalisms as these disciplines. The majority of this work has addressed the problem of text generation, in which the system either constructs or has passed to it a semantic content expressed in some (non-natural) symbolic language, which it converts into a printed monologue in a target (natural) language. Work in this vein includes [Davey 1979; McDonald 1983; McKeown 1986] and other more recent work (see, for example, many papers in [Zock and Sabah 1988]). Other work is more concerned with the planning and production of (spoken) discourse (for example, [Power 1974, 1979; Cohen 1978; Houghton 1986; Houghton and Isard 1987; Appelt 1985]. While discourse oriented, most of this work still produces only printed output, though Houghton and Pearson [1988] describe a system which produces spoken output and which attempts to integrate speech generation into a larger discourse model.

Despite the undoubted success of this work in establishing new research problems and the viability (or lack of it) of particular approaches, little of it sheds much, if any, light on the fundamental psychological, or neurophysiological, mechanisms which underlie the human capacity to produce sequentially structured behaviour such as language. The reason for this is that all such models take as axiomatic the existence of fully ordered objects (for example, ordered sets, lists etc.) and the serial control mechanisms provided by computer programming languages. Given serial mechanisms acting on and constructing ordered objects, the fundamental capacities required to generate language, or serially ordered behaviour generally, are essentially provided free and modellers and theorists can immediately start work on the higher level problems that concern them. However, these fundamental objects and processes have never been put forward as psychological theories in their own right, and the higher-level models, taken as psycholinguistic theories, thus rest on uncertain theoretical foundations. Many years of experimentation on serial recall reveal that human memory for sequences, while possibly hierarchical [Restle 1970; Rosenbaum, Kenny and Derr 1983; Gordon and Meyer 1987], is not well modelled by indefinitely long ordered structures containing 'passive' symbols. Models employing such devices do not shed much light on such phenomena as the various 'slips of the tongue' [Fromkin 1980; Cutler 1982; Aitchison 1987], or 'tip of the tongue' states whereby a speaker can often make accurate reports about certain aspects of the sound of a word which she cannot recall in full [Brown and McNeill 1966; Jones and Langford 1987]. This is not to say that attempts have not been made to understand speech errors using information processing models. However, these have been 'box and arrow' models (for example, [Garrett 1980; Shattuck-Hufnagel 1979]) and have never been developed to the point of being explicit, working, language production models.

An alternative approach to the predominant symbolic computational one is provided by a class of **connectionist** models which are variously termed **interactive** (or **spreading**) **activation** models [McClelland and Elman 1986; Dell 1986, 1988; MacKay 1987] or **adaptive resonance** models [Grossberg 1987, 1988a]. The basic elements from which these models are constructed do not contain ordered structures such as lists or serial processing mechanisms, but are inspired by fundamental discoveries in the neuro-sciences (see, for example, [Hinton and Anderson 1981; Grossberg 1982a; Kohonen 1984; Smolenski 1986; Anderson and Rosenfeld 1987]). Within this context, models may differ from each other in many ways, but they will generally share a number of basic features. Since connectionist models are still novel in the field of language production (particularly within that section represented by the majority of the contributions to the current volume), it seems unwise to assume that these basic elements will be widely known. In an attempt to make the chapter more accessible, I briefly introduce those aspects of connectionist models which figure most commonly in the following discussion, along with some relevant terminology and notation. For more detailed accounts the reader is referred to the works cited above and throughout the text.

Components of connectionist models

Nodes with activation values

The models consist of a finite set of nodes or units, $u_1, \ldots, u_n$, often arranged into **layers**. Each node u_i will be associated with an **activation value**, a_i, a real number often falling within some range, for example, [0,1]. Nodes are often no more than place holders for these values, though they may have other variable parameters associated with them; for example, a sensitivity parameter, or a specific 'resting' level activation. The activations of a set of nodes (in a layer, say) may be represented mathematically by a vector, $(a_1, \ldots, a_n)$, of activation values. This vector corresponds to a point in a state space of as many dimensions as there are units in the layer. The information processing which takes place in a network consists to a large extent of the moment by moment transformation of the activation state of the network (consisting of the activation levels of the constituent units). In principle, one may think of this transformation as occurring continuously, and hence the dynamical laws governing the state transitions would be expressed by differential equations. In practice, the states of models are generally updated in discrete time slices in which case these laws are expressed as finite difference equations (see, for example, equation (2) below). For a model to be behaviourally meaningful, some interpretation needs to be given to its constituent nodes and their states. In the simplest case, individual nodes may be taken to stand for individual entities in the behavioural domain under study. This is referred to as a **local representation** scheme and is the form employed in the model described below, where, for instance, individual nodes are taken to represent single phonemes.

Weighted connections

Nodes are connected to other nodes by **weighted links** which may be **excitatory** or **inhibitory** (i.e., have positive or negative values). Activation of a node spreads through the network along these links interacting with and affecting the activation levels of other nodes. In interactive activation models, nodes typically feed back activation to and from each other (unlike the more simple feed-forward nets found in associative learning models based on supervised learning (weight change) rules [Rumelhart and McClelland 1986b; Rumelhart, Hinton and Williams 1986]). In Grossberg's adaptive resonance models [Grossberg 1988a], nodes are usually embedded in lateral inhibitory (competitive) fields, as they are in competitive learning models [Kohonen 1984; Rumelhart and Zipser 1986] and more explicitly biologically motivated neural net models (for example, [von der Malsburg 1973]). This type of organisation is central to the model discussed later (see Figure 11.2). The set of connections within a

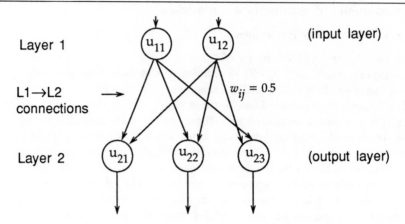

Figure 11.1: The connections from one layer of units (L1) to another (L2) in a simple network

Each of the six links shown is associated with a numerical value (the weight). The link from u_{12} to u_{23} (denoted w_{ij}) has the value 0.5. In the simplest case, the 'net input' to a given L2 unit u_j from L1 is computed by multiplying the activation level of each L1 unit by the weight of its connection to u_j and then summing the products; see equation (1).

tions within a layer or from a layer u to a layer v may be represented as a weight matrix W, each cell of the matrix containing a numerical specification of the weight from one unit to another. A set of one-way weighted connections between layers of a simple 2-layer net are shown in Figure 11.1.

Net input

Each unit u_i at any time t will have some net input net_i defined by

(1) $net_i(t) = \sum_j f(a_j(t))w_{ji}$

where w_{ji} denotes the weight from u_j to u_i and a_j the activation level of u_j. The function f (the **output** function) is generally either a threshold function or the identity function. In the latter case, (1) reduces to the Euclidean dot (inner) product $a.w$ where a and w are vectors of activation values and weights respectively (Figure 11.1). The fact that connectionist computations can often be conveniently represented as operations involving vectors and matrices accounts for the popularity of linear algebraic concepts in some formulations (see, for example, [Jordan 1986b; Smolenski 1986]).

Activation functions

The activation values of units in a net are updated by an **activation function**. This computes an activation value from the net input to a unit (as defined above) and its current activation (at least in continuous models such as that described later). In discrete time form:

(2) $a_i(t+1) = f(a_i(t), net_i(t))$

Activation functions vary considerably in complexity, from linear threshold functions of net input through to the baroque examples found in Grossberg's models (see [Rumelhart, Hinton and McClelland 1986; Williams 1986; Grossberg 1988b] for examples and discussion).

Learning (weight change) rules

In many models some (not necessarily proper) subset of the weights (such as those shown in Figure 11.1) are **variable parameters** whose values may be set during a **learning phase** by a learning algorithm. Referring to our simple net in Figure 11.1, since the effect an activity pattern in L1 has on the activity in L2 depends on the weights of the L1 → L2 pathways, changing the weights will change this effect. Learning algorithms attempt to change the weights so that 'desirable' effects are realised. That (some) connectionist models can learn forms a major part of their attraction and the study of learning algorithms is actively pursued. Current examples of learning schemes include unsupervised varieties, for example, Hebbian types, self-organising maps [Kohonen 1984], Grossberg's ART models [Grossberg 1988a], and error-based (supervised) associative learning [Rumelhart, Hinton and Williams 1986]. Associative learning rules allow input/output mappings to be learned, whereby an activation pattern on a layer of **input** units (Layer 1 in Figure 11.1) brings about an associated pattern on a set of **output** units (Layer 2 in Figure 11.1). To take a linguistic example, the input pattern might represent a set of grammatical features, each node corresponding to a particular feature, and the output pattern the selection of a closed class lexical item, for instance a pronoun. Such schemes associate spatial input patterns directly with spatial output patterns and hence implement a form of parallel, content addressable memory. When it comes to the recall of phonological word forms, however, we are faced with the task of recalling a temporal sequence of spatial patterns, and new algorithms must be devised. One of the goals of the current work is to do just that, and a novel learning algorithm is described later.

These models have the attraction of being built from elements with a neurally plausible mode of processing, and have already been applied with some success to a variety of issues in speech and word perception [McClelland

and Rumelhart 1981; McClelland and Elman 1986] and to some aspects of generation [Dell 1988; Stemberger 1985; Harley 1988; Kalita and Shastri 1987]. Nevertheless, many of these models contain a number of unsatisfactory features which are mainly due to the fundamental problem of serial order, which a number of the models do not attempt to tackle but rather avoid by recoding temporal information into a spatial form.[1]

In this chapter I will discuss a connectionist model of sequence learning and reproduction which I have been developing. The particular focus of the work, which I will refer to as the **competitive queuing** (CQ) model, is on the phonological retrieval of word forms, though many of the principles involved may be of use at higher levels of language generation.

11.2   The Competitive Queuing Model

In this section I provide a computational and mathematical specification of the CQ model. It is based on the intuition that sequencing can be effected in inter-active activation models by the activation of a node representing, say, a word, leading to the parallel activation of components of the word (phonemes in the case of the current model). The sequential selection of successive elements is then made on the basis of their level of activation. This intuition is shared with other connectionist models, in particular the Rumelhart and Norman [1982] typing model, and Dell's connectionist models of language production [Dell 1986, 1988]. However, these models have a number of shortcomings. For instance, neither can learn the connection patterns they presuppose. This problem is particularly acute in the case of the Rumelhart and Norman model, which does not contain stable internal representations from which sequences can be produced, but needs to produce a new connection pattern amongst sequence elements each time it is to output a new word (or part of a word). The Dell model, particularly in its 1988 version, appears in fact not to have an effective sequencing mechanism [Houghton 1989a]. Nonetheless, I believe it is important to attempt to retain the form of operation postulated in these models because it is central to many of the accounts of speech error data pro-vided by Dell [1986] and of typing errors provided by Rumelhart and Norman [1982]. Indeed, interactive activation accounts have hardly any competition in this respect. (Connectionist sequence models of the multi-layer perceptron type, based on back propagation learning [Jordan 1986a] do not strike me as likely candidates in this area.) For instance, while the Dell model employs an unsatisfactory position-specific 'phonemic' representation and does not specify

---

[1]Lack of space here precludes detailed discussion of other connectionist models of serial behaviour. See Houghton [1989a] for a discussion of the CQ model in relation to the models of [Rumelhart and Norman 1982; Dell 1986, 1988; MacKay 1987; Jordan 1986a].

an effective sequencing mechanism, its use of (what amount to) competing activation levels amongst phonemes provides its primary explanatory device for accounting for transposition errors: i.e., the wrong elements are most active at the wrong time. An entirely new mechanism would face the problem of providing a completely different account. In relation to previous work, then, my strategy here is to provide a model which is better defined and more effective at the level of its basic architecture and interactions, yet which produces the kind of run-time behaviour which makes so many error types comprehensible. The model is thus not intended to supersede interactive activation accounts, but rather to develop this particular line of theory.

The competitive queuing model, as described in this chapter, is specifically applied to the problem of the learning and recall of English monosyllabic words. The model has been constructed with the following constraints in mind:

1. Recall of a word should consist of the network, through its self interactions, going through a sequence of states which cause the phonemes of the word (represented by nodes of the type described earlier) to successively be the most highly activated. This changing location of an activation peak gives the associated unit the greatest degree of control over lower level units to which it is connected. Thus words are not stored in the form of copies or templates (as in classical symbolic models), but are rather recreated on-line as a dynamic activity pattern.

2. There should be no **position-specific coding** (PSC) of elements. As mentioned previously, problems of temporal order in neural networks have led to the use of a number of undesirable representational tricks in other work involving language. These include **wickelphones** ([Rumelhart and McClelland 1986b], criticised in [Pinker and Prince 1988]) and the use of separate nodes for what we would normally consider the same letter or sound occurring at different points in a word [Dell 1988].[2]

3. Upcoming phonemes in a word should be **pre-activated**, i.e., active before being produced. This appears to be a ubiquitous feature of human

---

[2]Dell's use of this scheme is motivated by a 'single speech-error phenomenon, namely that pre- and post-vocalic consonants almost never slip with one another'. He recognises that this imposes a 'considerable cost. The network no longer recognises the /k/s in *cat* and *tack* as being related sounds ... Thus the model's mechanism for handling syllable position effects in errors is not a very satisfactory one' [Dell 1988:132]. I believe this considerably understates the problems that the model faces in this respect, in that it suggests that the only consequence of removing the PSC scheme would be a slight decline in empirical accuracy (difficulty in accounting for an absence of one class of possible error). However, it is not clear how the model can specify sequential order at all without this coding, especially in a word such as *pip*, which contains the same phoneme twice. In the CQ model, producing the word /b I b/ (*bib*) must involve the activation of the same sound at the beginning and end.

speech (and other behaviour) and is essential to explain many phenomena (for example, pre-emptive articulations in speech production). This pre-activation *should not be an inessential or problematic aspect of the system*, but should be necessary for it to work at all.

4. The network should learn sequences through exposure to them followed by simple associative weight change rules, based on activation levels. (More powerful learning rules such as back propagation are not consistent with interactive activation (IA) type models. In addition, Grossberg [1987] argues that they are not compatible with biological constraints). The model was also formulated so that the feed-forward pathways used in recall should be purely excitatory, so that only learning of positive weights takes place.

5. Inhibitory mechanisms should be involved at all levels of operation. I believe some other models (for example, [Dell 1988; Mackay 1987]) suffer because they are basically excitatory models which draw on the notion of inhibition in a way which is not integrated, conceptually or mathematically, in the basic mode of operation of the model. Inhibitory mechanisms are ubiquitous in the brain, and I believe it is important that connectionist models reflect this and attempt to account for their role (see, for instance, [Shepherd 1974; Carpenter 1984; Sillito 1985] for discussion of inhibitory mechanisms in various brain areas).

In the following sections, I first describe the architecture of the basic model and then specify (a) the learning algorithm by which the network constructs a set of weights in the connections from word nodes to phoneme nodes, and (b) the run-time equations governing the interactions of the units during recall of learned sequences.

11.2.1   Architecture

In its simplest form the CQ model consists of a set of three layers of **on-center, off-surround** nodes. In such a layer each unit inhibits and is inhibited by the other units in the layer (off-surround), and feeds back positively to itself (on-centre) (Figure 11.2). Such a scheme is used, for instance, by [McClelland and Rumelhart 1982] and most extensively in Grossberg's ART models (for example, [Grossberg 1987]).

The model uses a local representation scheme whereby each node or unit represents some behavioural item at some linguistic level (for example, a phoneme or phonetic feature). Units should be thought of as standing not for individual neurons but for putative 'cell-assemblies': collections of excitatorily connected neurons whose firing is positively correlated.[3] The lateral

---

[3] Algorithms for the formation of such assemblies in response to structured input patterns

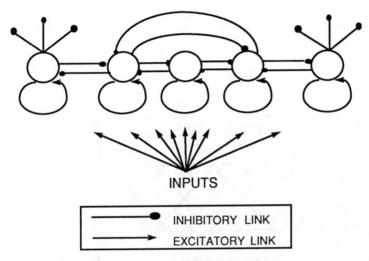

INPUTS

————————●	INHIBITORY LINK
————————▶	EXCITATORY LINK

Figure 11.2: On-centre, off-surround field

Each unit in the layer feeds back positively to itself and inhibits the rest. All units receive inputs in parallel along weighted input lines.

---

inhibition between assemblies (units) would be mediated by inhibitory inter-neurons, not by direct inhibitory connections between units [Sillito 1985].

Figure 11.3 shows the inter-layer connectivity. All top-down connections are excitatory.

Layer 1 is the layer of word nodes, each node representing a particular learned sequence of phonemes in layer 2. All L1 units connect to all L2 units and there are excitatory feedback connections from L2 to L1. It is in the L1–L2 connections that learning takes place when the net learns a new word, i.e. these weights are variable. Connections from L2 to L3 are one-to-one excitatory, and essentially copy the pattern of activation found at L2 to L3. Although L2 and L3 are architecturally identical, the parameters governing their lateral interactions are different. In particular, inhibition is stronger in L3, making it a 'winner-take-all' layer, i.e. one in which the highest activated node quickly suppresses all competition from other nodes. Competition at L2 is less fierce and a number of nodes can be active ('stored in STM') at the

---

are discussed in, for instance, [Kohonen 1984; Singer 1985; Linsker 1988], and in many other works on the self-organisation of neural networks. So far, they have been largely applied to problems in visual perception [Vernon and Rose 1985]. Whether such models can be applied to linguistic problems seems to me to be an interesting area for future work.

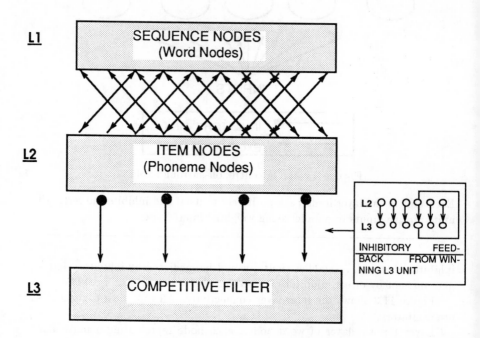

Figure 11.3: Inter-layer connections in the basic CQ model

All layers are lateral inhibitory layers. All top-down connections are excitatory. Connections from L2 to L3 are one-to-one, as are the inhibitory feedback connections from L3 to L2. Interactions between L2 and L3 lead to the suppression of the highest activated unit at L2. Connections between L1 and L2 are modifiable by a learning algorithm discussed in the text.

same time. Feedback from L3 to L2 is one-to-one inhibitory, and once a unit at L3 has won the competition it inhibits its corresponding unit at L2. (In the model, all activation values vary between 1 and -1, with 0 representing background, and negative values representing suppressed activation). L3 thus acts as a **competitive filter**. A key feature of the model is that L1 actually contains two node types: initiator (or start) nodes (which I will refer to as I-nodes) and end nodes (E-nodes), arranged in connected pairs. The precise function of this arrangement is described in the following section. Here I would note that these nodes are intended to capture the idea that sequences such as words are temporally patterned objects with 'temporal edges', i.e. they have a start and a finish which separates them out from an ongoing stream of events, just as physical and visual edges separate out objects in the spatial domain. The elements of a sequence may be thought of as being represented in terms of their relation to the edges of that sequence (see [Estes 1985] for discussion of similar ideas in modeling serial list learning).

11.2.2   Learning and recall

Activation range

All activation values in the model vary in the range $[-1, 1]$. An activation value of 0 represents background (spontaneous) levels of activation. Negative values represent below background levels, positive values excited states. Negative activations do not spread.

Parameters

Apart from the variable weights, the model contains a number of other parameters. The three layers in Figure 11.2 are all on-centre, off-surround layers and the inhibitory and excitatory weights in these layers can be varied. This provides six parameters, two for each layer. All units have a passive decay rate (see equation (6)). This may vary between layers and also may be different for decay from above background activation levels and for passive recovery from inhibition. In principle this provides another six parameters. The activation function described below contains a sensitivity parameter. Not all the above parameters will be different. For instance, the lateral weight parameters in layers 1 and 2 may be the same and all units may have the same sensitivity parameter. I will denote these parameters with the following symbols: $\tau =$ sensitivity, $\delta =$ decay rate, $\delta^+ =$ decay from excited state, $\delta^- =$ recovery from suppressed state, $w^+ =$ positive feedback weight, $w^- =$ negative (intra-layer) feedback weight. Typical values used are $\tau = 1.2$, $\delta^+ = 0.6$, $\delta^- = 0.8$, $w^+ = 0.4$, $w^- = -0.1$.

Learning

Learning takes place in two stages: initial exposure and practice.

Initial Exposure

The first stage of learning involves associating the phonemes comprising each word to be learned with a node pair in L1. At the outset all L1 $\leftrightarrow$ L2 weights are set to 0. An input word is represented as a sequence of unit vectors, i.e., vectors in which all but one element are set to 0, and the non-zero element has the value 1. The non-zero element represents the current input phoneme and activates the appropriate phoneme node in layer 2. The sequential phonemic input is presumed to come from a speech analysis system which divides a spoken syllable into its constituent phonemes. At the onset of a word, an uncommitted I-node is fully activated and thereafter decays with each successive time step. The phoneme input vectors are fed successively into the phoneme layer (L2) and the activation a_i of a unit u_i is updated according to:

$$(3) \quad a_i(t) = min(1, \delta a_i(t-1) + I_i(t))$$

where I_i represents the value of the ith element of the current input vector (1 or 0) and δ is a decay factor (for example, $\delta = 0.6$; given the way this is used in the above equation, the actual passive decay rate is given by $1 - \delta$). The function min returns the lower of its two arguments. The activation level of a phoneme unit thus goes to 1 whenever the value of the corresponding unit in the input vector is 1. Otherwise it remains at 0, or decays if it has been previously activated. The resulting behaviour is roughly in accordance with the activation function (7) below, with net_i set to 0 except when a unit receives external input. It should be clear that at any time t the most recently activated phoneme unit will have an activation value of 1 and earlier units < 1 (due to passive decay). If all input phonemes are different, their order of presentation will be the inverse of their current relative activation values. If lateral inhibition is included during the learning phase (and activations are updated using equations (7) and (8), rather than equation (3)), then successive phonemes achieve lower levels of initial activation due to inhibition from earlier items which are still active (**pro-active inhibition**) and past items decay more quickly (**retro-active inhibition**). I have not found that this makes any significant difference to the learning, and hence generally use the simpler equation (3) during the initial exposure.

   Crucial to the learning that takes place is the behaviour during input of the word of a selected pair of start and end nodes. At the onset of a word, an uncommitted start node is fully activated and thereafter decays with each successive time step. When the sequence ends, the associated E-node comes

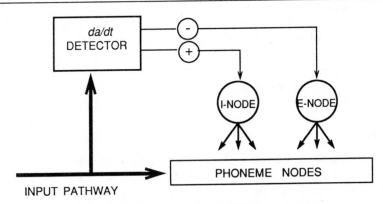

Figure 11.4: A da/dt detector

Start and end nodes respond to sequence onset and offset respectively. This activation patern can be achieved by a system whose output represents the first derivative of the activity along the input pathway.

on. I take this activation pattern to be achieved by a rate-of-change detector which monitors activity along the phoneme input pathways and responds to changes in its intensity. I shall refer to this as a da/dt detector, where a stands for activity. This has two excitatory outputs, one for positive da/dt (increase in activity) and one for negative da/dt (decrease in activity). The positive channel excites I-nodes and the negative channel E-nodes. This scheme is illustrated in Figure 11.4.

This word node pattern has functional properties similar to Grossberg's **gated dipoles** (see [Grossberg 1982b]). According to Grossberg, the properties of a gated dipole 'include a sustained on-response to cue-onset and a transient antagonistic off-response, or rebound to ... cue offset ...' [Grossberg 1982b:537]. In this model, the on-response decays.

As each successive phoneme of the word arrives the top-down weights w_{ji} from L1 to L2 are changed according to the simple Hebbian learning rule:

(4) $\quad \Delta w_{ji}(t) = \lambda a_i(t) a_j(t)$

where a_i is the activation value of the ith phoneme node (updated according to equation (2)), a_j the activation value of the jth I-node in the word layer and λ a learning rate parameter (in all simulations described later, $\lambda = 1$ during initial exposure). When the word ends, the drop in activity along the input pathway fires the negative da/dt, which activates the E-node, as described earlier. The L2 activations are decayed by one time step and the weights from the activated E-node to the L2 phoneme nodes changed according to equation (4). (The effect of this is that the E-node → L2 weight vector is a scalar multiple of the L2 activation vector at this point. If $\lambda = 1$, and the E-node has an activation level of 1, then the weight vector is simply a copy of the activation vector.) This part of the learning is unsupervised (i.e. no comparison of actual and target outputs from the net is made). For shorter sequences with no repeated phonemes it may be sufficient for correct recall.

Practice

The above exposure may not be enough for the network to learn some words (having learned a word means being able to recall it in the manner discussed in the next section). In this case, there is a practice phase which adjusts the weights formed initially until words are correctly reproduced. What happens in the practice phase is that the network is instructed to produce a given word by activating the appropriate I-node, which sends activation through to the phoneme nodes via the learned connections. The net starts to run through its version of the word, its output being taken to be the sequence of L2 nodes which win the competition at L3 (i.e., which manage to overshadow all concurrently activated phoneme nodes). The correct version of the word is presented concurrently so that the net attempts to predict the phonemes in it as they occur. When the net makes a wrong prediction, top-down weights from the start and end nodes are changed. Weights to the appropriate response (given by the input) are increased, and weights to the incorrect response are decreased. The weight change equations are, to the desired response:

$$(5) \quad \Delta w_{ji} = \lambda(w_{max} - w_{ji})a_j a_i$$

where w_{max} is the asymptote of associative strength (for example, $w_{max} = 2$); and, to the incorrect response:

$$(6) \quad \Delta w_{ji} = -\lambda w_{ji}a_j a_i$$

In both equations λ is the learning rate parameter, a_j is the activation level of the word node, and a_i the activation level of the phoneme node. At each weight change these rules are applied to the weights from both the start and end nodes of the word node pair. The learning rate during practice should be much smaller than during the initial exposure (for example, $\lambda = 0.1$) otherwise the weights will oscillate wildly and the net will generally alternate between incorrect versions of the word.

Since the net is told which word it is going to experience (by the activation of the appropriate sequence node pair) and compares its predictions with the input, this part of the learning algorithm should be considered a member of the class of supervised learning procedures. However, it should be noticed that the weight change rule does not include an error term, as in **delta rule** models [Rumelhart and McClelland 1986a]. Thus the learning is of the trial and error type, but does not require the numerical comparison of actual and target activation levels that the delta rule uses. (Indeed, an externally specified target activation value is not needed in this scheme. A phoneme node merely needs to be sufficiently more highly activated than its competitors to win the competition).

It is nevertheless possible to define an intuitively reasonable error measure for this system. When the net makes a mistake, it is because some element is more highly activated than the 'correct' one. If a_w is the activation value of the winning unit and a_t the activation value of the target or desired output (and $w \neq t$), then the error can be measured as $\varepsilon + a_w - a_t$ where ε represents some small, just noticeable, difference ($0 < \varepsilon \ll 1$); i.e. the error is the amount of additional activation unit u_t needs to win the competition at the competitive filter. If we take this measure during practice, we find that it gradually decreases, and thus that the learning algorithm implements a descent on the error surface (with respect to the weights), though without actually taking the size of the error into account. I would mention briefly that the mistakes the model makes are not random. Even after a single trial it has very good recall of word initial elements and tends to trip up on longer words by producing end of word elements too early.

The end results of successful learning can be discussed in terms of the weight vectors which connect individual word nodes to phoneme nodes. Suppose the net has learned the word /p a t/ (*pat*). There will be two vectors involved in recall: one from an I-node and the other from its associated E-node. Each vector contains values for connections to all nodes in the phoneme layer, but these equal zero for all phonemes other than /p/, /a/ and /t/. Thus the vectors have non-null components in three dimensions only (where each phoneme defines a dimension) and can thus be treated as 3D vector (Figure 11.4). The actual values of the weights represent the projections of the weight vector along the relevant dimensions. If we denote the projection of a weight vector w on a phoneme dimension by $w(/phoneme/)$ (for example, $w(/p/) = 1.2$) then for the I-node weight vector, $w(/p/) > w(/a/) > w(/t/)$ and for the E-node, $w(/t/) > w(/a/) > w(/p/)$. We could alternatively consider a related quantity, the direction cosines, i.e. the cosines of the angles formed between the weight vector and the three relevant axes. These would show, for instance, that the I-node weight vector for /p a t/ is nearest to (forms the smallest angle to) the /p/ axis and is progressively further away from later elements. Thus an I-node is most strongly connected to elements at the beginning of a sequence. Since initial access to a sequence is via activation of an I-node, this means that the most readily recollected portion of a learned sequence is its beginning. This result is in line with evidence from

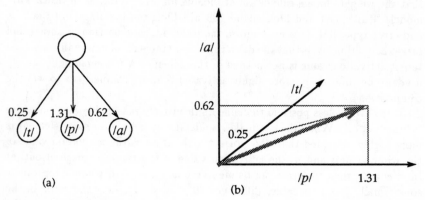

Figure 11.5: Depiction of the connection strengths from the I-node representing the word *pat* to the phoneme nodes /p/, /a/, /t/

The connections shown in (a) are represented in (b) as a vector in a 3D space, the axes of which are labelled by the phonemes to which the I-node has non-zero connections.

tip-of-the-tongue experiments [Brown and McNeill 1966]. In the model it is a consequence, ultimately, of the way in which learning takes place.

Recall

Recall of a sequence begins with the activation of an I-node in L1, which has its value set to 1. (This input may be taken to arrive via a learned connection from another system, say the semantic system for a content word.) This activation feeds through to the phoneme layer and elements here are updated according to the following scheme.

$$(7) \quad a_i(t+1) = \begin{cases} \delta a_i(t) + (1 - a_i(t))f(net_i(t)), \text{if } net_i(t) > 0 \\ \delta a_i(t) + (1 + a_i(t))f(net_i(t)), \text{if } net_i(t) < 0 \end{cases}$$

where δ is a passive decay parameter. The term $1 \pm a_i(t)$ acts as a gain control making the increase in activation proportional to the current activation level. To keep activation levels bounded, the function f should be a squashing function mapping net_i into the range $[-1, 1]$. The one used here is a sigmoid function with a variable 'temperature' parameter τ.

$$(8) \quad f(net_i) = \frac{2}{1 + e^{-\tau net_i}} - 1$$

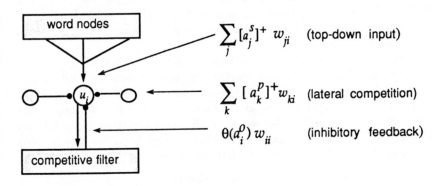

Figure 11.6: Sources of excitatory and inhibitory input to a phoneme node u_i

The parameter τ controls the gradient of the sigmoid and thus how sensitive cells are to their net input. It may be worth noting that there is nothing specifically sequential about these equations. For example, equations (6) and (8) are used in a model of visual selective attention by Houghton [1989b]. The net input net_i is generally contributed by a variety of sources. For instance, for a phoneme node we get:

(9) $\quad net_i = \sum_j [a_j^s]^+ w_{ji} + \sum_k [a_k^p]^+ w_{ki} + \theta(a_i^o) w_{ii}$

where the notation $[x]^+$ means $max(0, x)$, a^s denotes the activity of a sequence (word) node, a^p the activity of a phoneme node, and a^o the activity of the competitive filter node. The function max is applied to activation values so that negative values (which merely represent suppressed activation) are not passed on. If this were not the case, then sub-zero activity in a unit would have the effect of inverting the value of the weight of its links with other units; excitatory connections would become inhibitory and vice versa. The input sources represented by the three terms in equation (9) are illustrated in Figure 11.6.

The first term represents the top-down input from the word level and includes input from both start and end nodes. The second term represents both the lateral inhibitory feedback within the phoneme layer and the positive self feedback of a unit to itself. The final term represents the feedback from the competitive filter. The weights w_{ji} in the first term are variable parameters set during the learning phase. The weights w_{ki} in the second term are fixed parameters and all inhibitory weights have the same value, as do the self-feedback weights. The feedback weight from the output level (w_{ii}) is also fixed. The word level nodes are updated in a similar way receiving bottom-up excitatory feedback from the phoneme level and competing amongst themselves via lateral inhibitory feedback.

The question arises as to the pattern of activation in the word node pair during recall. Clearly the E-node must become active before the word finishes, otherwise it would exert no controlling influence on its production. Equally, it should not be (highly) active at the onset. Thus the E-node should have a low initial activation and become gradually more activated as the initially activated I-node decays. A number of schemes are possible, but for simplicity I have implemented this functional relationship using equation (10):

(10)   *E-node-activity*(t) = 1 − *I-node-activity*(t)

A consequence of equation (10) is that the total activity in a word node pair remains constant throughout the production of the word (and is equal to 1). This raises the issue of how a word is terminated when all phonemes have been produced, since, by (10), there will still be activity flowing from the word to the phoneme layer. Some of the possibilities include the use of an **efference copy** mechanism which compares the output to a target and generates a stop signal when the requirements of the target have been met. Another possibility is to include a special **junction** node in the phoneme layer which would be added to the end of all the words to be learned. When this junction node wins the competition it generates an off-signal terminating the sequence. The mechanism actually used in the examples given below is the inverse of this latter proposal. This involves an inhibitory control circuit which is suppressed by activity in the phoneme layer above a certain level (threshold). As a word is produced, the total supra-background activity gradually declines as elements become suppressed, and there are fewer phonemes still to be articulated. When it drops below threshold, this off-circuit is activated and resets the word node activations to 0, which prevents any further phoneme nodes becoming activated.

The mode of recall is, thus, that after activation of a selected I-node, a set of phoneme nodes become activated according to the learned weights in the L1 → L2 pathways. Due to these weights, items will generally be more highly activated the earlier they are to appear. Most importantly, the first element of the word must have the highest activation. Thus, at the onset of recall, word initial elements are most salient. The pattern of activity at L2 is passed onto L3 where, due to the increased competition, the highest activated node suppresses the rest. When the winning node reaches a threshold level it feeds back to L2, inhibiting its corresponding representation. This removes support for the winning L3 node, which rapidly decays. The temporal pattern of activity in the phoneme layer (L2) is thus the crucial controlling variable here,

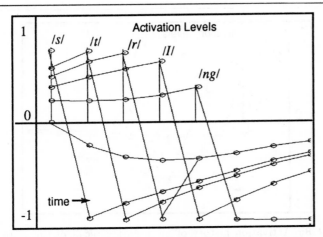

Figure 11.7: The activation history of units during recall of the word /s t r
ɪ n g/

Syllables in which all the phones are different are the easiest for the model to
learn and reproduce.

since it is the relative activations in L2 which provide the initial conditions for
the L3 competition.

Figures 11.7–11.10 provide a series of examples of the pattern of activation
over phoneme nodes during recall of certain syllables. In each figure, the
activation history of each phoneme unit is shown as a straight line joining a
series of circles. The phonemic value of the highest activated unit at each
time slice is shown by the symbol placed above the activation cross-section.
Figure 11.7 shows recall of the syllable /s t r ɪ ng/ (*string*) in which all the
phonemes are different. The following figures show three syllables in which
one or more phonemes is repeated. These are the more difficult cases for
models such as this, since the repeated units must be suppressed and then
reactivated to become the winning unit at just the right time. If all elements in
a syllable are different then the model has only to maintain their initial relative
activation values over time. These examples illustrate that the model does not
need to use a position-specific coding of phonemes. I would emphasise that, in
all these cases, the L1 → L2 weights necessary for setting up and controlling
these activation patterns were learned using the algorithm described under
Learning above.

The following features of the patterns may be noted:

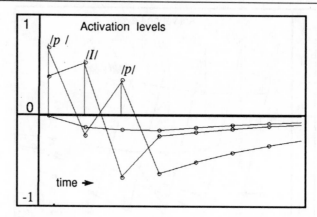

Figure 11.8: Activation history of units during recall of the word /p I p/ (*pip*)

This syllable requires that the /p/ be immediately reactivated after being suppressed. This shows clearly that the model does not require the use of a position-specific phonemic coding.

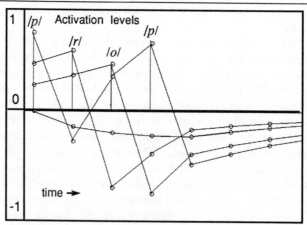

Figure 11.9: Activation history of units during recall of the word /p r o p/ (*prop*)

In this case, the repeated phoneme must not be reactivated so quickly that it overshadows the vowel.

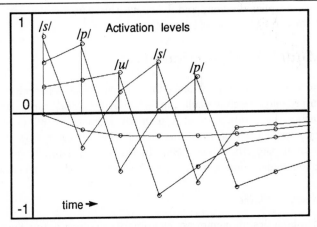

Figure 11.10: Activation history of units during recall of the nonsense syllable /**s p u s p**/

This shows that the model can handle double repetitions. A nonsense syllable was used here as I could think of no English monosyllable with this form.

1. All sequence elements (phonemes) are activated in parallel, but with a graded activation pattern which can be maintained over time. The initial activation gradient is the result of the learned weight gradient.

2. Elements become gradually more activated until they are the most highly activated, after which their activation is rapidly suppressed. There is thus 'more anticipation of future actions than perseveration of past actions' [Jordan 1986a]. The gradual increase in activation is due to both the decrease in lateral inhibition which comes from winning responses being suppressed, and to the gradual increase in the activation level of the sequence's E-node.

3. The relative activations at any time step generally reflect the order in which the associated units will become the winning units in succeeding time steps.

Evidence for this form of left-to-right bias in activation (or **access**) comes from a variety of sources. That word-initial phonemes have greater activation levels than do later phonemes is argued for by Brown and McNeill [1966] on the basis of tip-of-the-tongue data, by Stemberger [1983] on the basis of speech errors and by Fay and Cutler [1977] on the basis of evidence from malapropisms. However, none of these accounts provide any principled explanation of the phenomenon, and I believe this may be the first properly formalised (or even unformalised) model to do so.

11.3 Modeling Co-articulation

Some of the most convincing evidence for parallel access in speech production comes from pre-emptive co-articulations whereby the vocal tract configuration realised during the production of a phonetic segment is influenced by the articulatory specification of upcoming sounds [Perkell 1980; Roy and Square 1985; Lieberman and Blumstein 1988]. In this section I briefly describe how the basic phenomenon emerges naturally from the model described above.

Articulatory features

In linguistic phonetics phonemes are customarily mapped onto a lower level of representation, that of the articulatory feature. Each phoneme corresponds to a bunch of features which together specify an (abstract) articulatory target to be aimed at during production of the phoneme. The features cluster in groups depending on which aspect of the total articulatory gesture they relate to. For instance, there will be features for the various **manners** of articulation, for example, whether the sound is a fricative, a stop, a vowel etc. Manner features are roughly concerned with the what the upper vocal tract does to the air stream after it leaves the glottis: a stop closes it momentarily, a fricative adds turbulence. Other commonplace features include the presence or absence of **voicing** (glottal pulses) and the place of articulation (point of maximum closure of articulators), which may generally be at a number of places from the pharynx to the lips.

This level of representation is most naturally captured in a connectionist net by letting individual nodes stand for particular features and then grouping the nodes into clusters within which all nodes inhibit each other. For instance, one such cluster would contain all the nodes representing manner features, another would contain all the place features, and so on. In principle there could also be excitatory connections between elements in different clusters such that features which commonly co-occur would have mutually excitatory links. Such a connection pattern might be trained using an auto-associator, in which case the resulting net would tend to perform pattern completion. For instance, a net trained using English vowel specifications would form a strong link between the lip shape feature ROUNDED and the tongue position feature BACK (since all English back vowels are rounded). If the net was given a partial phoneme specification of the form [VOWEL ROUNDED] it would tend to spontaneously add the feature BACK (i.e., within the tongue-height cluster, the BACK node would become the most highly activated).

Networks which could self-organise to have such properties would clearly be well worth investigating in the construction of a connectionist phonetics/phonology. In the network described below I have employed only the inhibitory cluster element of this scheme and have divided up the feature nodes into inhibitory clusters by hand. The clusters and constituent features used are illustrated in Figure 11.11.

This is not intended as a definitive distinctive feature specification for English but simply serves to illustrate the way the model functions.[4]

Excitatory links between the phoneme nodes in layer 2 of the model described earlier and the feature layer (call it L4 for convenience) can be constructed using a variety of algorithms. The use of a local representation in L2 means that the activation vectors for individual phonemes will be orthogonal. Hence, the appropriate links can be formed by associating a phoneme vector with a co-occurring distinctive feature vector and updating the weights according to the Hebbian rule, equation (4), used with some asymptote of associative strength (limit on the weights). Alternatively, a supervised algorithm (for example, the Widrow-Hoff rule) may be used. By this means a pattern of activity in L2 will cause a pattern of activity to arise in L4 (the feature layer). If a single unit is on in L2 then the L4 pattern will correspond to the learned feature specification for that unit. If more than one unit is on, as when a syllable is initially accessed, the pattern will generally not correspond to that of a single phoneme but will instead reflect the competing influences of all activated phonemes. It is by this means that the model predicts co-articulation effects.

The CQ model in the form described above runs, so to speak, as fast as it can, suppressing one phoneme in every slice of its simulated (discrete) time. Assuming that states at a lower (more peripheral) level will be changing more rapidly, we need to translate one time slice at L2 into some number of time slices at L4. In the following simulations the ratio is 1:5, that is, from the point of view of L4, the L2 activation vector changes suddenly every 5 time slices. In between times it is constant. The state of L4 is updated at each of its time slices using the activation function (equations (7) and (8)) described earlier. The net input to a feature unit comes from the activated L2 nodes and from lateral inhibition from other feature nodes within its cluster.

A commonly observed co-articulatory effect is pre-emptive lip-rounding, where the lip rounding of a vowel spreads backwards to occur on preceding consonants whose feature specification is uncommitted with respect to lip shape. Figure 11.12 shows the activation history of the feature nodes ROUNDED

---

[4]Since there is no sub-feature level defined here, the actual labelling of the feature nodes relates only the phonemes which contain them. There is clearly nothing manner-like about the manner nodes nor place-like about the place nodes.

310

George Houghton

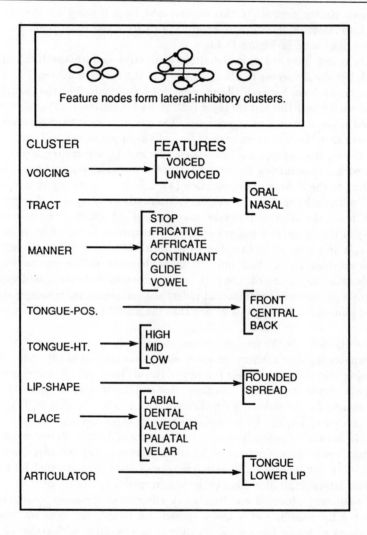

Figure 11.11: Clusters and features employed in modelling co-articulation

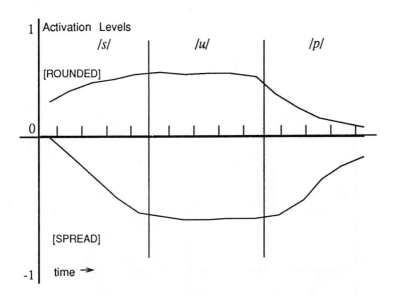

Figure 11.12: Activation levels of the features [ROUNDED] and [SPREAD] during production of the word /s u p/ (*soup*), showing pre-emptive lip rounding during the production of the initial /s/ due to the upcoming rounded vowel /u/

and SPREAD during the model's production of the word /s u p/ (*soup*), which shows the rounding of the initial /s/ due to the vowel and the decay of the feature during the following /p/. It is instructive to compare the feature pattern during the /p/ in this instance with that which occurs during production of /s u p i/ (*soupy*) shown in Figure 11.13. The final vowel in the word is specified as having SPREAD lip position, which causes the more rapid suppression of the ROUNDED feature during production of the /p/.

In this kind of model, the pressure for co-articulation arises as a natural consequence of the parallel access of phoneme nodes, all of which immediately begin to activate their associated feature nodes. The actual articulatory configuration settled on at any time represents a compromise between the specifications of all activated phonemes. Due to the phoneme activation gradient in L2, phonemes have a greater influence over the articulatory target the sooner they are to be produced, with the current phoneme having the overriding influence. Thus the basic features of co-articulation are a straightforward

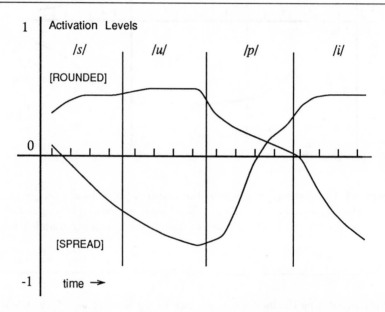

Figure 11.13: Activation levels of the features [ROUNDED] and [SPREAD] during production of the word /s u p i/ (*soupy*)

The important difference between this and the previous figure occurs during the production of the /p/. Due to the presence of the final spread vowel /i/, the lip rounding is suppressed more rapidly.

consequence of the way the model learns and recalls a phonemic sequence. This is in contrast to such models as the speech production model of Perkell [1980], which proposes a **look-ahead** component which scans upcoming phonemes held in a sequential buffer, and then adjusts the articulatory target for the current phoneme according to the contents of this buffer. The problem with such schemes is that they are essentially *ad hoc*. The system, if it could work at all, could probably work without its look-ahead component, which has no other function than to allow co-articulatory targets to be constructed. Further problems arise in constraining the extent of the look-ahead. Should it be restricted to two phonemes, or three or four or 20? Should the articulatory influence of a phoneme be a decreasing (linear or non-linear?), or a constant function of its distance from the current phoneme? All such decisions are bound to be somewhat arbitrary, motivated only by empirical fit to known data.

An alternative connectionist approach to this issue is provided by Jordan's associative chaining model [Jordan 1986a]. This model associates a **plan** (an arbitrary input pattern) with a sequence by first associating the plan with the first element of the sequence and then feeding back the first element (which appears on the output layer) to the input layer and associating the combination of the plan and the feedback with the second item of the sequence. This item in turn is fed back to the input layer to generate an association with the next item and so on. The net contains a layer of so-called **hidden units** between the input and output layers and is trained using the back propagation learning algorithm [Rumelhart, Hinton and Williams 1986]. Such a net can be trained to produce a sequence such as /s u p/ as a series of orthogonal output vectors (i.e., first the /s/ alone is produced, then the /u/ alone and so on). The problem with this as an account of speech production, of course, is that when the first element is produced there is no influence of upcoming elements and hence co-articulation effects cannot be explained. Jordan circumvents this problem by altering the training regime in such a way that, during recall, the net starts to anticipate upcoming elements by preactivating them, thus providing the basis for an account of co-articulation. While this is an interesting result, it would appear to be dependent on a somewhat arbitrary choice of training regime. There is nothing in the underlying dynamics of the network which more or less forces it to be the case (i.e., the network is quite capable of producing a sequence of elements with neither anticipation nor perseveration effects). The CQ model on the other hand, as a continuous, parallel, cascaded system, cannot function other than as it does in the above examples. The models in fact give quite different accounts of the origin of co-articulation. The Jordan model would produce lip-rounding during the production of /s/ in the word /s u p/ because the state of the input layer at the onset of the sequence is similar to its state during the production of the /u/. In such models, similar inputs tend to lead to similar outputs, if the training data do not explicitly act to prevent it. If, during training, the /s/ is not prevented from being rounded (i.e., no error is generated from a node representing the feature ROUNDED, whatever its value), then, due to the similarity of the input layer during the production of the /s/ and the /u/, features of the vowel that have not been explicitly disallowed during training will tend to appear in parallel with the features of the /s/. The explanation of the origin of co-articulation effects is thus quite different in the two models. In the Jordan model it is due to cross-talk between similar input states in an associative net, in the CQ model it is due to the temporal dynamics of continuous, parallel constraint satisfaction. In principle, it should be possible to distinguish empirically between the two models.

11.4   Conclusions

This chapter has described a new model of learning and recall of phonemic sequences. While falling within the general class of interactive activation models it attempts to improve on earlier applications of this class to sequential behaviour by:

1. Defining a learning algorithm so that sequences can be taught: the resulting coding scheme is stable and sequences sharing sub-elements do not interfere with each other (though co-activation of like sequences may occur due to bottom-up feedback, an aspect of the model not discussed here); and

2. Defining an effective sequencing mechanism so that recall of a sequence is genuinely a temporal phenomenon: the mechanism proposed avoids the use of position-specific encodings.

These two mechanisms are inextricably linked in that: (i) part of the learning takes place while the net is attempting to recall a sequence, i.e., the learning algorithm incorporates the recall algorithm; and (ii) as in all connectionist models that can learn, recall reconstructs the learned response from the weight changes wrought in the net during learning, and is thus dependent on the learning algorithm.

The basic architectural additions made to IA models in this work are (i) the use of paired start and end nodes (**temporal edges**) for the coding of a sequence; and (ii) the use of specific inhibitory feedback from a **competitive filter** to perform response suppression. I argued that the form of recall produced by the model is in line with psycholinguistic evidence from a variety of sources (TOT states, speech errors, malapropisms), and that the model thus provides a principled basis for the explanation of these data. From a consideration of the phenomenon of co-articulation I argued that the model provides a basis for understanding how parallel influences arise in speech production and how they may be controlled.

Further development of the model will involve increases in complexity in both and 'upward' and 'downward' directions. In the upward direction, we need to consider how polysyllabic words can be learned and recalled. I believe this will require more elaborate feedback control, possibly involving the use of efference copy mechanisms with internal (non-peripheral) feedback (see [Borden 1979] for discussion). In addition, this will involve consideration of stress patterns. In the downward direction, available evidence (see, for example, [Treiman 1984, 1986]) points to syllables having internal boundaries, at least between onset (everything up to the vowel) and rhyme (vowel and coda, if any). In some additional work not reported here, I have implemented a variation of the CQ model which learns syllables as a combination of onset and rhyme, instead of as an unstructured string of phonemes.

References

Aitchison, J [1987] *Words in the Mind.* Oxford: Basil Blackwell.

Anderson, J A and Rosenfeld, E [1987] *Neurocomputing: Foundations of Research.* Cambridge, Mass.: MIT Press.

Appelt, D [1985] *Planning English Sentences.* Cambridge: Cambridge University Press.

Borden, G J [1979] An interpretation of research on feedback interruption in speech. *Brain and Language*, **7**, 307–319.

Brown, R and McNeill D [1966] The 'tip of the tongue' phenomenon. *Journal of Verbal Learning and Verbal Behaviour*, **5**, 325–337.

Carpenter, R H S [1984] *Neurophysiology.* London: Edward Arnold.

Cohen, P R [1978] On Knowing What to Say: Planning Speech Acts. Unpublished PhD thesis, Department of Computer Science, University of Toronto.

Cutler, A (ed) [1982] *Slips of the Tongue and Language Production.* Amsterdam: Mouton.

Davey, A [1978] *Discourse Production.* Edinburgh: Edinburgh University Press.

Dell, G S [1986] A spreading activation theory of retrieval in sentence production. *Psychological Review*, **93**, 283–321.

Dell, G S [1988] The retrieval of phonological forms in production: Test of predictions from a connectionist model. *Journal of Memory and Language*, **27**, 124–142.

Estes, W K [1972] An associative basis for coding and organization in memory. In A W Melton and E Martin (eds), *Coding Processes in Human Memory*, pp161–190. Washington DC: V H Winston and Sons.

Estes, W K [1985] Memory for temporal information. In J A Michon and J L Jackson (eds), *Time, Mind and Behaviour*. Heidelberg: Springer-Verlag.

Fay, D and Cutler, A [1977] Malapropisms and the structure of the mental lexicon. *Linguistic Inquiry*, **8**, 505–520.

Fromkin, V (ed) [1980] *Errors in Linguistic Performance: Slips of the Tongue, Ear Pen and Hand*. London: Academic Press.

Garrett, M F [1980] Levels of processing in sentence production. In B Butterworth (ed) *Language Production* Volume 1: *Speech and Talk*, pp177–220. London: Academic Press.

Gordon, P C and Meyer, D E [1987] Control of serial order in rapidly spoken syllable sequences. *Journal of Memory and Language*, **26**, 300–321.

Grossberg, S [1982a] *Studies of mind and brain: Neural principles of learning, perception, development, cognition and motor control*. Boston: Reidel Press.

Grossberg, S [1982b] Processing of expected and unexpected events during conditioning and attention: A psychophysiological theory. *Psychological Review*, **89**, 529–572.

Grossberg, S [1987] Competitive learning: From interactive activation to adaptive resonance. *Cognitive Science*, **11**, 23–63.

Grossberg, S (ed) [1988a] *Neural Networks and Natural Intelligence*. Cambridge, Mass.: MIT Press.

Grossberg, S [1988b] Nonlinear neural networks: Principles, mechanisms, and architectures. *Neural Networks*, **1**, 17–61.

Harley T A [1988] Automatic and executive processing in semantic and syntactic planning: a dual process model of speech production. In M Zock and G Sabah (eds.) *Advances in Natural Language Generation*, Volume 1, pp161–171. London: Francis Pinter.

Hinton, G E, and Anderson, J A (eds) [1981] *Parallel models of associative memory*. Hillsdale, NJ: Lawrence Erlbaum Associates.

Houghton G [1986] The Production of Language in Discourse: A computational model. DPhil Thesis, University of Sussex.

Houghton, G [1989a] Connectionist models of serial order: A review and a new model. Unpublished manuscript.

Houghton, G [1989b] A connectionist-neuropsychological model of some aspects of visual selective attention. Unpublished manuscript.

Houghton, G and Isard, S D [1987] Why to speak, what to say and how to say it: Modelling language production in discourse. In P E Morris (ed), *Modelling Cognition*, pp249–267. Chichester: Wiley.

Houghton, G and Pearson, M [1988] The Production of Spoken Dialogue. In M Zock and G Sabah (eds.) *Advances in Natural Language Generation*, Volume 1, pp112–130. London: Francis Pinter.

Jones, G V and Langford, S [1987] Phonological blocking in the tip of the tongue state. *Cognition*, **26**, 115–122.

Jordan, M I [1986a] Serial Order: A Parallel Distributed Processing Approach. ICI Report 8604, Institute for Cognitive Science, University of California at San Diego.

Jordan, M I [1986b] An introduction to linear algebra in parallel distributed processing. In D E Rumelhart and J L McClelland (eds), *Parallel Distributed Processing*, Volume 1: *Foundations*. Cambridge, Mass.: MIT Press.

Kalita, J and Shastri, L [1987] Generation of simple sentences in English using the connectionist model of computation. In *Proceedings of the 9th Meeting of the Cognitive Science Society*, pp555–565.

Kohonen, T [1984] *Self Organization and Associative Memory*. Berlin: Springer-Verlag.

Lieberman, P and Blumstein, S E [1988] *Speech Physiology, Speech Perception and Acoustic Phonetics*. Cambridge: Cambridge University Press.

Linsker, R [1988] Self-organisation in a perceptual network. *Computer*, March 1988, 105–117.

MacKay, D G [1987] *The Organization of Perception and Action*. New York: Springer-Verlag.

McClelland, J L and Elman, J L [1986] Interactive processes in speech perception: The TRACE model. In J L McClelland and D E Rumelhart (eds)m *Parallel Distributed Processing* Volume 2: *Psychological and Biological Models*. Cambridge, Mass.: MIT Press.

McClelland, J L and Rumelhart, D E [1981] An interactive activation model of context effects in letter perception: Part 1: An account of basic findings. *Psychological Review*, **88**, 375–407.

McDonald, D D [1983] Natural language generation as a computational problem: an introduction. In M Brady and R C Berwick (eds), *Computational Models of Discourse*, pp209–265. Cambridge, Mass.: MIT Press.

McKeown, K [1986] *Text Generation*. Cambridge: Cambridge University Press.

Perkell, J S [1980] Phonetic features and the physiology of speech production. In B Butterworth (ed), *Language Production*, Volume 1. London: Academic Press.

Power, R [1974] A Computer Model of Conversation. Unpublished PhD thesis, University of Edinburgh.

Pinker, S and Prince, A [1988] On language and connectionism: Analysis of a parallel distributed processing model of language acquisition. *Cognition*, **28**, 73–193.

Power, R [1979] The organisation of purposeful dialogues. *Linguistics*, **17**, 107–152.

Restle, F [1970] Theory of serial pattern learning: structural trees. *Psychological Review*, **77**(6), 481–495.

Rosenbaum, D A, Kenny, S B and Derr, M A [1983] Hierarchical control of rapid movement sequences. *Journal of Experimental Psychology: Human Perception and Performance*, 9(1), 86–102.

Roy, E A and Square, P A [1985] Common considerations in the study of limb, verbal and oral apraxia. In E A Roy (ed), *Neuropsychological Studies of Apraxia and Related Disorders*, pp111-161. Amsterdam: Elsevier Science Publishers BV.

Rumelhart, D E, Hinton, G E and McClelland, J L [1986] A general framework for parallel distributed processing. In D E Rumelhart and J L McClelland (eds),

Parallel Distributed Processing, Volume 1: *Foundations*, pp45–76. Cambridge, Mass.: MIT Press.

Rumelhart, D E, Hinton, G E and Williams, R J [1986] Learning internal representations by error propagation. In D E Rumelhart and J L McClelland (eds), *Parallel Distributed Processing*, Volume 1: *Foundations*, pp318–362. Cambridge, Mass.: MIT Press.

Rumelhart, D E and McClelland, J L (eds) [1986a] *Parallel Distributed Processing*, Volume 1: *Foundations*. Cambridge, Mass.: MIT Press.

Rumelhart, D E and McClelland, J L [1986b] On learning the past tenses of English verbs. In J L McClelland and D E Rumelhart (eds)m *Parallel Distributed Processing* Volume 2: *Psychological and Biological Models*, pp216–271. Cambridge, Mass.: MIT Press.

Rumelhart, D E and Norman, D [1982] Simulating a skilled typist: A study of skilled motor performance. *Cognitive Science*, **6**, 1–36.

Rumelhart, D E and Zipser, D [1986] Feature discovery by competitive learning. In D E Rumelhart and J L McClelland (eds), *Parallel Distributed Processing*, Volume 1: *Foundations*, pp151–193. Cambridge, Mass.: MIT Press.

Shattuck-Hufnagel, S [1979] Speech errors as evidence for a serial-ordering mechanism in sentence production. In W E Cooper and E C T Walker (eds), *Sentence Processing: Psycholinguistic studies presented to Merrill Garret*, pp295–342. Hillsdale, NJ: Lawrence Erlbaum Associates.

Shepher [1974] *The Synaptic Organisation of the Brain*. Oxford: Oxford University Press.

Sillito, A M [1985] Inhibitory circuits and orientation selectivity in the visual cortex. In D Rose and V G Dobson (eds),*Models of the Visual Cortex*, pp396–407. Chichester: Wiley and Sons.

Singer, W [1985] Activity-dependent self-organisation of the mammalian visual cortex. In D Rose and V G Dobson (eds),*Models of the Visual Cortex*, 123–136. Chichester: Wiley and Sons.

Smolenski, P [1986] Neural and conceptual interpretation of PDP models. In J L McClelland and D E Rumelhart (eds) *Parallel Distributed Processing* Volume 2: *Psychological and Biological Models*, pp390–431. Cambridge, Mass.: MIT Press.

Stemberger, J P [1983] Inflectional malapropisms: Form-based errors in English morphology. *Linguistics*, **21**, 573–602.

Stemberger, J P [1985] An interactive activation model of language production. In A Ellis (ed), *Progress in the Psychology of Language*, Volume 1, pp143–186. Hillsdale, NJ: Lawrence Erlbaum Associates.

Treiman, R [1984] On the status of final consonant clusters in English syllables. *Journal of Verbal Learning and Verbal Behaviour*, **23**, 343–356.

Treiman, R [1986] The division between onsets and rimes in English syllables. *Memory and Language*, **25**, 476–491.

Whitsel, B L and Kelly, D G [1988] Knowledge acquisition ('learning') by the somatosensory cortex. In J L Davis, R W Newburgh and E J Wegman (eds), *Brain*

Structure, Learning and Memory. AAAS Selected Symposium 105. Boulder, Colorado: Westview Press.

Williams, R J [1986] The logic of activation functions. In D E Rumelhart and J L McClelland (eds), *Parallel Distributed Processing*, Volume 1: *Foundations*, pp423–443. Cambridge, Mass.: MIT Press.

Zock, M and Sabah, G [1988] *Advances in Natural Language Generation: An Interdisciplinary Perspective*, Volume 1. London: Francis Pinter.

von der Malsburg, C [1973] Self-organization of orientation sensitive cells in the striate cortex. *Kybernetik*, **14**, 85–100.

12 Parallel Incremental Sentence Production for a Model of Simultaneous Interpretation

Hiroaki Kitano

Abstract

This chapter describes a parallel incremental sentence production model. The model is designed as a part of a research effort to develop a speech-to-speech translation system with simultaneous interpretation capability. In simulating simultaneous interpretation, the generation system needs to satisfy several requirements obtained from the analysis of actual simultaneous interpretation sessions. The requirements include a capability of incremental and opportunistic sentence production, coupled with a parsing algorithm. In order to satisfy these requirements we employ a parallel incremental model of parsing and generation on a hybrid parallel paradigm which is a hybridisation of a parallel marker-passing scheme and a connectionist network. We also employ an almost concurrent parsing and generation model which allows us to attain simultaneity of translation because parsing and generation are integrated and run almost concurrently. Thus, a part of the utterance may be generated while parsing is in progress. Also, the model attains highly interactive processing of knowledge from morphophonetics to discourse by distributively representing that knowledge in a memory network on which actual computations are performed. An integrated use of case-based and constraint-based processing is one other important feature of our model. The model takes into account several psychological studies of sentence production. The model described in this chapter has been implemented as ΦDMDIALOG, a real-time speaker-independent continuous speech input speech-to-speech dialogue translation system, developed at the Center for Machine Translation at Carnegie Mellon University.

12.1 Introduction

This chapter describes a parallel and incremental model of natural language generation that was designed and implemented as a part of the ΦDMDIALOG speech-to-speech dialogue translation system [Kitano *et al.* 1989b; Kitano 1989b; Kitano 1989d]. ΦDMDIALOG is one of the first experimental systems that performs speech-to-speech translation, and the first system which demonstrated the possibility of simultaneous interpretation. Our model is intended to simulate a simultaneous interpreter at work. This is because simultaneity of translation is an essential factor in designing a practical speech-to-speech translation system in which real-time translations of utterances are ultimately demanded.

We found, as a result of analysis of several dialogue and speech corpora, that one utterance in a real dialogue can be quite long (15 seconds for one sentence is not rare in Japanese). This implies that if we adopt a sequential architecture, in which generation starts only after the entire parsing is completed, this inevitably creates an undesirable delay in translation. Suppose one speaker produced an utterance of 15 seconds duration, and the other responded with an utterance of 15 seconds duration; the first speaker would have to wait at least 30 seconds before hearing the translation of the utterance of her dialogue partner. It is inconceivable that such a system could be practically deployed. Thus, we claim that simultaneous interpretation needs to be accomplished.

Simultaneity of interpretation emerges from the fact that interpreters actually start translation before the whole sentence is spoken by the speaker. In designing the model, we advanced hypotheses that such activity is performed as a result of simultaneous interpreters' ability to process parsing and generation incrementally and concurrently with some interactions between these two, and that these interpreters' knowledge, especially discourse and world knowledge, enables them to predict what may be said in succeeding utterances. We also hypothesised that simultaneous interpreters have a huge amount of phrasal knowledge which can be used in both parsing and generation. These hypotheses were examined and verified by analysing transcripts of actual simultaneous interpretation sessions, and by introspective analysis by simultaneous interpreters including that of the author himself. Part of our analysis will be described in the next section.

The implications of these hypotheses for designing a speech-to-speech translation system are significant, especially in the designing of the natural language generation algorithm used in the system which has been substantially affected by these hypotheses and observations. In order to implement and actually test these hypotheses, we made several major design decisions employing the following features.

Almost concurrent parsing and generation

Our model employs a parallel and incremental algorithm, and the generation algorithm is coupled with a parsing algorithm in order to attain simultaneous interpretation. Unlike traditional methods of machine translation in which a generation process is invoked after parsing is completed, our model concurrently executes the generation process during parsing. This enables our model to generate a part of an input utterance during the parsing of the rest of the utterance.

Hybrid parallel paradigm

The model is built on a **hybrid parallel paradigm** [Kitano 1989c] which is a hybridised massively parallel processing scheme integrating a marker-passing algorithm and a connectionist network in a consistent manner. We employ this paradigm because natural language processing requires two different types of parallelism. One is parallelism at the symbolic operations level which builds up and constrains syntactic and semantic information; and the other is with respect to the competitive activations and inhibitions which select one hypothesis from several competing hypotheses. The marker-passing section of our model captures the parallel flow of information and symbolic operations during processing and the connectionist network acts as a discriminator which selects one hypothesis out of multiple hypotheses.

Dynamic participation of knowledge from morphophonetics to discourse

Knowledge from morphophonetics to discourse is distributively represented in the memory network and dynamically involved in parsing and generation, and makes predictions as to next possible utterances. This highly interactive structure is advantageous in resolving ambiguities as early as possible, thereby allowing generation of the translated sentences without significant delay.

Integration of case-based and constraint-based processing

In our model, the case-based and constraint-based processes of parsing and generation are integrated and treated in one scheme. While constraint-based processing, such as unification-based processing, allows wide syntactic coverage, case-based processing attains more efficient and more specific processing under contextual constraints. Our model takes advantage of both schemes by uniformly integrating the two. Linguistic and theoretical reasons for this scheme will be discussed later.

Learning by parsing and generation

Two learning schemes, learning by parsing and learning by generation, are incorporated. Each accounts for the acquisition of utterance cases and the learning of knowledge, in order to avoid faulty phrasal combinations.

In the following sections, we describe a part of our empirical investigations of simultaneous interpretation. Then, we describe a model of natural language generation which was designed to meet our hypotheses and the observed phenomena of simultaneous interpretation.

12.2 Empirical Studies of Simultaneous Interpretation

In this section, we will use transcripts from actual simultaneous interpretation sessions, and analyse requirements for the generator in simulating the simultaneous interpretation. We have English to Japanese and Japanese to English interpretation transcribed from recordings of actual presentations.

J shows source sentences in Japanese, **e** is an English annotation to the Japanese sentences, and **E** is the translation made by the interpreter. It is time-aligned so that the time before the interpreter starts translating the speaker's utterance can be analysed.

Table 12.1 is a transcript of English to Japanese simultaneous interpretation. Judging from this and other transcripts, there are substantial numbers of canned phrases used by the interpreter. The first two sentences are good examples. It seems that for some sentences, and typically in greetings, phrasal lexical items representing canned phrases may be useful even in computer-based processing. In the fourth sentence, we can see how parts of a sentence are translated and incrementally generated. In this example, a subject is translated before a verb is spoken. Due to the verb-final nature of Japanese, some parts of the sentence were not translated until the accusative was recognised in the source language.

The two transcripts of Japanese to English translation (Tables 12.2 and 12.3) show that the interpreter is dividing an original sentence into several sentences in translation. This is because a long Japanese sentence often contains several distinct parts, each of which can be expressed as a sentence, and translation of such a sentence into one English sentence is almost impossible. By subdividing a long sentence into multiple sentences, the interpreter (i) is able to produce understandable translations, and (ii) avoids delays in translation mainly caused by the verb-final characteristics of Japanese. Behind this, we can assume, is that the fact that the interpreter has a strong expectation about what can be said in the sentence currently being processed using discourse context and world knowledge. For example, in the second sentence (Table 12.3), the verb of the sentence, *motteiru* (*have*, or *hold*), comes at the very end of the sentence. Simultaneous interpretation is only possible because the interpreter made a guess, from the context, that issues of the Japanese labour system are to be described in terms of the images held by Western peoples. Thus, the interpreter made translations using ... *are what have been pointed to* or ... *It seems to those who say this* .... It is important to notice

E	On behalf of the Financial Times,
J	Financial Times sha wo daihyou itashimashite
e	Financial Times Co. -ACC represent -HUMBLE
E	may I welcome you all to the Imperial Hotel.
J	minasamagata wo teikoku-hoteru ni
e	you -PL -ACC the imperial hotel -LOC
E	It is a great pleasure to see so many people
J	gokangei itashimasu. Watashi ni torimashite
e	welcome -HUM I for
E	here today.
J	minasamagata ni omenikakaruno ha kouei de arimasu.
e	you -PL -DAT meet -HUM -TOP pleasure
E	Our presentation today is in three parts.
J	Kyou no puresenteishon ha mittsu no bumon kara
e	today -GEN presentation -TOP three -GEN part from
E	First of all, I would like to give you a brief
J	natteimasu Mazu saisho ni watakushi ga goku kantan ni
e	consists first of all, I -NOM briefly
E	historical review of the Financial Times —
J	Financial Times sha no rekishi ni tsuite no
e	Financial times Co. -gen history about -GEN
E	where we are today,
J	hanashi wo shimasu. Konnichi no genjou to
e	talk -ACC -HUM today -GEN status and
E	and what our plans are for the future.
J	shourai no keikaku ga dounatte iruka no
e	future -GEN plans -TOP what status -GEN
E	
J	hanashi wo shimasu.
e	talk -ACC -HUM

Table 12.1: Transcript: English to Japanese

J	Nihon no keizai hatten no seikou niha tashikani mezamashii monoga
e	Japan -GEN economy -GEN success -TOP actually remarkable things
E	The success of Japanese economic
J	atte, kokumin no seikatu suijun ha joushou shi, bukka shisuu ha antei
e	exist, people -GEN living standard -TOP improved CPI -TOP stabilized
E	development has actually been remarkable. The living standard has risen
J	shitekiteiru noha kekkouna kotodesuga seikou bakari deha nai to iukoto ha,
e	begin -TOP desirable thing success all not because,
E	and the CPI has stabilized. These are to be desired,
J	tatoeba, kokutetsu no baai wo mitemo akiraka desu.
e	for example, JNR -GEN case -ACC look-at obvious
E	but not all are successes.
J	
e	
E	JNR is an obvious example. (JNR: Japan National Railways)

Table 12.2: Transcript: Japanese to English (1)

J	Shuushin-koyou-seido ya shuu-kyou-futsuka-sei ga mada amari
e	lifetime employment and 5-days-a-week system -NOM yet not very
E	The lifetime employment system and the fact that the
J	jisshi sareteinai datoka, doumo nihon no roudousha ha kaisha ni
e	enforced not done yet somewhat Japanese workers -TOP company-BY
E	5-days-a-week system is not yet employed are what are being pointed to.
J	mibun wo kousoku sare rokuni yasumi mo torezuni hataraka sareteiru nado
e	status bounded -PASS hardly holiday -ACC can't-take work -PASS
E	It seems to those who say this that workers are tied to the company and
J	toiu imagi wo nihon no roudou shisutemu wo kikikajitta dakeno
e	such image -ACC Japan -GEN labor system -ACC scratched-the-surface
E	work like slaves without even taking holidays. This is the image of
J	oubei jin ha motteiru rashii wakedesune.
e	Westerners -TOP have it-seems
E	the working system held by European and American towards the Japanese
J	
e	
E	workers.

Table 12.3: Transcript: Japanese to English (2)

that these translations were made before the main verb was spoken.
Several observations can be made from these transcripts:

- Translation can begin even in the middle of the input sentence.
- The interpreter uses a phrasal lexicon of canned expressions.
- Translation generally starts after a phrase is spoken.
- Long sentences are translated into multiple sentences. (This is typically observed in Japanese to English translation.)
- The interpreter makes strong guesses as to what will be said.

These observations support our hypotheses described in the previous section. We can therefore derive several requirements that the generator of a simultaneous interpretation system must satisfy:

- the system must have incremental parsing capability;
- the system must be able produce sentences incrementally;
- the system must have an opportunistic sentence planning capability, in order to avoid syntactic dead ends;
- the system must be able to divide one sentence into multiple sentences; and
- the system must be able to predict what may be said.

12.3   A Model of Generation in ΦDmDIALOG

We describe here the model of generation in ΦDmDIALOG. ΦDmDIALOG accepts speaker-independent continuous speech and generates audio output of translated sentences. As a speech recognition device, we are currently using Matsushita's Japanese recognition system [Morii *et al.* 1985] for Japanese inputs. The recognition device takes voice inputs from a microphone and provides a noisy phoneme sequence to the main component of ΦDmDIALOG. The English translation is sent to a DECTalk speech synthesis system to obtain audio output of the translated sentence.

12.3.1   The organisation of the model

Both parsing and generation are conducted in a memory network using a parallel marker-passing scheme and the connectionist network. Major components of our model are the memory network and the markers which propagate through the memory network.

The memory network

The memory network incorporates knowledge from morphophonetics to plan hierarchies of each participant of a dialogue. Each node is a **type** and represents either a concept (**concept class** node; CC) or a sequence of concepts (**concept sequence class** node; CSC). Strictly speaking, both CC and CSC are a **collection** or **family** since they are, for the most of part, sets of classes. CCs represent such knowledge as concepts (e.g., *Conference, *Event, *Mtrans-Action), and plans (e.g., *Declare-Want-Attend). CSCs represent sequences of concepts and their relations such as concept sequences[1] (e.g., <*Conference *Goal-Role *Attend *Want>) or plan sequences (e.g. <*Declare-Want-Attend *Listen-Instruction>)[2] of the two participants of the dialogue.[3]

CSCs have an internal structure composed of a concept sequence, constraint equations, presuppositions, and effects. This internal structure provides our scheme with the capability to handle unification-based processing as well as case-based processing, so that typical criticisms against DMAP-type NLP [Riesbeck and Martin 1985], such as weak linguistic coverage and incapability of handling linguistically complex sentences, do not apply to our model.[4] Each type of node creates instances during parsing which are called concept instances (CI) and concept sequence instances (CSI), respectively. CIs correspond to **discourse entities** as described in [Webber 1983]. CSIs record specific cases of utterances indexed into the memory network. They are connected through labelled links such as IS-A or PART-OF, and weighted links which form a connectionist network.

The markers

A guided marker-passing scheme is employed for inference in the memory network. Basically, our model uses four types of markers. These markers are:

Activation markers (A-markers) which are created based on the input of the source language. These are passed up IS-A links and carry instance, features and cost. This type of marker is used for parsing.

---

[1] Concept sequences are the representation of an integrated syntax/semantics level of knowledge in our model.

[2] These should not be confused with **discourse segments** [Grosz and Sidner 1985]. In our model, information represented in discourse segments is distributively incorporated in the memory network.

[3] Use of plan hierarchies for each speaker as discourse knowledge is another unique feature of our model, whereas most other studies of dialogue have been dedicated to one-speaker initiative domains [Cohen and Fertig 1986; Litman and Allen 1987].

[4] Indeed, our model is substantially different from DMAP-type marker-passing or any other naive marker-passing models, because linguistic features are carried up by markers to conduct substantial linguistic analysis as well as case-based processing.

	Phonology	*Syntax/Semantics*	*Discourse*
CSC	Phoneme sequence	Concept sequence	Discourse plan sequence
CSI	——	Instance of concept sequence	Instance of discourse plan sequence
CC	Phoneme	Concept	Discourse plan
CI	——	Instance of concept	Instance of discourse plan

Table 12.4: Nodes in the memory network

Prediction markers (P-markers) which are passed along the conceptual and phonemic sequences to make predictions about which nodes are to be activated next. Each P-Marker carries constraints, cost, and the information structure of the utterance which is built incrementally during parsing.

Generation markers (G-markers) which show the activation of nodes in the target language, and each of which contains a surface string, features, cost and an instance which the surface string represents. G-markers are passed up through IS-A links.

Verbalisation markers (V-markers) which anticipate and keep track of verbalisation of surface strings. Final surface realisations, cost and constraints are carried by V-markers.

Besides these markers, we assume **contextual markers (C-markers)** [Tomabechi 1987] which are used when a connectionist network is computationally too expensive. The C-Markers are passed through weighted links to indicate contextually relevant nodes. Major features of each type of marker are summarised in Table 12.5.

12.3.2 A baseline algorithm

The basic algorithm employs a cycle of (i) marker creation, (ii) marker pass up, (iii) collision, and (iv) prediction or acceptance of CSCs. This process applys to both parsing and generation. In parsing, the sequence will be (P-1) A-marker creation, (P-2) A-marker pass up, (P-3) A-P-collision, and (P-4) prediction or acceptance of CSCs. In generation, it will be (G-1) G-marker creation, (G-2)

Marker	Passing direction	Information
A-markers	IS-A	Instance, features, cost
P-markers	The next element on CSCs	Constraints, cost, instances
G-markers	IS-A	Instance, feature, cost, lexical realisation
V-markers	The next element on CSCs	Constraints, cost, instances, verbalised words
C-markers	Contextual links	Activation level

Table 12.5: Markers in the model

G-marker pass up, (G-3) G-V-collision, and (G-4) prediction or acceptance of CSCs.

Although we are interested mainly in the generation algorithm, we need to explain briefly how our model parses utterances, because the generation algorithm in our model is coupled with the parsing algorithm.

In parsing, A-markers are created at CCs for phonemes, and the phonological level processing is performed. Details of this process are described in [Kitano, Mitamura and Tomita 1989]. When a word is recognised, the CSC representing the phonological realisation of the word (LEX node) is activated. An A-marker is created (A-marker creation phase) and passed up to a CC node which denotes an individual concept (A-marker pass up stage). When the CC is activated, the CI indexed under the CC is searched for in order to identify the discourse entity referred to in the utterance. The A-marker is passed up from the CC node through an IS-A link. When the A-marker activates the CC node which has a P-marker (A-P-collision stage), the information carried in the A-marker is merged into the P-marker and the P-marker is moved to the next element of the CSC (prediction stage). When the collision occurs at the end of the sequence of the CSC, the CSC is accepted, and a new A-marker is created which contains the established information structure. The new A-marker is passed up through an IS-A link. While each CSC may represent certain meanings, meanings of the utterance can be incrementally formulated.

Our generation algorithm takes advantage of this parsing mechanism and performs incremental generation. In the generation algorithm, G-markers are created when the CC node is activated by an A-marker (G-marker creation stage). The G-marker is passed up through an IS-A link (G-marker pass up stage). When the G-marker hits another CC node, which is a component of a CSC, the G-marker will be stored in that CC node, and a copy of the G-marker, which is also a G-marker with identical information content, is further passed up. When the parsing is finished or the partial parsing is completed, the whole or partial meaning of the utterance is already analysed, and that information is stored in an A-marker which eventually activates another CC node. When that CC node is activated, the information which represents the analysed meaning is passed to the V-marker on the first element of the CSCs linked under the CC node by the target language link. When a G-marker hits the CC node with a V-marker (G-V-collision stage), the information in the G-marker is merged into the V-marker and the constraint check, between the features and instance carried by the G-marker and the constraint equations stored in the V-marker, is performed. When the constraint check succeeds, the V-marker is moved to the next element of the CSC (prediction stage).

Generally, natural language generation involves several stages: content delineation, text structuring, lexical selection, syntactic selection, coreference treatment, constituent ordering, and realisation [Nirenburg *et al.* 1989]. In our model, the content is determined at the parsing stage, and most other processes are unified into one stage, because, in our model, lexicon, phrase, syntactic fragment, and sentence are treated in the same mechanism. There is no need to subdivide the generation process into text structuring, lexical selection and syntactic selection. The common thrust in our model is the hypothesis activation-selection cycle in which multiple hypotheses are activated and where one of them is finally selected. This cycle is adopted throughout parsing and generation. Lexical and syntactic hypotheses are activated at the same time and one hypothesis among them is selected to form a final output string. Thus, the translation process of our model can be viewed in the following processes:

Concept activation: a part of the parsing process. Individual concepts represented by CCs are activated as a result of parsing speech inputs. A-markers are created and passed up by activating the concept.

Lexical and phrasal hypotheses activation: hypotheses for lexical items and phrases which represent the activated concept are searched for, and G-markers are created and passed up as a result of this process. Usually, multiple candidates are activated at a time.

Propositional content activation: a part of the parsing process by which propositional content of the utterance is determined.

Syntactic and lexical selection: selection of one hypothesis from multiple candidates of lexical items or phrases. First, the syntactic and semantic constraints are checked to ensure the correctness of the hypotheses, and the final selection is made using cost/activation-based selection.

Realisation: the surface string (which can be either a sequence of words or

$$(a) \quad \overset{V}{<} a_0 \, a_1 \, a_2 \, \cdots \, a_n > \; \Rightarrow \; \overset{V}{<} a_0 \, a_1 \, a_2 \, \cdots \, a_n >$$
$$\uparrow$$
$$G$$

$$(b) \quad \overset{V}{<} a_0 \, a_1 \, a_2 \, \cdots \, a_n > \; \Rightarrow \; \overset{V}{<} a_0 \, a_1 \, a_2 \, \cdots \, a_n > \; \Rightarrow \; \overset{V}{<} a_0 \, a_1 \, a_2 \, \cdots \, a_n >$$

$$(c) \quad \overset{V}{<} a_0 \, \bar{a}_1 \, a_2 \, \cdots \, a_n > \; \Rightarrow \; \overset{V}{<} a_0 \, \bar{a}_1 \, a_2 \, \cdots \, a_n >$$
$$\uparrow$$
$$G$$

Figure 12.1: Movement of V-marker in the CSC

a sequence of phonological signs) is formed from the selected hypothesis and sent to the speech synthesis device.

The movement of V-markers is important in understanding our algorithm. First, a V-marker is located on the first element of the CSC. When a G-marker hits the element with the V-marker, the V-marker is moved to the next element of the CSC (Figure 12.1a). In the case where the G-marker hits an element without a V-marker, the G-marker is stored in the element. When another G-marker hits the element with a V-marker, the V-marker is moved to the next element. Since the next element already has a G-marker, the V-marker is further moved to the subsequent element of the CSC (Figure 12.1b). In Figure 12.1c, $\bar{a}_1$ is a closed class lexical item.[5] When a G-marker hits the first element, a V-marker on the first element is moved to the third element by passing through the second element which is a closed class item. In this case, the element for the closed class item need not have a G-marker. The lexical realisation for the element is retrieved when the V-marker passes through the element.

There are cases in which an element of the CSC is linked to other CSCs as seen in Figure 12.2. In such instances, when the last element with a V-marker

---

[5] **Closed class lexical items** are **function words** such as *in, of, at* in English and *wo, ga, ni* in Japanese. These words are non-referential, and their number does not grow, whereas open class lexical items are mostly referential, and their number grows as vocabulary expands.

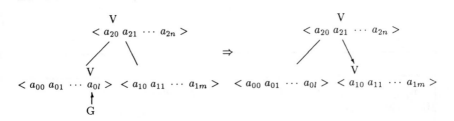

Figure 12.2: Movement of V-marker in the hierarchy of CSCs

gets a G-marker, that CSC is accepted and a G-marker containing relevant information is passed up through an IS-A link. Then an element of the higher layer CSC gets the G-marker and a V-marker is moved to the next element. Since the element is linked to the other CSC, constraints recorded on the V-marker are passed down to a lower CSC. This movement of the V-marker allows our algorithm to generate complex sentences.

Let us now explain with a simple example (Figure 12.3). In the following explanation, we will assume a consecutive interpretation mode from which translations are made after a whole sentence is parsed. The simultaneous interpretation mode is described in the next section. The major concern in this explanation is to describe the overall picture of how sentences are formulated in our generation scheme. Details of each process are described in corresponding sections.

Concept activation

Suppose the input is

(1) I want to attend the conference.

Parsing is performed by activating phoneme nodes and passing activations upward which eventually activate lexical nodes. When each lexical node is activated, it passes up activation through the memory network. The generation process runs concurrently. When the word *I* is entered, its lexical node gets activated. The activation is passed up and conceptual nodes, *I and *Person (superclass of *I), get activated as a part of the parsing process.

Lexical and phrasal hypotheses activation

When a concept is activated, the program searches for a Japanese lexical entry for the concept *I* and finds *Watashi*. A G-marker is created and includes an

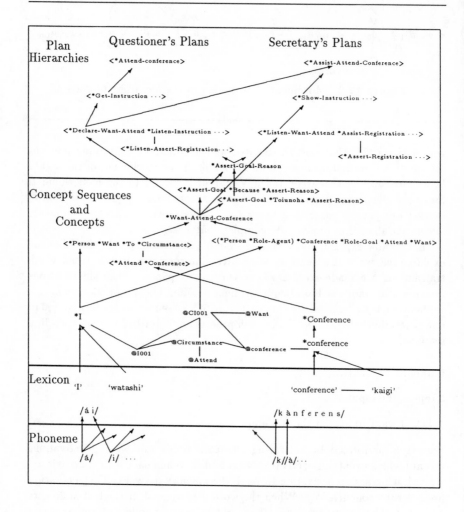

Figure 12.3: A process of concurrent parsing and generation

instance (@I001), features, and a surface string (*watashi*). The G-marker is passed up through the memory network, and is stored in the elements of relevant CSCs for the target language. When there is no direct translation of the word in the target language, a phrase or a clause may be activated which best expresses the meaning of the word in the source language. This process takes place for each word in the sentence.

Propositional contents activation

Next, the propositional content of the utterance is analysed as a part of parsing. P-markers are initially located on the first element of CSCs for the source language (in this example, a P-marker is at *Person of <*Person *Want *To *Circumstance> and <*Person *Attend *Conference>). When *Person gets an A-marker, the P-marker is moved to *Want. When *Want gets an A-marker then the P-marker is moved to *To and then to *Circumstance. The words *attend*, *the*, and *conference* would activate each element of the CSC (<*Person *Attend *Conference>). Thus, the CSC is accepted and furthermore an A-marker propagation will activate *Circumstance. Instantiation takes place when this sequence is accepted, i.e., the P-marker is placed on the last element of the sequence and that element gets an A-marker. As a result, a CI is created under the CC (*Want-Attend-Conference) which is a root node of the accepted CSC, and linked with relevant instances.

Syntactic and lexical selection, and realisation

When the propositional content is determined, the generation process selects the syntactic and lexical structure of the sentence to be generated. Knowledge of syntactic structure for a specific expression is represented as a hierarchy of CSCs in the memory network. In this simple case, the CSC which determines syntactic structure is stored under the *Want-Attend-Conference node. The CSC may look like:[6]

<(*Person *Role-Agent) *Conference *Role-Goal *Attend *Want>

Of course, this is simplified for the sake of clarity, and the real CSC has more information such as constraints, presuppositions and effects. V-markers are located in the first element of CSCs for the target language. The propositional content is passed to each V-marker of CSCs which are linked under the CC node. Since hypotheses for the lexical realisation of each concept are stored in each element, a surface string for an utterance can be created by concatenating surface strings stored in each G-marker on each element which meet constraints imposed by propositional content and the constraint equations. Details of the

---

[6]We use a very simple example here. A discussion of how to produce complex sentences, such as sentences with control, is provided in a later section.

constraint check will be discussed in a later section. Assuming the constraints can be satisfied, concatenation of a surface realisation from each element of the CSC will produce the final surface realisation. For instance, G-markers on `*Conference` and `*Attend` contain surface strings *kaigi* and *sanka*, respectively. Elements such as `*Role-Goal` correspond to closed class lexical items. The lexical realisation for such an element is retrieved by searching the link attached to the element, and activation from the source language is not necessary. The result of the concatenation is *Kaigi ni sanka shitai*. Notice that optional elements, (`*Person *Role-agent`), are not concatenated to produce a subject-ellipsed sentence. However, in concatenating surface strings in each G-marker, syntactic/semantic constraints are checked to ensure the syntactic and semantic accuracy of the produced sentences. Details of the syntactic and lexical selection are described in a later section.

12.4 Generation while Parsing is in Progress

Generation of a sentence while parsing is in progress is the central focus of our model. Of course, formulation of each part of the sentence takes place after it is processed and its meanings are determined. However, the processes are concurrent in the sense that the generation process does not wait until the entire parse is completed, so that the translated utterance is generated incrementally.[7] Lexical selection and partial production of utterances are conducted while parsing is in progress. Thus, in some inputs, a part of the utterance can be generated before parsing of the entire sentence is completed. We do this by verbalising a surface string or phonological realisation of the instance whose role is determined (i.e., not ambiguous), and hold verbalisation of ambiguous instances until they are disambiguated. In translating from English to Japanese, it is very likely that the subject can be translated and verbalised at the moment a verb is spoken to the system. Moreover, phrases can be translated before a subsequent part of the sentence is spoken to the system. The part of the sentence which is verbalised is recorded in a V-marker and the V-marker is moved to the next possible verbalisation element. This avoids redundant verbalisation, the phenomena by which the same words are articulated again. Only the element with a V-marker can be verbalised in order to ensure consistency of the produced sentence.

There is a question whether we can universally apply this idea in translating two languages which have very different linguistic structures. We chose to demonstrate the universality of our model by performing simultaneous inter-

---

[7] Unlike incremental generation by IPG [Kempen and Hoenkamp 1987], which assigns procedures to each syntactic category, our algorithm uses markers to carry information. Also, concepts to be expressed are incrementally determined as parsing progresses.

Input Utterance	Translation
I	
want	watashi ha (*I Role-Agent; this is ellipsed in the*
to	*actual translation*)
attend	
the	
conference	
because	kaigi ni sanka shitai (*want to attend the*
I	*conference*)
am	toiunoha (because)
interested	watashi ha (*I Role-Agent; this is ellipsed in the*
in	*actual translation*)
interpreting telephony	tuuyaku denwa ni kyoumi ga arukara desu
	(*interested in interpreting telephony*)

Figure 12.4: Simultaneous interpretation in ΦDmDIALOG

pretation between Japanese and English. It is widely accepted that Japanese and English have very different syntactic structure; Japanese is a non- (or weak-) configurational type language with case-markers playing an important role in its syntax and has an S-O-V type structure, whereas English is a configurational type language with an S-V-O type structure. Also, keeping semantic invariance in translation is not a trivial task. In the case of translation between English and French or other languages with similar linguistic structure, our model would trigger generation much more easily than is the case in Japanese-English translation.

Figure 12.4 indicates a temporal relationship between a series oᵢ words given to the system and incremental generation in the target language. An incremental translation and generation of the input

(2) I want to attend the conference because I am interested in inter-
     preting telephony.

results in two connected Japanese sentences:

(3) (Watashi wa) kaigi ni sanka shitai.
     Toiunoha (watashi ha) tuuyaku denwa ni kyoumi ga arukara desu.

During the analysis of utterances, there is a point at which the semantics of a part of the sentence is determined. For instance, *I* (@I001) can only be an agent of the action when *want* is analysed. At this time, *watashi ha* (I Role-Agent) can be verbalised. A V-marker, which is initially located on *Person is now moved to *Conference which is the next element of the CSC. The next verbalisation will not be triggered until *because* comes in, because the role of *I want to attend the conference* in the discourse is still ambiguous. At this moment, *Want-Attend-Conference gets activated and its superclass node including *Assert-Goal gets activated. A P-marker is now placed on *Because in a CSC (<*Assert-Goal *Because *Assert-Reason>) and a V-marker is still in place on *Assert-Goal of the corresponding Japanese CSC (<*Assert-Goal *Touiunoha *Assert-Reason>). Activation of *Because will determine the role of *Want-Attend-Conference. The word *because* acts as a clue-word which divides assertion of the speaker's goal and her/his reasons for it as represented in the CSC in the discourse. Verbalisation is now triggered; i.e.,

(4)   I want to attend the conference.

is vocalised, and the V-marker is moved the next element of the CSC. When a whole sentence is parsed, the entire meaning is made clear and the rest of the sentence is verbalised. This example illustrates generation in the target language at the earliest possible point. Although this is perfectly legitimate Japanese, this is not the best Japanese translation as far as style is concerned. In order to overcome this problem, we created an option to generate translation after waiting until a whole clause or sentence is parsed so as to enable generation of the best style under the given discourse situation. One option is to reverse the order of clauses, i.e. *Assert-Reason then *Assert-Goal, which realises perfectly fluent Japanese. One other example is when a topicalisation of the first clause is demanded, the translation will be

(5)   (Watashi ga) kaigi ni sanka shitai noha (watashi ga) tuuyaku denwa ni kyoumi ga arukara desu.
      The reason why I want to attend the conference is that I am interested in interpreting telephony.

Such constraints on generation scheduling are provided mostly from discourse knowledge and temporal constraints. Our model is basically *language-independent* so that it is applicable to Japanese to English translation or even English-French as well as English to Japanese. For a sentence such as

(6)   Tuuyaku denwa ni kyoumi ga arimasu node kaigi ni sanka shitai nodesuga.
      (I am) interested in interpreting telephony so (I) want to attend the conference.

our algorithm can generate *I am interested in interpreting telephony* before *kaigi ni sanka shitai nodesuga* (*I want to attend the conference*) is parsed.

12.5 Syntactic and Lexical Hypotheses Activation

When a concept is recognised by the parsing process, hypotheses for translation will be activated. The concept can be an individual concept, a phrase or a sentence. In our model, they are all represented as CC nodes, and each instance of the concept is represented as a CI node. The basic process is for each of the activated CCs, LEX nodes[8] in the target language would be activated. There are several cases:

Word-to-word: this is the case where a word in the source language can be translated into a word in the target language. In Figure 12.5a, the word LEX_{SL} activates CC_1. $LEX1_{TL}$ is activated as a hypothesis of translation for LEX_{SL} interpreted as CC_1. A G-marker is created at LEX_{TL} containing a surface realisation, cost, features, and an instance which the $LEX1_{TL}$ represents (CI). The G-marker is passed up through an IS-A link. When a CC_1 does not have $LEX1_{TL}$, CC_2 is activated and $LEX2_{TL}$ will be activated. Thus, the most specific word in the target language will be activated as a hypothesis.

Word-to-phrase: when a CC can be represented by a phrase or sentence, a CSC node is activated and a G-marker which contains that phrase or sentence will be created. In Figure 12.5b, LEX_{SL} activates CC_1 which has a $CSC1_{TL}$. In this case, the $CSC1_{TL}$ will be activated as a hypothesis to translate LEX_{SL} interpreted as CC_1.

Phrase-to-word: there are cases where a phrasal or sentence expression can be expressed in one word in the target language. In Figure 12.5c, CSC_{SL} activates a CC_1 which can be expressed in one word using $LEX1_{TL}$. $LEX1_{TL}$ will be activated as a hypothesis for translating CSC_{SL}.

Phrase-to-phrase: in cases where the expression in both languages corresponds at the phrase level, the phrase-to-phrase translation mechanism is adopted. In Figure 12.5d, CSC_{SL} will be translated using $CSC1_{TL}$ via CC_1. Such cases are often found in greetings or canned phrases.

12.6 Syntactic and Lexical Selections

Syntactic and lexical selections are conducted involving three processes: feature aggregation, constraint satisfaction, and competitive activation. Feature

---

[8] LEX nodes are a kind of CSC which represents a lexical entry and phonological realisation of the word.

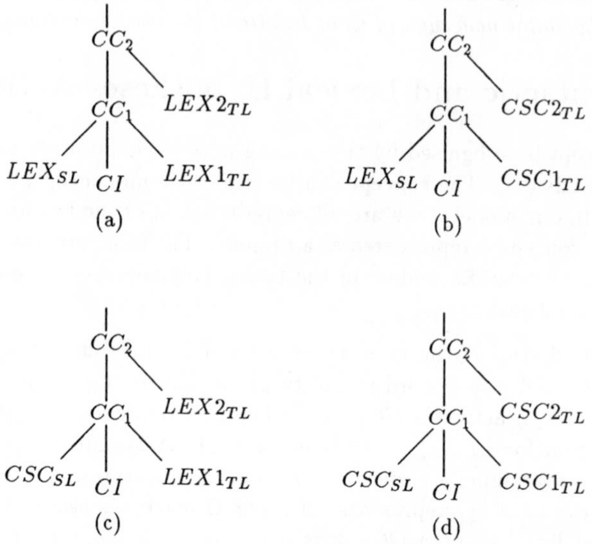

Figure 12.5: Activation of syntactic and lexical hypotheses

aggregation and constraint satisfaction correspond to a symbolic approach to syntactic and lexical selection which guarantees grammaticality and local semantic accuracy of the generated sentences, and the competitive activation process is added in order to select the best decision among multiple candidates.

12.6.1   Feature aggregation

Feature aggregation is an operation which combines features in the process of passing up G-markers so that minimal features are carried up. Due to the hierarchical organisation of the memory network, features which need to be carried by G-markers are different, depending upon which level of abstraction is used for generation. When knowledge of cases, similar to the **phrasal lexicon** [Becker 1975], is used for generation, features are not necessary because this knowledge is already indexed to specific discourse entities. Features need to be carried when more abstract knowledge is used for generation. For example, when translating the Japanese sentence

(7)   Kanojyo ha hashiru.
      She runs.

the parsing and the generation of the sentence can be handled at different levels of abstraction using the same mechanism. The word *kanojyo* (*she*) refers to a certain discourse entity so that very specific case-based parsing can directly access a memory which recalls previous memory in the network. Thus, the process activates previous memory in order to generate the translation using the same or similar cases in the memory network. Since previous cases are indexed into specific discourse entities, the activation can directly identify which memory to recall. When the word *kanojyo* (*she*) is parsed in a more abstract level, such as *Person, we need to check features such as number and gender. Accordingly, we need to check number and gender agreement in generation. Thus, these features need to be contained in the G-marker. Further abstraction requires more features to be contained in the G-marker. One of the advantages of this mechanism is that the case-based process and the constraint-based process are treated in one mechanism. Aggregation is a cheap operation since it simply adds new features to existing features in the G-marker. Given the fact that unification is a computationally expensive operation, aggregation is an efficient mechanism for propagating features because it ensures only minimal features are aggregated when features are unified.

12.6.2 Constraint satisfaction

Constraint is a central notion in modern syntax theories. Each CSC has **constraint equations** which define the constraints imposed for that CSC depending on their level of abstraction. CSCs representing specific cases do not have constraint equations since they are already instantiated and the CSCs are indexed in the memory network. The more abstract the knowledge is, the more they contain constraint equations. Feature structures and constraint equations interact at two stages. At the prediction stage, if a V-marker placed on the first element of the CSC already contains a feature structure that is non-nil, the feature structure determines, according to the constraint equations, possible feature structures of G-markers which subsequent elements of the CSC can accept. At a G-V-collision stage, a feature structure in the G-marker is tested to see if it can meet what was anticipated. If the feature structure passes this test, information in the G-marker and the V-marker is combined and more precise predictions are made as to what will be acceptable in subsequent elements. For generating *She runs*, we assume a constraint equation (agent num = action num) associated with a CSC, for example, <*Agent *Action>. When a V-marker initially has a feature structure that is nil, no expectation is made. In this example, at a G-V-collision, a G-marker has a feature structure containing (num = 3s) constraints for the possible verb form which can follow, because the feature in the G-marker is assigned in the constraint equation so that (agent num 3s) requires (action num 3s).

This guarantees that only the verb form *runs* can be legitimate.[9] Thus, the grammaticality of the generated sentences is guaranteed.

12.6.3 Competitive activation

The competitive activation process introduced either by a C-marker-passing or by the connectionist network determines final syntactic and lexical realisation of the sentence. We have adopted a cost-based scheme, like that which we have employed in parsing [Kitano, Tomabechi and Levin 1989]. In the cost-based scheme, the hypothesis with the least cost will be selected. This idea reflects our view that parsing and generation are dynamic processes in which the state of the system tends to a global minimum. In the actual implementation, we compute a cost of each hypothesis which is determined by a C-marker-passing scheme or a connectionist network. Since the least-cost hypothesis will be selected in the parsing process, the least-cost generation hypothesis that is linked to the parsing hypothesis will be selected as the final translation.

The C-marker passing scheme puts C-markers at contextually relevant nodes when a conceptual root node is activated. A G-marker which goes through a node without a C-marker will be added with larger cost than others. A pattern of linearisation is selected among CSCs linked with CC nodes representing the input utterance such as *Want-Attend-Conference. When there are multiple hypotheses for the specific CC node; i.e. when multiple CSCs are linked with the CC, the cost of each G-marker used for each linearisation and the preference for each CSC are added up to select a CSC with the least cost as the translated result.

The connectionist network will be adopted with some computational costs. When a connectionist network is fully deployed, every node in the network is connected with weighted links. A competitive excitation and inhibition process is performed to select one hypothesis. Our cost-based model can be used to determine the initial activation strength of the each node. When a lexical node is activated, associated CCs are activated according to the weights of connections. Activation of CCs will propagate to lexical nodes of the target language. A-markers are created when CCs are activated and G-markers are created when any lexical node of the target language is activated. Although both A-markers and G-markers carry cost information, its actual value changes over time according to changes in the activation level of the lexical and conceptual nodes. Activation levels of each node change through a spreading activation and inhibition process. Final interpretation and translation in the target language are selected through a winner-take-all mechanism.

---

[9]When we use abstract notation such as NP or VP, the same mechanism applies and captures linguistic phenomena.

12.7 Integration of Case-Based and Constraint-Based Processing

Unlike most natural language generation systems, which depend solely on syntactic knowledge in formulating sentences, we employ both case-based and constraint-based processing in generation. Case-based generation is an approach that stores many utterance cases (cases of actual utterances in the past), and uses these in order to generate sentences in the target language. Combined with probabilistic measures which are carried by markers, cases are a major source of collocational information. Cases of utterance or **utterance cases** are specific instances of CSCs which are indexed to each relevant CI. In addition to these instances, abstract knowledge of these instances, **generalised cases**, are created. The storing of specific cases and creation of generalised cases are based on the learning mechanism of our model which will be described later. These CSCs are hierarchically indexed and the most specific CSC will be selected in generating sentences. Our model encompasses approaches using a **phrasal lexicon** as a part of case-based generation.[10] Phrases such as *It is a great pleasure ...* or *On behalf of ...* are stored as phrasal lexical items. Phrasal lexical items are considered as generalised cases of utterances so that only common features are preserved, yet specificity of expression is not lost. These phrasal lexical items are expressed as CSCs and stored in the memory network.

There are two major advantages in using cases in generation. First, use of cases avoids over-generation by basing preference on the expression which appeared before over a newly generated expression using a syntactically-based process. When two hypotheses, one from a case and the other from a syntactic process, conflict, our system prefers a hypothesis from the case. Second, it improves efficiency of the generation process. The tradeoff between the productivity of knowledge and the efficiency of the process using such knowledge is recognised as one of the major bottlenecks of the knowledge-based system [Berliner 1984]. Natural language generation systems are by no means an exception. Use of cases is one way of minimising this problem. In our model, cases of utterance are stored in the memory network so that translation of a same or similar utterance will be handled by case-based processing; thus, there are gains in efficiency over a system that depends solely on constraint-based processing.

However, the problem of case-based processing is that it is only able to provide answers to variations of known situations, and pre-storing all possible cases is not a practical solution [Riesbeck and Schank 1989]. On the other

---

[10] Discussions on benefits of phrasal lexicons for parsing and generation are found in [Riesbeck and Martin 1985; Hovy 1988].

hand, constraint-based processing (which can be considered a kind of rule-based processing) is more flexible because it is based on rules and constraints that can be applied to many situations. The constraint-based approach is represented by various unification-based grammar formalisms [Pollard and Sag 1987; Kaplan and Bresnan 1982]. We use a semantic grammar which combines syntactic and semantic constraints.[11] In our model, propagation of features and unification are conducted as **feature aggregation** by G-markers and **constraint satisfaction** is performed by operations involving V-markers. This process allows our model to handle linguistically interesting phenomena such as control and unbounded dependencies in a linguistically sound manner.

This scheme is applied to discourse level processing and attains an integration of the syntactic/semantic level and the discourse level. At the discourse level, constraint equations are applied to establish discourse constraints and processing of discourse plans.

12.8   Learning Schemes for Generation

In this section, we briefly describe our model of learning schemes which we are currently investigating with regard to its feasibility. There are several motivations for developing a learning scheme for our model.

First, we want our system to automatically acquire phrasal lexical items. Our model requires extensive knowledge of specific instances of utterances, which we call utterance cases, in order to produce sentences. However, it is neither practical nor psychologically plausible to assume that all phrases appearing in the generated sentence are pre-stored in memory. Thus, a mechanism which can learn expressions from examples is necessary.

Second, we want to avoid the over-generation of sentences. Specifically, we would like to avoid the generation of utterances which it may be possible to generate with a given set of syntactic and semantic knowledge, but which are never used by native speakers.

Third, we want to maintain syntactic soundness even with a case-based generation process. Contrary to the problems which arise in syntax-based generation, case-based generation runs the risk of generating ungrammatical sentences because explicit syntactic knowledge is not incorporated. We need a mechanism to monitor such hypotheses using explicit syntactic knowledge, which will learn to avoid forming such hypotheses in the future.

Fourth, we want our system to be more efficient as it learns more expressions. By acquiring specific utterance cases that are linked to semantic

---

[11]This does not preclude use of a unification grammar formalism in our system. In fact, we are now developing a cross-compiler that compiles grammar rules written in LFG into our network. Design of a cross-compiler from HPSG to our network is also underway.

representation, recalculation to form surface realisation is no longer necessary. By having a large knowledge of utterance cases specific for each situation, efficiency of the generation, as well as the parsing process, would improve significantly.

Two types of learning mechanisms are considered in our model:

Learning by parsing: input utterances that are provided during the translation session are used for learning utterance cases. Since our system is a bidirectional system, both Japanese and English are provided to the system, and we can assume that speakers of each language are native. The purpose of learning from such examples is to acquire cases of utterances which are actually used by the native speaker. When such cases and generation hypotheses from constraint-based process conflict, we prefer to generate a sentence from the case, because these are actually used by the native speaker, and thus we avoid generation of sentences never used by native speakers. The process of acquisition consists of the following operations: (i) generation of utterance cases, whereby new utterance cases are generated from input utterances using syntactic knowledge, semantic knowledge and generalised cases; (ii) indexing into the memory network, whereby new utterance cases are indexed into the memory network so that they can be used in the parsing and generation processes; and (iii) generalisation, whereby a generalised utterance case is created by generalising specific cases using domain knowledge. This process is analogous to explanation-based learning [Mitchell *et al.* 1986, DeJong and Moony 1986].

Learning by generation: hypotheses which are generated during the generation process can be a source of knowledge for learning. Existing knowledge of cases is used for hypothesising a new pattern of sentence. Syntactic knowledge monitors this sentence to assure its grammaticality. Failures to meet the grammaticality judgement are recorded to avoid hypothesisation of ungrammatical sentences. Two stages are involved: (i) hypothesisation, whereby hypotheses for sentences are generated using the cases of past utterances; and (ii) monitoring, whereby syntactic knowledge monitors these hypotheses, and rejects those which violate syntactic constraints. Knowledge of failures is recorded in each case to avoid hypothesisation of syntactically unsound sentences in the future.

12.9 Discussion

12.9.1 Relevant studies

Since most machine translation systems assume sequential parsing and generation [Tomita and Carbonell 1987], a simple extension of existing systems to
combined speech recognition and synthesis would not suffice for interpreting
telephony. The main problem is in previously existing systems' inability to attain simultaneous interpretation (where partial translation is performed while
parsing is in progress), because in other systems a parser and a generator are
independent modules, and the generation process is only invoked when the
entire parse is completed and the full semantic representation is given to the
generator. Our model serves as an example of approaches counter to the modular approach, and attains simultaneous interpretation capability by employing
incremental parsing and a generation model. Pioneer studies of parallel incremental sentence production can be found in [Kempen and Hoenkamp 1987;
Kempen 1987]. They use Segment Grammar, which is composed of Node-
Arc-Node building blocks to attain the incremental formation of trees. Their
studies parallel our model in many respects. Segment Grammar is a kind of
semantic grammar since the arc label of each segment makes each segment a
syntactic/semantic object. Feature aggregation and constraint satisfaction by
G-markers and V-markers in our model corresponds to a distributed unification [De Smedt, this volume] in the segment grammar. However, their model
is limited to the syntactic layer and was not tested at the discourse level.

12.9.2 Psychological plausibility

Psychological studies of sentence production [Garrett 1975, 1980; Levelt and
Maassen 1981; Bock 1982, 1987; Kempen and Huijbers 1983] were taken into
account in designing the model. In [Kempen and Huijbers 1983], two independent retrieval processes are assumed, one accounting for abstract pre-
phonological items (L1-items) and the other for phonological items (L2-items).
The lexicalisation in their model follows: (i) a simultaneous multiple L1-
item retrieval; (ii) a monitoring process which watches the output of L1-
lexicalisation to check that it is keeping within constraints upon the utterance
format; and (iii) retrieval of L2-items after waiting until the L1-item has been
checked by the monitor, and all other L1-items become available. In our model,
a cc's activation stage corresponds to multiple L1-item retrieval, constraint
checks by V-markers correspond to the monitoring, and the realisation stage
which concatenates the surface string in a V-marker corresponds to the L2-
item retrieval stage. The difference between our model and their model is that,
in our model, L2-items are already incorporated in G-markers whereas they

assume L2-items are accessed only after the monitoring. Phenomenologically, this does not make a significant difference because L2-items (phonological realisation) in our model are not explicitly selected until constraints are met, at which point the monitoring is completed. However, this difference may be more explicit in the production of sentences because of the difference in the scheduling of the L2-item retrieval and the monitoring. This is due to the fact that our model retains interaction between two levels, as investigated by [Bock 1987]. Our model also explains contradictory observations by [Bock 1982] and [Levelt and Maassen 1981] because activation of CC nodes (L1-items) and LEX nodes (L2-items) are separated with some interactions. Also, our model is consistent with a two-stage model [Garrett 1975, 1980]. The **functional** and **positional** levels of processing in Garrett's model correspond to the parallel activation of CCs and CSCs, the V-marker movement which is left to right, and the surface string concatenation during that movement.

Studies of the planning unit in sentence production [Ford and Holmes 1978] give additional support to the psychological plausibility of our model. They report that the **deep clause**, rather than the **surface clause**, is the unit of sentence planning. This is consistent with our model, where the CSCs account for deep propositional units and the realisation of deep clauses as the basic units of sentence planning. They also report that people plan the next clause while uttering the current clause. This is exactly how our model performs, and is consistent with our observations from transcripts of simultaneous interpretation.

12.9.3   Current implementation

The model of generation described in this chapter has been implemented as a part of ΦDMDIALOG, a speech-to-speech dialogue translation system developed at the Center for Machine Translation (CMT) at Carnegie Mellon University (CMU). ΦDMDIALOG is implemented on an IBM RT-PC workstation using CMU CommonLISP running on the Mach operating system. Speech input and voice synthesis are carried out by connected hardware systems, in this case Matsushita Institute's Japanese speech recognition hardware and DECTalk. The memory network is based on hierarchies described in [Tsujii 1985], with domain knowledge and world knowledge added. We are currently interested in implementing our model on a parallel machine. We believe direct implementation of our model on a parallel computer will incur significant advantages in overall performance. We have partially verified this by implementing a part of our model (a part of the parsing stage) on special VLSI chips [Kitano 1988].

12.10   Conclusion

We have described a parallel incremental model of natural language generation which is designed for the speech-to-speech dialogue translation system ΦDMDIALOG. The system is intended to model simultaneous interpretation. We put forward some hypotheses as to what made simultaneous interpretation possible. These hypotheses are supported by the analysis of transcripts from actual simultaneous interpretation sessions. The analysis of the transcripts also provides us with several requirements that the model must satisfy. Such requirements include incremental parsing and generation capability, needs for discourse and world knowledge, and the coupling of parsing and generation. Integration of parsing and generation based on a massively parallel computational model enables us to execute the parsing and generation processes almost concurrently, and to attain some of the required features. Generation is integrated with the parsing process and uses both surface and semantic information carried by G-markers and A-markers. Predictions and tracking of verbalisation are done by V-markers. In our model, the case-based processing and the constraint-based processing were integrated, providing flexibility in generation while maintaining specificity of expression. Two learning schemes were briefly described. These schemes are designed to improve the system's competence and performance during the actual exposure to the inputs and generation process. A cost-based disambiguation scheme and a connectionist network are useful faculties in dynamically selecting one hypothesis among multiple hypotheses. Psychological plausibility is another notable feature of our model since most research in natural language generation has not taken into account psychological studies. We believe our parallel incremental generation model is a promising approach toward the development of interpreting telephony where simultaneous interpretation is required.

Acknowledgements

The author would like to thank Teruko Mitamura, Lori Levin, Masaru Tomita, Jaime Carbonell, James McClelland and Hitoshi Iida for fruitful discussions. Yoko Kadota provided us with recorded tapes of actual simultaneous interpretation sessions. Lyn Jones was a patient proofreader.

References

Becker, J D [1975] The Phrasal Lexicon. Bolt, Beranek and Newman Technical Report 3081.

Berliner, H J [1984] Search *vs* Knowledge: An analysis from the domain of games. In A Elithorn and R Banerji (eds), *Artificial and Human Intelligence*, pp105–117.

Amsterdam: Elsevier Science Publishers.

Bock, J K [1987] Exploring levels of processing in sentence production. In G Kempen (ed) *Natural language generation: New results in Artificial Intelligence, psychology and linguistics*, pp351-363. Dordrecht: Martinus Nijhoff Publishers.

Bock [1982] Toward a cognitive psychology of syntax: Information processing contributions to sentence formulation. *Psychological Review*, **89**, 1–47.

Cohen, P and Fertig, S [1986] Discourse structure and the modality of communication. In *International Symposium on Prospects and Problems of Interpreting Telephony*, ATR Interpreting Telephony Research Laboratories, Osaka, Japan, 1986.

DeJong, G F and Mooney, R [1986] Explanation-based learning: An alternative view. *Machine Learning*, **1-2**, 47–80.

De Smedt, K J M J [1989] Distributed Unification in Parallel Incremental Syntactic Tree Formation. In *Extended Abstracts of of the Second European Workshop on Natural Language Generation*, Edinburgh.

De Smedt, K J M J [1990] IPF: an incremental parallel formulator. This volume.

Ford, M and Holmes, V [1978] Planning units and syntax in sentence production. *Cognition*, **6**, 35–53.

Garrett, M F [1980] Levels of Processing in Sentence Production. In B Butterworth (ed), *Language Production*, Volume 1: *Speech and Talk*, pp177–120. New York: Academic Press.

Garrett, M F [1975] The Analysis of Sentence Production. In G Bower (ed), *The Psychology of Learning and Motivation*, Volume 9. Academic Press.

Granger, R H [1977] FOUL-UP: A program that figures out meanings of words from context. In *Proceedings of the Fifth International Joint Conference on Artificial Intelligence*, MIT, Cambridge, Mass., 22–25 August 1977, pp172–178.

Grosz, B J and Sidner, C L [1985] The Structures of Discourse Structure. CSLI Report No. CSLI-85-39.

Hovy, E H [1988] *Generating Natural Language Under Pragmatic Constraints*. Hiilsdale, NJ: Lawrence Erlbaum Associates.

Kaplan, R and Bresnan, J [1982] Lexical-Functional Grammar: A formal system for grammatical representation. In J Bresnan (ed), *The Mental Representation of Grammatical Relations*, pp173–281. Cambridge, Mass.: MIT Press.

Kempen, G [1987] A framework for incremental syntactic tree formation. In *Proceedings of the Tenth International Joint Conference on Artificial Intelligence*, Milan, Italy, 23-28 August 1987, pp655-660.

Kempen, G and Hoenkamp, E [1987] An incremental procedural grammar for sentence formulation. *Cognitive Science*, **11**, 201–258.

Kempen, G and Huijbers, P [1983] The lexicalization process in sentence production and naming: indirect election of words. *Cognition*, **14**, 185–209.

Kitano, H [1988] Multilingual information retrieval mechanism using VLSI. In *Proceedings of RIAO-88*, Boston, Mass.

Kitano, H [1989a] A massively parallel model of natural language generation for interpreting telephony: almost concurrent processing of parsing and generation. In *Extended Abstracts of the Second European Conference on Natural Language Generation*, Edinburgh.

Kitano, H [1989b] A model of simultaneous interpretation: a massively parallel model of speech-to-speech dialog translation. In *Proceedings of the Annual Conference of the International Association of Knowledge Engineers*, University of Maryland, June 1989.

Kitano, H [1989c] Hybrid parallelism: A case of speech-to-speech dialog translation. In *Proceedings of the IJCAI-89 Workshop on Parallel Algorithms for Machine Intelligence*.

Kitano, H [1989d] A Massively Parallel Model of Simultaneous Interpretation: The ΦDMDIALOG System. Technical Report CMU-CMT-89-116, Center for Machine Translation, Carnegie Mellon University, Pittsburgh.

Kitano, H, Tomabechi, H and Levin, L [1989] Ambiguity resolution in DMTRANS PLUS. In *Proceedings of the Fourth Conference of the European Chapter of the Association for Computational Linguistics*, Manchester 1989, pp72–79.

Kitano, H, Tomabechi, H, Mitamura, T and Iida, H [1989] A massively parallel model of speech-to-speech dialog translation: a step toward interpreting telephony. In *Proceedings of the European Conference on Speech Communication and Technology (EuroSpeech-89)*, Paris, pp198–201.

Kitano, H, Mitamura, T and Tomita, M [1989] Massively parallel parsing in ΦDMDIALOG: Integrated architecture for parsing speech inputs. In *Proceedings of the International Workshop on Parsing Technologies*, Center for Machine Translation, Carnegie Mellon University, Pittsburgh, pp230–239.

Levelt, W J M and Maassen, B [1989] Lexical search and order of mention in sentence production. In W Klein and W J M Levelt (eds), *Crossing the Boundaries in Linguistics: Studies Presented to Manfred Bierwisch*. Dordrecht: Reidel.

Litman, D and Allen, J [1987] A plan recognition model for subdialogues in conversation. *Cognitive Science*, **11**, 163–200.

Mitchell, T, Keller, R and Kedar-Cabelli, S [1986] Explanation-based generalization: a unifying view. *Machine Learning*, 1(1), 47–80.

Morii, S, Miyada, K, Fujii, S and Hoshimi, M [1985] Large vocabulary speaker-independent Japanese speech recognition system. In *Proceedings of the 1985 IEEE International Conference on Acoustics, Speech, and Signal Processing*, pp866–869.

Nirenburg, S, Lesser, V and Nyberg, E [1989] Controlling a language generation planner. In *Proceedings of the Tenth International Joint Conference on Artificial Intelligence*.

Pollard, C and Sag, A [1987] *Information-based Syntax and Semantics*. CSLI Lecture Notes No. 13.

Riesbeck, C and Martin, C [1985] Direct Memory Access Parsing. Yale University Report 354.

Riesbeck, C and Schank, R [1989] *Inside Case-Based Reasoning.* Hillsdale, NJ: Lawrence Erlbaum Associates.

Schank, R [1982] *Dynamic Memory: A Theory of Learning in Computers and People.* Cambridge: Cambridge University Press.

Tomabechi, H [1987] Direct memory access translation. In *Proceedings of the Tenth International Joint Conference on Artificial Intelligence*, Milan, Italy, 23-28 August 1987, pp722–725.

Tomita, M and Carbonell, J G [1987] The universal parser architecture for knowledge-based machine translation. In *Proceedings of the Tenth International Joint Conference on Artificial Intelligence*, Milan, Italy, 23-28 August 1987, pp718–721.

Tsujii, J [1985] The roles of dictionaries in machine translation. *Jouhou-syori* (Information Processing), Information Processing Society of Japan, 26(10). In Japanese.

Webber, B L [1983] So What Can We Talk About Now? In M Brady and R Berwick (eds), *Computational Models of Discourse*, pp331–371. Cambridge, Mass.: MIT Press.

Index

propositional attitudes 199, 200
psycholinguistic constraints 4
psycholinguistic data 12, 52, 287, 321, 346
psycholinguistic models 48
psychological justification 208
psychological plausibility 347
psychological theories 288

quantification 199, 219

raising-to-object 152
referring expressions 9, 194, 195, 214, 223, 229, 231, 235, 243, 245, 252, 258, 270, 283
remediation 92
repair 201
response determination 194
rhetorical function 29
rhetorical markers 50, 51, 64
rhetorical predicates 201
rhetorical relations 3, 25, 53, 77, 98, 110
rhetorical structure 48, 71, 259
Rhetorical Structure Theory 3, 4, 19–21, 48, 75, 77, 80, 86, 110
right dislocation 183

salience 209, 304
satisfiability 280, 281
Segment Grammar 6, 168, 346
semantic grammar 344
sentence boundaries 53, 55
short term memory 295
simultaneous interpretation 321
speech acts 26, 27, 84, 115, 194, 198, 200, 201, 206, 210, 222
  indirect 26, 77
speech errors 11, 167, 288, 292, 307, 314
speech output 287, 321, 327
story grammars 19, 79

strategic generation 1, 141, 195, 220
style 4, 38, 39, 48, 71, 211, 338
stylistic blunders 58, 60, 70
stylistic criteria 215, 218
subsequent reference 115, 244
supervised
  learning 300
systemic grammar 7, 113, 117

tactical generation 1, 5, 141, 167, 195, 220
terminological gaps 198
terminological transformations 10, 199, 201, 203, 206, 222, 258
text grammars 79
text organisation 200, 331
text planning 3, 20, 25, 29, 48
text schemas 3, 5, 18, 19, 24, 31, 76, 104, 105, 110
theme 33, 35, 68, 217
threshold function 290
top-down generation 8, 145
top-down planning 4, 10, 20
topic 184
topicalisation 153, 154, 158, 184, 185, 219, 338
Tree Adjoining Grammar 169, 174
tutorial dialogues 94
tutorial discourse 88
type raising 152
typing errors 292

unification 6, 7, 112, 120, 135, 141, 167, 213, 328, 341
  grammar 6, 143, 170, 243, 251, 344
  local 169
Unification Categorial Grammar 141, 146, 151, 152
user modelling 49, 79, 81, 96, 106, 110, 198, 262, 266, 283